On
SACRED
GROUND

On
SACRED
GROUND

A 7,000-Mile Walk of Discovery into the Heart of Wild Nature

ANDREW TERRILL

Enchanted Rock Press

Golden, Colorado

DEDICATION

For Berry and for Sam.
You and you alone know your path.
Never doubt it. Follow it.

CONTENTS

AUTHOR'S NOTE

On Sacred Ground is the second of two books that describe a 7,000-mile walk across Europe. For full enjoyment of this book, readers are strongly encouraged to read *The Earth Beneath My Feet* first.

This is a true story, but to preserve the privacy of individuals and improve the clarity of storytelling some names and locations have been changed. A small number of villages are composites and won't be found on any map. The wild locations all exist.

Readers should note that this book is written in British English, but that imperial units of measurement are used, just as they were during The Walk. Metric units are occasionally given, but for readers who struggle with Fahrenheit, miles and feet, please don't worry: as readers of *The Earth Beneath My Feet* already know, this journey isn't about the numbers.

One final note: this is a long book—intimidatingly long, perhaps. But this is appropriate. A condensed book wouldn't do justice to the journey that took place. My advice—for whatever it is worth—is to travel slowly. After all, even three miles an hour will get you across an entire continent.

Then again, this is your journey now.

FOREWORD

ACCOUNTS OF LONG-DISTANCE journeys have been a standard format in English writing for centuries. They've produced classics of our literature: Borrow's *The Bible in Spain* and *Wild Wales*; Boswell's and Johnson's 18th-century Scottish travels; Walter Starkie's *Raggle-Taggle*; Laurie Lee's 1930s Spanish wanderings; Paddy Leigh Fermor's masterful pre-war trilogy on walking through Europe; Colin Fletcher's *The Thousand-Mile Summer* and *The Man Who Walked Through Time*. The latter two books inspired an immense body of work within the sub-genre of outdoor writing. Hamish Brown, Chris Townsend, Cameron McNeish are among the notable names here. Recently they've been joined by a young man from Pinner who bids fair to become the most impressive and accomplished of all outdoor writers.

When I read *The Earth Beneath My Feet*—the first part of Andrew Terrill's entrancing account of a walk from the Mezzogiorno to the North Cape—what immediately struck me were its novelty, clarity, lack of inflation, principled ethical approach, and sureness of tone in describing his monumental undertaking. An additional virtue already apparent in the first volume is his effective plain style; its modesty, honesty, accessibility. Not for Andrew the contorted syntax, preciosity, academic posturings, derivative content and exhibitionist lexis that so mars the major literary fad of the early twenty-first century—that which goes under the highly dubious description of *The New Nature Writing*. Instead, Andrew's writing is grounded in qualities more crucial: substance and direct experience. There's the substance of what he describes, and substance sums it up. He notes at the outset of his book that it's about a 7,000-mile *journey*, whilst adding rightly that his book is not about numbers.

It certainly isn't. It's about rigour, human tenacity, resourcefulness, connection and perhaps above all good humour and forward-looking optimism. He recounts his impressions and emotions *en route* in so straightforward and honest a manner that you can't help but be charmed by his company and good-natured intent. He's not out to impress. He simply wants to see for himself what's out there in Europe's few remaining truly wild places, and in turn to convey a vibrant sense of them to us, his armchair readers. In this he succeeds beyond all expectations I had of his story. In the course of those thousands of miles he grows as man and writer, and we grow with him, as though we too were wading knee-deep through snow, or rising to another day bright with possibility. This is relatable adventure, devoid of bravado, a walk undertaken for love of being out in wild nature. You feel you'd like to be keeping him company. Though how we, his readers, might get on, hefting Ten Ton onto our shoulders each morning or putting up a tiny tent to give scant protection against the incessant deluges of northern Norway, scarcely bears thinking about. I'm glad I'm too old and feeble even to consider doing it for myself. But I'm supremely grateful that such an engaging and observant character as Andrew has done it for us, and told us about it in vivid, glowing prose.

Here, then, is the newest classic of our outdoor literature.

—Jim Perrin, Radnorshire, 2022

Jim Perrin is a two-time winner of the Boardman Tasker Prize for Mountain Literature, and a winner of the Mountaineering History Prize, and the Mountain Literature Prize, at the Banff Mountain Book Festival.

PART IV

THE HEART OF EUROPE

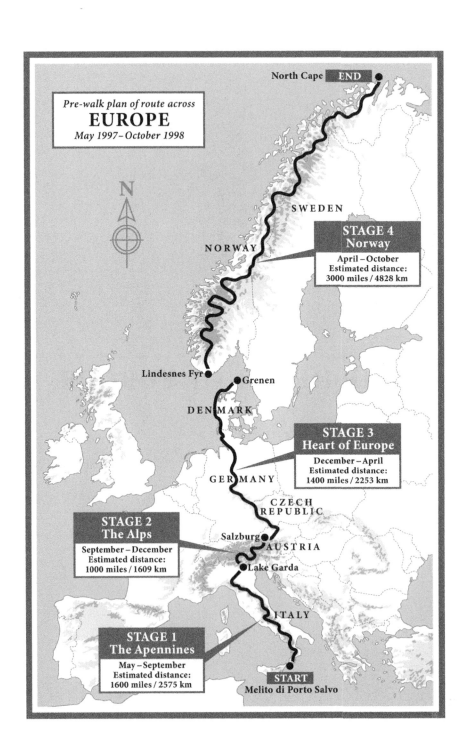

North Cape END

Pre-walk plan of route across
EUROPE
May 1997–October 1998

N

SWEDEN

STAGE 4
Norway
April – October
Estimated distance:
3000 miles / 4828 km

NORWAY

Lindesnes Fyr
Grenen

DENMARK

STAGE 3
Heart of Europe
December – April
Estimated distance:
1400 miles / 2253 km

GERMANY

CZECH
REPUBLIC

STAGE 2
The Alps
September – December
Estimated distance:
1000 miles / 1609 km

Salzburg

AUSTRIA

Lake Garda

ITALY

STAGE 1
The Apennines
May – September
Estimated distance:
1600 miles / 2575 km

START
Melito di Porto Salvo

DEEP IN THE FOREST:
THE AUSTRIAN ALPS, MID-NOVEMBER
Chapter 1

THE ALPINE FOREST surrounded me, swirling with wind and snow. Towns, roads, houses, central heating, carpet—such modern inventions were worlds away. This was the Europe of old.

I stole through it quietly, awash with gratitude. Even after seven months on foot I still couldn't take for granted that I was here, walking across wild mountains, living my dream. This—the life of a long-distance wanderer, living outside no matter the weather, moving on day after day—may not have been easy or comfortable, and may even have appeared daft from the outside, but it was the life I'd chosen. It was an existence to celebrate, every aspect of it, even the raging elements that many people preferred to shut away outside.

Out here, I followed my own path, unrestricted by society's normal rules and routines. My days could be whatever I wanted them to be. Each one was slow, straightforward, uncluttered. Each was different. I rarely knew what lay ahead, what I'd see, who I'd meet, what events would unfold. My maps gave only the smallest of hints. My expectations meant little. The possibilities were practically endless.

On this day I hadn't seen any other people—a rare occurrence in modern Europe, supposedly a crowded continent, but not unusual for me on this journey into Europe's wild side. I'd begun the day in a quiet valley above any settlements, had spent most of it making fresh tracks across a snowbound plateau, and was now heading up a side valley. The valley hadn't been part of my original route, but it had caught my interest on the map. There was no trail marked, and the promise of passing through another of Europe's secret corners was too tempting to resist. Months earlier it might have been too intimidating, but since beginning my journey I'd grown in confidence. Experience had taught me how to read the land and find my way. It wouldn't matter if progress was slow—there was no destination that I had to reach. I carried everything I needed on my back—my shelter, food, warm clothes—and I could stop whenever I found a location that called to me as though I belonged.

Finding places that called as though I belonged was one of the reasons I'd started The Walk. I'd set out from Calabria in the spring to do more than walk to the North Cape in Arctic Norway. In truth, I was walking to *be* somewhere, not *get* somewhere. My goal was to seek out the continent's special places of natural wonder, then lose myself within them. Over the miles, I'd come across many special places—more than I'd dared hope for. They'd held me spellbound, but they'd also kept me moving forward, fuelling my desire for new experiences and fresh discoveries.

I'd been through a great deal since the start. Since plucking five small pebbles from a quiet Mediterranean beach—done with the intention of delivering them to the North Cape—I'd walked the entire length of the Apennines and had weaved across the Alps. I'd traversed forests, summits, valleys, plains, glaciers and ridges. I'd been baked by the sun, blasted by the wind, deluged by rain, plastered by snow. I'd bled within the tangled *sottobosco*, dripped sweat in the Mezzogiorno, blistered in the Val Padana, and been feasted upon by *zanzare*. I'd received glares from the mafia, kindness from strangers, rejection from hoteliers, and hospitality from shepherds. I'd found paradise in beech woods, detachment above cloud seas, perspective on summits, and humility in blizzards. There'd been numerous ups and downs—physical *and* emotional—and I'd soared and suffered from them. But I'd learnt from both. Both, I'd come to see, were essential. Without lows there are no highs. Without valleys, no summits. Without struggles, rewards mean little.

The rewards from this day's struggle, from a long day trudging through shin-deep snow, were becoming clear. *Just look where I am!* My muscles ached with tiredness, but what did that matter when I was surrounded by

Snowstorm in the Hohe Tauern, November 16, 1997.

a forest that I had to myself? The landscape touched all my senses. I could feel the softness of freshly fallen snow underfoot, taste the sweetness of snowflakes in the cleansing mountain air, and hear the music of the wind as it rose and fell like the voice of some omnipresent being. The wind set spruce trees swaying, their branches creaking, their limbs sweeping to and thro as though beckoning me forward. Falling snow hung suspended in the air when the wind ebbed, sped by in a blur when the wind flowed. Even the snow underfoot stirred in motion. It shifted in mesmerising spirals and waves. The entire environment was alive and moving, and I felt alive and moved because of it.

There was nowhere else I would rather have been.

For a while, progress was uncomplicated. I weaved around trees, always searching for the easiest line, grinning with satisfaction each time clearings appeared where needed. But I reached an obstacle eventually: large boulders spilled across a steep slope. Many were precariously balanced, and the cracks and holes between them were hidden by snow. For a moment, the valley felt wilder than Alpine valleys typically feel. I wavered, experiencing doubt for the first time all day. No one knew where

I was; no one would come to help if I slipped and hurt myself. The lack of safety net wasn't entirely by choice—it was merely a byproduct of the kind of journey I wanted: a loosely structured walk that I could alter on a whim. I couldn't tell other people where I was going because *I* didn't always know where I was going. But the benefits outweighed the risks. I had a walk that was free from constraints and could evolve naturally. I'd learnt to assess, understand, and trust my own capabilities. And I had a growing appreciation for mountains and forests as they truly are. Alone, I was forced to examine the landscape intently—safe travel depended on it. I saw so much more because of it.

I paused and surveyed the boulder field, comparing it with other obstacles I'd overcome, as well as others I'd retreated from. Was I comfortable carrying on? Was I capable? I decided I was. I'd overcome stiffer challenges, and had come to terms with wilder places. This was only the Alps after all —I hadn't reached the vaster wildernesses of the Arctic yet.

I proceeded carefully, considering each step, just as I'd been doing since starting The Walk—just as I'd been doing since falling down a mountain in Switzerland four and a half years earlier. It was because of that accident that I was here. The accident—an out-of-control 1,000-foot bounce down a glacier beneath the Hohtürli Pass—could have ended my life, but through good fortune and clawing fingers I'd survived. Survival filled me with exhilaration: I was alive! The accident had revealed a profound truth: that life is a fragile gift too precious to waste. In the years before Hohtürli I'd been wasting my life, or so I'd believed. I'd been stuck in the suburbs, going nowhere. I'd felt trapped. But the accident had shaken me awake. It had pushed me to take control. After Hohtürli, I chose to live life on *my* terms.

It only took five minutes to negotiate the boulder field, and I did it with ease. It was another example of what my journey had often demonstrated: that most obstacles aren't as difficult as they appear. The first step usually reveals the truth. Plucking up courage to take the first step is often the hardest part.

Above the boulders, the valley levelled off. A broad, snow-smothered meadow came into view, and the moment I saw it I knew that I was done walking for the day. It felt like a hidden sanctuary far removed from the outside world, a reward for heading up the trailless valley in a snowstorm when common sense might have argued for an easier route. The meadow called out a welcome, and I was all too happy to accept it.

I chose a sheltered spot on the meadow's edge and began setting up camp. Thousands of snowflakes dusted my tent while I pitched it, blanketing it before it was fully up. Moving swiftly to stay warm, I stamped down snow anchors to hold my shelter in place, emptied my embarrassingly large backpack, Ten Ton, brushed snow off my shoulders, and retreated under cover. I was home. *This is so perfect*, I thought, chuckling, knowing that not many people would agree, or understand—my father among them.

'I think you're mad,' he'd said more than once before the journey had begun. He'd often shaken his head in mild disapproval at my foolish choices. 'A year and a half in a tent! Absurd!'

I'd laughed then and I laughed now. He, and all the others, were probably right. Then again, for the life I craved, it was Pinner—the London suburb I came from—that was absurd.

I cooked dinner while snow settled upon my ceiling mere inches overhead. The flakes landed with a whispering, fluttering murmur. Despite the limited space within my home, and the layer of hoar frost that soon coated the walls inside it, I felt warm and comfortable. I'd changed into dry thermals and lay within a thick sleeping bag. Dinner was filling and piping hot. I had a good book to read, and candlelight to read by. I'd carved out a nest of comfort in the heart of winter and had everything I needed—and nothing I didn't. It was all a matter of perspective, and mine had changed over the miles. The journey's experiences had added up and my needs were simpler than they'd ever been. I even felt I had more here than I'd ever had back in the suburbs. There were treasures everywhere, often right before my face. Like the frosted tent walls, a sparkling fur of exquisite artistry. I was warm, fed, and surrounded by beauty. Truly, I had everything I needed.

Most of all I had freedom, a rare prize in the modern world. Out here, I had control over every minute of my day.

Yes, I thought, *give me absurd*.

At some point during the night the wind died and the snow stopped falling. I awoke to sagging tent walls, biting cold, and throbbing silence. As I reached out to light my camp stove, my movements sounded supernaturally loud.

By the time I emerged into the new day the storm clouds were clearing. Down the valley, a glacier appeared, hung upon a high peak. It looked heartbreakingly pristine. Tearing my gaze away took considerable effort.

I dismantled camp and it was a struggle—as always, a fight to dismantle my ice-encrusted shelter and pack all my gear into Ten Ton before my fingers and feet lost all feeling. But I barely noticed the discomfort. Excitement and expectancy overwhelmed it.

In less than three weeks I'd be across the Alps and walking north into a different range. There'd be new places to explore, new people to meet, new experiences to have. And *far* ahead was the Arctic, a fabled realm—the ultimate wilderness, as I saw it. The Arctic had featured in dreams of longing for decades. I still couldn't believe that I was walking toward it. Would it feel as much like a reward as this secret Alpine sanctuary?

Only time would tell.

I set out with a wolf howl of delight. The day was a blank slate and I was ready to write upon it. I had no idea what lay ahead—and I couldn't wait to find out.

Clearing storm in the Hohe Tauern, November 17, 1997.

SALZBURG:
WHERE THE WILD THINGS ARE
Chapter 2

I REACHED THE city of Salzburg nineteen days later with ice frozen to my clothes and pack. I'd done it—I'd crossed the Alps! It's fair to say that I was delighted to arrive.

Salzburg looked massive to my eyes. Tall buildings, traffic, noise, crowds—they weren't what I'd grown used to. Deliberately entering the city might have felt like a betrayal of everything my journey stood for—*if* I'd stopped to think about it. But I didn't, not for a moment. All I could think about were the comforts waiting ahead. The developing winter had taken a toll; the final Alpine weeks had been a roller-coaster ride through some fierce conditions. As a result, everything I owned was either icy, wet or in need of repair—my own body included. I needed a break before the next stage of The Walk began. The next stage was certain to be even snowier.

I'd started my walk to escape cities, wanting to live in freedom and simplicity with the untrammelled earth beneath my feet. Over 2,650 miles and two mountain ranges I'd achieved what I'd sought. I'd also found something unexpected and greater: meaning and purpose, two reasons to live that had been lacking for me back in Pinner. Meaning had come from giving everything I had to a single all-consuming task, and purpose had come from the simple act of moving forward.

Except it wasn't a simple act at all, as I'd only just realised hours earlier on my approach to Salzburg. I wasn't only moving forward *physically*—I was also moving forward *as a person*. I was growing, becoming a fraction more each day than I'd been the day before. Everything that I'd done since Calabria, everything endured and experienced, every moment good and bad, had moved me forward. Each step had expanded my knowledge of the world; each experience had added another layer to who I was. Understanding this had transformed the journey. It had turned it into a quest.

And it was a quest that had now brought me to Salzburg: the kind of environment I'd begun the journey to escape. Only this time it was different. This time I was merely passing through.

I arrived on December 6, Saint Nicholas Day, the feast of jolly old Saint Nick, and the start of the Christmas season. After so long on foot, and so many moments of hunger, I'd come to treasure feast days—and gifts. My gift to myself after successfully crossing the Alps was four nights indoors.

A tourist office provided directions to a cheap *Gasthof*, although I still cringed at the nightly rate. I'd begun The Walk with £2,000 saved—enough for only six months of food and expenses, not enough for the full eighteen months the journey would last. Starting had been a huge leap of faith, but so far it had worked out. Extra funds had trickled in from trail reports that I'd written for newspapers and magazines, from sales of my photos through a photo library back in London, and from a handful of extra sponsors. But I was still desperately short. I only had enough money to last to northern Germany four months away, but not for Denmark and Norway beyond it—and I'd only reach northern Germany if I reserved my funds for essentials like food. After Salzburg, extravagant expenses like indoor accommodation would have to remain a rare treat.

A short, bald man with a neatly trimmed moustache and a tidy waist-coat welcomed me to the *Gasthof*. Talkative and friendly, he asked a long string of questions about my walk as he guided me to my room. At last, I settled in. I eased off my boots, stretched long and slow, and felt a great sense of release as I sloughed off the winter. I'd woken with frost on my sleeping bag and a pool of water beneath my camping pad. In comparison, a creaky bed and a heap of rough blankets in an old hotel was the height of luxury. I lay down, and for a moment considered the two charities that I was walking to help. The Passage and the Cardinal Hume Centre offered shelter and support to homeless people in the centre of London, and my appreciation for their work, and for what a home was, had grown beyond measure since beginning The Walk. Life outside in nature by choice was one thing—life on a city street with no escape was quite another. As I thought about it, my appreciation for the hotel bed grew even greater. I'd write about it in my next trail report, I decided—see if I could prompt extra donations for the charities. It was worth a try.

I lay in gratitude for a long while, happy for once to step away from adventure.

But, as it turned out, I hadn't stepped far. Adventure waited right outside, and I should have known. From Salzburg I'd expected an uneventful stay—time off from drama. But what I expected and what The Walk delivered seldom matched. The Walk had been shattering expectations since the very first step.

I might have guessed that something unusual was on the cards from my approach into the city. People had given me strange looks as I'd waltzed cheerfully along the banks of the River Salzach. They'd made comments I didn't understand.

'Ah,' a passing stranger had exclaimed. 'I thought you were one of the monsters!'

Another had said: 'You look dangerous... like one of those fanatics... with these huge things on their heads.'

What on earth had they meant? Someone had mentioned *crampons*, but I didn't get it. I had crampons—they were strapped to the top of Ten Ton. I knew that I looked unusual carrying my ridiculous load, but monstrous? Dangerous? It made no sense.

At 8 p.m. I grew aware of commotion outside the hotel: agitated voices, distant shouts and screams. I peered through my window to the street two storeys below. It was black outside, but in the amber glow cast by street lights I noticed figures in heavy coats standing shoulder to shoulder, lining the street. Oddly, there was no traffic. Earlier it had roared; where had it gone? After throwing on my warmest layers I stepped out to investigate.

Icy air hit my face and snow crunched underfoot, but despite the cold the street was crowded with adults and children. Two policemen stood on the corner, radios crackling. A babble of voices filled the air. 'They're coming, they're coming,' a stranger told me, nervous laughter in her voice. 'Who is?' I asked, but screams and shrieks and a crash of cowbells down the street drowned her reply. It was possible she too had said *crampons*, but that couldn't be right. How could crampons be coming down the street? It sounded like a riot, whatever it was, and it was approaching fast. I hung back from the crowds and waited, for what I wasn't sure.

And then *they* came…

Like creatures from a nightmare sprung to life.

All at once the street was in uproar. Dark figures appeared in the road— heavy-set bear-like shapes running and roaring, clawing at the crowds. Mayhem erupted. People scattered. *What the hell?* I thought as something rushed past in a blur, chasing a group of youths. I caught a glimpse of long matted hair, muscular arms, stomping feet, and a demon's head topped with stabbing horns. I saw another: a hideous face with red eyes and sharp teeth, the mouth fixed into a rabid snarl. It passed swiftly, but others followed— massive horned monsters leaping at Salzburg's citizens like outraged bulls. Fixed to their backs were large cowbells that clanged and clattered, kicking up an almighty din. Unable to look away, I watched the nightmarish beasts run amok, swinging birch whips at bystanders. Shouts and screams filled the air. And… laughter. Most of all laughter. Everyone seemed to be having a grand old time.

I scrambled onto a tall stone pedestal that supported a light post. A cowardly local joined me. Through gleeful laughter he explained all.

'You do not do this back in England? No? You should! This is *Krampus-lauf*—the Krampus Run. These monsters are Krampusse. We do this every year on this night, the first Saturday each December, *Krampusnacht*. It is wonderful, yes?'

I nodded. Wonderful, yes. But terrifying, also.

'We tell our children that Krampus will come and take them away before Christmas if they have been bad. And then gobble them up.' My eyebrows shot up at that. What a thing to tell kids: be good, or else a monster will kidnap and devour you! Austrian children must be the best behaved in Europe—or perhaps the worst, if Krampusse were needed in the first place.

'But it is all to celebrate Saint Nicholas,' my companion continued. He paused when he saw my look of confusion. What, I wondered, did these creatures have to do with Saint Nick? 'You know,' the man continued, 'Santa Claus? Look…'

Out in the street, unmolested by any of the rampaging Krampusse, was an old man with a long white beard. He wore priestly robes, a mitre upon his head, and held a crosier in one hand—an ornate stick shaped like a shepherd's crook. The man was moving with calm reverence, an island of solemnity amid a sea of chaos. He stopped often to bend down and talk to the smallest children.

'He is granting the *Kinder* their wishes,' my companion explained. 'But the Krampus also is good. If one swats you that is good luck for a whole year.'

Well, I thought, picturing the long winter ahead, *I could do with some good luck.* I eased myself down from my perch but jumped straight back when a creature from hell lunged at me. What else to do? The Krampusse were only men in fur rugs and carved wooden masks, but if one ever lunges at you, you'll see; you get out of the way damn fast.

As I later learnt, Krampus has inhabited Austrian folklore for centuries. The creature originated thousands of years ago in pagan rituals as a horned wilderness god. In medieval times, Christianity appropriated them, inserting them into religious plays as servants of the Devil. By the seventeenth century, Krampusse found themselves paired inextricably with Saint Nicholas, and celebrations on Saint Nicholas Day soon featured saint and monster side by side, the evil Krampus a useful tool for convincing doubters to follow a righteous path. Some people, however, took Krampus celebrations too far, or so the Church thought, and attempts were made to kill it off. Following the Austrian Civil War in 1934, the Krampus tradition was outlawed; even in the 1950s Austria's government was still distributing anti-Krampus leaflets. But some traditions are hard to suppress. Clearly, you can't keep a good monster down. As decades passed, Krampus celebrations resurged in popularity, and despite modern debates that question the tradition's suitability for children, *Krampusnacht* became an annual family event.

Stumbling upon the Krampus Run was one of the rewards of travel, I thought, as I watched the mayhem. But it was more than just delight at discovering a colourful tradition. I sensed something deeper. Before reaching Salzburg I'd had no idea that wild Krampus existed, but I knew that wild Europe did—I'd just spent seven months immersed in it. Krampus was arguably a symbol of wild and untameable natural forces beyond our control. Even though wilderness isn't something modern Europeans need to

Salzburg and the River Salzach, December 8, 1997.

fear on a day-to-day basis as their ancestors had, I found it telling that these people had so enthusiastically embraced a representation of it. Perhaps it was more than just a fun tradition. Was it possible that, on some level, fear of the wild was still needed? Could it be that it remains a part of who we are? Despite the walls we live behind, we are still creatures of the planet; we are still bound to natural forces beyond our control. Civilisation is but a recent invention, and a fragile one at that. Older, deeper-rooted instincts live on within us all—as I'd been discovering for myself since Calabria.

Later that evening, reliving the night's events, I found myself wondering what effect Krampus would have had on my own childhood. I hadn't thought much about wild nature while growing up in suburban London. I'd barely known it existed, and had certainly never experienced a fearful symbol of it charge at me from the night. But perhaps, beyond the simple fun of *Krampusnacht* (and beyond the nightmares that would inevitably have followed), a reminder of the wild would have been a beneficial thing. The culture I'd been raised within insisted that I was separate from nature and above it; that it existed for my use. But the threat of Krampus might have helped me question that, might have hinted at my true place in the natural order of things. It might have reminded me that nature could never be controlled. That it deserved great respect. Perhaps it was something the human race needed too, and desperately; a critical reminder that wild nature would run rampage and devour us all if we stepped too far out of line.

———

Salzburg, beautiful Salzburg, was a fine place to temporarily escape my walk. Historic buildings, easily attained food, a delightful *Gasthof* bed—I made the most of it all.

But when the morning of departure arrived I was ready. I lay for a moment and considered everything ahead: the depths of winter, and all the discomforts that come from living outside, but also new landscapes, new adventures. The Walk would surely change in personality as it had changed several times before, and I couldn't wait to find out how. After four days' rest I was raring to go. The next stage was going to be good. I could feel it.

At 8 a.m. I launched myself from my room and saw the *Gasthof* manager—the short, bald man with a neatly trimmed moustache and tidy waistcoat—stepping from a room down the hallway. He looked up as I strode in his direction. Wearing a broad grin, I halted right before him and grabbed his hand as though greeting an old friend. '*Guten Morgen,*' I exclaimed loudly, pumping his hand up and down. 'How are you? What a GREAT day this is!'

To my surprise, the manager didn't react with the open friendliness he'd shown each time we'd spoken before. Previously, he'd laughed and joked, showing great interest in his English guest, but now he looked surprised, nervous—scared, even. He dropped my hand quickly and backed towards the room he'd just left. It seemed strange, but perhaps he simply wasn't a morning person. That had to be it. Shrugging, I didn't give his reaction any more thought. I was glad I'd found him. My tent, sleeping bag and waterproofs were still locked in the drying room and I needed the key.

As the manager backed away I stepped after him, and asked if he could give me the key.

'I... I... don't think so,' he stammered, eyes darting about. Moving furtively, he reached for the door handle behind him. 'Perhaps you should ask downstairs,' he murmured, and with an impressive turn of speed he darted through the door and swung it shut behind him.

Oh-kay then, I thought, *I'll ask downstairs*. What a peculiar encounter.

Downstairs, I approached the reception desk, and to my surprise the manager—short, bald head, neatly trimmed moustache, tidy waistcoat—was already standing behind it. How had he got there so fast? The manager smiled broadly when he saw me. '*Guten Morgen, Herr* Andrew!' he exclaimed with enthusiasm. 'Are you well today? Did you *schlafen gut?*'

'But...' I blubbered. 'But... you were upstairs... how... why... who...?'

Then it dawned: the man upstairs hadn't been the manager. He'd looked like him, but it hadn't been him. Mixing up faces was something I'd done throughout my life. I never made such mistakes with mountains. I was good at places, not faces. Places were so much easier.

What must the poor man have thought, to have been accosted so energetically outside his room? To have had his hand hijacked? To have had a complete stranger demand his key? I almost shrivelled with embarrassment. Thank the stars I'd never see him again.

Except I saw him at breakfast. I was already seated, and when he entered the room our eyes locked. He tensed, turned to flee, but finally steeled himself and marched to a seat in the farthest corner, then sat facing directly away. Feeling flushed, I stared at his stiff back, and knew that *he knew* I was looking at him. I considered walking over to offer an explanation and an apology, but instead did what all brave long-distance mountain walkers do when the chips are down: I wolfed down my sausages and headed for the hills as swiftly as my skinny legs could carry me.

Civilisation was too damned complicated. It always had been. It was one of the reasons why I'd begun my walk.

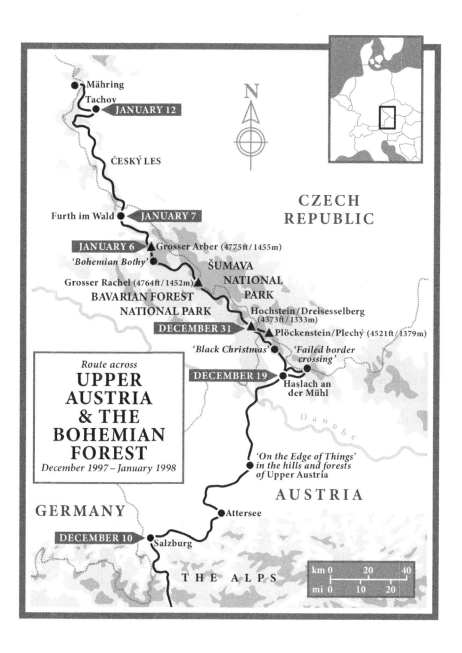

Mähring
Tachov
JANUARY 12

ČESKÝ LES

N

CZECH
REPUBLIC

Furth im Wald ● JANUARY 7

JANUARY 6 ▲ Grosser Arber (4775ft / 1455m)
'Bohemian Bothy' ●
Grosser Rachel (4764ft / 1452m) ▲   ŠUMAVA
BAVARIAN FOREST   NATIONAL
NATIONAL PARK   PARK
   Hochstein / Dreisesselberg
   (4373ft / 1333m)
DECEMBER 31 ▲   ▲ Plöckenstein / Plechý (4521ft / 1379m)
   'Black Christmas'   'Failed border
   crossing'
Route across   DECEMBER 19
UPPER   Haslach an
AUSTRIA   der Mühl
& THE
BOHEMIAN   Danube
FOREST
December 1997 – January 1998   'On the Edge of Things'
   in the hills and forests
   of Upper Austria
GERMANY   AUSTRIA
   ● Attersee
DECEMBER 10
   Salzburg
   km 0   20   40
THE ALPS   mi 0   10   20

17

BACK ON THE TRAIL
Chapter 3

I STRODE OUT of Salzburg swiftly, anticipation hastening my steps. Cobbled city streets gave way to soft, muddy paths. Exhilaration surged. I felt as though I was starting a new journey. The Apennines had been one distinct walk, the Alps another, and the stage ahead was going to be different again. Sure, an unbroken line of footsteps connected all the stages, but it didn't feel as though much else did.

I'd labelled the journey's next stage 'The Heart of Europe'. Arguably, it wasn't a geographically accurate label, but it felt fitting for a route across the centre of the continent. The stage would take me on a four-month, 1,800-mile journey through four different landscapes: the rolling hills of Upper Austria, the forested mountains of Central Europe, the expansive North German Plain, and Denmark's windswept North Sea coastline. I felt mounting excitement for the variety ahead. I had high hopes that I'd once again be able to lose myself within the *other* Europe.

The *other* Europe was the side of Europe that I'd begun my walk to find, the hidden wild side that still existed beyond road's end. I'd found it throughout the Apennines, especially in the trailless *sottobosco*—the infamously tangled Apennine underwood. I'd even found it in the better-known Alps. I'd passed through the Alps out of season, crossing mountains emptied of their summer crowds. Through a glorious autumn that I'd named the 'Endless Summer', then in the deepening snows of November, I'd found a wilder range, an Alps from centuries past.

I was confident I'd find the *other* Europe in the Böhmerwald, the first of the Central European mountain ranges, now lying ten days ahead. The Böhmerwald—or the Bohemian Forest—is an ancient range that curves along the Czech, Austrian and German borders. My maps showed large forested areas devoid of roads and settlements, especially in the Czech Republic. The mountains weren't going to be Alpine in shape, but Apennine-like remoteness looked entirely possible. Once I reached the Bohemian Forest I faced six weeks of forest walking *and* the coldest months of the year. I felt nervous and excited at the prospect.

After the Böhmerwald I'd traverse two further ranges, the Thüringerwald and Harz. Beyond them I'd have easier travel, or so I hoped. By mid-February I'd leave the mountains, cross the North German Plain, then tramp for a month up Denmark. I imagined I'd be ready for a break from winter *and* mountains by then, and I saw this flatter stretch as a holiday from strenuous walking—recovery time before Norway. I considered Norway 'The Prize': the reward my efforts would earn. In Norway I'd enter Europe's emptiest mountains, and the thought of exploring the forests, fjordlands and fjells, and especially the Arctic, set my gut churning with excitement. If all went to plan—and if my finances allowed—I'd reach the top of Denmark by mid-April, take the ferry to Norway, and begin the toughest but most rewarding stage of the journey.

But for now, Upper Austria was the only landscape that mattered. I paced into it, and found it attractive from the start. The path I picked led into a valley of farms and fields, with forests capping the hills above and the Alps rising sharply to the south. I was keen to return to wilder places, but happily embraced this gentle beginning. It was certainly better than plunging into the deep end, as I'd done in Calabria at the journey's start. Back in The Walk's first mountain range, the Aspromonte, I'd spent two days completely lost—an unforgettably stressful way to start. I didn't mind not going through that again.

In this less wild landscape it would have been easy to race north on roads, but I chose a slower route along footpaths and forest trails instead. As I'd been doing since Calabria, I wanted to travel in *good style* and not tempt fate or the wrath of the mountain gods. I'd sensed from the start that if I stuck to the highest and wildest route I'd earn rewards, but if I took the easy option I'd be punished. It was an illogical belief, but events this far had seemed to prove it. When I'd detoured through low-level valleys I'd often suffered negative consequences. Blisters had formed thanks to hard-paved roads, and farm dogs had attacked, but when I'd ventured into the wildest corners I'd won rewards: moments of exhilarating connection with nature.

Here, an accurate map made good style easier to achieve—it made avoiding pavement simple. The map was detailed and reliable, two useful qualities that I'd never again take for granted after the fiction-filled maps of southern Italy. I'd examined the map before breakfast back in the *Gasthof*, identifying the wildest-looking areas and the most interesting paths through them. I'd also chosen a possible destination: a forest roughly fifteen miles from Salzburg. On the map, the forest wasn't named, and yesterday I hadn't known it existed—which made it all the more appealing. Finding new places to explore was one of the perks that kept me walking forward.

Of course, there was a good chance that I might not reach the forest—I often changed destination on the spur of the moment. My route had never been set in stone. The overarching aim was to walk the length of Europe from south to north via a roughly defined route, but the details were entirely flexible. It was exactly like the path I'd taken away from Pinner—mine to choose and change whenever I wished. Recognition of choice, then exercising it—that was where real freedom lay.

The first miles felt easy, thanks in part to a reduced load on my back. Ten Ton was noticeably lighter than it had been back in the Alps. There, with villages further apart, I'd packed more food. I'd also carried snowshoes, crampons and Alpine climbing gear, but those items had been posted back to London. All I'd kept was Excalibur, my trusted ice axe, and as usual that was in hand, not on my back. I'd been using Excalibur as a walking stick for so many months I felt undressed without it.

I crossed the first hills beneath an unseasonably warm sun. Soon, my coat and fleece were removed and stowed inside Ten Ton, and within another mile my sleeves were rolled high—a happy state of affairs for December 10. I weaved into the Austrian Lake District and skirted the fjord-like Fuschlsee, Wolfgangsee, and Attersee lakes, watching snow thaw before my eyes. After so many weeks of Alpine snow the sight of bare earth emerging from the snowpack was a welcome sight. My feet crossed damp woodland floors softened by fallen leaves, trekked over carpets of pine needles, mats of green grass, and acres of chocolate-brown soil, all surfaces

Leaving Salzburg on a spring-like day, December 10, 1997.

to treasure. I couldn't get enough of the snow-free ground. After jettisoning Ten Ton, I dropped to my knees and ran my hands over the earth, caressing and exploring it. I pushed my fingers through mulchy forest litter and on-wards into soil, relishing the fibrous textures and sticky softness, inhaling the heady organic smells my probing unleashed. Back in the Apennines, The Walk had changed my perception and appreciation of water. In the Alps, it had changed how I valued shelter and warmth. And now it altered how I regarded the very earth I walked upon. Each square inch had become a surface to never again take for granted—especially when it ought to have been buried beneath snow.

For once I stuck with the morning's plan, and by late afternoon entered the unnamed forest. As December's early twilight darkened the shadows, I stepped off a narrow path and began casting around through shrinking snowdrifts, seeking a good spot for camp. There was always a perfect pitch somewhere—I just had to look. What I wanted was a location that was flat, sheltered and had a strong sense of place, and after a few minutes I found it: a small clearing enclosed on three sides by thick young spruce, almost like a nest. I named all my campsites, and naming this one was easy. I'd enjoyed my *Gasthof* room, but 'The Spruce Nest' felt far more like home.

I pitched my tent, the Blob, with practised efficiency, knowing that the job would grow harder when winter weather returned. The Blob was the second tent of The Walk, and better at shedding snow than the tent I'd used throughout the Apennines. It would probably seem small and laughably inadequate to most people, but to me, after three months' use, it felt familiar and safe. It was my castle—albeit one that was now dubiously scented.

Once I'd unpacked all my gear I collected snow from a drift and began melting it for water. This task was always slow, and while I waited I celebrated the eccentricity of what I was doing—sleeping in a forest, choosing solitude over company, cooking dinner with thawed snow. *Mad Mountain Jack*, I mocked myself, *you are a complete idiot!* Mad Mountain Jack was the name my three brothers back in England had given me. It suited. I wasn't the same person out here as I'd been back in the suburbs. Here, I was free to be myself. And I was happier—most of the time.

Out here, my previous existence had little relevance. It barely seemed real. I still phoned my parents—Base Camp—every week, swapped letters with my brothers and a few friends, stayed in touch with sponsors and the charities, so I wasn't entirely cut off from the outside world. But for most of the time I felt as though I was. The journey had evolved into an entirely separate existence, but I didn't find this surprising—I was far more embedded in *this* life than I'd ever been in the suburbs. Back there, I hadn't been attached to my job, and thanks to my stammer and lack of social skills hadn't lived much of a social life. Aside from my family, I'd had no strong ties to hold me, and certainly no girlfriend. The days had been repetitive and predictable, dominated by routines, work obligations, restrictions. I'd slept every night in the same house, travelled every day to the same office, and had lived with carpet and concrete underfoot. I'd felt as though I were going nowhere fast. But out here, I *was* going somewhere—and I was going somewhere incredibly slowly. Time runs at a different pace in nature. Attention narrows to the immediate environment, and expands to fully encompass it. There's less room for outside distractions. For me, this made every waking second richer and longer lasting, and it made suburban London feel like a distant, faded dream.

The only time London intruded was when loneliness hit, as it had on a handful of occasions. I'd felt it first after leaving home in April, and again in September after my parents had visited me at the foot of the Alps. And I'd felt it most intensely in October after one of my brothers and a friend had walked with me for a week. Their visit had passed in laughter, but when they'd left the cold reality of my aloneness had hit hard. With a long solitary winter stretching ahead I'd teetered on the edge of a black pit of despair, unsure how I was going to avoid falling in, until the remarkable rock peaks of the Dolomites had pulled me back from the brink.

I'd survived, but the loneliness remained—a shadow that I couldn't entirely shake. I feared and resented it. It didn't match who I wanted to be. I saw myself as a happy-go-lucky wilderness wanderer who needed no one. But the loneliness suggested that I was someone who couldn't manage alone, someone who might even be following the wrong path. I knew that at some point I'd have to confront it. But I was too scared to try. The loneliness was a monster, and I feared unleashing it again. I wasn't certain that the journey would survive.

In the blackness of my forest camp I felt a sudden return of it—a dark hint, not a full-blown attack—but steam rising from my stove, and the act of cooking dinner, worked as a distraction.

Soon, I had a mug of scalding tea to sip and a steaming-hot bowl of eat-it-if-you-dare stew to devour. My standard dinner was a stodgy mush of pasta, powdered soup, meat and vegetables, and as always it tasted far better than it looked. Afterwards, I kept myself busy. I scrubbed my pots with snow and zipped shut the Blob's entrance. I spent half an hour jotting notes in my journal, fifteen minutes practising German, twenty minutes examining the map, then two hours reading a trashy adventure thriller by candlelight. By the time I was ready for sleep the loneliness was buried.

Finally, I lay with my eyes closed, wrapped in my sleeping bag, listening to light rain brushing my roof. I breathed deep the damp air, welcoming it, remembering the heat and dryness of the Apennines. Beyond the rain I could hear soft rustling sounds—the night-time forest going about its business. These sounds now brought great comfort. Back in Calabria, the forests of the Aspromonte had prompted a very different response. Lost for two days in an unfamiliar environment, I'd dashed through the Aspromonte in fear —a victim of an upbringing that had taught me to see the wild as inhospitable, if not dangerous. At first, I'd felt I didn't belong among the trees, but now, after seven months of forest immersion, I saw things very differently.

Here, in this small Upper Austrian forest, I felt comfortable and safe. I pulled the forest tight around me like a blanket, relishing how far I'd come.

It was great to be back on the trail.

ON THE EDGE OF THINGS
Chapter 4

BY THE MORNING, rain was falling in torrents. I delayed striking camp, giving the rain time to relent, a tactic that had worked many times before, but this time it didn't. I set out into a deluge.

'*Gutes Wetter für Fische!*' ('Good weather for fish!') observed a bedraggled farmer as I sploshed by after an hour's progress, and he had that right. The Alps were still visible to the south, but they were wreathed in fog and looked grey and indistinct like old memories. Gloom soon consumed the forests too, but I didn't mind that—I liked how it made them feel wilder. I imagined Krampus moving furtively through the trees just beyond vision's edge, but I stopped my fantasies when a deer with massive antlers burst suddenly from the undergrowth, bringing Krampus to life for a heart-palpitating second.

The rain continued, and during the second and third nights the Blob leaked. I awoke to puddles within the tent, but a little water was nothing compared to the Alpine cold I'd grown used to. I splashed through woods and over hills feeling invigorated by the mild conditions. It was no worse than a typical summer's day back in Britain's mountains—a familiar and manageable discomfort, and still a delight after Mezzogiorno heat and dust.

But the warmth couldn't last. Winter's return was inevitable. On the fourth day from Salzburg it reasserted itself—with a vengeance. Hounded by a cruel wind, pelted by horizontal snow, I cinched my hood tight and kept my head down. I marched north across a pastoral landscape that soon resembled the Arctic. Escape from the biting cold didn't come until my camp in a sheltering forest that night. I burrowed into my sleeping bag like a hibernating bear and listened to the wild ruckus outside: trees thrashing, broken twigs falling, ice pellets flying. The wintry conditions were harder to deal with than warmth and rain, but they *were* what I'd come for. In truth, I didn't want warmth for this stage of my journey. I wanted piles of snow and intense cold. I didn't want a smooth ride—I wanted to be tested by a long, hard season, to feel that I'd *earned* the spring. How else could I grow? How else could I move forward? Winter was supposed to be *winter*, after all.

Winter had always been my favourite season. Throughout my child-hood, snowfalls had been rare and fleeting, which made them a special treat whenever they occurred. Snow transformed the suburban landscape into something new and thrilling, and it always seemed to arrive with sensational media fanfare: *Arctic Blast Screams In!* Snow became one of the highlights of the year, alongside Christmas and family vacations, but arguably greater because I never knew when—or *if*—snow would fall. The excitement of waking to discover that the Arctic had arrived overnight was uncontainable, and it usually took stern parental voices to pull me inside from the back garden at day's end. *But Mum, I'm a polar explorer—do I really have to come inside?* Years later, when I finally discovered mountains, I treasured them the most in 'Arctic weather'. Mountains felt wilder in deep snow, and this was why I wanted snow now, here in Upper Austria. I was here because I wanted a *wild* walk.

Once again, I found myself living a life very different from everyone else around me. Other people had homes, buildings, cars, but I was living entirely outdoors and the weather affected every single part of my day. Just as I'd done in the Alps, I began asking everyone I met for the forecast. A happy, roly-poly man in the village of Attendorf supplied the most memorable forecast.

'The weather tomorrow,' I asked in German, my phrasebook in hand. 'Will it be sunny?'

'*Ja-ja-ja!*' the man replied with a cheerful expression, nodding his head vigorously.

'Or... snowing?' I asked, just to make sure.

'*Ja-ja-ja!*' The man nodded again and beamed at me.

'Or... rain, perhaps?'

'Ah! Rain! *Ja-ja-ja!*'

'Foggy? Windy? A thunderstorm?'

'*Ja-ja-ja!*'

As forecasts go it wasn't especially useful, but when the following morning's weather struck I reflected that perhaps it was better that I hadn't known in advance. I set out into a ferocious wind that whipped up a ground blizzard so fierce it practically blinded me. I couldn't face forward when walking but had to keep my head down, bent sideways. Lurching forward, I felt like a deranged Arctic crab.

I continued north. One foot in front of the other, the most natural thing in the world, but made harder by conditions. Salzburg quickly faded from memory, becoming as dreamlike and distant as London. I'd returned to the *other* Europe far more swiftly than I'd expected. Here it was, even among the farms and villages of Upper Austria. I'd rediscovered it by travelling slowly and on foot, and also by hiding away in the forests at night. Even by day, I rarely saw people in the forests, but at night I had them entirely to myself, unsurprisingly—Austrians had far more sense than Mad Mountain Jack. In fresh snow, with paths hidden, I saw no evidence that people had ever visited, and the landscape's true nature—its wildness—was revealed. My unusual approach turned the forests into environments from another, older time.

Back in the Alps in the autumn, I'd felt as though I'd discovered a secret, as though I were getting away with something: having the landscape entirely to myself. And now the feeling had returned. Once again I was getting away with something, carving out an existence on Europe's wild margins, living in freedom on the edge of things. Admittedly, the forests weren't comfortable, but they were *forests*—the environment I'd grown to love. Over seven months they'd become my home, and a change in seasons couldn't alter that. Home was home, even when the heating failed.

The forests may not have been vast, but the local inhabitants added a dash of wildness. I saw deer every day and listened to owls screeching by night. And then there were foxes, hundreds of them from the sound of it, barking and screaming from sunset to sunrise. They were so vocal —and often sounded so unhealthy, if not unhinged—that I began to wonder if some were sick, and possibly even rabid. The foxes frequently ventured closer to camp than seemed normal; wildlife usually kept away.

My home in the 'other' Europe at the 'Sprayed With Foam Camp', December 15, 1997.

At a camp I named 'Mad Fox Wood', the resident fox sounded so sick that it *had* to be suffering from rabies. Shortly after midnight it crept towards my tent and unleashed a torrent of abuse from close range, shattering my sleep. The barking continued for several minutes and showed no sign of ceasing. Eventually, feeling annoyed, I barked right back, and at that the fox fled, which I presumed meant it was rabies-free. The encounter reminded me of a similar experience in the northern Apennines. I'd camped where a wolf symbol appeared on my map, and for several hours I'd endured a wolf-like howl. I'd tossed and turned, unable to sleep for the racket, until finally I'd had enough. *'SHUT UP!'* I'd screamed at full volume—in Italian, of course, *'STA' ZITTO!'*—and to my amazement it worked; the rest of the night passed without a whimper. Unfortunately, most Austrian foxes ignored a similar request—*'KLAPPE HALTEN!'*—and they robbed me of many hours' sleep. Perhaps my German accent still needed work.

On December 17, 120 miles from Salzburg, I crossed Europe's second-longest river, the Danube. From its source in the Black Forest, the Danube flows east for 1,780 miles through ten countries en route to the Black Sea. Running through a deep valley beneath snowline, the 100-yard-wide river was an impressive sight—a powerful, unstoppable force, even with a determined wind trying to blow it back the way it had come. The river felt like a natural border, as though it marked a change in the land. South of the river sunlight seemed brighter, the environment gentler, but beyond it a suggestion of harsh northernness permeated everything. Perhaps it was all in my mind—but then again, perhaps not. The ancient Roman Empire had once stretched to the Danube at this location, but not any further, and the Romans seldom stopped unless there was good reason. Beyond the Danube lay wild northern lands and fierce, uncivilised barbarians. Cross the Danube at your peril.

Not that I met any fierce barbarians north of the Danube. Fierce weather, yes, but also welcoming, generous people; typical Austrians, in fact. From the moment I'd entered Austria five weeks earlier its citizens had offered spontaneous help; on the approach to my first Austrian village, Mayrhofen, I'd had to turn down three rides. The offers continued in Upper Austria whenever I reached a road. I appreciated the generosity, but there was a downside: the length of time it took to decline a ride. It was all very well for drivers inside their vehicles with heaters blazing and windows opened a tiny crack, much less pleasant for me standing outside in the numbing blast of winter. But if someone offered a ride the least I could do was explain why I couldn't accept it.

My route each day led along forest trails, across open fields, and by road into small villages. The reaction I got from villagers often provided light relief.

'So, where are you walking?' a middle-aged lady in a town square asked in German. 'The train station?'

'Nein,' I responded. 'Norwegen. Nordkapp.' ('Norway. North Cape.') The lady's eyes widened, then she laughed. 'What, today?'

A shopkeeper had a different response: 'But why would you do that? Are you being punished for something?'

And then there was the man who simply shook his head in disbelief. *Yeah right*, his sarcastic expression said, and that was arguably the most satisfying reaction of all.

Earlier in the journey I'd learnt not to mention Norway. The mountain gods seemed to punish me whenever I did. But now, after all I'd been through, it felt less risky, as though I'd earned the right. And I wasn't in Calabria anymore. Norway wasn't that far ahead.

Rolling hill country in Upper Austria near Hofkirchen, December 17, 1997.

Eight days from Salzburg I entered Hofkirchen, a typical Upper Austrian village. I walked to the centre and looked around in appreciation. Modern development hadn't marred this corner of Austria. Most of the houses were simple and square to the point of being severe, with large steep roofs and tall narrow windows, but there was something appealingly Germanic and northern about them. They were also painted in cheerful pastel hues that offset winter's glowering skies and beat back the darkness of surrounding forests. I wasn't crossing Europe for the villages, but I felt drawn to this one. In fact—hard as it was for me to admit—I felt drawn to *all* the villages, a symptom of an issue I was finding increasingly hard to bury.

I lingered longer than necessary inside the supermarket, taking time over my choices. The hum of the freezers and flicker of neon lights felt alien, but also comforting. Leaving the shop was disturbingly difficult, and walking away from the village produced a burst of loneliness. I stopped and stared back at the houses and warm lights. I caught the scent of wood-smoke, and imagined crackling fires and stockinged feet stretched toward glowing embers. Turning back to the woods took an act of strength—or was

29

it an act of foolishness? I couldn't tell. I *loved* the wild margins, *loved* being alone on the edge of things, but I had to accept that villages were growing increasingly attractive. Voluntarily leaving them had begun to feel like an exceedingly odd choice.

The next day, loneliness tugged at my gut once again. In less than a week it would be Christmas, a holiday that had been the happiest time of the year throughout my life. It had always been a family celebration, with parents, brothers and grandparents all coming together, but this year I'd be spending it alone. As the day went on, other small things also set off loneliness: the sight of someone stepping into a warmly lit house on a village's edge; the suggestion of music and laughter from behind a window; the aroma of home-cooked food. *Damn civilisation.* Loneliness didn't strike in the forests.

In the day's last village, I stopped at a phone box to make my weekly call to Base Camp, and that definitely didn't help.

'Hi Mum, hi Dad! It's only me from over the sea!' I sang in cheerful greeting, before launching into descriptions of beautiful winter forests. We talked a while, and I carefully hid my loneliness. My parents would only worry, and that wouldn't achieve a thing. I wasn't walking to make other people suffer.

Only myself, it seemed.

Back in the forest, I wrestled with the growing loneliness. I suspected that it was the greatest difficulty I'd face, far more dangerous than the fiercest winter storm or steepest mountain. Forget Krampus—loneliness was the beast that could destroy The Walk if I let it. In an attempt to overcome it I resorted to harsh words. *Don't be so childish*, I told myself. *Stop being so self-absorbed.* I also tried a more positive approach. *Remember, you've chosen to be here. Remember the homeless that you're walking for. This is nothing compared to what they go through. And just look around at where you are!*

When I'd been lost in the Aspromonte I'd struggled to appreciate where I was because it wasn't where I had wanted to be. Was this a variation of the same theme? I told myself that focusing on what I didn't have instead of the many treasures I did was nothing but an indulgence—and a foolish one at that—but it was an indulgence I found increasingly hard to resist. When the short December day ended, and icy darkness took hold, my thoughts darkened to match. As I pitched the Blob I tried *not* thinking, but the trouble was that I had endless time with nothing to do *but* think.

The winter night—fifteen hours of darkness—seemed desperately long.

The next day went better. Blue skies and a cessation of the wind brought a dash of holiday cheer, and I strode up and down the hills feeling free once again, able to laugh at my up-and-down moods. Christmas carol singing entertained the local crow population, and a signpost with 'Grub' printed on it entertained me. Grub is something most long-distance walkers spend entire days dreaming about.

But, ironically, Grub's village food shop was closed.

By day's end, with the wind picking back up and weariness pulling heavily at my spirit, the loneliness returned. *Again?* I thought in annoyance. *Why isn't this forest enough?* As usual, I was too scared of the answer to honestly reach for it. And, as usual, I tried pushing the loneliness aside. But this time I failed. Disappointment surged. I'd believed that I could handle aloneness. I'd been deliberately choosing it for years. For most of my life aloneness had been a positive state of being.

I'd grown up with a stammer, a mild affliction in the scheme of things, but it had shaped me into a solitary person. The stammer had rendered most social situations desperately stressful, and the taunts and mocking laughter I'd experienced throughout childhood had become a torment to avoid at all costs. I'd been safe at home with my three brothers and parents, even though my stammer still regularly intruded. But I'd rarely been safe anywhere else. Because of it, I'd gone out of my way to be alone.

Life alone was better and safer in every way. It was one of the reasons why I'd fallen so hard for mountains, for the solitude they allowed. There were other reasons too—deeper reasons that I didn't fully understand— but the solitude was a significant part of it. In the mountains I could wander without fear of embarrassment. I could be myself, able to fully relax. For years, being alone in the mountains had been easy. Aloneness had nothing to do with loneliness. Aloneness had become a state of being where life was at its very best.

But now, distressingly, this state of being was cracking apart.

Back in October, when the distracting scenery of the Dolomites had helped me overcome the biggest crisis of loneliness I'd ever experienced, I'd realised for the first time that I needed more than being alone. Yes, I was someone who *could* live alone. But there was also a side of me that needed something else.

But I was still too scared of falling back into the black pit of loneliness to fully acknowledge or examine that side of me. I'd built myself into an island and I didn't want to risk washing it away.

The next day I couldn't still my troubled mind. For once, the landscape wasn't enough to distract me. The simple act of walking didn't distract me, either; in fact, it did the opposite. The meditative nature of putting one foot before the other focused my thoughts in ways I didn't welcome. And the thoughts nagged. *You are an imposter*, they told me. *You are not who you think you are.*

I tried singing cheery tunes, tried every pep talk I knew. But the negative thoughts kept on coming. *A six-month walk would have been fine. You could have pretended to be a free spirit for six months. But not for eighteen. You've been found out.*

My head spun.

You've made a REALLY bad choice.

The hills around me rose and fell, but their ups and downs were nothing compared to my up-and-down mood.

———

Six days before Christmas I tramped into the village of Haslach an der Mühl. My mood had sunk to an all-time low the evening before, but arrival raised it again. In Haslach I'd collect my fourteenth resupply parcel —containing essential maps and film—as well as whatever Christmas post friends and family had sent. The promise of it had me racing through the streets with the exuberance of a child bounding down a staircase on Christmas morning.

At first, I had a hard time finding the post office, but a kind lady went out of her way to show me where it was. I took that as a good omen and decided I liked the village. But then I discovered that the post office had closed early for a village event and wouldn't re-open until after the weekend —three days away. Suddenly, I didn't like Haslach after all. I stood outside feeling uncertain, assaulted by a cold wind and a splattering of sleet. What to do? How could I retrieve my mail? This wasn't in the script.

Snow-covered hills rising above Haslach an der Mühl, December 19, 1997.

Seeking a solution, I came up with Plan A: find someone who spoke English, explain my predicament, and ask for help. Asking for help hadn't been something I'd done much of. Back at the start I'd decided that standing on my own two feet was the purest path to take, the *only* path. Self-sufficiency was something I'd needed to prove. But hadn't I proved it? Three thousand miles of self-sufficiency was surely enough to earn the right to reach out. And reaching out wasn't giving in. It certainly wasn't taking the easy option. As a stammerer, approaching strangers was *never* an easy option.

Across the street from the post office was a small bookshop, and inside it I hesitantly explained my situation. The owner, a blond-haired man about my age, listened impatiently. He spoke good English but failed to comprehend my dilemma. 'Yes-yes,' he finally shouted, losing patience, his wispy moustache bristling, 'but what is the *problem*?' He turned on his heels and stomped away.

So much for asking for help.

Plan B was to write a note and push it through the post office door. *Hello—I'm on a long walk and need help. You were closed when I came for my post. Please forward it URGENTLY to the Czech Republic town of Vyšší Brod.* I sat under cover of a bus shelter attempting to piece together the correct words from my English-German dictionary, but then gave up. It would never work. Even if they understood my note and acted on it the parcel would never arrive in time. But what else could I do? Damn, I wanted my Christmas post.

Just across from the bus shelter was Haslach's town hall, the *Rathaus*. Its entrance was bustling with activity—people coming and going. I approached a lady walking down the stone steps and asked if Haslach had anywhere cheap to stay. 'Wait here,' she replied kindly in German. 'My daughter speaks English—she can help.'

The daughter soon appeared. She had short dark hair, an open face, and was young, perhaps eleven, but her English was near perfect and she quickly translated my question. After a quick-fire exchange between mother and daughter she made an unexpected offer. 'So...' the daughter said cheerfully, 'would you like to stay with us?'

The question was so unexpected that I had to ask the girl to repeat it. But once repeated I didn't hesitate. 'Yes please! I would love to!' The overcast day suddenly brightened. The sleet may even have stopped. I *did* like Haslach after all.

Leaving her mother at the *Rathaus*, the girl, Veronica, guided me across the village to her large home. She led me through a grand entranceway, then pointed me towards the dining room, saying she'd be right back. Into the dining room I stepped, and stopped dead; it was jam-packed with an intimidating crowd of at least forty adults, as well as two dogs. The babble of conversation ceased, heads turned, frowns appeared, the dogs barked, and I swallowed hard, aware of how out of place I must have looked—a dirty vagabond bursting in unannounced. 'Er...' I began, stammering, wondering how to explain, but just at that moment Veronica returned with her older, blond-haired, twenty-something sister, Julia, and to my relief they pulled me back and led me upstairs. *Close call*, I thought.

My room for the night was the 'sewing room', a space overflowing with odds, ends, bric-a-brac and junk. A full-size tailor's mannequin dominated the room's centre, and reams of colourful fabric buried the small bed, but a few minutes' work from the sisters created room enough for their English guest. 'So,' Julia said with a glorious smile, 'you must make yourself at home. But first,' she continued, 'you are walking *how far?*'

With Julia leaning close, her golden hair spilling down, I pulled out my European map and traced my finger along the entire route. This wasn't like explaining it to motorists while standing in a biting wind. This time, I didn't care how long it took.

After a series of questions and some of my best stories, the two sisters led me back to the dining room—thankfully now empty. They salvaged some leftover food—hearty sandwiches, spicy coleslaw, and still-warm potato salads—and the three of us tucked in. Halfway through the feast Julia's boyfriend arrived, along with her mother. The boyfriend, Levente, was from Hungary, and Julia proudly told me he made pottery for a living and would be selling it today at the big Christmas market back at the *Rathaus*. 'You can help us carry it there,' Julia suggested, 'and also there will be a man there we know who works at the post office…'

A man from the post office? I jumped straight up. 'Well… let's go!'

We squeezed into Levente's matchbox-sized white van and drove back to the *Rathaus*. While Julia ran an errand I helped Levente carry clinking boxes of delicate pottery up the stone steps, praying I wouldn't trip. Julia returned shortly after we'd safely completed this task, leading a middle-aged man. He was holding a large crate in his arms—a crate filled with mail.

Julia laughed. 'You must have a lot of friends, *ja?*'

My eyes widened. The man was from the post office and the mail was all for me. There were twenty-five items; a great pile of packages and envelopes. I could scarcely believe it. How the day had changed! What a great place Haslach was!

Little Veronica led me back across town once again, let me in to her home, then left me alone in the sewing room. Laughing aloud, I tore into my parcels, but not the letters—those I'd save for Christmas Day.

With brown paper shredded and cast aside I worked through the gifts: a new sleeping pad, several books, a traditional British Christmas cracker (of all things) from my mother, a box of English shortbread, a Christmas fruit cake with a Santa on top (but no Krampus), some chocolate liqueurs, a party whistle, and three smaller gifts in wrapping paper that I decided I'd also save for the Big Day. For a few hours, it was Christmas come early.

Following Julia's suggestion, I returned to the town hall at 5 p.m. 'There's going to be a Christmas show,' she had said. 'It will be on the steps. You *must* come and see it. My mother is in charge.'

Darkness had descended by the appointed hour and sleet was falling hard, but neither dampened the spirits of the gathered crowd. Parents and grandparents sheltered beneath a sea of umbrellas, and the performers were all children, arranged beneath a stone arch at the top of the steps. After a short delay the show began. First came a brass band, not entirely in tune, then carol singers, not exactly in harmony. Next were several mumbled speeches and readings, followed by a short and chaotic nativity play. The grand finale was the appearance of a large, wheeled swan, upon which sat a small girl dressed in white. For some reason she wore a crown topped with five burning candles, and the crowd greeted her with a long round of applause. The show lasted less than twenty minutes, and it should have been underwhelming—but I looked around at the glowing faces of adults and children, at a community come together, and I felt myself glowing too. The festivities may have been gentler than those of *Krampusnacht*, but it was an event of warmth and magic.

I ambled 'home' afterwards and let myself in. Later, Veronica fetched me from my room and soon I was downstairs with the family, devouring the tastiest sauerkraut and bratwurst I'm ever likely to eat. The following hours passed in easy companionship, the gentleness of it helping me overcome my stammer. Veronica had me play her favourite game, a Japanese pick-up-sticks game called Mikado. She was an expert; I didn't stand a chance. Photo-album viewing came next—family snaps and stories—followed by television, an Austrian chat show that by some bizarre coincidence featured nothing but English-speaking guests. Elton John appeared first, rainbow-heeled and frilly cuffed, talking about how he'd escaped Pinner, the very same London suburb I too had fled; then Pierce Brosnan, 007, arrogantly puffing a cigar. The Backstreet Boys performed, to Veronica's delight, then the Spice Girls, delighting Levente. I sat enjoying it all, treasuring the understated everyday normality of it.

Without any fuss they had made me a family member, and I was awed and humbled by the hospitality. I was just a passing stranger—a foreigner, a tramp, unkempt and unknown—but they had taken me in and treated me with unconditional acceptance and astonishing trust. I'd been living a voluntary form of homelessness and had been struggling with it. But the family had given me a home. For a few hours loneliness was utterly banished.

No Christmas gift I'd ever received had been finer.

Day's end on the forest's edge, December 18, 1997.

BLACK CHRISTMAS
Chapter 5

NORMAL LIFE RESUMED the next morning, although when was The Walk ever normal? A few brisk miles had me back in forests, nearing the Czech border. With each stride my energy surged: the Czech Republic, a new country, new people! There was even a chance I'd find someone I'd met before, a wise Czech mountaineer named Frantisek. We'd met during my 1994 walk across the Alps, sharing a winter room beneath Grossvenediger, and the man's live-life-to-the-full attitude was something I'd been unable to forget. Frantisek had suffered a heart attack three years before I met him, and for a while his existence had been touch and go. He'd been a climber all his adult life. When his doctor ordered no more climbing, Frantisek had refused to listen. Accepting the risks, making his own choices, he climbed on regardless, *living* life, not just surviving it. He was sixty-four when I met him, but possessed a twenty-year-old's spirit and zest. He lived in a town a day's march from the Czech border, and although I didn't have his address tracking him down seemed feasible. How fantastic if I could see how he was doing!

My route to the Czech border followed a forest road. The surface was sheet ice, more glacier than pavement, and progress was precarious. I had the road to myself for several treacherous miles until a police car appeared ahead and slid carefully to a halt. Two policemen emerged. They wore immaculate grey coats and long black boots, and their highly polished holsters were unfastened as though ready for use. Their appearance was intimidating, but it was lessened by the comedy of their approach across the ice. As they wobbled and teetered, waving their arms to stay in balance, it was all I could do to stifle my laughter.

Finally, they reached me. '*Guten Tag*,' one of them said politely, and with great dignity. 'Please, may we see your passport?'

I dropped Ten Ton and dug it out. While one of the policemen returned carefully to the car with my passport to confirm by radio that I wasn't a wanted criminal or illegal immigrant, the other stayed with me, happy to pass the time of day. We chatted amiably about the weather, language, London, football, and eventually The Walk.

'You are going… *where?*' the policeman exclaimed, and I grinned. I'm human—the reaction was never going to grow old.

I asked if crossing into the Czech Republic anywhere in the forests was allowed. I'd grown used to doing this elsewhere in Europe during previous walks, popping over international borders at remote mountain passes without formalities. But that wasn't the case here.

'*Nein*,' the officer replied seriously, 'you can only cross at official control points. Our laws are quite strict on this.'

I nodded. It was what I'd expected. The Czech Republic wasn't yet part of NATO or the European Union and had only recently escaped imprisonment from behind the old Iron Curtain. I was intrigued to reach the border and see what evidence remained of Cold War defences. The Cold War and its threat of nuclear annihilation had been a constant feature during my teenage years. I'd seen endless clips of the Iron Curtain on the news and in movies. Images of people trying to flee communism flashed before my eyes. It was understandable that I'd have to take a long detour to officially cross it—but also a chore. The actual border lay half a mile ahead, but I'd have to walk fifteen miles in the wrong direction to legally reach the other side.

Eventually, the policemen handed my passport back and wished me luck. Fifteen minutes later I reached the border, site of the Iron Curtain. I stood before it thoughtfully. Just eight years earlier it had been heavily militarised and fortified. Two barbed-wire barriers had run through a cleared stretch of forest, and the open space between them had been seeded with mines. There'd been guard towers and guard dogs, and regular foot and armoured-vehicle patrols. Soldiers had been authorised to shoot anyone

Site of the old Iron Curtain, December 20, 1997.

trying to cross. But now, nothing remained of the defences—the border was an inconspicuous clearing running through a peaceful forest. The only evidence left were unassuming signs posted every fifty yards: *Pozor! Státní hranice* (Attention! State border). I looked left, right, left again. There was no one in sight. I still planned to cross where I was supposed to but couldn't see the harm in popping over right here for a few seconds. Carefully, I stepped over, and stood breathlessly in the Česká Republika, feeling like a naughty schoolboy breaking a clearly stated rule. After ten seconds I stepped back, but the moment I re-entered Austria the silence of the woods was shattered by a blood-chilling Cold War sound: the rising wail of a siren. The suddenness of it set my heart a-thumping, had me staring in all directions at once. It *had* to be a coincidence—I couldn't possibly have set it off, could I? But I didn't linger to find out. I dashed away through the Austrian woods with all the speed I could muster.

It took two days to reach the official crossing point, although I could easily have reached it in one. I was slowed by an unplanned rest day on December 21, the winter solstice. I woke in camp—the 'Little Spiders Wood'—and instead of packing Ten Ton and striding on I simply stayed in bed, eating and reading. The day off surprised me—it wasn't planned. Although keen to reach the Czech border, I felt controlled by other forces. Amused by my laziness, I wondered if it had something to do with it being the year's shortest day. Perhaps staying in bed was instinct. A token day of hibernation in the middle of winter.

The following day couldn't have been more different. I was up early and heading for the border with energy and purpose. Conditions had warmed again and snow was melting fast. Ahead, exactly where the border lay, overcast skies gave way to startling blue, and I took that as a promising sign. My pace picked up. I loved approaching new countries! I loved not knowing what lay ahead! Wasn't *this* the point of travel?

The Austrian border crossing was a formality. I lined up behind three cars, and when the guard took my passport he stamped it and handed it back without sparing me a glance. On I walked. The Czech control lay a mile inside the country, and I marched down the shoulder of the road towards it, thrilled to be across the Iron Curtain in the old Eastern Bloc, doing something that for most of my life had been beyond the bounds of possibility. Incredibly, the landscape already looked different. The spruce and fir hadn't changed, but the forest looked less managed and visibly wilder. Shortly before the control point I passed a roadside duty-free shop and grinned at the signs featuring unpronounceable words and unrecognisable symbols. *Bring it on*, I thought.

When I reached the Czech border control a stern guard took my passport and stared at it long and hard. The guard's face looked like one that had never smiled.

'What is your destination?' he asked brusquely, in Czech first I guessed, then in German.

'Norway,' I replied, hoping to break the ice. But I didn't achieve even a hairline crack.

'No,' the guard snapped. 'Your destination. Today. Where are you staying?'

'Well… I'm camping. In the forest.'

The guard looked me up and down, officiously, assessing. 'That is not allowed.'

Silence followed; I didn't know what to say. Awareness that things weren't going to plan suddenly overcame me.

'You must tell me where you are staying,' the guard said again, growing impatient.

'Um,' I mumbled, 'er...'

'If you cannot do that you cannot enter.'

'Well, you see, I'm walking from Italy to Norway. I can't really plan ahead.'

The guard shook his head and handed back my passport. 'You must go back now. Go. GO!'

I looked around desperately, wondering if there was anything I could do. I didn't want to go back to Austria. Wasn't there someone else I could talk with, some way of explaining? I tried, but no—there was nothing to be done. The guard waved me away, pointing back towards Austria, and back towards Austria I walked, cursing my ignorance, cursing my inability to think on my feet. I was too law-abiding. I should have lied, made up something. Dammit! But it was too late now. No new country. No Frantisek!

I paced back towards Austria and stared at the only snatch of *Česká* forest I'd likely see. I hadn't noticed before, but the road margins were fouled with litter, beer cans, cigarette packets, and torn pornographic magazines. *Humph*, I thought. It didn't look like a particularly nice country anyway.

Back in Austria, I examined my map and chose a new route that led north-east toward Germany, picking trails that stayed south of the Czech border. Adapting my route was something I'd been doing all journey, in ways small and great. I'd changed plans because of the weather, the mafia, misleading maps, and often because I'd simply wanted to see what lay on the other side of a hill. Missing out on the Czech Republic was a crying shame, but it wasn't the end of the journey. My route had never been set in stone.

In any case, a flexible route had its benefits, as I proved once again the next day when I retraced my steps to Haslach. Although I was too embarrassed by my failure at the border to call upon Julia and Veronica's home, I made certain I stopped at the post office. Amazingly, there was more Christmas mail for me: another six spirit-lifting envelopes. Being turned back was a failure, but I rationalised it away. If I'd crossed the border, the extra post would never have reached me. Everything happens for a reason —or so it sometimes seems.

Looking south toward the Alps from the foothills of the Bohemian Forest, December 20, 1997.

The following day was Christmas Eve, and upon it a bleak light shone, and across it a chill wind blew. The winter landscape was now *brown*, and it wasn't what I wanted to see. I'd been dreaming of a white Christmas my entire life—and *this* Christmas should have been white.

Just twelve hours earlier there'd still been some snow streaking the hillsides, resting in clumps on trees. But then came a harrying wind, tossing the trees about overnight, knocking most of the snow down. A few stubborn clumps still clung to branches at dawn, but while I was packing away camp, trying to keep my gear dry, a joker of a gust dislodged one final dollop and it avalanched into my open pack. Some even went down the back of my neck. If I hadn't been fully awake before, I certainly was after.

Following my new route, I strode across the now-familiar Austrian landscape. It offered farmland at first, but as I entered the Bohemian Forest the edges grew wilder, the hills larger, the forests thicker, the shadows darker. To the south, the Alps were still in view, jagged and gleaming; north lay the forests of the Czech Republic, for me forbidden country. But it didn't matter. As I'd learnt in the Apennines, it was where I was that counted, not where I wasn't. Also, my revised route didn't lack interest. I passed an old stone farmhouse, smoke puffing from its chimney. A hundred yards past it I came to a wooden bench and took a break, spreading out gear to dry on the skeletal limbs of a spiky hawthorn. Within minutes an ancient farmer ambled over, creaking down onto the bench beside me. He wore an oversized cap and tattered clothes, but it was his thick socks and fluffy carpet slippers—both bright pink—that caught my attention. He lacked teeth, he had trouble hearing, and the words he slurred were utterly indecipherable. But that was okay—he couldn't understand me either. Despite our mutual incomprehension we passed a happy half hour together, talking and grinning into each other's faces. When finally I pushed on the man appeared disappointed; I got the feeling he wanted to sit and not quite communicate for hours. Later, I wished I had.

Brightness faded shortly after noon and fog seeped across the hills. Now that the solstice had passed the days were supposedly growing longer, but by 1 p.m. dusk had already begun. Down in the valley, farmhouse lights flickered on one by one. As the gloom deepened so did my mood. I couldn't stop picturing an alternative reality: myself indoors, feet stretched towards a roaring fire, a decorated Christmas tree shimmering in the corner. Angrily I punctured the image. Didn't I have real Christmas trees all around?

Mid-afternoon I reached a road and followed it briefly. Another patrol car pulled over and two policemen climbed out—a welcome distraction from my dark thoughts. The officers were different from the pair that had stopped me days earlier, although one recognised me, saying he'd seen me back at the official border crossing.

'I'm not planning on it,' I said, 'but do people ever cross illegally?'

'Yes, they try. People from Hungary and Romania mostly. But we catch them and send them back.'

'Can't be much fun working on Christmas Eve,' I observed, trying to share a little of my holiday misery.

'Oh, we have Christmas Day off,' the policeman replied with a smile, before continuing more seriously: 'But some of our colleagues don't.' The message was clear: don't get any ideas.

With drizzle falling I pulled on waterproofs and slouched along a well-marked trail, the Saint Oswald's Way, according to a sign. It led uphill into murky forests. Over two lonely hours I thought about all the people I'd encountered that day: the toothless old man, the police officers, a young farmer who'd gushed about a surfing adventure he'd once had in Australia, a hand-in-hand couple seeing only each other as they walked, and a family with three excited kids. Every one of them would close a door at day's end, shutting out the darkness. They'd sit down to dinner indoors in a familiar place, surrounded by comfort, warmth, and people they loved, and probably wouldn't think anything of it. But not me. I had a small, dirty, soggy tent, and a cold, damp, foggy forest. I still wanted to be on The Walk, but suddenly didn't want to spend Christmas alone.

No forest clearing has ever been murkier than the clearing I chose for my Christmas Eve camp. And it was the brightest clearing I could find. Tall spruce surrounded it, their trunks rising like pillars of dark stone, fog sucking at their tops. Daylight died hours early, and while I ate my miserable stew heavy rain began, large droplets hammering onto my tent's roof. But at least I had a roof. At least I had that.

At no time had walking to raise money for the homeless felt more appropriate. My own home was a world away, and I felt completely cut off from it, from everything and everyone I knew, and the fact that it was by choice only made it harder to bear. When first I imagined spending Christmas alone in the woods the idea had appealed. How romantic: the 'hero' alone in the wilderness on his big adventure! I'd anticipated coping effortlessly with the solitude. I had even pictured myself enjoying it. But how wrong I'd been! There was nothing romantic in this isolation, nothing clever in what I was doing. It was self-punishment, pure and simple. I'd willingly chosen this unique form of homelessness, and I cursed myself for it.

And I wasn't homeless, as well I knew from the many times I'd thought about it since Calabria. But I *was* lonely—goodness was I lonely. For all my life I'd taken the people around me for granted, but my final thought on this dark Christmas Eve was that I'd never take them for granted again.

Dawn was slow in coming; the sun appeared as unwilling to face Christmas Day as I felt. With fog pressing heavily, the forest was stuck in a grey and depressing twilight. Choosing a name for the camp wasn't necessary. 'Camp Gloom' named itself.

'Camp Gloom' on Christmas morning, December 25, 1997.

For an hour, the task of opening and reading my Christmas post distracted me from the abyss that threatened to swallow me. Love and support poured forth from friends, family, neighbours, even complete strangers who were following The Walk. I was an inspiration, according to one kind lady—and for a few minutes the comment raised my morale, even though I felt like a fraud. But when I read that my family were going to raise their glasses and toast me at exactly 2.30 p.m., and that I should raise my mug at the same moment, darker emotions welled and almost overcame me. Somehow, I kept them in check.

I escaped 'Camp Gloom' mid-morning and headed for the valley, leaving my sodden shelter and gear behind. But I couldn't escape my own gloom. Carrying it with me, I reached the closest village in under an hour, and the monastery in the centre of it in time for Christmas mass. I crept into the church at Stift Schlägl and sat discreetly at the back, an interloper and non-believer, but a man craving comfort and familiarity. The church, right then, was the closest thing I had to home.

I'd been raised a Roman Catholic, and for much of my life had been one. I'd attended mass each week, performed an altar boy's duties, had gone to a Catholic school, and had been part of a wonderful, warm-hearted and welcoming religious community. I'd been brought up to believe, and believe, I suppose, I had—until I began thinking for myself. It had taken years before I'd developed sufficient intellectual curiosity to question my faith. Questioning it, I had once been admonished, was 'a dangerous path to follow', and finally I discovered why: the answers that had been calculated for me didn't remotely add up. A difficult but honest journey had followed, spread over several years. Ultimately, it revealed that my religion was built on sand—sand that a rising tide of rational thinking washed away. Left behind were rocks the tide couldn't shift: ethical values that supported themselves, and morals that were right because they were quantifiably right, because of the net positive effect they had, not because a powerful institution said they were right. My entire view of the world—and of existence itself—changed profoundly. Understanding that I, and not some omnipotent deity, was in control of my life only strengthened my determination to live that precious, fleeting life to the full and celebrate it to its utmost. Instead of guilt I found a new innocence, and instead of rules I found freedom of choice. The meaning of life, I discovered, was to live a life of meaning, and meaning was something we created for ourselves.

And yet, I found great comfort when I stepped into the church at Stift Schlägl. Within seconds the familiarity soothed my troubled mind. How well I knew the smell of incense, the reverent atmosphere, and the powerful pull of a community come together for a shared purpose. I sat at the back and let the intimately known rituals banish my loneliness. It was like watching a movie I'd seen a thousand times before, a welcome distraction from thinking my own thoughts. When a little girl stood and sang 'Silent Night' it brought tears to my eyes. The performance was hauntingly beautiful, representing everything Christmas had ever been, but the tears it prompted weren't just tears of appreciation for the singing, or even of loneliness, but also of mourning for the easy end-of-life safety net of a faith I no longer had. I couldn't go back, and didn't want to, but it was something I suspected I'd always miss.

Once mass had finished I rose to go. The people in church were probably all good people, and I had no doubt any number of them would take me in if I revealed my situation, but it felt wrong to take advantage of them. Instead, I scoured Schlägl's streets, hoping to find a restaurant and treat myself to a meal I hadn't cooked myself. I came upon a Chinese restaurant first, but it was closed and empty, then a pub, but it was being cleaned. 'We open at six,' I was told coldly. 'Disco at nine.'

After a few more turns I reached an expensive-looking hotel and thought: *to hell with my funds.* But the meal wasn't a success. The food was heavenly, and the large whisky that accompanied it a glorious indulgence. But each bite and sip only brought home how *far* from home I was. I sat alone and isolated, the only single diner in a crowded restaurant, separated from everyone else by a gaping chasm. At first I tried to savour the meal, to fully taste each morsel of food and relish the indoor warmth, but the familiarity pushed me too close to the edge, reminding me too powerfully of all it was not, and I ended up rushing it to have the anguish over and done. Stepping outside was a relief.

Before returning to camp I phoned home, aiming to reassure Base Camp that all was well. Back in Pinner, the entire family had gathered together. I spoke to everyone in turn—brothers, grandparents, and parents—listening to happiness in their voices and Christmas energy in the background. How I managed to get through the call without breaking down I cannot say. It was touch and go, and when finally the call finished I barely had seconds spare to crash down the handset before all the emotions I'd been holding back burst forth. I fell against the dirty glass inside the phone box, head in hands, and sobbed and moaned in torment. For long, uncounted minutes my world was as black and desolate as outer space.

Camp when I regained it was drained of light, colour and warmth. Still desperate to escape my thoughts I tried keeping myself busy for the few hours of daylight that remained. I wandered about the grey woods, sorted gear, reread my post. Nothing helped. The minutes passed like hours, the hours like months, and the evening darkness like an eternity. I couldn't imagine how I was going to get through it, couldn't picture The Walk ever again being the same. I'd push on, I knew I would; I'd push on until the end or until I ran out of funds, whichever came first. But there'd be no pleasure in it. No real point. I'd be alone, forever alone, because alone was how I lived. It was what I'd chosen, it was who I was, and it was all I deserved. Loneliness was my curse, my eternal penance and punishment, and nothing

I could do would ever change it. There was no way out.

Darkness swallowed me long before nightfall. I'd imagined that The Walk would give me a white Christmas, but I got the exact opposite: a *black* Christmas.

It was the blackest Christmas imaginable.

Fog still clung to the Bohemian Forest the next morning. If anything, the murk was even dimmer, the dampness more penetrating, the temperature colder, but—unexpectedly, astonishingly, gloriously—I awoke to feelings of unbounded lightness, to irrepressible optimism, to streaming internal sunlight, to high spirits that wanted to soar.

The foggy dawn was simply dazzling. It was the extreme opposite of everything I'd expected it to be. I could scarcely believe how I felt.

I lay with the stove humming and laughed aloud in surprise. I wanted to get up and run around and scream with happiness. I wanted to raise my arms to the sky. *Look—I survived!*

As I devoured breakfast I checked myself over mentally, the way someone checks their body after taking a hard fall, looking to see what had been broken, feeling immense relief that nothing had. I felt great. No, greater than great. I was a new man; renewed if not reborn. It was as if all the emotions that had washed through me on Christmas Day had washed me clean. Loneliness was gone, as though it had never existed. It was extraordinary. I couldn't even *imagine* it anymore.

I was soon underway, striding forward with enthusiasm and delight. As I weaved through the fog-bound forest I delved deeper into the Christmas low, no longer scared to explore loneliness, no longer fearing what I'd find.

After two miles I had my answers. I concluded that it had been an ordeal I'd had to face—an essential part of my quest to move forward. It had been a learning experience, necessary and ultimately beneficial. I'd needed it for the altered perspective it provided. If I hadn't fallen so low I may never have truly appreciated everything I had both here in the woods and, more importantly, back in civilisation. I now understood that I wasn't an island, and never had been—an instinctive understanding for most people, perhaps, but to me a monumental discovery. For years, I'd been fighting for a belief that had never been true, and now that I understood the truth there was no longer any need to fight. Without conflict, there was peace.

Company, I now saw, was as essential as food. But that didn't mean I needed it constantly. Just as I didn't have to miss food between meals, so I didn't have to miss company when I didn't have it. It always lay ahead, and knowing this was enough. The distance no longer mattered.

From the Christmas low I now understood the importance of family as I never had before. I saw that I was fortunate beyond measure. I had a family. And they supported and loved me. How could I ever feel lonely, knowing that? I wanted to sing with joy because of it.

I am not alone.

The entire Christmas season had forced me through an emotional wringer, and it had thoroughly reshaped me. It reminded me of my Hohtürli accident, for how it had altered my place in the world. For the experience I'd gone through I felt grateful beyond words.

Loneliness had died, and I felt confident that its power over me would never again be the same.

BOHEMIAN RHAPSODY
Chapter 6

AS A NEW man, I strode into the Böhmerwald, a range as little known to most outsiders as the mountains of Calabria. My own knowledge was equally limited. I knew there'd be forests of course, and mountains—but little else. As always, finding out was why I was walking.

Being realistic, I knew that the Böhmerwald was not going to be Europe's last great wilderness. Then again, I suspected it was *not* going to be the overcrowded, over-industrialised Europe that most people know either. And so it proved.

At first it was a hidden world—grey, damp and smothered. Rain fell with determination and fog remained stubbornly in place. But conditions failed to dampen my soaring post-Christmas high. If anything, they added to it. The perpetual twilight made the forest a place of mystery, a wild Krampus realm from ancient legends. As I weaved through a labyrinth of barely seen trees, with rain-streaked trunks rising into fog, spruce boughs dripping, and mossy boulders looming, I imaged myself in a world from millennia past, traversing the original primeval forest. A woolly mammoth might appear ahead, or a fierce-eyed sabre-toothed cat, or a Neanderthal cloaked in heavy skins. I felt isolated from my own species, removed from normal society—but unlike at Christmas I rejoiced in that aloneness. I felt alive, fully engaged in the here and now, no longer thinking about things I didn't have.

Miles passed and little changed. I paced along soft paths, trees appearing and vanishing in moments, the environment forever altering but always the same. The forest *felt* vast, as though the range were nothing but trees—which wasn't far from the truth. As I later learnt, eighty per cent of the Böhmerwald is forested. At lower elevations, the forests are rich and varied, filled with spruce, white birch, alder, beech and willow. Higher, conifers dominate, and on the highest ridges spruce cloaks all. Though the Böhmerwald is far from pristine—civilisation has reached far up many valleys—large areas have never been felled. Stands of old-growth forest shelter ancient giants 180 feet tall. These living cathedrals are as sacred as any on Earth. By European standards the forests *are* vast. Between the Atlantic and the Urals no other forests come close in size—or in wildness.

But it's not all trees. There are open spaces: upland plateaux studded with lakes and blanketed in peat and bogs. There are also eroded outcrops of granite and gneiss rearing above the trees like goblin castles. These coarse-grained tors hint at the mountain range the Bohemian Forest once was, a mightier range that predates the Alps by hundreds of millions of years. The Böhmerwald was once sharp and jagged, but time beyond human comprehension has worn the hills down. The mountains are old—something I felt with every step. Here, there was no hum from traffic, no gleam from electric lights, no walls—and there never had been. The trees around me were going about their unhurried business as their ancestors had for thousands of years, and as their descendants might for thousands of years more. The sense of continuity was all-pervasive.

On December 27 rain fell without let-up from dawn to dusk, slowly dampening my body beneath my waterproofs. But then, as darkness approached, it turned to snow as though a switch had been flicked. Within minutes the forest was transformed. Conditions that had merely been wet and uncomfortable edged towards serious. Feeling damp and chilled, I began looking for a sheltered site for camp. I paused several times, considering the wintry forest. Since turning white it had grown wilder, but not in a way that made me comfortable. All at once, a voice inside began arguing for retreat—the voice from my upbringing, the voice of anxiety insisting that the forest was a place where I didn't belong. It was the old Aspromonte fear, and its return annoyed me. Would I never get over it? I stared into the forest, unsettled, but knew enough now to question my fears. Was this forest *really* a place I needed to retreat from? I compared it to the Aspromonte and saw that it wasn't as vast. Here, civilisation only lay a few hours below. Conditions were serious, but not unmanageable. *I belong here*, I reminded myself, *even in a snowstorm*. I began walking again, onward and upward, further into the wild. *This* was what I'd come for, after all: to experience a place wild enough to stir my senses and emotions. If I'd felt absolutely nothing, there would have been little point being here.

The snowstorm grew in severity, but the reward for pushing on eventually came, just as it always did. This time it took the form of a rickety lean-to: three wooden walls and a roof. It appeared at exactly the moment I began wishing for a more solid shelter than my tent, and although it wasn't a natural part of the forest I welcomed it. It was a reassuring sign of civilisation—although I didn't want to accept that I needed it for that reason. Instead, I focused on its practical benefits: the shelter it gave. I pitched the Blob inside the lean-to on bare earth, although the tent's rear end stuck out into the storm. But it was shelter enough. Soon, I lay in relative comfort, and listened to the wind roaring, trees thrashing and snow flying—winter being unleashed. This was the Central European winter I'd been waiting for, and I celebrated its arrival. It made my final night in Austria suitably memorable.

The storm eased by dawn, although snow still floated gently down. I crossed into Germany mid-morning and descended to the small Bavarian municipality of Neureichenau to stock up on fresh supplies. At first glance *Deutschland* was little different from *Österreich*. The buildings looked similar, stores and banks displayed the same corporate logos, the trees were identical, and the cold numbed my fingers just as effectively. I only found one small difference: the state of a local bus shelter. I paused within it for a rest and discovered walls covered with obscene graffiti and an overflowing rubbish bin—two things I hadn't seen in neat-and-tidy Austria. It felt very urban, and I left quickly. Neureichenau sat beneath snowline. Village residents stared at me as I trekked along their rain-washed streets. There was no snow down here, but snow lingered in soggy clumps on my shoulders and pack. I imagined how out of place I must look.

Far above, back in my familiar fog-bound forest home, I made my first German camp. Scattered about the forest were the first of the Böhmerwald's tors: looming outcrops weathered to look like giant skipping stones stacked one atop another. They bore a striking resemblance to tors

Looming granite tors in the forest, December 28, 1997.

on Dartmoor back in England, but here, instead of standing proud above windswept moors, they lurked among trees. The '*Other* Dartmoor' camp felt like a truly ancient spot.

The next day, instead of walking on, I left camp pitched and set out to explore the area. Travelling light, I followed a meandering make-it-up-as-I-go route through the forest and around the tors. Moisture from the fog had frozen onto every surface, frosting spruce-needles, twigs and tors. Fresh snow carpeted the ground underfoot. Aside from deer and fox tracks, mine were the only prints, and I enjoyed the illusion of being the first human to visit. The fog grew thicker as I climbed, and when I reached the day's first summit—4,373-foot Hochstein (also known as Dreisesselberg)—the swirling cloud was so dense I could only see fifteen feet. Hochstein's outcrops were impressive, even in the fog. They rose above the trees and I suspected they'd give a sensational view—*if* the fog ever cleared. Hoping it would, I decided to stay camped in the area for a second night. It wasn't as though I had to rush on. Norway wasn't going anywhere.

A short distance below Hochstein I stumbled upon an unexpected outpost of civilisation: a small restaurant. Outside, a family were playing in the snow, acting as though they had never seen it before. A laughing father explained that this was *almost* the case.

'This is our first heavy *Schnee* of the winter. Normally, it would be a metre deep by now.' He held his hand waist-high to demonstrate. 'But this winter's been slow getting started.'

His wife chimed in. 'But it *has* been cold,' she said. 'Compared to the lowlands it's *always* cold up here.' She looked less happy about it than her husband. 'Usually, it is winter for three quarters of the year here in the Böhmerwald.' She paused a moment for dramatic effect. 'And cold the rest of the time.'

Smiling at the joke, I pushed east from Hochstein and soon reached a broad, treeless ridge. It definitely *was* winter now. In the snow and fog, the landscape was a blank sheet of paper, an environment of absolute simplicity. The ridge marked the Bohemian Forest's watershed—the Black Sea–North Sea divide—as well as the international boundary. To the north lay the Czech Republic, and Šumava National Park, part of a protected area of 385 square miles. The mountains of Šumava (which means 'dense forest') are even less disturbed than those in Austria and Germany. The Šumava border regions have always been sparsely inhabited, and they became sparser still when the Iron Curtain was drawn tightly across them. German-speaking inhabitants were expelled, restrictions put in place, and an empty buffer zone was created where East meets West. But what was damaging to the local population became beneficial for the landscape—it suffered few of the ravages of the modern age, becoming a wilderness preserved almost by accident.

Following the ridge, I walked with one foot in Šumava, one in Germany, but saw nothing of either. Two miles east of Hochstein I crossed back into Austria for a brief hour and climbed to the summit of Plöckenstein, known as Plechý to the Czechs. At 4,521 feet Plechý is the highest point in Šumava, but for the view it gave it might as well have been at sea level. For a moment, I considered stepping further into the Czech Republic, until I remembered the wailing siren. But I felt gratitude—even for this. If this wild summit was all I ever experienced of the country, that was at least something. The remoteness stirred me.

Fog still clung to the forest the next day. I decided to linger beneath

Hochstein a third night. The Böhmerwald only rises above tree line in a handful of locations, and I didn't want to miss the view. I had a hunch that The Walk would reward my patience—and anyway, after so much progress, staying in one place was reward in itself. Learning the intimate details of one small patch of forest made that patch comfortingly familiar. I wasn't quite ready to put down roots, but I enjoyed imagining that I could.

When the third Hochstein dawn arrived—the final dawn of 1997—it was clear from the second I opened my eyes that the decision to wait had been a good one. In place of twilight gloom, brightness filled my tent. Peering out the frosted entrance I discovered a brilliant sky overhead, and sunlight so intense after seven days of greyness that I had to squint. I rushed breakfast, barely tasting it, grabbed my camera, and set out for Hochstein's summit. I gained altitude swiftly, and was soon sweating—something I normally tried to avoid for how dangerously chilling sweat could be when I stopped—but for once didn't care. After a week of fog I didn't want to waste a second of this miracle-clear morning.

As I sped uphill, the hoar frost that coated the forest grew thicker. Soon, trunks, twigs and pine needles were festooned with ice. I stared around in awe as I raced by, and on any other occasion would have slowed or even stopped to enjoy where I was, but instead began moving faster. I felt certain that even greater sights waited on Hochstein's summit. In a fever of excitement I pushed on, reached the base of the summit rocks, scrambled upward—and finally, *finally* stopped dead. I stared out across a winter landscape unlike any I'd ever seen. The summit was a sparkling wonderland. The trees weren't just glazed with ice. They were completely encased in it. They barely even looked like trees—they looked like sculptures made of glass.

Beyond the trees the frosted Böhmerwald swept downwards to great banks of valley fog. I could even see the Alps again: a notched line on the southern horizon, some of the peaks an incredible 150 miles distant. After an entire week seeing nothing further away than thirty feet the view was so immense that I almost doubted it. How could this be real? I didn't notice that my clothes were damp with sweat, and for two wonderful hours forgot I was engaged in a 7,000-mile walk, forgot I still had months more of winter to face, forgot I'd ever been sad or lonely—I simply lost myself in the joy of being exactly where I was.

The Hochstein Miracle, December 31, 1997.

A year earlier, while planning the route, I'd thought of the Böhmerwald as an in-between place, a range that had to be crossed because it lay between the Alps and Norway. Perhaps it would give a few days of remoteness, maybe a fleeting snatch of wildness. But it wouldn't likely deliver The Walk's most memorable moments or affect my emotions as powerfully as bigger mountains. How could it? But Hochstein's ice-enveloped summit confounded my expectations. It was as extraordinary as anything experienced further south, and it transformed the in-between Böhmerwald to a place valuable for its own sake. The Hochstein Miracle reinforced a lesson I was finally coming to understand: that no single part of The Walk was ever going to be ordinary.

January 1 dawned—and it was a cold one. I opened my eyes and examined the tent's zipper, inches from my face. Frost completely encased it. I wondered if it would open. It looked frozen solid.

Lying still, I thought about starting my day—starting the year—and doing it right. I'd set a precedent for 1998 by setting out early. I'd jump up, pack away camp, then put in an epic day. I'd cover some miles. I'd show the wilderness who was boss. Mad Mountain Jack, unstoppable wilderness wanderer!

It was a great image. I spent half an hour enjoying it. And then I went back to sleep.

The problem was, my sleeping bag was so warm that I found it almost impossible to get up. It seemed unfathomable that a damp sleeping bag in a squalid, ice-encrusted tent could provide such comfort, but it did—too much comfort. This wasn't the first time I'd slept late since winter had begun back in October. *Just five minutes more* had become a familiar refrain. And five minutes often meant an hour, sometimes more. Most mornings I burrowed deeper into my sleeping bag than more determined adventurers might have. Norwegian explorer Roald Amundsen probably didn't loiter in his sleeping bag each morning, nor Sir Edmund Hillary. They probably jumped straight up and got at it. But not Mad Mountain Jack. Most days started far later than I care to admit.

I always roused myself eventually, and once I was up the cold usually prompted great haste. 1998's first morning was no exception. From slow and lazy I became speed-obsessed within seconds. Working swiftly to complete my chores before frost claimed ownership of my fingers and toes, I mopped up the puddles that always formed overnight, stuffed away my sleeping bag and gear, packed Ten Ton, de-iced and dismantled my shelter, and grimaced in pain as frost took control of my hands.

Moving urgently, I crunched away into the forest, leaving little puffs of breath behind as though I were a steam locomotive. Soon, blood was coursing through my veins, warming my hands, and dawn's reluctance had vanished as though it had never existed. Sleeping in meant nothing. I wanted to be walking, no question. Even after 3,000 miles I still set forth excited by the day ahead, ready to take on the world, feeling utter amazement that I was living my dream. The morning may have started slowly, but I embraced the miles that followed as eagerly as any that had preceded them.

Over the next few days my route across the Böhmerwald rose and fell with the hills. I followed marked trails, took frequent shortcuts through the forests, and only occasionally resorted to minor roads. I loved the shortcuts best, picking my own route the way deer do, sinking into soft snow that no one else had disturbed. Progress wasn't fast, and the deepening snowpack tested my determination, but the forests were open and easy to negotiate compared to those back in the Apennines. The freedom to choose my own path, to not feel restricted to lines others had blazed, to let the land show the way, matched everything I'd wanted The Walk to be. I found it deeply reassuring that this freedom was still possible in the heart of modern Europe. Even here, the continent was demonstrably wilder than most people supposed.

I reached a village every day or so and usually picked up a few extra supplies. But I rarely lingered now, and never looked back. I'd changed since Christmas. My perception of villages had changed too. To the residents of Haidmühle, Philippsreut and Mauth the world most likely centred around human-made things and was lived mostly indoors. But to me, villages were no longer central to existence. They'd become mere outposts resting on the edge of the Real World. The real world was trees and snow, earth and water, wind and air, the sun and moon. I felt as though a shift had occurred, as though I was now viewing villages the way a creature of the land might—as something inconsequential, an environment that didn't really impinge upon normal day-to-day living. I felt as though I was standing outside of what had once been normal and was now looking in *at it* instead of out *from it*, and finally understood that my view had been back to front all along.

Miles passed. Before long I entered the Bavarian Forest National Park —Nationalpark Bayerischer Wald. Established in 1970, the park was Germany's first, and its creation took quite the battle. Many Germans opposed it: local people and politicians who feared losing control of the land; hunters who feared losing access to their prey; foresters who feared losing access to timber; and citizens across the country who didn't believe their heavily populated nation had enough land spare to set aside for nature's sake, even though nature and *der Wald* (the Forest) are key parts of German cultural identity. There were even disagreements between park proponents on its purpose. Some saw the park as a playground for recreation, and wanted to create a manicured, heavily managed park. Some thought it should be a wildlife preserve almost like a zoo, designed to bring in tourists, repopulated with moose, lynx, wild boar and wolves. And some foresaw a park where development should be limited, where nature would truly come first. Despite the many conflicting interests the national park was eventually born, and the wild ultimately benefited. Management of the park now revolves around a simple but profound philosophy: *let nature be nature.* To someone seeking the *other* Europe, such a philosophy was something to cheer.

When I entered the park I was pleasantly surprised by the number of walkers I found following its trails. Despite my preference for solitude, it was heartening to see so many other people choosing to travel on foot. The summits of the park's two highest mountains—Lusen and Grosser Rachel—weren't places of silence, but I didn't begrudge having to share them. Mutual enthusiasm improved the views, and I still got to experience them in solitude at day's end. When sunset neared, I didn't have to descend like everyone else. I was free to camp nearby and sit upon the summits for as long as I could stand the cold; free to stare across the world in quiet contemplation. And the views were worth contemplating. Grosser Rachel's 4,767-foot perch gave a panorama across the vastest cloud sea I'd ever seen. The inversion lapped against the Böhmerwald's foothills, stretched south across Germany to the distant Alps, and reached south-east to a barely discernible range of hills that—according to my compass and map of Europe —was the Black Forest. But seeing so far was hard to believe. The Schwarzwald lay 250 miles distant. Still, as the sun sank and the cloud sea turned pink I didn't worry which hills they were. I couldn't worry about anything.

The landscape the following day was less elevating. North of Grosser Rachel, I crossed an entire mountainside covered by dead trees. Once-majestic spruces were now skeletons; black stalks pointed skyward like accusing bony fingers. Thousands of fallen trunks lay scattered across the mountain like matches spilled from a box. It was a disturbing sight, a horrifying glimpse of the future, a clear example—I thought—of the world our massive greed and polluting civilisation was creating. It reminded me of the cirque beneath Königspitze back in the Alps. There, what had once been an arena of gleaming ice was now a place of dirty rubble, a change almost certainly attributable to human-influenced climate change. There, we'd hastened the demise of glaciers. Here in Bavaria, we'd killed an entire living forest. The sight of it darkened the day.

Acid rain and a warming climate are serious issues in the Böhmerwald, affecting the forest's health in many ways. The dead trees around me had suffered years of acid rain, had been torn apart by hurricane-force winds in August 1983, and then decimated further by bark beetles, a plague that winters were no longer cold enough to keep in check. Still, there was a chance that the forest might recover. New plants would probably take root amid the bones of the old, insects and birds would recolonise the dead trees, and although it would probably take decades the forest would eventually return in some form. Scientists working for the national park understood this, and resisted demands made by the public that they repair the forest more quickly. *All that timber going to waste*, people raged, *all that ugliness*. But the park's philosophy—*let nature be nature*—demanded a more hands-off approach. When I later learnt that the forest was being given time and space to heal itself the situation became marginally more positive. Here was evidence, at last, that humankind could do more than take-take-take. Even when timber was available—a material often seen as an economic resource—we had the wisdom to leave it be. The forest may have been ugly, but even ugliness has its place. So does death. Death to one species is merely an opportunity to another—a fact humans might do well to remember.

Leaving the national park, I continued north into healthier forests, approaching Grosser Arber—Great Arber—the Böhmerwald's highest summit. Appropriately, the weather grew worse, and soon a fierce wind was screaming across the landscape, shaking trees as though trying to uproot them, whipping snow into the air as though seeking to suck every flake back into the sky. Criss-crossed by well-groomed Nordic ski trails, the forests beneath Great Arber are less wild than those in the national park, but in the storm they felt like the wildest forests I'd ever traversed. The wind's roar was so loud I could barely think. Its physical violence was worse. I couldn't get warm no matter how many layers I pulled on, no matter how briskly I walked. Suddenly, camping was a daunting proposition. I'd known a storm like this could hit; but, just like spending Christmas alone, the idea of it had appealed. Now it was upon me I wasn't so sure I could cope.

But there was nowhere to hide.

Head down, face stinging, ears ringing, stumbling from the wind, I battled on, delaying camp. But I couldn't keep walking all night. Once daylight started to dim I knew the time had come. Steeling myself, I stepped from the hard-packed ski trail I'd been following and cut into the trees through knee-deep snow. After fifty yards a clearing appeared ahead, and I started to turn from it—open space was the last thing I needed—but then stopped, and did the classic double take. There was a cabin across the clearing. It didn't look like much, just a beat-up shack, but if unlocked it might solve my problems.

I've always treasured 'arrival'; it is one of backpacking's greatest joys. Finishing a day's miles, finding a spot for camp, sliding off my pack, sinking into stillness after motion, ease after effort—nothing is better than that. There'd been some memorable arrivals during The Walk, the best of them after the hardest days, but none that compared with arrival at 'The Bohemian Bothy'.

The door was unlocked. I cheered as it swung open easily, then cheered again as I closed it on the outside world. What a contrast a few steps made—from chaos into calm, from a fearsome din into peace, from dangerous exposure into the sanctuary of shelter.

I pulled off Ten Ton, then looked around. The cabin offered a single room, small, cluttered and dirty. It was furnished with a wooden table and stools, a bed covered by tatty blankets, a kitchen counter and shelves. There were old pots and pans, mugs, plates and empty jars. Tacked to the walls were old posters of Alpine glaciers and Dolomite walls, a few of them places I'd seen myself just months earlier. A wood-burning stove sat in the centre, and beside it a stack of wood and a hatchet. Space was limited, dust and grime covered every surface, I could see mouse droppings in corners, but to me it looked like the world's finest mansion. And it was free—perfect for a cash-strapped vagabond. I could hardly believe my luck.

Grinning broadly, I settled in, confident that no one would mind me staying. Soon, candlelight filled the interior with a flickering glow, and once I lit the stove a crackling fire spread Mezzogiorno heat into the room's farthest corners. Stripped to shorts and T-shirt, I thought back to all the simple shelters I'd ever slept in, to all the Scottish bothies, Alpine winter rooms, old barns, cabins, shacks, lean-tos and caves. Severe weather had assaulted many of them, but none had been as fiercely assaulted as the cabin I sheltered in now.

Singing with contentment, I pushed aside a voice of dissent that suggested I was cheating, retreating indoors when I ought to be sleeping outside. *No*, I argued, *this isn't cheating*. I'd already experienced the storm —I'd been out in it for hours. And it would have gone against every instinct I possessed—it would have been *un*natural—to turn down shelter when it appeared. Plus, was my tent really any different from a cabin? Both were human-made and both, to some degree, cut me off from the natural world. If anything, the cabin allowed better access on a night like this. Camping, I'd have hidden until dawn, but in the cabin, no longer battling for survival, I was free to enjoy the conditions, free to step into them every so often. After dinner I opened the door and stood in the entrance, and felt the full force of winter's power. From 'The Bohemian Bothy' I was able to revel in the storm as I never could have from my tent.

I revelled in the fire, too.

Fires were something I never lit in camp—they left far too much trace. But it was different in the cabin. With the stove door open, I sat before the flames and relived the entire day, extending its pleasures far into the night. The flames hypnotised me, touched something primitive inside, satisfied an ancient half-forgotten instinct I barely knew that I possessed. The fire got me thinking about our ancestors, and how greatly they too would have appreciated it on a night like this. They'd have experienced similar winter winds, and sought shelter from them, and relied on a fire's life-giving aid. With the storm raging, and the fire crackling, I felt kinship with all those that had gone before. Tens of thousands of years may have passed, but fire, warmth and shelter were still essential human needs.

I stayed up late, not wanting to waste the cabin by actually sleeping. But by midnight tiredness finally won and I let the fire fade. And that was when 'The Bohemian Bothy' revealed that it wasn't entirely perfect. As I settled down, the cabin's residents began stirring. First came a tell-tale patter of tiny feet overhead in the attic, followed by—strangely—a rattle of claws within the stove's rapidly cooling metal flue. Mice—and from the sound of it hundreds of the buggers. The noise grew steadily louder, and from the depths of my sleeping bag I pictured them entering the room, darting over the bed, rummaging through my gear, tearing into my food. Sleep soon became impossible. Camping might have been a better option after all.

Leaping up, I threw more wood on the fire, and as it burst back into life and sent heat shooting up the flue the scampering sounds died away. Perhaps that was secret—keep the fire burning! This I did for the rest of the night. I set my alarm to go off every hour and each time I woke I added fuel to the blaze. Happily, it worked—the mice stayed away. It didn't make the night the most restful ever—but pretty soon it was the hottest.

At some point I must have sunk into deep sleep, for suddenly dawn was upon me. And it didn't arrive slowly or peacefully, but with heart-palpitating abruptness, louder even than gunshots in Calabrian woods.

KER-RACK!—an explosion so loud that its vibrations shook dust from the rafters. I sat straight up, staring around in confusion at an unfamiliar room. Ah, the cabin. But the explosion? Had I inadvertently entered a military training zone?

FLASH!—a blinding light directly outside, along with another cabin-shaking CRACK! I nearly fell out of bed.

I rose quickly and dashed to the dirty window, then wiped clear a patch of glass. Outside, the forest was white, blurred by snow and fog. The wind had lessened, but the storm had intensified to a new level of violence, spitting bolts of electricity 50,000-degrees hot. Lightning flashed every few seconds, leaving after-images, and thunder exploded simultaneously, making me jump each time. For once I had good reason to hold back from the day's miles. And if I'd been glad that I'd stumbled upon 'The Bohemian Bothy' the evening before, now I was ecstatic.

The storm lasted an hour, and I cheered it on from my secure haven. But eventually it fizzled out. The lightning and thunder ceased, the fog thinned, although the wind picked back up in strength, harassing the trees once again. I decided it was time to go, while I could. After sweeping the cabin clean, and building a cone of kindling within the stove for the next visitor, I stepped outside. I staged a quick photo, then walked away, leaving behind my deepest gratitude.

Underway now, I considered the day's goal: the Great Arber, summit of the entire range at 4,775 feet. It rose 1,000 feet above the forest, consumed within raging clouds. Climbing it wasn't going to be comfortable, but I had to try. Reaching the highest point of each range I visited had always been a goal. I'd managed it in the Apennines on Corno Grande, had summited Mont Blanc in the Alps during a previous walk, and couldn't possibly skip the Böhmerwald's highest peak.

In normal conditions, Great Arber isn't an especially difficult mountain to climb. There are no plunging crags to overcome or glaciers to ascend. My map showed forested slopes, a summit capped by rocky outcrops, and nothing else. It should have been easy.

'The Bohemian Bothy', January 6, 1998.

But it wasn't. I didn't have normal conditions. What I had were knock-you-over winds, fill-your-eyes-with-ice spindrift, can't-see-twenty-yards fog, and sink-to-your-knees snow. What I had was winter at its very worst. Or, as I suddenly saw it, at its thrilling best.

Working hard, I gained altitude, partially sheltered by thick forest. Five hundred feet beneath the summit I dropped Ten Ton and stowed it beside a rock. I'd be returning the same way and saw little point carrying the load if I didn't have to. Turning into the full force of the storm I continued uphill, too engrossed in progress to feel any of my old fears. With Excalibur in hand I picked my own line. I was approaching Arber from the south-east, and in the swirling whiteness saw no evidence anyone else had ever visited the mountain. It might have been a peak that had never been touched or climbed.

The ascent was a genuine struggle. Conditions were soon *epic*. Thigh-deep drifts bogged me down. Spindrift blinded me. Twice, the wind bowled me over. I had to stop frequently and cower, hands over my face, crouched

Savage conditions beneath Great Arbor, January 6, 1998.

low to the ground. On several occasions the wind managed the impossible: it blew from four directions at once. There was even an electrical charge to the atmosphere that suggested lightning could strike again at any moment. But I pushed on regardless, not just throwing caution to the wind but letting the wind tear caution away and whip it east to some far-distant land. *Who the hell cares? You only live once!* The elements raged, pounding my senses, but they didn't weaken my desire—they strengthened it. And the storm didn't sap my energy—it fuelled it. Soon, a kind of madness enveloped me, an exuberant pig-headed nothing-can-stop-me determination that had me fighting upwards as though nothing else mattered in the world. Soon, I was utterly consumed by the ascent, more lost to the moment than I'd ever been. I fought my way uphill, past wind-bent trees and whirlwinds of snow, and howled at the sheer idiocy and soaring exhilaration of what I was doing.

The summit eventually appeared: an ice-veined outcrop rearing above the trees. Now on exposed ground, the wind was even fiercer. With the wind shrieking, snow flying and visibility at fifteen yards, it was the wildest environment of the journey so far. Progress slowed, but nothing could stop me now. I scrambled up a crown of rock that rose above everything else in sight, and finally stood atop it.

And still the wind blew. It screamed like a banshee, hurling spindrift at my face, smashing into me as though air had become a solid entity, almost knocking me off the perch. But it wasn't an unpleasant wind. It wasn't something to fight any longer, and it wasn't out to get me; it was only the wind. Setting my feet firmly, rooting myself into the rock, I let the elements rush at me. Facing them, I threw my arms wide and stood exposed, thinking: *why should we cower from the worst weather, from winds like these, from pouring rain, from driving snow? Instead, why shouldn't we embrace such storms, and let them run around us and into us so that they can touch every sense we are lucky enough to possess? Why shouldn't we put ourselves out there sometimes and let the world remind us that we are here, that we are truly alive?*

And so I stood on the summit of the Böhmerwald. I faced the storm and lived it, and after a while it became hard to tell where I ended and the wind began. Was it for a minute I stood, or an hour? It could have been an entire lifetime, the way the moment stretched out. But it didn't matter. I stood and grabbed the moment and held onto it for all it was worth, as alive as I'd ever been.

And when the time came, and I left the summit, and ran back down the mountain with great bounding strides, I possessed all the energy in the world. Nothing seemed impossible.

***

Years later, I discovered with absolute astonishment that there is another side to Great Arber, a side I completely missed. Lacking protection as a national park or nature reserve, Great Arber has been heavily developed. On the mountain's northern side a ski resort breaks the integrity of the forest. On the south-western slopes there's a winding road. And upon the summit there are signs, paths and fences. And there are buildings: a cable-car terminus, a large restaurant, an ugly garage, and two massive golf-ball-shaped military radar stations built during the Cold War.

But, incredibly, I'd seen none of it. My map hadn't shown any of it, and the savage storm had hidden it completely. By some stroke of fate I'd experienced a wilder mountain, a truer summit experience, a Great Arber from years gone by. Once I learnt the truth I marvelled at my summit experience. For a short while I even began doubting it, but then shook the doubts away. My Great Arber *had* been as wild as I remembered. The more I relived the experience the more it seemed like a rare gift, something seldom, if ever, given to visitors. I concluded that its extraordinariness was all down to my approach—not just the physical approach up Arber's undeveloped side, but the approach *inside*. It was all down to The Walk—down to every one of its cumulative, transformative moments. They'd added up, come together, and they'd changed me *and* the mountain.

My Great Arber wouldn't have been possible any other way. The soaring experience had been a reward I'd earned.

CZECHING OUT THE 'FORBIDDEN ZONE'
Chapter 7

THE VERY NEXT day winter loosened its grip. The wind died, the air warmed, the snowpack began thawing. Conditions changed so rapidly that the savagery I'd experienced on Great Arber seemed like unlikely events that could only have occurred in a dream. Life eased, and damp conditions that might once have felt uncomfortable became ridiculously easy to bear —a testament perhaps to the intensity of the preceding days. The miles that ticked by underfoot felt as easy as any I'd walked.

North of the village of Furth im Wald I neared another official entry point into the Czech Republic. After three weeks spent gazing with great longing into forbidden Czech forests I knew I had to try again. Looking from afar wasn't enough; I needed to touch. From a distance, the Czech forests appeared different, not so much greener on the other side of the hill as wilder and less maintained. Perhaps the Czech officials would turn me back again, but as with Great Arber I had to make an attempt. What finally swung it was the way the Czech Republic basked in perpetual sunshine while Germany sulked beneath a persistent grey pall. Towards the border I walked.

This time, my story was ready. I'd explain that I had rooms booked in several small hotels, arranged by telephone months earlier. If asked, I'd pull out my map and point to the towns where I'd stay. My plan had flaws, but it might work.

I reached the German border control first. My passport was demanded by a guard who was probably used to being obeyed. Almost seven feet tall, built like a granite outhouse, and dressed in black military fatigues and combat boots, he would have made a great villain in a Bond movie. He gave my passport the third degree, eyeballed me just as intently, but I almost burst out laughing when he asked if I was transporting drugs or guns. I thought about replying *only biologically hazardous socks and underwear*, but decided against it. Perhaps sensing how close he'd come to suffering one of my jokes he ordered me to proceed.

If the German guard was dressed for combat the Czech officials were dressed for a parade. Their uniforms were immaculate: spotless peaked caps, polished shoes, sharp creases, shining buttons; they were definitely putting on a show. But their boredom spoilt the effect. The guard that I reached stared at me blankly, then yawned a lion-sized yawn. Still, it was too early to celebrate. There were bound to be questions similar to those I'd faced three weeks earlier.

But there weren't. No words were exchanged. I held up my passport but the guard waved it away as though he didn't care. Then he waved me away too, pointing me east into his country. I didn't argue.

From the checkpoint I marched full speed down the road for half a mile, keen to vacate the border area before some other official called me back. I passed roadside markets filled with tourist junk, and three dumpy-looking hotels. I aimed for a forest path, but unfortunately it didn't exist where my map marked it. I cast around for long minutes, kicking through piles of roadside litter, and began wondering if I'd made a mistake. Was the Czech Republic going to be a place of trash, inaccurate maps and non-existent paths? The litter didn't fill me with optimism. There were torn pornographic magazines, soggy cigarette packets, piles of discarded beer cans. Two beer brands dominated. There were 'Flirt' cans featuring a scantily dressed woman, and neon-yellow 'Erectus' cans featuring a highly exaggerated side-view of a man with his equipment at full salute. What this first glimpse of Czech culture said about the country I couldn't quite decide.

On the verge of giving up, I stumbled over a post lying on its side. *Aha!* It was the trail marker indicating the start of the path. The road soon fell behind, and I finally entered the Český les, literally 'Czech Forest'. I breathed out, relaxed. I felt I'd passed a particularly severe test.

The first miles were uneventful, but intriguing. I was now in the

Wild Czech forest, January 10, 1998.

'Forbidden Zone', the strip of forest beside the old Iron Curtain that prior to 1989 had been a fortified and mined no-man's land.[1] The communist regime had emptied it of people, and to walk where I now walked wouldn't just have been forbidden—it might have got me shot. And yet here I now was, enjoying the benefits of a failed ideology. And what benefits! The land *was* wilder than back in Germany. There was no sign of forest management, no stumps from felled trees, no cleared undergrowth. The meadows were rough and unploughed, the trees shaggy, the grass coarse and tussocky. It was wild nature, left to do its own thing.

The difference was thought-provoking. The soil, climate and underlying rocks were identical to those back in Germany, but the environment was entirely different. Two contrasting worlds sat side by side, and it was all down to us—down to intensive management one side of the border and decades of 'neglect' on the other. Seeing such stark evidence of our influence should, perhaps, have been troubling. Was it a fool's errand to seek the wild in a Europe so thoroughly shaped by humankind? But instead

---

1. Years later, I learnt that not all the landmines had been cleared at the time I passed through, especially deep in the forests where few people ever went. My blood ran cold at the idea that my gentle steps could easily have not been gentle enough.

71

it prompted optimism. It didn't only reveal how domineering we are but also how quickly nature could bounce back. The Český les had once been developed, but it was now reverting to wilderness. The sight of it kindled a powerful response: hope. If the wild could return here, why not elsewhere? Why not in patches small and great right across the globe? Tiny squares of wasteland in cities, road and field margins, any area of land no longer in use, no matter the size, could all become wild oases. It *was* possible. These Czech forests proved it.

Early in the afternoon I reached my first Czech village and encountered neglect of another kind: pot-holed roads, cracked walls, missing roof tiles, leaning utility poles, weeds everywhere. Homes resembled cheaply built council flats, and the entire village looked like an impoverished inner-city estate that had been dumped in the forest and left to fend for itself. Times, evidently, had been hard.

But the most notable feature was the peacefulness. The sound of cars, engines and machines—the omnipresent drone that usually accompanies civilisation—was entirely absent. The village may have been run down, if not ugly, but the hush was deeply appealing.

Fascinated, I walked down the main street. There was no traffic, but I saw an elderly couple shuffling side by side, several free-range chickens, and a pack of dirty dogs too busy chasing one another to notice me. Down an alley I noticed a young scrawny girl in olive-green fatigues pushing a squeaky wheelbarrow. *What*, I thought; *no school?* Come to think of it, I couldn't see any shops, restaurants or churches either. The worn, sleepy ambience reminded me of villages back in Calabria, until I considered the comparison more carefully and realised that no Calabrian village had been as quiet or run down as this. And as for comparing it with nearby Germany, well, the gulf was so wide that Germany might have been a thousand miles away, not three.

Near the centre of town I caught up with an old man. He was short and stooped, and also dressed in olive green. He looked over his shoulder when he heard my footsteps, smiled broadly, then spoke a string of utterly incomprehensible words.

'I'm sorry,' I said in German. 'Do you speak German? Or English?'

Predictably, it was no to the English, but his German was better than mine, and he agreed right away to teach me some Czech. We started with 'hello', then 'goodbye', and then 'thank you', but none of the Czech words stuck. They featured a curious blurring of consonants and vowels—too blurred for me to grasp or repeat. Fortunately, I was spared embarrassment when a second pedestrian approached us, a silver-haired man with a neatly trimmed goatee. 'Ah, here comes Stefan,' my Czech friend said in German, 'I must go, but he *can* speak English.'

Stefan could indeed speak it. 'Would you like to come home with me?' he asked with perfect pronunciation. 'For a cup of tea? If you have time?'

'Definitely!' I replied. 'Thank you!' It wasn't just the hospitality that appealed but the opportunity to get to know a Czech citizen. I knew so little about the country.

Curious to see inside one of the crumbling tenements, I was disappointed when Stefan led me to the newest and best-maintained house in the village. 'I built it myself,' Stefan explained with quiet, inoffensive pride. 'It took three years. My wife and I lived in a van during the work, but it was worth it, don't you think?'

My disappointment grew another notch when Stefan explained that he was German, not Czech, but I quickly pushed it aside. Stefan waved me to an armchair in a comfortable living room and picked up a phone to call his wife.

'Anna, we have a guest here,' he murmured gently. 'Will you come?' She stepped through the front door a minute later, back from a neighbour's house. Her gentle smile and shining brown eyes radiated warmth and hospitality—she seemed delighted to have a guest. She disappeared into the kitchen without a word, and returned in a few minutes bearing a tray of tea and biscuits. It amused me that Stefan couldn't have put together the refreshments himself.

Feeling that I was visiting elderly grandparents, I sat back and relaxed, sipping my tea. A clock on the mantle ticked hypnotically while my hosts told me about their lives. Originally from a small city near Munich, they'd grown disillusioned with the endless development, noise and pace of late-twentieth-century German life.

'And so we came here to find something quieter. Back in Germany people no longer have time for anything. But our new neighbours are always ready to talk. Once you get to know them the Czechs are very friendly. Their language isn't easy, but almost everyone here speaks German.'

Stefan had spent most of his working life as an engineer on merchant ships. This explained the eclectic mix of ornaments decorating his walls: spears, masks and other souvenirs gathered from sailing around the world. 'I understand the lure of travel,' he said. 'It wasn't something I could resist. Especially after... after... well.' I guessed he was going to say 'the war', and was intrigued he didn't. 'I visited many countries, but fell in love with the tropics and the bright sunlight. I miss it, especially during our winters here. They are so grey and dark.'

He paused, then smiled as he and his wife shared a look. 'But now I have settled and found something *far* better than travel.'

Anna asked if I'd ever settle down, and I answered that I might, if I ever found what I was looking for.

'Well, what *are* you looking for?' she asked.

'Can I tell you when I find it?' I joked. Anna and Stefan laughed.

Time slipped by. While Stefan continued with his stories, I studied my hosts discreetly. There was a beguiling gentleness to them, along with an unusual desire to please. It seemed like more than natural kindness—as though something else underpinned it, but I didn't dwell on it. Being treated like an honoured guest was too much of a treat to question.

By my estimate, Anna and Stefan were in their late seventies, which would have put them in their early twenties at the outbreak of World War Two. I wanted to ask about the war, but sensed that it was a sensitive subject. My own grandparents talked about their war years more than any other time of their lives, and this was a rare opportunity to hear a first-hand account from the other side. I approached the subject obliquely, asking about their lives when they were younger, and about the world they'd grown up in, but they wouldn't be drawn. It was understandable—and perhaps revealed more than straight answers would have. Not wishing to cause offence, I willingly let it go.

After a while, it was time for me to go too.

'But you are sure?' Stefan protested. 'We...' he hesitated, but Anna nodded when he looked her way. 'We would be honoured if you would stay the night.'

The offer was sorely tempting, and if a Czech had made it I might have said yes. But I'd only just arrived in the country and was itching to keep going. Plus, conditions were simply too good to sleep inside. For a fleeting moment I remembered Christmas when I'd longed for someone—anyone —to invite me in. It seemed like years ago.

'Well, you must at least take extra food with you,' Anna insisted, wrapping some home-baked bread.

The couple accompanied me outside. I thanked them for their hospitality, and they wished me good luck.

As I turned to go Stefan reached out and placed a gentle hand on my elbow. His eyes suddenly filled with emotion. 'You *will* tell them back in England, won't you, that we are not *all* bad?'

Surprised, moved, and thoroughly educated by the plea, I assured him that I would. I told him how friendly and hospitable the German-speaking world had so far been. I told him about help that had been offered, the homes opened, and about the numerous rides I'd had to turn down.

'Thank you,' Stefan murmured, looking as though my answers meant a great deal. 'You are a good man. Our blessings go with you. We hope you too find somewhere to settle down.'

———

Settling down, of course, was the last thing on my mind. Moving on was all I wanted, and on I moved, back into my forest home. I had the 'Forbidden Zone' to explore, a week's food on my back, and didn't honestly care where exactly I was going so long as it was roughly north, and so long as no border guards caught me camping illegally along the way.

I pitched my first Czech camp deep in the forest, far from any road or track—or so I thought. Water came from a small stream, golden sunlight spilled through the trees. Quietness reigned. I ate dinner outside the tent, something conditions hadn't allowed in months, and I stayed up late, reading in the tent by candlelight, too content to sleep. But the tranquillity ended when I heard a vehicle approaching. Hastily, I extinguished the candle, and listened in the dark to an engine drawing nearer. From the sound of it the vehicle was moving slowly. Its speed dropped to a crawl as it approached, but then the engine revved and the vehicle motored swiftly away. Was it some kind of border patrol? Had they seen my light? I decided that it had nothing to do with me, but didn't relight the candle, and slept less soundly than I'd hoped.

There were no dramas overnight, and dawn was glorious: clean, crisp and bright. Delicate feathers of frost decorated the landscape, but the rising sun soon turned frost to dew. By the time I'd dismantled the 'Crawling Car Camp' steam rose from the dewy landscape. Everything looked new and pristine as though it was the first morning ever.

I found the road fifty yards west of camp. It was barely wider than a car, the pavement was cracked, and twigs reached across it. It struck me as an extremely odd route for anyone to drive at night, but I didn't worry further. It made no difference now that I was underway.

The day that followed was just about perfect, and it set the template for all the Czech days after it. Progress was easy, on narrow trails and quiet tracks, chosen for the way they reached into the remotest corners. The weather was shockingly unseasonable: warmer than it had been in three months. I wandered through forests that felt ancient, crossed wide-open meadows where rough grasses grew, and climbed to ridge-top woodlands filled with streaming sunlight. I paused for the longest lunch break I'd taken in 1,000 miles, sitting still for three hours just because I could, resting with my back against a huge old oak, staring out across a forgotten land. Closing my eyes I turned my face to the sun, cherishing its warmth. It felt like a summer holiday.

Every so often the Český les gave way to small villages, each as neglected as the first. It seemed obscene that the countryside could be so achingly beautiful and the villages so painfully ugly. Each village offered pot-holed streets lined with crumbling, utilitarian apartment buildings, and most had abandoned factories on their outskirts, each one a desolate shell. Poverty was apparent in the rough clothes people wore, in their bent backs, and in the ancient, rusty Škodas they drove. The cars roared like lawnmowers and belched sooty black clouds. Fortunately, traffic was light, and engines weren't always used. On several occasions I saw cars freewheeling downhill, engines off, saving petrol. It reminded me of southern Italy where drivers did the same thing.

The Czech dogs reminded me of southern Italy too. They ran about the villages unrestrained and barked long into the night. I made my second Czech camp in a scrubby patch of woodland within earshot of a village, and as I lay in my sleeping bag after dark I experienced a powerful sense of déjà vu. It was an illegal forest camp, I'd carried water to it from a village, and the

Taking it easy outside a small Czech village, January 12, 1998.

baying of dogs filled the night. It took me right back to the Mezzogiorno.

On the fourth day I reached the ugliest settlement of all. Hoping to find somewhere attractive, if not historical, I detoured to Tachov, a town of 12,000 people. It came into sight as I crested a hill, sitting in a bowl far below, but the first impression wasn't good. Where I stood the air was clean and clear, but down in the bowl it was greyish-brown, stagnant with smog. Tall apartment buildings and factories stabbed through the pollution, many of them adding to it, their chimneys pouring smoke. This time, the monotonous hum of traffic, factories and machines reached my ears. I almost turned about on the spot.

Bracing myself, I descended anyway. Grimy apartment blocks lined the road into town, and the pavement underfoot was cracked, uneven and strewn with litter. I passed several factories. They reared overhead, blank-walled and inhuman, spewing noxious yellow gasses through countless pipes and ducts. As I later learnt, heavy industry in the Czech Republic had blossomed following the fall of the Iron Curtain. Many German businesses had relocated their manufacturing plants across the Czech border, taking advantage of a cheap workforce and less stringent environmental laws.

Tachov's struggling residents had gained employment, but from what I saw they were paying a heavy price for it.

I reached an area of shops, but didn't reach for my wallet. The shops were small, dirty and spartanly stocked, and I decided to make do with the supplies in my pack. Škodas rattled along the street, adding filth to the air, and locals rushed by, serious-faced, dressed in clothes decades out of fashion further west. Trying to break the ice I smiled and nodded at several people, but was thoroughly ignored. I might have been invisible.

The town centre was a touch more attractive. Older buildings surrounded a large square, and the focal point was a sharp-steepled stone church. But I didn't linger; the air tasted too foul. I suspected that I was experiencing the city at its worst. After almost a week without wind the pollution must have built up, filling Tachov's bowl to the brim, but even without the smog I couldn't imagine wanting to stay. I'd been spoilt by everything I'd seen elsewhere, and in a region of wild beauty Tachov was appallingly out of place. Reckoning I'd seen enough I retreated with all the urgency of someone running out of oxygen, finally bursting free into clean, upland air.

For the rest of the day I walked in deep appreciation, wondering what my own life, and health, would have been like had it all been lived somewhere like Tachov.

I spent the remainder of my 'Forbidden Zone' stay soaking up less industrial sights and scents. Sparkling dawns in sun-dappled forests, intense colours and shining skies, waves of warmth radiating from peaty soils, woodsy aromas, hawks overhead, deer in sunlit glades, moonlit meadows, hooting owls: it was idyllic, a glorious spring interlude in the depths of midwinter. If it hadn't been for the border patrols I'd have stayed in the country *far* longer.

A patrol almost caught me camping on the fifth evening. They appeared just as I was setting up the tent. I'd found a beautiful pitch in the middle of a meadow offering warm sunlight and sweeping views, but as I began unrolling the Blob I heard a vehicle approaching. Its engine was off and the vehicle was creeping on brakes down a nearby hill, following a narrow track. Fortunately, the crunch of gravel gave it away. Instinctively, and perhaps foolishly, I crouched down into the long grass. A black police van appeared. Had they seen me? It seemed hard to believe they hadn't. I lowered myself further, realising that hiding made me look *really* suspicious, but I stayed down anyway. The van reached the base of the hill, coasted a little, then roared into life. It raced up the next hill and away. I waited a few minutes, then withdrew, choosing a more hidden spot for camp.

I encountered more border police the next morning. I woke to a police helicopter overhead, buzzing like a frustrated bee that couldn't find any flowers. I struck camp quickly, keen to move on before I was spotted. Once underway I powered through the woods, but almost ran into a crowd of police a mile later. It happened when I left the trees and began crossing an open field. After twenty paces I noticed several parked police vans and a large group of policemen on the field's far side. Smoothly, without breaking stride, I turned on the spot and ambled back the way I'd come as though that had been my plan all along. Someone had to have noticed my comical change of direction, but no shouts came. I tramped away, determined to stay more alert.

Of course, I failed. The final decisive encounter occurred the next day. I was marching down an old military road, picturing a Russian platoon once doing the same, when I slowly grew aware of figures ahead. As I drew closer they came into focus—two border policemen—and I slowed, but this time didn't try to hide. That would have been silly; the policemen were staring straight at me.

Trying to walk casually I continued toward them, wondering if they'd let me pass. The pair weren't especially intimidating. One looked too old and frail to be out in the wilds on foot, and the other sported a moustache that belonged on a Mexican bandito, plus an impressive paunch spilling over his belt. Unfortunately, both carried guns, and when they commanded me to halt it seemed wise to obey.

Speaking sharply, the mustachioed bandito demanded my passport— or, at least, I guessed he did. He spoke in Czech, but might just as easily have asked if I'd seen his dog, or was engaged in gun running, or had any 'Erectus' beer spare. I responded in German, but both policemen shook their heads. '*Nein sprechen Deutsch,*' they replied, a surprise, given that they were patrolling the German border.

El Bandito made another demand, and held out his hand, clearly requesting documentation. I dug out my passport, handed it over, and the policemen leafed through it, leaning together. I stood to the side, snacking on raisins, trying to look unconcerned. What could happen, anyway? What could they do? The answer, I realised with sudden horror, was a great deal. They could take me to their headquarters, hold me for who knew how long, figure out I'd been breaking the rules, kick me out of the country, create a gaping hole in my hard-won line of unbroken steps across the continent—in short, seriously compromise the integrity of The Walk.

I waited. Every so often I felt their eyes upon me, but whenever I looked up they looked away. Eventually, they came to the page that held the two Austrian stamps I'd received three weeks earlier at the failed Czech border crossing. There was an EXIT stamp from Austria, then an ENTRY back into Austria timed thirty minutes later.

Puzzled, they turned my way and asked a question, eyebrows raised. I merely shrugged. What else could I do?

Turning back to my passport they flicked through it, possibly searching for a matching Czech stamp. How I wished there was one. Even a recent stamp would have helped. But when I'd entered the country the German officials hadn't stamped my passport and the Czech guard hadn't even touched it. I'd been relieved at the time, but now wished the official had been less bored.

The policemen huddled in conference, and I could see them reaching an obvious conclusion. On December 23 I'd left Austria but had returned to it within minutes. The question 'Why?' seemed logical, followed by 'Were you turned back at the Czech border?' leading to 'And if you were turned back *there* what are you now doing *here*?' They asked questions, perhaps these very ones, but once again the language barrier saved me. I just smiled what I hoped was an innocent sort of smile, and carried on snacking as though I hadn't a care in the world. If either spoke German I'd tell the truth—well, a version of it. But as it was?

The older policeman pulled out his radio and spoke rapid-fire Czech into it, reading from my passport. Five minutes passed, during which El Bandito asked me further unanswerable questions. Finally the radio crackled back into life. After listening intently, the old policeman closed my passport. It seemed that I wasn't a known or wanted criminal.

But they still seemed unsure about letting me proceed. It was almost as if they could smell that I'd done something wrong. (I was certain they could smell something.) Hoping to break the deadlock, I pulled out my map, pointed to where we stood, and walked my fingers towards Germany, just two miles west. Next, I pulled out my small-scale map of Europe, and used sign language to explain the entire route. The old policeman looked utterly confused, but El Bandito caught the gist. *That's quite something*, his expression said.

And that was that. He scribbled in his notepad, handed back my passport, let me go.

Once out of sight I strode toward Germany at full clip, and passed both the Czech and German customs without incident.

Germany seemed comfortingly familiar once I was back in it—safe and very much like home. It was clean, prosperous, friendly. Its stores were well stocked with treats. Locals returned smiles and greetings. On reflection I realised that I preferred Deutschland. The wild landscapes of the 'Forbidden Zone' were all very fine, but hiding from border patrols had been too stressful. And then there were the poverty-stricken towns; it had been unsettling to feel so well-off in comparison to the locals.

It was so much easier being the tramp.

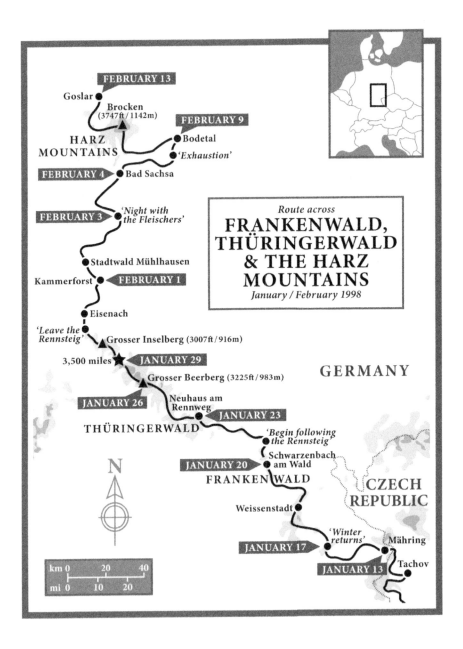

FEBRUARY 13

Goslar
Brocken
(3747ft / 1142m)

FEBRUARY 9

HARZ
MOUNTAINS

Bodetal
'Exhaustion'

FEBRUARY 4   Bad Sachsa

Route across
FRANKENWALD,
THÜRINGERWALD
& THE HARZ
MOUNTAINS
January / February 1998

FEBRUARY 3

'Night with
the Fleischers'

Stadtwald Mühlhausen

Kammerforst   FEBRUARY 1

Eisenach

'Leave the
Rennsteig'   Grosser Inselberg (3007ft / 916m)

3,500 miles   ★   JANUARY 29

Grosser Beerberg (3225ft / 983m)

GERMANY

JANUARY 26

Neuhaus am
Rennweg

THÜRINGERWALD   JANUARY 23

'Begin following
the Rennsteig'

Schwarzenbach
JANUARY 20   am Wald

FRANKENWALD   CZECH
REPUBLIC

Weissenstadt

'Winter
returns'   Mähring

JANUARY 17   Tachov

JANUARY 13

N

km 0   20   40
mi 0   10   20

82

HALFWAY
Chapter 8

THE RESTLESS WINTER wind was back. It rushed through the night and set the forest into motion; it probed, teased and roared. Falling snow came with it, growing the snowpack once more, settling on pines. Massive clumps built up on the trees, and every so often the wind dislodged them, setting avalanches into motion. From around the forest *thwumps* could be heard from near and far, sounding from within my tent like the footfalls of passing giants. Frost tightened its grip, creeping across the Blob, glazing it with ice. Winter had returned.

I lay within my sleeping bag, thrilled by the change. I was now in the Thüringerwald—the ancient granite mountains of Central Germany—and they looked better dressed in white. It was hard to accept that they merged into the Czech mountains and forests I'd recently left. I might have been on a different continent in a different season. Had it really felt like summer only four days previously?

By my reckoning, I was halfway to the North Cape—more or less. It was impossible to say exactly where halfway lay because I didn't know how many miles I'd walk or when I'd finish walking them. If I finished walking in early October then I'd already reached halfway in terms of *time*. But if I ended up walking 7,000 miles then I'd pass halfway in *distance* 100 miles ahead. All of which made a halfway celebration due. *I'll celebrate it tomorrow*, I decided. A youth hostel lay on my route and I'd treat myself to a night indoors. My funds were still shrinking horribly, but I'd earned a break.

Winter resumes, January 16, 1998.

Snow was still falling at dawn, settling heavily upon my shelter. To clear it I thumped the sides, and as the *Schnee* slid away the gentle murmur of falling flakes resumed. As usual, I burrowed deeper into my sleeping bag instead of jumping up. Rushing headlong into the world was what *other* people did. It was for people with commitments and jobs, people living indoors. For me, this wasn't the season for rushing.

Two and a half hours later I was wallowing through the forest, knee deep in winter. With snow clinging to every twig the forest had been transformed into a work of art, but it wasn't easy to traverse. Half my usual speed was about the most I could manage, and at that pace I found it difficult to stay warm. Carelessly, I'd lost my heavy winter mittens in the Czech Republic, and the replacement pair weren't up to the job. To keep blood flowing I raised my effort level. It didn't really help. My body overheated but my fingers remained cold. The typical morning battle to strike camp had chilled them, and they would likely stay chilled until the day was done and I was back in my sleeping bag. This wasn't the season for rushing, and it clearly wasn't the season for warm extremities either.

Picking my own path through the forest, I accidentally knocked aside a snow-laden branch. It sprang quickly up and for a split second the snow that had covered it hung in the air unsupported, before finally falling to the ground. It was like something from a children's cartoon. Amused, I tried it again, but the second branch set off a chain reaction that led to volumes of snow cascading onto my shoulders and head. This was like something from a cartoon too. I didn't try a third time.

After a while I reached an easier route: the Rennsteig, a 110-mile trail that runs the length of the Thüringerwald. Keeping to the high spine of the mountains, the Rennsteig follows the medieval boundary path that once divided the regions of Franconia and Thuringia. The path existed as far back as the 1300s, but its usage surged after a cartographer, Julius von Plänckner, mapped and publicised it in 1832, and after an author, August Trinius, hiked it in 1889 and wrote a book about his journey. The book brought fame to the trail, and six years after its publication the Rennsteig Club was founded. For the next forty-six years the club organised *Der Runst*, a popular six-day trek along the route—until World War Two brought the tradition to a close. Following the war, the Iron Curtain was drawn across the range and complete Rennsteig hikes were no longer possible. But then came reunification in 1989, and the reopening of the trail in 1990. Hikers soon returned, keen to step into the past and find *früher*, a bygone era when life was simpler and slow-paced travel in nature was the rule not the exception. Few regions in modern Germany offer *früher* more completely than the state of Thuringia, and few locations in Thuringia allow *früher* more completely than the Rennsteig.

Walking along the Rennsteig, I made reasonable progress. The snow was well compacted by *langlauf* skiers, and I encountered several of them, individually and in groups—cheerful, red-faced travellers who were fascinated by my less-than-usual approach to *Der Runst*.

'What, you are not on skis?' they asked. 'And you are *camping*! Ah...' they concluded, shaking their heads. 'You are so odd... so British!'

Perhaps they had a point—skiing would have been easier. By late morning, with snow still wafting down and growing ever deeper underfoot, my legs began to feel day's-end heavy, even here on the established trail. Seeking a temporary reprieve, I descended to a village, Oberland-Hasenthal. By the time I arrived the sheer quantity of snow falling from the sky meant that I couldn't see thirty yards. Each individual flake was such an insignificant thing by itself, but it became hugely significant when joined to millions more.

Back in London, such a snowfall would have brought chaos, but Oberland-Hasenthal's residents were coping with practised efficiency. Ploughs had already cleared the roads once and were doing it again, pushing up high banks either side. Locals were at work, too. No matter where I looked I saw shovels in hands. There were frail-looking old ladies clearing garden paths, shopkeepers removing snow from in front of their shops, couples shovelling outside their homes, even small children getting in on the act. One short and heavily muffled child was grunting and groaning behind a two-handed metal plough as she public-spiritedly cleared a long stretch of pavement. Singing happily between her grunts and groans, she was obviously enjoying the labour. I watched as her little brother toddled into view, and soon he too was grunting, mimicking his sister, although the snow plough he pushed was entirely imaginary.

Taking the easy option, I stuck to roads for the rest of the day. I should have known better. Everything went well—but only at first. Footing was secure, traffic was minimal, and the snow-hushed landscape was easier to enjoy without having to wallow through it. I even came across shelters every few miles—local bus stops that let me escape the falling snow. I was becoming quite the connoisseur of bus shelters as winter progressed. I'd sampled many different kinds since Salzburg, turning my nose up at some, accepting the offerings of others. Once I'd even found one with a heated bench, and I'd seriously considered staying the night—but its location in the middle of a town finally dissuaded me. I wasn't that much of a vagabond, and I hoped I never would be. Then again, who knew what the future had in store? Most people sleeping rough on bus shelter benches weren't doing it by choice.

The roads became less pleasant as I neared the day's goal: the town of Neuhaus am Rennweg. Traffic increased dramatically, and from my perspective all of it was in a hurry. Cars, vans and juggernauts barrelled by, flinging up dirty grey slush, pummelling me with air, filling my lungs with fumes. Approaching town, I found myself stuck following a main road. It was the only possible route. I kept off it as much as I could, but the massive snow banks either side often made this impossible. Several times I had to stop and climb onto the bank to give cars space to pass, but I received no nods of acknowledgment, just glares. Horns blared. One motorist rolled down the window of his van, shook an annoyed fist, and screamed angrily in German: 'Get off the *VERFLUCHT* road!' I felt bad, and wished I could, but there was nowhere else to go.

By the time I reached the centre of town I was feeling thoroughly fed up. Neuhaus was larger than it had looked on the map, and busier than I'd expected. With its harsh-edged buildings and roaring traffic, *früher* definitely didn't exist here. The weather didn't help. Daylight was fading fast and the storm was worsening. Dense fog billowed along the streets, grimy snow covered the pavements, rime ice coated parked cars, and snow flew parallel to the ground, stinging my face. It wasn't a good night to camp. Fortunately I wouldn't have to: my halfway treat—the youth hostel—waited right ahead.

I found the *Jugendherberge* on the far side of town and stepped indoors with relief. The storm fell from my shoulders and warmth enveloped me. Arrival: how I loved it!

A woman about my age stood behind a tall reception desk, busily riffling though papers. From a hallway behind her, from up a flight of stairs, and from every corner of the building came the echoing sound of loud voices, laughter, and thumps. The hostel sounded busy.

But it was worse than that.

'We are full,' the receptionist stated, and my joy in arrival, and my hope for a night indoors, came crashing down.

'Full?' I stammered. 'Completely full? There isn't room *at all*?'

'*Ja*,' she answered, matter-of-factly. 'Every bed is taken.'

She looked down at her papers, showing no concern for the snow-plastered traveller standing before her.

'But...' I stammered again, looking down the hallway, 'couldn't you find space somewhere?' I could see a bench thirty feet away that would do just fine. There had to be a free corner *somewhere* in the building. 'I could manage without a bed...'

'Oh no, we cannot do that,' she said with a hint of reprimand in her voice. 'That is not allowed.'

I stared into her eyes, willing her to understand. Darkness was falling. The storm outside howled. I needed shelter. This wasn't a night for camping.

'Look, I'm walking,' I pleaded, putting up more of a fight than I had seven months earlier when hotel receptionists in the Apennines had turned me away. 'There's nowhere else I can go.' I cringed inwardly at the begging, but heading outside again was unthinkable.

'I am sorry,' she said, not sounding sorry at all. 'We cannot help you.'

Outside, the night was now black. The storm raged with 'Bohemian Bothy' fierceness. But this time no lean-to, cabin or shelter magically appeared to meet my needs. In disbelief, I tramped from town, picked up the Rennsteig, and followed my headtorch beam into a swirling maelstrom. I wasn't sorry to leave Neuhaus, but I wasn't happy about camping. Until now, The Walk had rescued me every time I'd needed rescuing, rewarded me every time a reward was due. But now I felt deserted, cast out. Even the mountain gods had abandoned me. But perhaps it was my fault. After all, I'd chosen to follow roads that afternoon, not the trail I should have stuck to. This was my comeuppance.

Grimly, I chose a spot and set up camp—and finally found my reward. But it took an unusual form. When I unzipped the inner tent I caught sight of a strange grey creature lurking within it. I cried out in alarm, fell backwards into snow, and reached instinctively for Excalibur. The creature clung upside down to the ceiling like a cross between a hairy bat and a giant slimy leech, and it seemed to be grinning rabidly. It was a horrible, terrible sight. But then I paused, looked again, and realised the truth. It wasn't a creature, and it wasn't alive. It was just a sock, a dirty frozen sock! I'd missed packing it away that morning and it was now glued by ice to the tent's ceiling, guarding the entrance. Laughter erupted—I lost it completely. I laughed long and hard, at myself most of all. The Frozen Vampire Sock of Neuhaus may not have been a typical reward, but it worked as effectively as any.

By the time I settled comfortably into the 'Halfway House' camp I was ecstatic to be outside. Not only was I proving that I *could* cope with the fiercest weather, but also this was the halfway point of an *outdoor* adventure. Celebrating it in a frost-encrusted tent in a winter-locked forest in a raging snowstorm was perfect. This was where I belonged, not in a jampacked hostel. The mountain gods hadn't abandoned me—they'd merely nudged me in the right direction.

I received further rewards the following morning. The frozen forest was as magical as the forest back at Hochstein, every surface glazed with ice. I'd still have seen it had I stayed at the hostel, but I wouldn't have woken

The ice-encrusted forest, January 21, 1998.

to it, wouldn't have breakfasted within it, wouldn't have squatted for my morning constitutional surrounded by it. It would have been a place I'd stepped into, not a place I felt a part of. The miles that followed were spellbinding, unworldly. Being turned away was the best thing that could have happened. The hostel receptionist had done me a good turn.

Still, when I reached a second youth hostel later that afternoon I didn't walk by. A temporary reprieve from winter was still attractive—*and* needed. My tent was soaked inside and out, pretty much all my clothing and gear was wet too, three straps on Ten Ton needed to be repaired, my boots required drying and waxing, and—honestly—my body was *long* overdue a shower.

The *Jugendherberge* in Katzhütte was an unpromising-looking establishment at first sight—austere, grey and dark—but it was open, had plenty of vacancies, was reasonably affordable, and above all it was receptive to snowmen. Unfortunately, a bed wouldn't be available until 4 p.m., but the warden explained that I could wait in the common area or have something to eat across the street in Katzhütte's cosy little restaurant.

I chose the restaurant. It offered huge servings of down-to-earth food, as well as beer, perfect for a celebratory halfway feast. I marched over and entered, nearly demolishing a low-hanging chandelier with my pack. 'HALT!' the manager screamed in German, running up, arms out. 'Stop-stop-stop! DON'T MOVE!' He pointed behind me, and I looked in horror at the wildly swinging chandelier, as well as a trail of mud that I'd left on the polished wooden floor. Deeply embarrassed, I retreated and removed my boots. I was appalled—my manners were failing me. I may not have been enough of a vagabond to sleep in bus shelters, but apparently I *was* enough of one to have forgotten how to behave in civilisation.

Despite taking great care, I left my mark at the youth hostel too. My room was soon littered with pine needles and clumps of earth, mud from my tent smeared the drying room downstairs, and I even managed to leave gravel in the shower. Gravel? Where on earth had that come from? And then there was the less-than-subtle eau-de-long-distance-hiker cologne that followed me everywhere I went.

'Hmm…' the kindly hostel warden had murmured thoughtfully when she'd checked me in. 'You should probably have a room to yourself?'

'Oh yes please!' I'd answered, not wanting to listen to other people's snores.

It was only later that I realised she wasn't just being kind to me.

———

For the next three days snow continued to fall. Before long, the snowpack was Alpine-deep and the landscape oozed Apennine-like remoteness. Every natural water source had now frozen over, and tree limbs were breaking under the weight of the snow and ice. I heard the gun shot retort of snapping wood several times, and frequently saw the aftermath: large branches lying where they'd fallen, their yellow splintered wood standing out against the snow.

As the snow continued to fall, the landscape grew in wildness. The mountains of Thuringia are only 3,000 feet high, and the range is only twenty miles wide. It isn't the Alps or the Apennines, or even the Böhmer-wald, but in full-on winter conditions it felt as wild as them all. I was impressed I'd made it so far into Europe's most industrial and most populated nation and yet still felt I was on a wilderness walk. The Heart of Europe was working out better than expected.

For eight days snow fell, and by the end I'd almost forgotten the sun existed. But finally the storm clouds rolled aside, and on January 26 I awoke to brittle silence and blinding light. I emerged from my snow-smothered home into the winter wonderland I'd always dreamt of as a child, and I celebrated my good fortune. Winter, I discovered over the following five days, can be the most spectacular and colourful season of all.

Following the tracks of deer, foxes, and skiers, I weaved along the fabulous Rennsteig, thinking about Norway, The Prize. I'd been dreaming of Norway for months and the Arctic for years, but from the look and feel of it, from the sparkling wintry wildness of it, I might already have arrived.

Winter wonderland along the Rennsteig, January 27, 1998.

KEEPING OUT THE CHILL
Chapter 9

THE FIRST NIGHT of February was another night of creeping frost.

It advanced steadily like a white tide inside the tent, and short bursts from my stove merely postponed the inevitable. The clothes I'd worn the day before, damp from falling snow, stiffened into armour; the snow-water I'd thawed ready for breakfast refroze; and my well-worn sleeping bag proved itself no longer equal to the task. Shivers interrupted sleep. By midnight, the thermometer read zero Fahrenheit, minus seventeen Celsius, and that was *inside* the tent. Those stupefying hot-house nights of the southern Apennines felt a lifetime ago.

By dawn the air was crackling with cold, and I hid inside the tent considering hibernation until the late-rising sun found a gap between surrounding trees and shone upon my home. But the sunlight made little difference. Dismantling camp was even more of a battle than usual. Ice had locked the poles so that they wouldn't spring apart, straps wouldn't undo, and the tent's walls were rigid as board. But I persevered, singing and cursing in equal measure to maintain my spirits, and at last, just before eleven, I had Ten Ton packed. I crunched off into the forest without further ado, feet and hands practically useless in the cold.

A foot of snow hid the forest trails, but the trees were well spaced and I chose my own way, not bothering with the map. The sun's position and long blue shadows guided me in the right direction, more or less, and—as always—I celebrated the vagueness of not knowing what lay ahead. Who knew what would happen next, who I'd meet, what I'd see, where I'd spend the night? Letting The Walk take charge was now second nature. I felt light-hearted and alive, inexplicably happy for someone with numb extremities.

Tracks of countless mammals and birds twisted across the snow's surface, a join-the-dot testimony to the abundance of forest life. I couldn't read all the signs, but felt less alone for seeing them. And yet, perhaps because of the day's great cold, nothing stirred, no bird sang. The forest was gripped in an almighty hush. The crunch of my feet, the swish of my clothes, and the sound of my breath seemed intrusively loud. I felt as though I were moving through a sacred place, and any unnecessary sounds would be disrespectful. I fought down the urge to sing.

The winter light shimmered with ice crystals—a visual feast. Moisture was freezing from the air and falling like diamond dust, sparkling with rainbow colours as it fell. Beams of sunlight cut through the trees, catching on the descending crystals. The beams swept along with me as I walked, bright strobes glittering with light.

I hadn't anticipated such beauty from this obscure corner of East Germany. I was in lower country now, a rolling landscape between the Thüringerwald and Harz. It was just another 'in-between' stretch, and my expectations had been low, but here I was, entranced by the unexpected wildness of it.

To keep warm I moved briskly, overtaking clouds of my own breath. Sensation slowly returned to hands and feet, preceded by waves of throbbing pain that forced me to finally break the silence. Staving off frostbite had become a constant task. Through great care, through movement, through frequently taking off my gloves, breathing hot air into them, and pulling them back on, I somehow managed it, although my hands were seldom truly warm. Striking camp was always the most difficult part, and rewarming my hands afterwards the most painful.

After a couple of hours the trees thinned and I found myself on the forest's edge, facing open country. A cruel wind sent spindrift hissing across fields, but a village with a tall church spire half a mile away looked worth a short detour.

With the wind rattling my hood and thrusting daggers of cold through my balaclava I paced to the village and cowered in yet another bus shelter, watching the world blow by. It was Friday, but oddly all the shops were shut, and despite the intense cold plenty of locals strolled by, looking curiously re-laxed. I wondered if it was a regional holiday—a sledding-fest, maybe! Almost everyone, young and old, possessed a sled. The elderly were leaning on walker-sleds, mothers were dragging children on smaller models, older kids were flying down ice-rutted streets on race-car versions, and most memorable of all were two small girls, wide-eyed with excitement and terror, bouncing along on a sled attached to a car. There was little German sobriety there!

On the way out of town I stopped and spoke briefly to a young couple, although talking wasn't easy. My jaw had been anaesthetised by the cold and it led to slurred speech, but a broad smile and friendly persistence finally convinced them that I wasn't a lunatic, or drunk, merely English.

'Why are there no shops open?' I asked. 'Is today some kind of holiday?'

'Well… yes, in a way.' They looked at me with patient, good-humoured tolerance. 'Today is Sunday.'

'Oh!' That explained it—it wasn't Friday, after all. Somewhere along the way I'd lost a couple of days.

Before pushing on I had one other question. 'Please, what is this village called?'

The couple laughed and shook their heads. 'Kammerforst,' the man said, then asked a question of his own. He spoke with mock seriousness. 'And… would you like to know the country too?'

The following days were cast in a similar mould: long nights of biting frost, perishing days, silent forests, and underfoot snow—deep-lying, never-thawing snow. I developed an easy-going rhythm, and twenty-mile days were common, but conditions made it impossible to physically relax. More than anything I longed now for spring, for a bank of luxuriant grass to sink onto, for the caressing warmth of sunshine on bare arms and legs. I began fantasising about the colour green. I'd wanted a long hard winter—but now I'd had enough of it.

Late one afternoon my ever-evolving route led to a hamlet sheltering in a forest hollow. Hansel-and-Gretel-styled cottages clustered loosely around a pub. Warm light spilled from its windows. After carefully kicking snow from my boots I stepped inside.

'The Painted Snow Camp'—a sparkling winter camp at sunset, January 27, 1998.

The interior was plain and nearly empty. Evening sunlight streamed through condensation-soaked windows, illuminating a group seated beside a roaring fire. The heady scent of a meat stew hung in the air, and music drifted down faintly from upstairs, John Lennon singing 'Imagine'. It was worth stepping inside just to hear that.

A woman about my age stood behind the bar and smiled a welcome, and after gentle persuasion agreed to fill my water carrier with tap water. I rested in ease while she did it, enjoying the pub's warmth. But I knew I couldn't stay. The fire looked wonderful, and it would have been so easy to sink into the simple comforts of the pub and forget the harsh winter outside, but I'd be a weak-willed fool to do it. I'd have to return to the cold eventually, and the longer I spent inside the colder outside would feel. Plus, darkness wasn't long off. It was easier to find a spot for camp while I could see what I was doing. The water was all I'd stepped in for. Thawing enough snow for my needs always took time, but tonight I wouldn't have to.

Staying strong, I heaved on my pack and strode towards the door, but a voice from the group in the corner stopped me before I reached it. 'Hey,' a young man called out in German. 'Do you want a drink?'

To be honest, I didn't really. What I wanted was to have the day done, and get into camp, curl up in my sleeping bag, and above all relax. I wasn't certain that beer and winter camping were a sensible mix. But fortunately my polite and very British 'No thank you' wasn't accepted. The offer came again and I reconsidered—then caved. *After all, why not?* An extra chair was pulled over to the fire, and into it I flopped. Someone thrust a beer into my hands. It tasted rather fine.

'There now. That will keep out the chill,' the young man said.

Exhaling slowly, relaxing into the chair, I looked around at the group. Five faces returned my gaze: a middle-aged couple, grey-haired and genial; two young men close to my age, one with dark curly hair, the other shaven headed, both with moustaches that stretched to their jawlines; and a young woman with a warm smile and striking blond hair.

The group had questions. Backpackers were *not* common in the area, especially in winter. As usual, my answers only prompted more questions, but soon disbelief gave way to laughter, and eventually I was free to ask questions of my own. I learnt that the group were a family, the Fleischers. Wilfred and Elma were the parents, Ricardo and Carl the sons, and Katrina was Carl's girlfriend. Then there was Max, a large Alsatian curled beneath the table courting sleep. His tail thumped briefly when Carl mentioned his name.

Carl—the shaven-headed son—spoke good English, and translated my words when needed. At twenty-one he was the youngest of the sons, but not the quietest. His energy dominated the table, a life force that couldn't be contained. Muscles knotted his tattooed arms, his neck was wide, and when he spoke the others listened. It was Carl who'd called over to offer the drink.

Carl explained that the family was enjoying a rare day off work.

'It is not often we go for a walk together. We all work too much.' He paused for a moment. 'And so here *you* are, and you say you haven't worked since this time *last year? Scheisse!* I think *I* need to walk to Norway!'

The family lived just over the hill in the next village, in a 400-year-old house.

'Also, we have a small cabin in our back garden. It has a light, heating and a bed.' Carl looked across at his father, who nodded, seeing where Carl was going.

'If you like, you can come back with us and spend the night there?'

It was ten Fahrenheit outside (minus twelve Celsius), growing colder, and I was being offered a cabin all to myself with heating and a real bed. I didn't try to say no to that.

Once we'd downed our drinks, off we tramped along a snow-covered forest path. Carl and Katrina walked with me, the parents ambled along at the rear, Ricardo strode out far ahead, and Max raced everywhere, all energy and muscle.

'Could we train him to carry my pack?' I asked.

'Of course!' Carl said, laughing. 'I can train him to do anything.'

Carl was a butcher by trade. 'I was born to it!' he exclaimed theatrically. 'Our family has lived in the same village for five hundred years. There is a record in a book in the church, and beside our name is also our profession, butcher, every single generation for five hundred years. It is our family job!'

Carl told me he'd just returned home after a year in the German Army, and was glad to be back doing his real work. Usually he was at the butcher's by 5 a.m. and had slaughtered several pigs by the time I was up.

'You will eat dinner with us, of course,' he declared, and he listed the many meats we'd eat. My eyes widened with delight, but Carl must have misread my expression because he suddenly stopped and held my arm in a vice grip. 'Hey, you're not a vegetarian, are you?' he asked fiercely, but a mischievous smile gave him away. 'I *hate* vegetarians,' he joked. 'They say they love animals, but they don't, you know. They eat all the food the animals would eat and so the animals have nothing!' I laughed at his mock rage.

We walked on, laughing often. One of the few things The Walk didn't provide that I actually missed was shared laughter, but Carl and Katrina helped with that—my underused laughter muscles were well exercised. We talked about work, the forests, wildlife, distant places, the German Army, languages, dogs, books—and the jokes came thick and fast.

'I am not tall,' Carl began, 'and in bars people used to pick fights with me.' He paused, then grinned. 'But never the same people twice!'

'My Katrina!' he laughed fondly, a little further down the trail. 'She is always reading. Always, her nose in a book. In bed even! *In bed!*'

'And what's wrong with that?' I asked, chivalrously defending both Katrina *and* books, but falling right into Carl's trap. 'There's nothing like a good book late at night.'

'Oh, books have their place. But they do... not... belong... in... bed,' Carl lectured. 'A bed is good for two things only, two things: sleep... and... well...' Carl looked over at Katrina, who blushed. 'But *not* reading!'

It had been another long day and my body was feeling it. The village was a welcome sight when it appeared below. With the western sky on fire we descended to it down an ice-chute path that would have better suited sleds than people. Top-heavy Ten Ton made balance precarious, and I nearly fell; Carl and Katrina looked on and laughed. But it was Katrina who fell first, and when she did she dragged Carl with her.

'What, here?' he asked. 'Can't you wait until later?' Every comment was a gem.

The village was a community of 500 people, and the Fleischer family seemed to know every one of them. Progress through it was slow—stop start, stop start—with handshakes and conversation compulsory each time. It wouldn't do to be in a hurry if you lived here.

'Do you know everyone in the village?' I asked Carl.

'Well... almost!' he said. 'But I do know all the dogs! Here they have an Alsatian, here a Dobermann, here a Scottish terrier...' The list went on. Carl told me he belonged to a dog-training club, and when we stopped to talk with another villager Carl began training her 'little fat dog' on the spot. The dog had been pulling at its leash, but after thirty seconds Carl had it walking to heel. Carl warned me that his own hound was trained in police work. Max could bring a man down if needed.

'So, you must behave yourself, *ja*?' he suggested with a cold glint in his eye—and a grin.

We walked on. 'Look, there's my old school.' It was a large, barracks-like building. 'I hated that place! I still see my teachers about and many of my friends are still here, but our village is changing. People are moving away and there are so many empty houses.' There were. The village was full of half-timbered homes—buildings that were deeply attractive to my eyes—but many were unlit and looked vacant, and a few were falling into decay.

'It is criminal, but there is no one to look after them. Since Germany was unified everything costs more but there is less work. Some families cannot afford to keep up their homes. They are forced to leave.'

'Where do they go?'

Carl shrugged, for a moment despondent. 'Who knows? They just go. In some ways life was better under the communists.'

'Can you remember when the Berlin Wall came down?' I asked. 'What did you think?'

Carl was silent for a moment, recalling the past. 'I was at school when I heard, in a classroom. A teacher came in. She was crying when she told us. I was young and didn't fully understand. But I *do* remember the street party that followed. I have never, *ever*, eaten so much. And I have *never* seen so many happy people in one place. It was the most fantastic party ever.'

The Fleischer family home was a fine old place, an ornate wood-beamed building with a date—1592—carved above the front door. Carl and Ricardo gave me the grand tour before leading me round back to my cabin. It was smaller than I'd imagined, more a garden shed than a cabin, and like many garden sheds it was stuffed to the rafters with junk. But Ricardo and Carl soon cleared out the worst of it. They unearthed some unusual objects, including a large skeleton held together by wire.

'Yes, of course it is real,' Carl said, laughing. 'It is from the local hospital.' Carl held up his hand and smiled as my mouth formed another question. 'It is Ricardo's, and it is better if you don't ask!'

Once enough space had been cleared they turned on an electric heater and told me to make myself at home. Dinner wouldn't be long. 'Come over when you are ready.'

Dinner, served in a toasty-warm kitchen, was mostly meat—ham, pork, beef, lamb and possibly other meats too, offered with fresh bread and a limitless supply of tea. For a famished wanderer there couldn't have been a better spread. My chair began to creak.

After dinner, before we could all relax, we went shopping—of all things. Back in the forest I'd extolled the virtues of Scotland's single-malt whiskies, and Carl was now keen to track one down. We piled into Ricardo's battered old BMW and roared helter-skelter down narrow, snow-packed lanes towards the nearest large town before its only supermarket shut. It was a black night and I could hardly see a thing in the headlamps. 'Don't worry, I can't either!' yelled Ricardo, who was driving, but fortunately the car seemed to know the way already. Frenzied heavy-metal music exploding from the stereo added to the sensation of anarchy. It was a world away from the previous night's silent forest camp.

We returned to the house baring a bottle of Talisker aloft.

'Okay,' I said. 'I'd suggest a tumbler of whisky *and* a glass of water. Take turns sipping from each. The water clears the palate. It's a good way to really appreciate each sip.'

'Right,' Carl answered thoughtfully. He picked up his glass for his first wee dram—and threw back the entire contents in one go. 'Ahhh!' he said, grinning devilishly. He picked up the bottle, peered at it, then crashed it down on the table. 'This bottle? We must kill it tonight!'

And so we set to it.

Events blurred from that point on. But I know that I laughed more than at any time since my brother Paul's visit back in the Dolomites. I'd been longing for a break from winter, for a burst of spring, and the evening of laughter became that spring, better in many ways than the one I'd dreamt of. Conversation flowed, jokes flew, whiskies were downed. A couple of friends breezed in and joined the party. Carl and Ricardo attempted to teach me two local games—one with dice called *Schock*, another with cards known as *König*—but the rules eluded my grasp, adding to the evening's hilarity. Katrina spent an age on one slow monologue, carefully explaining every detail of the games, ignoring Carl and Ricardo's impatience to just begin playing. 'So,' she finally said, 'I think you have it now?'

'I'm sorry,' I murmured, woolly headed. 'Could you just go over it one more time?'

'Noooo!' everyone else cried.

And yet, somehow, we got the games started—and what entertainment they brought. Somehow, inexplicably, embarrassingly, I won game after game after game.

They couldn't touch me, even with my clueless playing.

'*Scheisse!* Not again!' they all shrieked at what must have been my tenth triumph. At last Carl could stand it no longer. Faking a dark Teutonic rage he jumped up and rushed from the kitchen, returning quickly with a broad leather belt that he threw onto the table. It was an impressive sight, a thing straight from a horror movie. Hanging from it were the gruesome tools of the butchering trade: vicious-looking knives, serrated saws, evil spikes, torture-chamber hooks, murderous cleavers. Slowly, Carl slid out a curved knife eighteen inches long. It gleamed in the kitchen light as he placed it deliberately on the table in front of him.

Scowling darkly, he dealt the cards.

'Okay,' he said, softly, menacingly, his accent becoming exaggerated for effect. 'Zis... time... I... vin... zee... game!'

And he did!

We all roared.

This wasn't the first time I'd been made to feel like an honoured guest, but no one had been more hospitable than the Fleischers, and they weren't done yet. During a short break from the drinking they wondered if I wanted to shower, and I jumped at the opportunity. I stood beneath stinging water and sluiced away two weeks of forest dirt. Being clean was like being reborn. I giggled in the ecstasy of it—or perhaps it was the whisky taking full hold.

'You know,' I joked, when I returned to the kitchen, holding onto walls and chair tops for support, 'you've given me everything I need. A bed, food, drink, a shower. I don't suppose you do haircuts too?' My hair was doing a fine impression of a gorgon's; my third trim of the walk was long overdue. A selection of scissors in the bathroom had prompted the question, but I didn't expect the answer I got.

'YES!' Carl shouted, raising both arms as though he'd just scored a winning goal in the World Cup final. 'We do!'

'It is my job,' Katrina explained.

'Really?'

'Really. I work as a hairdresser. It is what I do.'

The evening had taken on a dreamlike quality. Before I knew what was happening I found myself perched upon a high stool with the whole family seated around, looking on benignly while tangled wisps of hair floated to the floor. Katrina, fortunately, hadn't been drinking to excess, and any doubts I'd had about the wisdom of being trimmed were soon dispelled. As she snipped away I was quizzed further on the journey, although it took increasing effort to answer the questions clearly and not to simply sit and laugh. A few hours earlier I'd been all alone in a snowy forest, and now here I was in someone's kitchen having my hair cut, sipping whisky, surrounded by friends—by family. I made a mental note to step into more East German pubs.

As usual, the goodbyes the next morning were hard. After so much time alone it was easy to become attached to people, especially people as hospitable as the Fleischers. I was leaving behind a string of friends the length of the continent. The urge to prolong each encounter was growing harder to resist. But I had to keep in mind The Prize. The only way I'd reach it was by walking on.

I'd taken some rousing: sleep had rarely been deeper. The successful demolition of one large bottle of Talisker left no hangover, however, and after a huge meat-based breakfast I stood outside with Ten Ton on my back, ready to go. It weighed more than it had done on arrival. The family had been generous again.

'If I make it that far,' I said, 'I'll send a card from the top of Europe.'

'Yes, we will expect it.'

Carl had the last word, and his simple statement echoed the words of Stefan back in the Czech Republic. It confirmed that the tumultuous twentieth century had left a hangover of another kind in Germany's young as well as old.

'You see…' he said quietly. 'Not all Germans are bad.'

Katrina, Carl, Ricardo and Max (seated), February 4, 1998.

THE HARZ
Chapter 10

WITH SNOW BENEATH my feet I walked, and upon snow I camped. I was getting to know the stuff well. Since leaving Italy I'd covered 1,250 miles, 1,100 of them on snow. It's said that Eskimos have fifty words for snow, and although linguists dispute the number I could believe it. From what I'd seen, snow came in *at least* that many varieties. It changed by the minute, by how it fell, by where it lay and by how long it lay there. The diversity was practically endless.

As I continued across snow-covered hills I thought about the many varieties I'd encountered. They ranged from snow that hindered progress—such as 'sloppy-porridge snow', teasing 'trapdoor snow', and treacherous 'skating-rink snow'—to firmer 'rock snow' that eased it. I thought about the snow I loved, such as the exquisitely rippled 'wind-art snow', glittering 'moon-dust snow', and my favourite of all, 'storybook snow'—snow that had been written upon by countless passing creatures. Reading the stories, adventures and dramas was an entertainment I never tired of.

I thought about 'fern snow', 'sugar snow', 'pillow snow' and 'cut-your-shins-on-the-crust snow'. There was 'crystal snow', 'downy snow', 'mirror snow' and 'speckled-dust snow'. There was 'ankle-twisting-rutted snow', 'crunchy-gravel snow', 'squeaky-styrofoam snow' and 'dirty-old-town snow'. I'd come across all these kinds, and *many* others besides—so many that I'd almost forgotten what bare earth looked like.

As I climbed into the Harz the snow softened into the soggy-porridge kind. For the first time in three weeks the temperature edged above freezing, and while the warmth was welcome the thaw came as a curse. Even trails packed by cross-country skiers became soft and wearying to follow.

The Harz was the final mountain range to cross. Beyond it lay the North German Plain, a landscape that was sea-level low and billiard-table flat. Once there I'd be away from mountains for *two whole months*, and although flat hadn't ever been my favourite topography I couldn't wait to walk upon it.

I'd wanted a long, cold, snowy winter—and now I'd had one. I'd found much within it to treasure, but it had taken a toll. Damp clothes, numb extremities, a squalid tent, overused muscles, a feeling of always being on, seldom able to fully relax—the discomforts had worn me down. Like the boots on my feet and the pack on my back I was slowly coming apart at the seams. I wasn't sure how much more I could take.

But I had the Harz to cross first—five final mountain days—and I wanted to walk them in good style. This meant following the longest route and reaching the highest summit, the Brocken. But then came the thaw, and masses of 'bog-me-down swamp snow'. Step by step my energy waned and my desire faltered. Mile by mile good style grew less and less appealing.

I began making mistakes—simple errors that dented my resolve. I knocked over a mug of tea inside the tent after spending days carefully drying it. I hiked for five hard miles in the wrong direction after misreading the map. I wandered right through a town with my flies open. It was worse than embarrassing—it was worrying. These were all symptoms of deep fatigue, signs I'd been underway too long. I even began stammering more, regressing into an affliction I thought I'd almost escaped. The more tired I grew the more I stammered, the more I stammered the more my confidence waned, and the more my confidence waned the more I stammered. Several people I met looked at me with pity. I imagined their thoughts: *Oh, this poor homeless foreigner, struggling to talk. He probably has mental-health issues.*

The frustration of it sat heavily upon my shoulders. Ten Ton was nothing in comparison.

Wearily, I crossed the Harz. The thawing snow sucked momentum from my steps, and even at a sluggish one mile an hour I found myself sweating hard. For the first time in three weeks I changed out of thermals, but then instantly froze. Once underway again I rapidly overheated. What was going on? Why couldn't I regulate my temperature? Soon my right knee began throbbing. My left ankle ached. My concentration was failing, too. When I stopped for food it took ten minutes to remember why I'd stopped. And then I almost didn't bother eating. It was far easier to simply sit and stare.

On the second morning in the Harz, I reached a road, and across it found hundreds of skiers. Dressed in figure-hugging Lycra with numbers pinned to their chests, the skiers were bobbing and stretching, preparing for a cross-country ski race. I envied them their energy and enthusiasm. Music and instructions blared from loudspeakers, and race marshals with clipboards minced about importantly. One of them called me back when I stepped onto the snow trail beyond the crowds. '*NEIN*,' he shouted, waggling a finger. 'You cannot go that way. It is *VERBOTEN* for non-racers.' The man ordered me away. Soon I was following the only other option, an unbroken trail of knee-deep 'pig's-slop snow'—the very last surface I wanted to be wading through. Then, half a mile further, a buckle that held one of Ten Ton's shoulder straps in place snapped.

That was the last straw. *Forget it. Forget the bloody Harz.* Feeling defeated, I revised my route. Instead of the longest path I settled on the shortest. Instead of climbing the Brocken I turned for the plain. It was the opposite of good style and it didn't sit comfortably. Mad Mountain Jack protested, but I was too tired to listen.

I pushed north and lethargy settled even deeper. The broken strap, partially repaired with a spare bootlace, gave Ten Ton a ridiculous sideways lean. Unbalanced, I stumbled over rocks hidden beneath the snow, and expended outrageous amounts of energy for each small step. This was the other side of walking, the slog, the very opposite of everything I was here for. My world shrank, time slowed, darkness descended, and when finally I found a remote forest clearing suitable for camp I ground to an emphatic halt.

And barely moved again for forty hours.

The Harz, February 11, 1998.

The break, of course, did me good. All I'd really needed was time off from exertion, and an epic amount of sleep—a holiday from my journey. Afterwards, I looked at the mountains with renewed interest, but didn't revert to the original plan. I was done with winter. I still wanted to escape it as soon as I could.

I examined my map and picked a new route. It led downhill to a gorge, the Bodetal—a dramatic way to leave the mountains. Vertical rock had been scarce since the Alps, but it wasn't lacking in the Bodetal. Granite spires a thousand feet tall reared upward. Down in the gorge's depths a half-frozen river plunged over numerous falls. A trail led the length of the Bodetal, and I walked it in solitude, enjoying the sheer-sided scenery. But progress wasn't straightforward. Pale green ice covered the trail's final mile, and where it traversed steep slopes my pulse soared to levels not attained in half a year. At the most exposed sections I held tightly to Excalibur and inched forward carefully, feet skittering in a way that might have looked comical to a casual observer but wasn't remotely funny to me. There were jagged rocks far below and a slip was unthinkable. It felt like mountaineering again, and I reached the end with relief. A barrier with a sign blocked the trail where the gorge finished: 'Trail Closed. Dangerous Ice Conditions'. *Now you tell me*, I thought.

But it didn't matter. I was done with mountains, done with ice and snow. I'd survived the winter and was free to push on across the wide North German Plain.

Except I wasn't done. Not quite. The mountain gods wouldn't let me. Neither would Mad Mountain Jack, damn him to hell. *You cheated*, he observed reproachfully. *You followed the shortest line. And you avoided the highest mountain. Oh no, you're not done.*

He was right, I realised. I couldn't live with leaving the Harz unfinished. I'd always regret it.

And so back to the mountains I turned. Map in hand, I chose a new route, picking trails that led back to the highest ground, avoiding the icy Bodetal. For three days more I wallowed and camped in snow. But I was glad I did. The mighty Brocken wasn't what I'd expected, but the gentle wildness of the forests made up for it. They helped me remember all I'd achieved and learnt. They gave me an opportunity to say farewell to the mountains of Central Europe. They turned defeat into triumph and sent me out into the plains with my head held high. The final loop through the Harz reminded me of my final loop through the Alps. There, as here, I'd almost finished with a whimper, but instead went out in style.

I fell in love all over again with the forests, with the shelter they offered and the peace they bestowed. But I didn't fall for the Brocken. The mountain should have been great, and once upon a time it had been, but I reached it 260 years too late.

The Brocken sits all alone, a bulky mountain of modest altitude but immense stature. At 3,747 feet it would barely count as a foothill in the Alps, but in the middle of Germany, as the highest peak for hundreds of miles, it stands out. The summit rises above tree line and experiences an impressively severe microclimate. Extremes include a record low temperature of minus nineteen Fahrenheit, minus twenty-eight Celsius, and a record wind gust of 163 miles an hour. Snow can cover the summit for 200 days each year, fog for eleven months out of twelve. The Brocken is colder, wetter, snowier, windier and foggier than the plains at its feet, making a short climb up it comparable to travelling 1,000 miles north.

Among mountaineers, the Brocken is famous for giving its name to a rare atmospheric phenomenon, the Brocken spectre. A Brocken spectre occurs when an observer's shadow is cast from above onto clouds or mist. The shadow can look enormous, and a bright rainbow halo often appears around the shadow's head. To some, the sight can seem threatening, even supernatural; legend tells that a climber on the Brocken panicked and plummeted to his death after seeing a giant ghostly figure. The phenomenon was reportedly named by Johann Silberschlag, a German pastor and scientist who witnessed it in 1780. Also called a Brocken bow, or a glory by meteorologists, it can only be seen when specific atmospheric conditions are met—conditions that frequently occur on the Brocken. I'd been fortunate to see Brocken spectres several times in other places, and I was intrigued by the possibility of witnessing one here.

I approached the Brocken from the south, excited by the summit ahead —although I knew it wasn't going to be entirely wild. My map marked a narrow-gauge railway leading to the summit plateau, and a building right at the top. But I imagined I'd be able to ignore them. On paper they looked small in scale, similar to the railway and café on Snowdon in North Wales —intrusions I'd barely noticed when I'd climbed the mountain at the age of fifteen and had fallen in love with the wild.

Unfortunately, I noticed the Brocken's railway right away. It was impossible to miss. I heard it several miles before I could even see it—echoing horn blasts that shattered the forest's peace. Soon I heard the thunder of locomotives, then smelled their smoke, then felt the ground shaking. At that, the wild began slipping away.

It was the weekend, the weather was perfect, and crowds had converged on the Brocken. I reached a well-packed snow trail and joined a line of walkers heading upward. The trail ran near the railway tracks. Twice, trains rumbled by, far larger than expected, and their passage assaulted all the senses. Keen to escape the noise and smoke I climbed at full speed, overtaking my fellow hikers. Despite their slower speeds and smaller pack sizes I suspected that we shared a great deal. Like me, they were probably looking forward to an elevating experience on top.

But the summit wasn't elevating. It barely looked or felt like a summit. It was a circus, teeming and noisy, with horns blasting, people shouting, dogs barking, engines roaring, steam erupting. And worse, it had been built upon, transformed, urbanised. The scale of development was obscene.

I stared at it in shock.

Instead of the single building marked on my map there were several, and they weren't small. There was the train station, bustling like an inner -city *Bahnhof* at rush hour. There was a stark six-storey wooden tower, dark and depressing. There was a massive radio tower, and beneath it a cluster of ugly industrial-style buildings. A futuristic dome capped one nine-storey monstrosity—it resembled an airport control tower. An enclosed obser- vation deck was wrapped around its top floor, and I saw visitors peering through its windows. I found it hard to believe that hundreds of people would choose to visit a mountain to follow paved paths to a concrete building and then squint at the view from behind dirty glass.

This wasn't the mighty Brocken I'd expected—it was pretty much the opposite. My expectations were shattered. For nine months, The Walk had been shattering my expectations, but embracing it and moving on was one of the key lessons I'd learnt. But I couldn't do that here. The summit had been treated too badly to embrace.

As I later found out, it had all begun centuries earlier. In 1736 a rich local nobleman, Count Ernst, had built a small cabin at the summit. He called it *Wolkenhäuschen*, or Clouds Cabin, an affectionate name. No doubt the count had loved the summit for its wildness, but by building upon it he did what our species too often does: he *un*wilded a place through loving it too much. The cabin may have seemed inconsequential compared to the summit environment, but it wasn't like a cabin in the woods or a valley —both natural places for a shelter or a home, both environments better able to survive disturbance. His cabin was out of place. It was a prominent structure that altered the summit completely.

The cabin was an imposition enough, but the count soon added a lodge. In 1800 another building was constructed, the first of several summit inns, and in 1899 the railway was opened, bringing trampling crowds to the fragile top. Further buildings followed, including a weather station and, in 1936, the world's first television tower, from which the Berlin Olympics were broadcast live, increasing Hitler's propaganda reach. The summit suffered further indignities during World War Two. In April 1945 it was bombed by the U.S. Air Force and the inn and weather station were destroyed. After the war, American forces occupied the summit; they rebuilt the structures, but then disabled them again when they left. In 1947 the entire mountain was transferred into Soviet hands. For a while civilian visits were still permitted, although a pass was necessary, but from 1961 onward, as the Cold War intensified, the mountain and entire border region became a fiercely guarded no-man's land. The Red Army stationed a platoon at the train station and covered the summit with utilitarian military structures. These included two powerful listening posts that were used for surveillance and espionage, turning the Brocken into a modern-day mountaintop lookout. A second, even taller television antenna was built in 1976. For security, the entire summit plateau was surrounded by a massive concrete wall eleven feet high. By this time, any real sense of nature or wildness was long gone. Count Ernst wouldn't have recognised the place. And it would have served him right.

Following the fall of the Iron Curtain in 1989 the summit was reopened. The wall was removed, military installations were dismantled, and in 1990 the Harz National Park was born. The last Russian soldier left in March 1994, less than four years prior to my visit. From 1990, millions of Deutsche Marks were spent 'renaturalising' the summit—although it was difficult to imagine what had been done. It didn't look natural to me.

In great dismay, I stared at the ugliness, trying to picture how the summit might once have looked. But I failed. The place was degraded—no, *ruined*—and it made me seethe. But no one else seemed to care. To a visitor fresh from a city the summit might have offered a hint of wild, or a packaged version of it—I could see that. But to me, fresh from nine months in the wild, the summit resembled a city. It wasn't merely a spoilt view or a shattered expectation—it was a wrecked environment. The Brocken was a perfect example of what we as a species all too often do to natural environments and their plant and animal communities: we transform them for our own use with bludgeoning disregard for every living thing present before us. My fellow human visitors didn't appear to see it, but I was painfully aware of the harm that had been done and the treasures that had been lost. I wanted to grab everyone by their shoulders, shake them awake, and yell: 'IT'S NOT SUPPOSED TO BE LIKE THIS!'

I felt resentment, but not for my fellow visitors. It was the opposite, in fact—I wished there were more of them. But I didn't wish there were more *here*. I wished there were more elsewhere, more visitors on other, wilder mountains. If more people climbed mountains more people would fall in love with them. More people would reap the incredible benefits that come from being among them. And more people would fight to protect them. The world would be a better place.

No, what I resented was that *their* summit experience and *my* summit experience was *this* summit experience. For some, this was likely their only summit of the year, and with all my heart I wished them something better. I wished I could wipe the Brocken clean and grant the other visitors the kind of summit I'd experienced elsewhere, a summit that offered an immense range of natural gifts—gifts that couldn't be found in noisy built-upon places. Gifts that only come in the wild.

I couldn't stay. The weather was beautiful and I could see 100 miles, but the damage was too upsetting. And, yet, I was glad I'd come. As much as I loathed what had been inflicted upon the Brocken, and as much as I wished to banish it from memory, I vowed instead to keep it in mind. It would be a counter to complacency, a reminder of what was at stake. Enough wild places had already been lost, but that didn't mean more had to be. The Brocken's *broken* summit reminded me that I too had a role to play, however small. Instead of sitting quietly by I needed to share with honesty and passion exactly how I felt. Only by showing that I truly cared could I hope to sway others into caring. Why should the destroyers of the wild stop if they don't believe that people object? But if they learn *how much* people care, if enough of us show that we care, changes can be made.

My anger and sadness faded once the Brocken fell behind. Within an hour I was back in pine-scented forests that showed little sign of damage. They felt even more precious than usual, and for this heightened appreciation I was gladder still that I'd re-engaged with the Harz. I'd seen the best of wild Europe, and now the worst. And I'd learnt from both.

I made my final mountain camp for two months on a quiet ridge at 1,500 feet—the 'Spring Ridge Camp'. At this lower altitude snow was melting fast, subsiding into the earth and forming streams, filling the valley below with the song of snowmelt. I ate dinner outside and spent the night tossing and turning, unable to sleep in the warmth.

I descended to the plains the next morning, walking from Thuringia into Lower Saxony, and soon it wasn't snow beneath my feet but earth—the much-missed, half-forgotten, instantly familiar, deeply cherished earth. It was carpeted with pine needles, softened with grass, speckled with stones, padded by moss, textured with endless organic matter. It was gentle and forgiving, rich and welcoming, intricate and fascinating. It gave off intoxicating scents that enlivened the air, eased every step, left me giddy with happiness, set me grinning and singing, banished weariness as though it had never been.

It wasn't concrete, hadn't been built upon, and it wasn't altered for convenience or pleasure. And it wasn't snow, either.

With the earth beneath my feet I was free.

View from the 'Spring Ridge Camp' on the edge of the Harz, February 12, 1998.

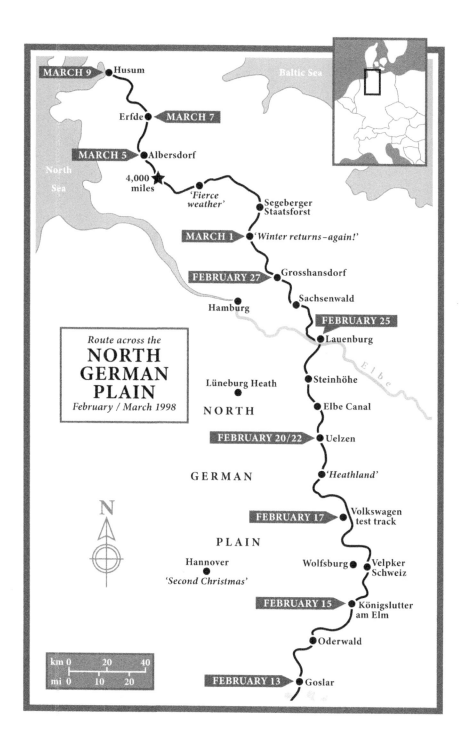

MARCH 9 — ● Husum

Erfde ● ◀ MARCH 7

MARCH 5 ▶ ● Albersdorf

4,000 miles ★

'Fierce weather'

● Segeberger Staatsforst

MARCH 1 ▶ ● *'Winter returns – again!'*

FEBRUARY 27 ▶ ● Grosshansdorf

● Sachsenwald

Hamburg ●

FEBRUARY 25

● Lauenburg

Route across the
**NORTH
GERMAN
PLAIN**
February / March 1998

Lüneburg Heath ●

N O R T H

● Steinhöhe

● Elbe Canal

FEBRUARY 20/22 ▶ ● Uelzen

G E R M A N

● *'Heathland'*

FEBRUARY 17 ▶ ● Volkswagen test track

P L A I N

Hannover ●
'Second Christmas'

Wolfsburg ● ● Velpker Schweiz

FEBRUARY 15 ▶ ● Königslutter am Elm

● Oderwald

FEBRUARY 13 ▶ ● Goslar

Baltic Sea

North Sea

Elbe

N

km 0   20   40
mi 0   10   20

113

ACROSS 'THE GREAT IN-BETWEEN'
Chapter 11

'YOU'RE GOING TO walk across northern Germany?' queried one of my few good friends, Charles, two months before the journey had begun. 'Well… that'll be dull!'

Which only goes to show how little imagination some people have.

Then again, it was an understandable reaction. I'd shared it. After all, the top half of Germany doesn't exactly top every walker's must-visit list. It offers no soaring mountains or plunging canyons; it's just a wide, flat, human-altered landscape, and the only reason I was going to cross it was to get to the far side. Clearly, it wasn't just *another* in-between stretch, it was the longest and *greatest* in-between stretch—and, yes, it probably would provide the dullest month of the journey.

Or so I'd thought in my previous life: BC, Before Calabria. But now, after almost ten months on foot, after finding wildness and beauty in so many unexpected places, I had higher hopes. Sure, the Great In-Between wouldn't give the remotest miles, but I had a sneaking suspicion there'd be more to it than dull farmland. I'd show my friend Charles a thing or two.

The stretch began in Goslar, a mid-sized town at the foot of the Harz, and it was a treasure—the first unexpected treat from the Great In-Between. Filled with medieval charm, gothic splendour and a maze of cobbled lanes, it was the most fascinating town I'd entered since the hilltop villages of the Abruzzo. Once I'd deposited Ten Ton at a cheap private *Zimmer*, a rare but overdue luxury, I stepped back outside and spent long hours exploring.

Rest would have made more sense, but Goslar was too much of a feast to resist. I binged.

Goslar reminded me that the human world, not just nature, could offer beauty and rewards. One of the rewards was logistical: a well-stocked bookstore, and within it maps for the next 400 miles. I bought five sheets covering the entire route to Denmark. Unlike the maps I'd used in southern Italy, these were incredibly detailed, and one specific detail filled me with optimism. For the Great In-Between I'd had two major concerns. One was that I'd struggle to find fresh water each night, and the other was that I'd struggle to find hidden spots for camp. But the map dispelled the latter concern in an instant; it showed forests *everywhere*. From northern Germany I'd expected a similar landscape to Britain's flatter agricultural spaces: that is, mostly treeless. But, as usual, my expectations missed the mark. Germany, it turns out, is thirty-seven per cent wooded, significantly more than Britain's paltry eleven per cent. Detailed pre-trip research might have told me this, but it was far more fun to find out the way I did.

High on optimism, I paced from Goslar early the next morning, keen to engage with the flatlands, keen to walk from forest to forest—a game of join the green dots on my new maps. From the first step, I felt as though I'd entered an entirely new country, and an idea I'd been pondering for some time finally emerged into full clarity. Human-drawn political borders, I saw, weren't the real boundaries that mattered on my walk. They were artificial and inconsequential. No, the boundaries that made the real difference were those formed by nature, topography and climate. When I'd stepped from nation to nation very little that truly affected me had changed, but when I'd transitioned from environment to environment *everything* had changed: the climate, the plant and animal life, the routines and character of daily existence. The very earth I stood upon. From mountains to plains, from forests to open country, from summer to winter; these were the boundaries that meant something. This simple observation completely altered how I looked at the continent, changing it from a politically divided landmass into something more whole, something more *real*. As human-drawn boundaries faded in relevancy a curious sense of unity and belonging grew. I would never belong to Italy, Austria or Germany—but I *did* belong to the land, no matter what nation claimed ownership of it. Belonging to nature, to the land itself, made every single part of Europe feel like home.

Down here in my new low-altitude home spring was definitely in the air. I no longer needed to wear a fleece while moving. I saw fresh buds on shrubs and new stems of grass pushing aside old. Just as winter had lowered my energy levels so the promise of spring now raised them. Rational thinking told me it was too early to celebrate the passing of winter, but other instincts developed over thousands of miles told me otherwise. And I trusted them; I'd learnt to. They were better attuned to the rhythms of the land than my thinking mind, and if they urged me to sing then I bloody well would. And so I sang; as I strode across the land I sang in company with all the uncaged birds.

Twenty miles passed with rare ease, but soon my legs, unaccustomed to ticking across flat terrain, were hinting that enough was enough. When I reached a small village—Flöthe—I set to the task of acquiring water for camp. This was to become a regular feature of the journey until Norway: collecting water from civilisation and carrying it off into the woods for camp. Occasionally, I'd find a natural source, but more often I got it from petrol stations, supermarkets, pubs, or simply through knocking on someone's front door. In the weeks ahead, water was to come from many varied sources, and it became a light-hearted game, a test of ingenuity to acquire it from someplace new. *Okay*, I'd reason at day's end, *so I've already sourced water from a florist, a vet's office, a retirement home, a fire station, and a kindergarten, but how about this: an undertakers?* It wasn't as rewarding as pulling fresh water from an untamed mountain stream, but it always provided entertainment.

Occasionally, the people that gave water would also give more: a cup of coffee, slices of home-baked bread, and a patch of lawn for camp. 'Excuse me,' I'd ask meekly, standing back a respectful distance. 'I'm walking across Germany. I need water for camp. Is there anywhere I can fill my water carrier?' The answer was almost always 'Yes, follow me'. I was often led indoors, shown to a kitchen sink, helped without hesitation. The process became so easy, and introduced me to so many Germans from so many walks of life, that I wished I'd asked for water back in southern Italy. Sure, I'd wanted to do things the hard way back then and stand on my own two feet, but looking back now it was clear I'd made a huge mistake. If I'd approached more people it would have been a far richer journey.

On this first occasion I wasn't yet bold enough to knock on someone's door, but when I came upon a small butcher's shop I reckoned it was worth a try. The shop wasn't yet open, but a woman standing outside said it soon would be.

'*Fünf Minuten*,' ('Five minutes,') she declared, so I lined up behind her.

Six other women were also waiting, lined up with military precision. Oddly, no one spoke. The women all carried shopping bags, looked as though they'd come on foot, and must all have been locals, but they stood stiff and upright, distant from one another like strangers waiting for a city bus. It wasn't what I would have expected from a tiny rural town, but it appeared to say a great deal about German orderliness.

The shop eventually opened. When my turn came the butcher let me use his tap as though he dealt with long-distance hikers every day of the week. And that was that—wild camping on the plains clearly wasn't going to be a problem. Half an hour later I was alone in a forest, pitching my home behind a thick stand of spruce. I had clean water, a soft mulchy bed to sleep upon, and nothing but natural sights, sounds and scents all around. I couldn't have asked for more.

As motion ceased, and time slowed, I gazed around at my new forest home. To my eyes it looked well established and thoroughly natural, even though I guessed it probably wasn't. Natural tree cover across the North German Plain should be deciduous, with beech and oak the dominant species, but after 10,000 years of human intervention very little natural tree cover remains. From early hunter-gatherers, who burnt forests to create openings for game, to twentieth-century foresters who planted fast-growing spruce in endless straight lines, humankind has altered and reinvented the woods. As I was to discover over the next month, conifers vastly outnumber deciduous trees, although in a season without leaves this worked in my favour—conifers make better screens for illegal forest camps. But despite their altered state many forests still *felt* natural. They were frequently filled with trees of different ages and species, they often provided a multi-storeyed canopy, they regularly showed evidence of self-regeneration, and almost all teemed with life. Modern German foresters were increasingly practising close-to-nature management. Many were harvesting individual trees selectively instead of clear-cutting entire forests, and were also allowing natural long-term processes to run their course. Clear-cutting was still taking place, and I was to come upon many single-species single-age plantations,

A discreet woodland camp in a peaceful spot, February 17, 1998.

but they were fairly easy to avoid. Most of the forests I walked through and slept in over the next month showed little evidence of heavy-handed management. This was one of the greatest surprises—and pleasures—of the Great In-Between.

The first forest night passed peacefully, with slumber broken only by barking foxes and screeching owls. Dawn arrived a couple of hours before I was ready for it, but I couldn't complain; the dawn chorus was a symphony of such optimism I could only listen in appreciation. Soon, crisp sunlight and heady morning scents completed the job the birds had begun. Rising was easier than it had been since the Endless Summer in the Alps. Striking camp was a cinch. Only two weeks earlier I'd been battling zero-Fahrenheit dawns, but now there wasn't even a hint of frost, and by early afternoon the temperature had climbed to the sixties. The change was life-altering; it made me feel fitter, stronger, *happier*. I'd hoped for spring beyond the Harz. Never in my wildest dreams had I expected *this much* spring.

Feeling that I'd rather dance than walk, I set off through sunlit woods; alone, but not for long. An unusually large fox stepped onto the path twenty yards ahead. I slowed and walked quietly, watching it pad along for a full minute until finally it caught my scent. It looked back in surprise, and took off to the side. *Hey*, I thought, *I don't smell that bad. I had a shower in Goslar!* A few minutes later I came upon eight red deer, the largest sporting impressive antlers. The deer watched me enquiringly as I approached, ears twitching, nostrils flaring, and then sprang away into the trees. I found more wild companions three miles further, out in open space: skylarks, filling the air with song. I listened with surprise and joy to a sound that I associated with spring sunshine, freedom and wild open places. I'd had no idea I'd hear them in February in rural Germany. Skylarks had provided the soundtrack to some of the finest miles I'd ever walked, miles along high mountain ridges, dramatic ocean-top bluffs, and lonely heather-cloaked moorlands. Hearing them here took me straight back, linking so many different places and moments in time together.

Skylarks aren't much to look at—they're just small brown birds with no extravagant plumage—but once soaring they enter a class of their own. Their flight song is continuous and flowing, energetic and youthful, light-hearted and optimistic. It pours forth and fills the sky, sounding the way sunlight feels. It may just be a declaration of territory and a call to mate, but to me it has always been a celebration of freedom, and it never fails to carry me away.

Feeling carried, if not elevated, I walked on. It became a day of fields and forests, warmth and sunlight, earthy scents and cascading song. I spotted the first flowers of the year: white snowdrops growing in delicate clumps on grassy verges. I disturbed the first frog, by a pool, and the first rabbits, in a field, and the largest herd of deer so far—more than thirty on the edge of a forest. I met others of my own species, locals also out and about enjoying the sun: cyclists and dog walkers, horse riders and runners. Two girls ran by, blond hair flying behind them. 'Hallo!' they called cheerfully, flashing dazzling smiles. When I came upon a phone box later that afternoon I stopped to call Charles, to tell him that northern Germany was *far* from dull. But, alas, his line was busy.

Grinning with contentment, I settled into another peaceful forest camp that evening. I felt fully embedded in nature, I was warm and dry, and I didn't have to struggle for any of my comforts. Life was ridiculously easy.

The journey no longer felt like an adventure—it had become a *vacation*. But I didn't mind that one bit. I reckoned I'd earned it.

Basking in sunlight near Wolfsburg, February 18, 1998.

The first full week on the plain passed without drama, at least for me. But for my fellow creatures and plants the struggles, tragedies, comedies and successes were never ending. I noticed a fox with a mouse in its mouth, two squirrels angrily chasing one another around a tree, a woodpecker drilling into an old stump for insects, a leaf-shaped bug trying to avoid attention, a hawk shooting downward like a lightning bolt to pluck a small furry being from the centre of a field—life and death, everywhere. I watched a blackbird pulling a worm from the earth and imagined the incident from the worm's perspective: how fearsome the blackbird must seem, how horrible to have one's body so stretched! I watched crows mobbing a northern goshawk, and imagined what the attack felt like to the raptor as it twisted to get away. I watched a tiny, fuzz-covered fly writhing in a web while a spider inched closer, and I swear I could sense *understanding* in the fly's desperate attempts to escape. I stared at a tiny shoot of green that had curled upwards toward the sun from beneath a rock, and to me the joy the shoot exhibited at its escape from coldness and darkness was palpable. And I watched a ladybird drowning in a puddle, unable to swim to safety —and for once watching wasn't enough. Afterwards, the ladybird sat on a leaf that from its point of view must have seemed like divine intervention. It remained motionless in warm sunlight, wings half open, drying off, its entire life altered by chance. Everywhere I looked I saw drama, on each patch of earth and in each quarter of the sky, and I thought to myself: *the North German Plain, dull?*

On the fourth plains day the temperature cooled and a soft rain fell. But compared to conditions back in the mountains it still felt like spring, and I received the moisture as I would a treat. Gentle against my upturned face, lulling upon the roof of my tent, the fine drizzle only increased my sense of well-being. It wasn't snow, frost or ice; it didn't lock my home rigid or impede progress. It added diamond-bright droplets to hawthorn twigs, increased the richness of scents rising from the earth—and, in any case, sunlight the next day quickly banished it. For the kiss of moisture my world was renewed once again. Who would have guessed how many first dawns there could be?

The landscape continued to surpass my expectations, especially when I chanced upon an area of heathland north of Wolfsburg. The heathland was a sparsely inhabited stretch of semi-open country, and it felt wild and elemental. It was covered in acres of purple heather, sprinkled with shapely junipers, edged by pockets of silver birch, chequered with pinewoods. The sandy earth felt soft and gentle beneath my feet, and I walked it in solitude, feeling awe at my good fortune to have chanced upon such a wild place in a land that I'd presumed would be entirely farmed.

The heath was part of the Lüneburg Heath, an extensive tract of wild land much treasured by Germans of the north. The heath looked natural, but it wasn't—like every environment across the North German Plain it owed its appearance and existence to humankind's influence.

After the retreat of the last ice sheet 16,000 years ago, successive waves of trees colonised the plains. Birch and pine woodlands appeared first, evolving into forests of hazel, then sessile oak, then beech. The first human inhabitants, Mesolithic hunter-gatherers, had minimal impact on the forests, burning only small clearings, but the Neolithic farmers that followed made a lasting difference. They brought livestock and overgrazing, and over time the forests died back, making way for open heathland.

The heath expanded to its greatest extent roughly 1,000 years ago, and farmers were partly responsible, albeit unintentionally. They removed turf from large areas to enrich smaller fields for crops, and the sandy, nutrient-poor soil they left behind was an ideal environment for heather to occupy and thrive. Heather dominated for the next 850 years, and humans came to regard the heathland as a barren and inhospitable wilderness, a waste-land to avoid. But that changed with the industrial revolution, and the romantic ideas about wild landscapes that came with it. Soon, the heath was seen by some as a valued place, a refuge for body and spirit—a view that I well understood.

By the early 1900s the heath was under threat, shrinking yearly before an advancing tide of cultivation and reforestation. To counter this, organisations like the Verein Naturschutzpark, the Nature Park Society, sprang up to preserve Germany's few remaining wild corners. The society developed bold plans to create national parks across the country, and by 1913 they had the support of thousands of German citizens. Progress was difficult, but they managed to achieve small gains. In 1921 a 77-square-mile parcel of the Lüneburg Heath was designated a nature reserve, a first for German conservation. But attacks on the heath continued. The fiercest came from the military who, in the run up to World War Two, considered the unpeopled 'wastes' a perfect environment for training. After the war, British, Canadian and American forces also trained on the heath, spending several decades tearing the environment to shreds. In the 1970s and 1980s, growing protests by the public and burgeoning environmental organisa-tions eventually led to a reduction in training, and in 1994 a return of the heath to the Nature Park Society. With assistance from the government, rewilding began.

The heathland I crossed wasn't part of the official nature reserve, but it was being protected and maintained in a similar way. One of the tools was controlled grazing by flocks of Heidschnucke, a hardy breed of moorland sheep. I passed one large flock, all ragged fleeces and curved horns, their lower incisors trimming back tree saplings to keep the land open. It struck me as wonderfully ironic, how a land that had once been entirely forested was now treasured for what we'd turned it into, and was being actively pre-served in an artificial state. But I completely understood. The open heath *was* attractive, and it did *feel* wild. When I considered it further, I acknowl-edged, begrudgingly at first, that many of the landscapes I'd treasured since Calabria had likely been artificial too.

That night, while camped amid the heather, my thoughts kept returning to this. Artificial, I finally accepted, didn't have to be a negative state, the way it had been on the Brocken's summit. In fact, it could be the opposite—when there was room within it for nature to flourish. When I set out the following morning, heralded by another glorious dawn chorus, I sensed that a profound paradigm shift in my outlook was taking place. It reminded me of how, earlier in The Walk, my outlook on forests had also changed. Before Calabria, I'd thought of forests as second-tier environments to pass through swiftly en route to the only environments that really mattered: high mountains. But months of forest living had woken me up, revealing their true value. Was I now reassessing human-altered landscapes in the same way?

It was a radical idea, that unnatural landscapes could also offer 'wild' nature, and something within me resisted it. It didn't match what I'd believed for so many years. But it was an idea I couldn't now shake.

The heath fell behind, and I tramped on, from farmland to forest and from village to village. It wasn't all peace and beauty. On February 20 I bedded down within earshot of the Mittelland Canal, the longest artificial waterway in Germany, and spent a disturbed night listening to barges blowing their horns. I spent further noisy hours the following day trapped between the famous Ehra-Lessien Volkswagen test track on one side and a military firing range on the other, committed to a badly chosen, dead-straight road until I reached its end. To my left cars screamed as test drivers pushed their vehicles to the limit; to my right machine guns went *rat-a-tat-tat* and explosions boomed. It was possibly the oddest and loudest five miles of the entire journey.

I came upon another man-made straight line later the next day: the Elbe Canal. This I followed to the town of Uelzen, and in Uelzen I took a temporary break from The Walk. I bought a ticket, jumped aboard a high-speed train, and was spirited south to the city of Hannover at unsettling—if not terrifying—velocity. I had an appointment to keep.

Six weeks earlier, The Passage and the Cardinal Hume Centre had hatched a joint plan to fly my parents to Hannover for a (slightly delayed) halfway celebration. The aim was to use photos of our reunion to generate extra publicity and encourage extra donations, and the plan worked—donations for the homeless far exceeded the budget plane fare. The plan worked for me too. I was treated to a weekend with Base Camp—a second chance at Christmas. I hadn't needed time off from The Walk, but I wasn't going to complain at interrupting it for this.

We met at the Hotel Viel Essen in the city centre. I tramped into the lobby, feeling thoroughly out of place amid so much polished wood and gleaming tile, but instantly forgot my discomfort when my parents rose from the plush seats where they'd been waiting.

I didn't notice walking towards them, but I did notice the tight group hug I suddenly found myself a part of. I happily lost myself within the life-long familiarity of it. Mad Mountain Jack felt warm inside and curiously safe.

'Well,' my mother finally said, her head tilted as she inspected me. 'You don't look too bad.'

I laughed. 'You know, I'm not sure that's a compliment!'

'We've read your reports,' my father explained. 'The cold and snow! We were expecting something more abominable. We thought you'd look *even more* weather ravaged than you do.'

I laughed again. 'I'm not weather ravaged. Most of what you see will come off in the shower!'

'Andrew, you look okay, really,' my mother said gently, ignoring the jokes. 'You *are* okay, aren't you?'

'Mum—I really am. The journey's been extraordinary. I'll tell you all about it.'

Putting their questions on hold, my parents guided me to the front desk. As we walked, I reflected on the things I wouldn't tell them. I'd leave out the worst moments, especially the loneliness. They'd worry no matter how much I tried to reassure them, and there'd be no need. Loneliness lay in my past. At least, I hoped it did. My return to the trail after a weekend of company would soon reveal the truth.

After checking in, Base Camp led me to my room, then left me alone for half an hour so that I could 'un-weather ravage' myself. We met back downstairs for dinner.

'You *do* look hungry,' my mother observed before the meal. Afterwards, I read awe in her eyes. 'You *were* hungry! How on earth did you fit all that in? I wouldn't have thought it possible.'

'Um...' I said, furrowing my brow as though concerned. 'But that was only the starters, right? I thought you were going to take care of me?'

'We are,' my mother answered earnestly, and I saw from both of my parents' expressions that they truly meant to.

———

The weekend passed with stories and laughter, with epic volumes of food forming the backdrop. To me, it truly felt like Christmas—a celebration of togetherness, a gift of family time that I appreciated with an intensity I'd never before felt. Time slowed, just the way it does in nature, and the weekend felt longer than two days. I savoured every minute, deliberately storing away the details so that I could carry my parents with me when I returned to The Walk. As I child, I'd taken my privileged home life for granted. As a young adult, I'd wanted to escape it. But now I felt nothing but gratitude for everything I'd had growing up, and for parents who still gave unconditional support even when I was following a path they didn't understand or like.

We only touched on my perplexing choices once, and then only briefly. There was no need for a long and deep discussion about what I was doing. My father already understood that I was moving in a direction I'd chosen. He was a realist, one of his many strengths. He saw things as they were. But at the same time, my choices were so contrary to his that he couldn't entirely let them go. Questioning them was a well-intentioned parental duty.

'Life is risky enough,' he'd said before The Walk. 'Adding extra risk is foolish.' He'd attempted to instil in me that his own rational and pragmatic approach to life was the only sensible approach. 'Andrew, you have to work hard to create a secure future for yourself—because no one else will. Compromising your entire future because all you want to do *right now* is walk doesn't make sense. Honestly, it's a short-sighted choice with serious long-term consequences.'

So I wasn't remotely surprised when he finally brought the subject up in Hannover.

'Andrew, have you got this out of your system yet?' he asked late on the final afternoon.

I'd attempted to prepare for the question by getting ahead of it with my stories. As I saw it, they were my best bet. They explained the *whys* far more clearly than any distilled answer ever could. From the moment we'd met I'd shared tales of Alpine cloud seas and ice-glazed Bohemian forests. I'd described the kindness of strangers, the hospitality of families. I'd talked about growth, about learning to understand and trust my own capabilities, about becoming *more* with each step, about finding meaning and purpose in moving forward. At times, I could have sworn I'd detected the light of understanding in my father's eyes. *At last!* But then he asked his question and it showed that he hadn't understood.

In truth, I wasn't surprised. When considering what to say I'd come to believe that there simply wasn't a convincing explanation for a journey like mine. It was beyond words. It was something that could only be experienced and felt to be understood. Or it was something that had to be yearned for, and without that yearning it would never make sense. A person either understood it, or they didn't. Trying to explain was arguably pointless, either way.

So I answered the way I'd learnt to over the years. I laughed the question off.

'Have I got this out of my system? Hmm, let's see.' I paused a moment for dramatic effect. 'Of course not! It's stuck there. My system's broken. And probably always will be.'

'Yes,' my father said, nodding, willing to play along, but still making his point. 'You *are* broken. I think we can all agree on that.'

We laughed—as we usually did. My mother made a face that told me not to worry. *I don't care about the reason*, her expression said.

My father had the final word, before the conversation moved on. 'I still think you're completely mad.'

I walked away from my parents on Monday morning, my stomach churning with nerves. Would loneliness strike now that I was back on my own? But it didn't. Not in the first few minutes as I paced along Hannover's hard paved streets, not in the train back to Uelzen, and not when I picked up the trail exactly where I'd left it. Instead, I felt strengthened by the laughter and love I'd just enjoyed. This was an immense relief. I'd hoped to walk away unscathed, but hadn't been 100 per cent certain that I would. But what I'd learnt from my Christmas low was now confirmed. Yes, I needed people, and yes, I *was* a member of a social species—the joy I'd felt in Hannover proved it. But no, I didn't need people all the time. As I walked back into nature I celebrated the company I'd just enjoyed, and I celebrated nature, too. But most of all I celebrated my freedom—freedom from having to suffer a belief that I'd mistakenly clung to for so much of my life: the unnatural belief that I was—and needed to be—an island.

The Christmas-in-February visit from Base Camp hadn't just delivered emotional gifts but material gifts, too. I returned to the trail bearing several items of new gear, much of it sorely needed. Top of the list was Ten Ton Mark II, a replacement for Ten Ton with its broken shoulder strap. Gear and clothing sponsor Lowe Alpine had willingly donated a second pack, and Base Camp had delivered it. As I walked north, I was shocked by how balanced and comfortable this new pack felt. The broken strap had given Ten Ton an awkward sideways lean. A pack that let me walk upright felt strange, if not wrong!

On February 25 I crossed the Elbe, swapping Lower Saxony for Schleswig-Holstein, the final German state on my route. At first the landscape was wide-open; so broad and flat that I imagined I could see the curve of the earth. I paced north in watery light, smiling at memories from Base Camp's visit, marvelling at the excessive space all around. After two days I reached Grosshansdorf, a commuter village on the outskirts of Hamburg. Grosshansdorf felt disorientingly familiar. It was a mirror image of Pinner, the London suburb I'd grown up in. Walking through it, I saw clean residential roads with grass verges, and well-maintained homes with immaculate gardens. It oozed the sleepy atmosphere of a bedroom community, a quiet, respectable place where change was slow and drama remained hidden. With each step, I found myself imagining that I was almost back at my parents' home, that The Walk—like all the walks before it—was finally over. A small part of me wanted it to be true, wanted to discover that the effort was done, wanted to be able to jettison Ten Ton II and all the journey's discomforts and take life easy. I was unsettled by the way Grosshansdorf called.

But a greater part wanted the opposite, screamed at me to escape while

I still could. The real truth came when Grosshansdorf fell behind: I felt nothing but relief. I wasn't ready to return to the suburbs, and I definitely wasn't ready to end my walk.

On February's last day winter returned. Westerly winds raked the land. Lashing rain turned into sleet, then snow. I woke on March 1 to a sodden cover of white. Progress became a battle once again: uphill walking on flat terrain. The snow thawed, returned, thawed, returned—but it was wind and rain that became the fiercest opponents. The wind tried its damnedest to blow me back to the Harz. For a week I squared off against the elements, staggering at each blast, bending before the onslaught, energy fading once again. Head down, boots squelching, I slogged on, enduring the miles now, not enjoying them. Ideas previously entertained came back to haunt me. *Why should we cower from the worst weather?* I'd asked on Great Arber.

I'll tell you why, I responded now, *because life in the worst weather can be unutterably miserable!*

The landscape soon disappeared beneath water. Fields flooded, paths ran like rivers, a rain-filled sky merged with the earth. The North Sea lay less than fifty miles west—but with so much water around it felt much closer. My waterproofs began soaking up moisture like sponges, and by each day's end I was more chilled and uncomfortable than I'd been at any point during the winter. I took refuge whenever I could, rarely passing a bus shelter or open shed without stopping. I trembled at the thought of similar conditions in Norway. I was barely coping down here where I could find frequent shelter, but Norway's fjells would be exposed, and weather like this up there was guaranteed—Norway was infamous for it. The idea of crossing Norway suddenly seemed borderline suicidal. This wasn't what I wanted to feel. Norway was supposed to be The Prize, not a place to fear. But I couldn't help myself. Fear was what I was now feeling.

Happily, my tent was doing a slightly better job than my waterproofs, although puddles still washed the floor each morning and wet streaks darkened the walls. But despite the leaks I felt secure inside. It repelled the worst of the rains, shrugged off the fiercest blasts, and the storms outside *almost* became something I could forget. Of course, I never could entirely, because dawn would always come with more miles to be walked. Twice, however, I woke to conditions so severe I hid in camp all day. The only problem with staying put was that I seldom had enough drinking water.

I could only smile at the irony of having to ration water while endless amounts sheeted from the sky.

On March 5 the elements adopted a new approach, alternating short bursts of calm with even fiercer storms as though hoping a good-cop-bad-cop routine would finally break me. But the ploy didn't work. The calm interludes only reminded me that the sun would *always* come out again eventually, no matter how bad things got, and the storms themselves were so biblical in scale that I felt nothing but awe. Towering cumulonimbus cloud monsters built on the horizon, drifted closer, and when they hit it was as though hell had been unleashed. In an instant the sun disappeared, twilight descended, and raging violence replaced peace. The wind roared, tearing at trees, flinging rain, hail, sleet and snow, mixing earth and sky into one writhing mass, setting *everything* into motion. But then, as suddenly as they had arrived, the storms passed, leaving behind sunshine and calm as though nothing had happened. One after another the storms barrelled in; soon I felt I was watching the seasons sped up, time-lapse photography in real life. It was invigorating stuff—so *un*-dull that I tried phoning Charles yet again, but his line was still engaged.

The skies eventually gave up on the good-cop-bad-cop routine and resumed a drenching rain. I splashed on, lamenting my all-but-useless waterproofs, forever soaked to the skin, feet white and wrinkly in sodden socks. Twigs flew by in the wind, telephone wires wailed desolately, birds were silent, and I could see only one colour to the land: grey in a million shades. I escaped my wet clothes each evening, but cringed each morning when I pulled them back on. The leaks in the tent grew worse. Puddles spread further. Water and wind dominated my existence. The vacation was clearly over, and the journey had become an adventure once again. But that was fine; it was still better than the other life I could have been living.

When I reached the town of Albersdorf I caught an unhappy glimpse of that other life. It began with a middle-aged lady. I asked her for directions to the food shop, but she was in too much of a rush to help. I found the shop eventually, but once inside wished I hadn't. It was huge—a disturbed ants' nest of consumerism. Like several other supermarkets I'd visited since January, it didn't cater for people who wished to purchase goods in small amounts. What good were sealed bags of twenty-four apples to someone who only wanted two? And the prices were mostly unaffordable. Still, it was the only option in town, so I made do, filling a basket with food not on my usual list. Every so often I stood aside to let shoppers in more haste go first, but nobody thanked me for it. I gave way to one old lady but she showed me no courtesy when we met again. She ended up directly behind me at the checkout line, both of us many customers back from the front, but when a neighbouring checkout opened she—and several other shoppers—rushed straight for it, elbowing me aside. Even sadder was the way customers treated checkout staff. The girl working my line looked pale and exhausted as she frantically scanned items to keep up. No one spoke to her or said thank you. When my turn came I tried desperately to connect, to share a simple smile, but she was too harried to look up. Afterwards, back outside in the wild weather, my tramp-like existence didn't seem so bad. There were worse things than being cold and wet.

The reality was, foul weather or not, I was free—more so with each passing day. I had time on my hands and clean air to breathe and wonders all around. When I pitched my tent later that afternoon in a sheltering wood my attention was caught by a small patch of earth. I stared at it for long minutes, and the more I stared the more remarkable the spot became. Fallen beech leaves covered it. The leaves were dead, but they weren't dull or grey as one might expect: they were full of colour and texture, each one an exquisite work of art. Rising through the leaves was a tree stump, a decaying cathedral of sponge-soft wood and emerald moss, a biome crawling and sprouting with life. I stared at the fallen leaves, at the old stump, at the small patch of earth, and although I knew it was all ordinary, replicated innumerable times across the continent, I also saw that every single part was unique and had value, that it was a complete wilderness, albeit in miniature. It revealed the truth: that wildness existed everywhere in nature. It was present in a blackbird's dawn song, in soft haze that blurred the horizon, in rattling reeds that edged a pond. It was present in every corner of the landscape, from one tiny leaf to an entire forest, from a trackless mountain to a human-altered heath. The Great In-Between had taken me far from the kind of environments I'd previously considered wild, but I'd found wildness anyway.

Walking isn't just walking; it is thinking too, and as I walked across Schleswig-Holstein and drew ever closer to the North Sea I thought about the wild. Of course, I'd thought about it *many* times before, but never with such intensity. This time I probed it, turned my assumptions upside down and shook them. *What exactly IS the wild? I asked. What is it to me? Why does it affect me the way it does?*

The answers came slowly—at three miles an hour. But they came all the same, and they arrived with more clarity than ever before, informed by 3,700 miles in nature. I saw that the wild wasn't any single easily defined landscape, as I'd once thought. It had nothing to do with scale, nothing to do with remoteness. Instead, I saw that it was a state of being, a natural order—the way *all* things had evolved to be. The wild was simply the natural world going about its business, regardless of, and alongside, the human-influenced world.

I saw that the barriers I'd been brought up behind—the walls, comforts and distractions, and also the beliefs I'd been taught—had separated me from this natural state of being. It wasn't that the barriers had all been bad. Some were obviously necessary, and some were simply fun, but many of them had cut me off *too thoroughly*. They'd stopped me from being what tens of thousands of years of evolution had made me to be. They'd separated me from the environment I'd been shaped to fit into, and as a result I'd been severed from who I really was. I'd been incomplete. And I'd struggled because of it.

And this, I now saw, was the main reason why I was drawn to the wild: to remove that separation, to reconnect. It seemed laughably obvious now I'd seen it.

Yes, there were other reasons. I also went for the sensory joy of being in the wild, to simply *feel*—to feel alive. I went to have ancient instincts and physical abilities brought back to life, to discover that I could *do* more than I'd thought. I went to reap the numerous health benefits that I suspected were always being given by the wild, even if many were too subtle to notice. And I went for the adventure and challenge of negotiating the wild, for the journey itself—to be in motion, moving forward, finding out. This was where larger areas of the wild would always be important, for the freedom and space they gave.

But above all I went for connection.

The idea sounded ridiculously simple on the surface, a cliché almost. But it was also profoundly true. When I stepped into nature and felt the boundaries between myself and the natural world blur it was like entering a parallel existence. It left me feeling complete—not complete as an individual but complete as an integral part of everything. No longer separated, I knew with every ounce of my being that I'd found my true place, my home, and the emotions that accompanied that homecoming were exhilarating beyond expression. Away from the wild I was limited; in it I was expanded. Yes, it was simple. But the most profound truths usually are.

This was why I needed the wild: to be complete. And this was why I would always keep returning: *because life without the wild is a mere shadow of all it can be.*

Such were my thoughts as I tramped through rain, wind and snow across the not-remotely-dull reaches of the Great In-Between.

On Monday, March 9 I reached the town of Husum on the North Sea coast. For once it was a clear day with air diamond-sharp, and although a biting wind blew I felt energised by the sunshine. The thick, briny scent of the sea and the azure skies took me straight back to childhood holidays. In memory, the sun always shone at the seaside, and it was wonderful to discover that memory hadn't been false. Perhaps the next four weeks of the journey along the North Sea coastline would be the brightest since September.

Husum is popularly known in Germany as 'the grey town by the grey sea', but on this day it was ablaze with colour. The painted wooden buildings fronting the harbour, the bright hulls of boats, the shimmering reflections in water, the vivid blue sky—all these were the exact opposite of grey. It was novelist Theodor Storm who coined the 'grey town' epithet. Storm was born in Husum in 1817, back when it sat under Danish rule, and lived and worked in the town most of his life. He no doubt knew Husum in *all* its moods, but the inaccuracy of his description on the day I arrived did his hometown a disservice. No other town I'd visited since Calabria had offered such a richness of light or range of colour, and no other town was so wonderful for this particular long-distance walker to behold.

For me, Husum marked the end of the North German Plain and the start of a new journey: the month-long walk up the North Sea coast. It was another natural frontier, another character-changing boundary. Beyond Husum I'd move from farmland to dunes, from forests to mudflats,

Husum harbour, March 9, 1998.

from earthy tones to shimmering light, from crows to gulls, from limited horizons to endless space. For the next 400 miles I'd be on a coastal walk, living beside the greatest wilderness on the planet—the sea—and at this first sight of it I couldn't stop grinning. For a brief moment I imagined myself back at Melito di Porto Salvo beside the Mediterranean, preparing for The Walk's very first step, and then I returned my focus to the colder waters of the North Sea and truly appreciated how far I'd come.

I pushed north from Husum, passed whitewashed cottages with thatched roofs, passed futuristic turbines pulling energy from the wind, and finally landed on a tall dyke directly beside the sea. From it, I quickly lost interest in the view inland. The immense space to the west and the clamour and abundance of avian life captured my attention. Just as the plain's birds had made the mountains seem quiet, so too the coastal birds made the plains seem quiet. Nowhere else across the entire continent had I seen such a pulsating throbbing mass of life. It was tumultuous, unrelenting, cacophonous. My eyes and ears were almost overwhelmed.

Mudflats and open space along the North Sea coast, March 10, 1998.

Mudflats woven with the paisley designs of twisting, silver channels stretched west to open water, and open water stretched further to a dark line of distant land—the North Frisian Islands, a small remnant of the ancient Doggerland that once linked mainland Europe to Britain. Since 1985, the mudflats, salt marshes and islands had been part of the Schleswig-Holstein Wadden Sea National Park, and soon-to-be-realised plans to expand the park from the Danish border to the Elbe Estuary would ultimately make it not just the largest protected area in Germany but also the greatest nature reserve anywhere between Calabria and Norway: over 1,700 square miles where nature comes first. It is a park mostly of water—more than two thirds of it is underwater—and it's a park of birdlife, especially during the spring and autumn migrations when an estimated twelve million birds pause to refuel. A fair number were feasting as I passed, while others filled the sky in pulsating waves, thousands of birds changing direction as one. I walked entranced, not noticing the effort or the biting north wind, thinking to myself: *for this I could even give up mountains.*

I camped a short distance inland in a small beech wood, and picked up a few extra supplies early the next morning in a village, Langenhorn. Full of exuberance and wanting to share my happiness, I paused on the road from Edeka when I saw an elderly lady approaching on a bicycle. I stuck out my right thumb playfully, as though hitching a ride. The lady appreciated the joke. Laughing, she pointed to the little wicker basket fronting her bike. *If only I had more room*, her expression said.

Back on the windswept dyke I paced north, entertained by thousands of singing companions. It was my penultimate day in Germany, and one of the most memorable—a twenty-six-mile epic through arguably the richest natural environment of the journey so far. But it also became one of the hardest. Shortly after noon grey clouds blotted the sky, the wind picked up, and rain began falling. By late afternoon my energy was flagging and I returned inland to seek a sheltered camp. My map showed an official campsite, but on arrival I discovered it closed. Not that I minded once I saw it. The site sat beside a road and it was an ugly, weed-filled yard crammed with mouldy caravans. Paying to camp would have been hard enough, given my tight funds, but paying to stay *here* would have been ridiculous. After filling my water carrier at a nearby supermarket I tramped on.

Another wind-blasted rain-washed mile passed, and it soon became obvious that a discreet and sheltered wild camp wasn't going to be easy. There was no cover anywhere on the wide-open land. When I passed a garage a short distance down the road I stopped on the spur of the moment and asked if I could camp in the field beside it, but the owner, in grease-stained overalls, shook his head apologetically.

'There is a campsite three kilometres north,' he told me. 'It is open and has a restaurant. Try there.'

The walk to it drained the last of my reserves, but I was delighted to see lights upon arrival. Optimistically, willing to accept the damage to my limited funds and pay whatever was needed, I stepped from wind and rain into the restaurant, but found little hospitality. The dark-suited owner, whose heavily lined face looked as though it had endured decades of hardship, replied: '*Nein...* tent camping is not possible at this time of year.' He gave a grim, mirthless, condescending laugh, as though such a thing should have been obvious.

'But all I need is a small patch of grass...' I explained. There was plenty of space outside, a field as broad as a football pitch. How hard would it be to let me stay? 'I've been camping all winter,' I added.

'Until May, only caravans,' the man replied sourly. He looked me up and down, disdain clear in his eyes. I felt judged, and found to be inferior, but I couldn't understand why. Because I was living out of a backpack?

I tried one more time, explaining how far I'd come. But he wouldn't budge. Disappointment washed through me—and sadness, for the man as much as for myself. From his mocking, sneering expression I sensed that he was pleased with himself for being in a position to turn me away.

I stood, dumbfounded. The site was open, and the man could have helped. But he was deliberately choosing not to. It was his right, I knew, but it was hard to take. I could only wonder at the reasons behind his behaviour. I walked away, feeling deflated and heavier, as though I were carrying some of the man's misery with me.

Trying to find some adventure in it, I dragged my weary limbs on. Once I'd settled into a hidden but fiercely windy pitch on the seaward side of the dyke, I was soon glad, after all, that I was camping wild. The wind bent and shook my home, but it was a clean wind, a free wind. It carried with it the song from thousands of birds—a song of joy, not misery.

The following morning I found a phone box and tried for the sixth time to call Charles and tell him about the many adventures I'd had in 'dull' northern Germany. This time, at last, I got an answer. It was sharp and to the point.

'Charles Weaver's phone.'

'Charles?' I asked, confused. It didn't sound like my friend's voice, but it could have been the line.

'No. Charles Weaver's... *phone*,' replied an annoyed, *why-are-you-bothering-me* voice.

'Is Charles there?'

'Who is this?' Short, ill-mannered, unfriendly.

'I'm a friend of his, Andrew. I'm in Germany. I'm on a long walk...'

There was no answer, and I waited a moment, hearing voices in the background: '...some person from Germany... you'd better take it... we don't want this on the bill.'

Finally, my friend came on the line. 'Andrew,' he said—a wonderful, familiar voice, but unusually tense and impatient. 'You couldn't have called at a worse time, mate.' And before I could manage even a quick 'okay' a dial tone filled my ear.

Well, I thought, staring at the receiver, *WELL!* That wasn't the reaction I'd expected.

I stood motionless, feeling rejected. It was followed hotly by anger—an overreaction maybe, but I couldn't help it.

Charles worked hard, this I knew. He was single, career-minded and had a prestigious job in the music industry, a job that undoubtedly had challenges. But he was a good friend, one of the small number I had. He knew what I was doing, had travelled a great deal himself, and also knew from experience what hearing a familiar voice from far away could mean. We'd talked about it before I'd begun The Walk. 'Call,' he'd said. But now he'd hung up. An apology would have taken mere seconds.

He must be having a really bad day, I thought, but was too annoyed to feel sympathy—that came later. For now, I was having a bad day, too. His stress, shared.

It was another glimpse of the life I could have been living, a life of careers and stress, a life that people chose however much that choice was rationalised as a necessity. The encounter sucked the wind from my sails. It left me stuck in the doldrums. I tried shrugging it off the way I might have been able to back in London, but couldn't. Back there, connections were relatively easy and frequent, no big deal. But out here, after ten months away, being rejected by a friend was a very big deal. My situation blew it out of all proportion.

Walking on, I thought hard about choices. I probed the reasons that underlay them. What was it that made some people willing to help or talk, and some unwilling? Why did one person open their home to a complete stranger without hesitation, and another person turn them away? Of course, there were too many answers, most of them impossible to know. A lifetime of experiences led to most choices. This I could see. But it was now clear: experiences make us who we are. *Choose your experiences,* I thought, *and you choose who you want to be.*

By late afternoon my anger and dejection were fading, and the day's last human encounter finally banished both. Seeking water, I approached a man on the outskirts of the bouncily named village of Humptrup. He was muscular, red faced, and working outside a farmhouse, busily chopping a massive pile of firewood. Probably, he was too busy to stop, but did he have any water?

'Yes, yes, yes!' he replied cheerfully in German. 'Of course you can have water!' He broke into a broad smile and lay down his axe. 'And you must come in and have some coffee...'

Which I did, and for the next half hour the man, Kurt, laughed with me about the inconsistencies of the world, and together we raised each other's spirits and improved each other's day. Friendliness, shared.

I spent my final German night camped in a pine forest amid unexpected patches of old snow, and imagined that I was back in the mountains. For long hours I thought about moods and behaviour. Both had great impact, I saw, just like experiences. Both were contagious. Rudeness, I realised, led to more rudeness. Anger bred anger. And friendliness bred friendliness. I thought about all the times I'd been turned away, but also about all the smiles that had lifted me. *Actions make the world*, I thought, and I drifted off to sleep with the happy idea that I—small insignificant me—could make the entire world a better place one small action at a time.

All I had to do was smile.

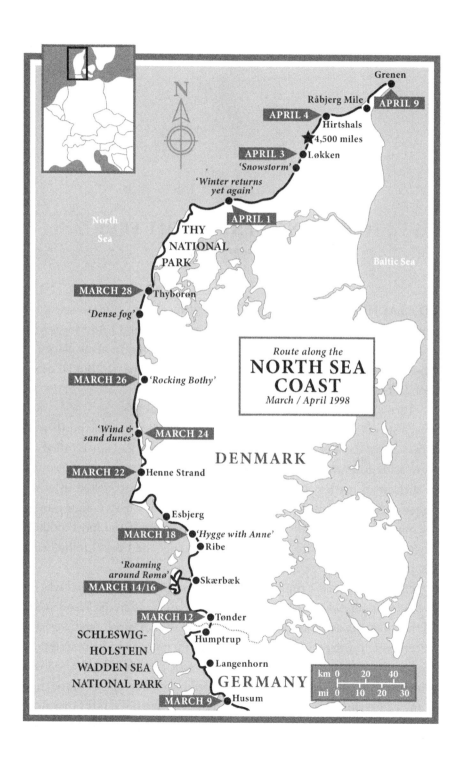

Route along the
NORTH SEA COAST
March / April 1998

Grenen

APRIL 9

Råbjerg Mile

APRIL 4

Hirtshals

4,500 miles

APRIL 3

Løkken

'*Snowstorm*'

'*Winter returns yet again*'

APRIL 1

THY NATIONAL PARK

North Sea

Baltic Sea

MARCH 28

Thyborøn

'*Dense fog*'

MARCH 26

'*Rocking Bothy*'

'*Wind & sand dunes*'

MARCH 24

MARCH 22

Henne Strand

DENMARK

Esbjerg

MARCH 18

'*Hygge with Anne*'

Ribe

'*Roaming around Rømø*'

MARCH 14/16

Skærbæk

MARCH 12

Tønder

SCHLESWIG-HOLSTEIN WADDEN SEA NATIONAL PARK

Humptrup

Langenhorn

GERMANY

MARCH 9

Husum

km 0   20   40
mi 0   10   20   30

THE SAND BENEATH MY FEET
Chapter 12

I'D REACHED DENMARK, The Walk's fifth country. (Or the sixth, if I counted the forty-seven minutes I'd spent in Switzerland.) And I was lost, *again*. But I was used to that. Since Calabria I'd been lost in many places: in tangled forests, on remote mountains, at snowbound passes. But I'd never been lost on a *beach* before.

Then again, I'd never been on a beach as wide as this.

I'd set out across the beach twenty minutes earlier, heading north-west across a vast expanse of waterlogged sand, but mist had since rolled in. Now, aside from my compass, the only guide to direction was the sound of surf far to my left, pounding away unseen. Sand stretched in every direction, blurring into mist, its surface firm but awash, its colour grey as the mist itself. It was without doubt the wettest, flattest and most unlikely environment of the entire 'mountain' walk so far—and I didn't mind being lost in it one bit.

Of course, I wasn't *entirely* lost; I knew *roughly* where I was. I was on Rømø (pronounced something like *hroy-mu*), an island in the Wadden Sea off the Jutland coast, and I was on Danish soil. Well, Danish sand. Perhaps 'uncertain of my exact whereabouts' would be a more accurate description. The beach measured eleven miles long by a mile and a half wide, and I was somewhere in the middle of it, surrounded by a landscape as untouched as any I'd previously walked. As I stole quietly across the sands I treasured the thrilling sensation of being completely alone in an unknown and not entirely hospitable place.

On the beach, Rømø, March 15, 1998.

I was here on Rømø on another whim. The island was well off route, but after noticing it on the map I realised that I couldn't pass by. Compared to Denmark's mainland, it looked intriguingly undeveloped. After 4,150 miles I'd learnt that I wasn't taking a walk; the walk was taking me. Chance and instinct showed the way, not logic, and if instinct urged 'go to Rømø' then to Rømø I went. Three days previously I hadn't even heard of the island. Discovering it was travel at its very best.

Rømø lies five miles out at sea, just north of the German border. The island began life as a modest sandbank, but one with ambitions, and aided by currents and drifting sands it eventually built itself into a landmass of almost fifty square miles. It is connected to Denmark's Jutland peninsula by a long causeway: a paved umbilical cord that allows cars (and long-distance walkers) to ply the route ships once sailed. As I crossed the causeway I smiled ruefully at the ridiculousness of choosing a route I'd have to retread. I hoped that the island would be worth it.

It certainly began well. Wild camping was banned on the island, according to a sign, and so my first stop was an official campsite. Would it be open? Would I be turned away again? Happily the answers were 'yes' to the first question, 'no' to the second. A grandmotherly lady strode out from a small cottage when I stepped onto the campsite's grounds. She greeted me with twinkling eyes and a gentle smile.

'It is unusual to have tent campers during the *silent wastes of March*,' she observed poetically in English. After offering me a generous discount, she guided me to a sheltered spot on the edge of a sandy field, then left me to settle in. Peace reigned. I marvelled at what I now had: easy access to drinking water and hot showers, plus a legal camp that I didn't have to hide from sight. It was a luxury—I felt spoilt.

Feeling in need of a holiday, I decided to stay on Rømø for three days. On the first day I walked twenty miles, an easy distance without Ten Ton on my back. Meandering without a plan, I roamed around Rømø, exploring dunes, heathlands and pine forests, quickly falling under the island's spell. Aside from a few inevitable signs of tourist development, the island looked as though it belonged to another era. It felt unhurried, detached from the pressures of the modern world.

'It's an island thing,' a quietly spoken local explained when I paused to say hello. 'Life is slower here, friendlier. We have a small population, only 850 permanent residents. Few of us would rather live anywhere else. Once Rømø gets into your system you've pretty much had it.' The man paused for a moment. 'You'll see,' he added.

On the second day I cheated and rented a bicycle, and in unshackled freedom pedalled wherever fancy took me, on sandy paths through rolling moors and primeval forests, exhilarated by unfamiliar wind-in-my-hair speeds. But I also stopped often, sampling the island's many wild environments. Beneath a huge sky I sat for lunch on a dune, my back resting against a salt-pruned birch, looking across a pond edged by reeds. Geese, swans and other waterfowl paddled the water; smaller birds flew overhead, constantly singing, skylarks among them. Nearby, a mass of wood ants swarmed industriously upon their nest, a sure sign of approaching spring. Two deer emerged from a pine thicket, their white tails standing out prominently against the trees, then retreated. A fox padded by and disappeared into a mass of coarse yellow grass that swayed hypnotically in the wind. At so much wildness an emotion that had been building since I'd first stepped onto Rømø finally erupted—pure joy. I was glad I'd come.

I thought about it as I sat on the dune: *what is it about this place?* The answer came quickly. Rømø felt like the first real outpost of the north, like the true start of Scandinavia. It may simply have been because it was so different from the North German Plain, so undeveloped. But I sensed more to it than that. The island's landscape *called* to me, as though I already belonged. There was something mysterious *and* familiar to it. It was like meeting someone for the first time but feeling I'd known them all my life. The call was so powerful that my gut churned. I'd felt nothing like it further south. And yet, there was an edge, too, as though I wasn't just welcomed but also warned, not just called to but also challenged. Rømø reminded me that Norway and true wildness lay just weeks ahead: environments less forgiving than any so far encountered. Heading toward them felt right, but also intimidating.

I cycled on, and eventually reached the beach. Once I'd stashed the rented bicycle behind a distinctively shaped dune I set out on foot across the broad sands. I aimed for a half-glimpsed island of dunes far across the flats, but halfway to them mist materialised from the salty air and my world shrank, becoming a surreal void of water, sand and flat light. Giving up on the dunes, I turned directly toward the sea, and let the sound of crashing waves guide me. Unsettled by the eerie nothingness, by the growing crescendo of the surf, by an increasing sense of not knowing exactly where I was, I pushed on regardless, unwilling to give up on so rich an experience. I wondered what would happen if the tide turned and came racing in, but told myself that the sand was so flat it wouldn't matter. I'd surely be able to wade back to solid land. In any case, the beach was so wet that I might already have been walking in the sea. I'd never felt so disconnected from the surface of the earth while still standing upon it.

The closer I drew to the sea's edge the fiercer the waves sounded, until soon I imagined ten-foot breakers erupting into explosions of foam. The reality, however, was far milder: when finally the sea appeared the waves weren't even eighteen inches high. And, yet, I still sensed untameable power behind them. The sea stretched from my feet into the mist, and its unknowable wildness stirred exactly the same emotions that wild mountains also touched. Standing before it I felt hugely insignificant. As I stared out to sea I felt it call me forward. I experienced a strong urge to keep walking, to enter the water, to find out what lay beyond the misty horizon.

Instead, sensibly, I remained rooted where I was, and for a long while let the surf hypnotise me. Unmeasured time passed.

At length I noticed a shape moving slowly in my direction. It evolved into a man wearing a heavy coat, looking down at the sand as he walked. Soon he stood at my side. Like everyone I'd met since crossing the Danish border four days earlier he was perfectly happy to speak English. '*Hej!*' quickly became 'Hello!'

'Have you seen anything like this yet at the water's edge?' the man asked, and he opened his hand to show three angular, golf-ball-sized pebbles. I told him I hadn't.

'I collect them. Here, take one. Hold it up, have a look.'

The man passed over one of the pebbles and I raised it to the light, dim though it was. The pebble was a rich orange colour and semi-transparent. Inside were tiny bubbles and flecks of black; it seemed to glow from within. The man smiled at my expression of surprise.

'It is amber,' the man explained. 'Formed from tree resin. The amber in your hand might have come from a tree two hundred million years ago. Sometimes you can even find insects caught in it. The resin flows over an insect, traps and preserves it… and then washes up on the beach.'

It was beautiful, and I said so. It would have made a worthy addition to the five small pebbles I'd collected on The Walk's first morning from the beach at Melito di Porto Salvo. Reluctantly, I handed it back.

'I take them home and polish them,' the man continued. 'Then my wife makes them into jewellery.'

'How large can the pebbles get?'

'Sometimes as big as a potato. But that is rare. The winds have been strong recently'—as I well knew—'and the waves big. The waves stir up amber from the seabed and carry it in. Amber is lighter than rock. And it can be soft. If you bite it your teeth can leave a mark.'

'Well,' I said, 'I'll keep my eyes open.' I paused and smiled at a thought. 'Treasures from the deep!'

The man laughed. 'Yes, treasure. We call it Danish Gold.'

We spoke some more, the man revealing that he was a Rømø resident, but German by birth.

'I first came to Denmark to buy a car. The cost was much less than in Deutschland. Then I returned to get married. Back home my wife and I would have had to wait eight weeks, but we wanted to do it right away, and in Denmark we could. When you are young and in love, why wait, *ja?* And then we visited Rømø and decided to stay. The island is… what is the right word? Ah, *enchanted*! And now it is my home. I don't ever want to leave.'

I could believe it. I wasn't sure I wanted to either.

Once the man walked away I studied the wash intently, as if expecting the gods of the sea to deliver a perfect specimen of amber directly to my feet, but of course they didn't. I continued looking even once I began the long trek back to solid land. I found no amber, but saw plenty of other treasures: colourful shells, delicate worm casts, intricate ripples in the sand, endless prints from shore birds. I didn't need amber. Each square yard was as priceless as the finest jewellery ever made.

After a mile and a half the dunes marking solid land appeared from the fog and I felt a touch of relief. Supposedly, the sea only covers the entire beach during winter's fiercest storms, but I'd still felt exposed and at risk. The amber collector had laughed when I'd admitted this. 'This is a safe place! The sea is so shallow you could probably walk from here to England. You'd just need stilts!'

Finding the rented bicycle was easy. I deliberately regained the dunes further north than I'd departed them, which meant the bike had to be south. Sure enough, after 200 yards I came across my own prints. Navigating to a particular spot by purposely missing it, by aiming off, is a useful trick. If I'd arrived too close it might not have been obvious which way to turn.

For the rest of the day, and all of the next, I immersed myself ever deeper into Rømø's rich northern landscapes and fell ever deeper in love. When the time came to leave I regretted that I had to. Rømø was small and unassuming compared to the soaring Gran Sasso, the Dolomites, or any number of other places I'd visited, but I'd never walked anywhere finer. I could easily imagine it becoming home. As I recrossed the causeway and turned north up the coast I took Rømø with me, not just in memory but physically too; sand from the island was in my boots, my sleeping bag, my pack and my pockets. Even the holes in the twenty-five øre Danish coins had sand in them. Small grains of Rømø would probably accompany me all the way to the North Cape, but that seemed appropriate. Some places are impossible to leave behind. Visit them and they become part of who you are for the rest of your life.

Breezy afternoon in the village of Kirkeby, March 18, 1998.

So far, Denmark was treating me well. From the moment I'd entered the country I'd been welcomed with warm smiles that countered its bracing winds. From the first Dane I'd spoken with—a laughing customs official at the border—to the residents of Tønder, Højer, and Skærbæk, to the gentle inhabitants of Rømø, to the many cyclists I'd encountered atop the coastal dyke, I'd received nothing but friendliness.

From what I could see, the Danes were different to their neighbours in the south. They dressed more for the outdoors than for the city, three out of every four heads were blond, they were by and large rosy cheeked and healthy looking, and their approach to life seemed appealingly exuberant. They spoke English with pleasure, quickly brushing aside my suggestion that I try to learn Danish.

'Learn Danish?' I was told. 'No, don't be silly. It would be a waste of your time!' Several people even made me feel that by speaking my own language I was doing the Danes a favour. 'We are happy to speak English. It is very useful for us to practise.'

I stopped at a campsite north of Rømø and the owner treated me like

146

an honoured guest. She was bursting with a desire to help.

'Denmark is such a small country,' she explained. 'We are pleased when someone comes to visit. We don't take our guests for granted.'

Even the owners of unofficial campsites were welcoming.

'Do you know if there is anywhere near here where I can camp for the night?' I asked a farmer the following evening. There were no forests now, nowhere discreet or sheltered to hide away.

'What kind of location do you need?' the farmer asked.

'Just a small corner of a field. And water.'

'Okay... you can camp right here,' he replied, nodding to the field behind him. 'Only, camp high. It will rain hard tonight! And you'll find water from a tap over in that barn.'

Offers for camp even came unsolicited. A frail elderly couple pulled over in their small car early one afternoon and invited me to camp in their garden just down the road. I almost burst out laughing with delight. Where had all the fierce Vikings gone?

I even received an invitation to marriage. On the outskirts of a small village, three ten-year-old girls on rollerblades joined me for half a mile. Speaking impeccable English, they asked endless questions as they skated alongside. Most importantly, they wanted to know if I was married, or had children of my own, and if not could I please marry Abigael's mean big sister and take her away!

Encouraged by the hospitality, I put a plan I'd been considering for a while into action when I reached the village of Brøns. Standing at a bright red phone box, I called several of Denmark's leading national newspapers, hoping that I'd be able to talk one of them into financing the Danish leg of the walk. If I succeeded, I'd do the same in Norway.

The calls were necessary; my funds were now critically low. Since starting the journey I'd known that a lack of money could end it prematurely. I'd begun with that huge leap of faith, setting out with funds enough to see me across the Alps, trusting that everything would somehow work out, banishing from mind the idea that it wouldn't. Through photo and story sales, a trickle of extra sponsors, and most of all through frugal living, the funds had stretched thousands of miles further than I'd originally imagined possible. But from the small amount left it was clear that they'd been stretched almost as far as they could go.

If I only spent money on food then I had funds left for six weeks—reserves enough to get me to the top of Denmark and two weeks into Norway, but definitely no further. The idea of failing to reach the North Cape because of *money* was hard to accept. I wanted to be above such things, live life on *my* terms. The wilderness was free—but the trouble was I couldn't eat it. The idea of living off the land *had* occurred, and aspects of it were attractive. But it would be a completely different kind of wilderness journey. Even if it were possible on the Danish coast in March, and even if I had sufficient knowledge, gathering food would be a full-time occupation, leaving little room for progress. As someone who wanted to keep moving, I needed to buy food, not find it—that was the reality.

Having already failed to land a major sponsor before starting The Walk, I didn't see a renewed search for one as an option. And neither did I follow up on my father's suggestion that I ask the charities for support. As I saw it, every single donation needed to go directly to The Passage and the Cardinal Hume Centre—anything else was unthinkable. There was only one other option: sell my story to local news outlets. Weren't newspapers rich? Wasn't my story *different*? Hadn't I proved something by making it this far? Surely they'd jump at the chance!

And so, emboldened by the hospitality of Denmark's ordinary citizens, I began making the calls. But they went as you might expect.

I wasn't helped by my stammer. For me, a telephone was Arch Enemy Number One. It always made my stammer worse, especially when calling strangers. The pressure didn't help either. These calls really *mattered*—the success of The Walk hinged on them. Plucking up courage, I rang several papers, but each time my stumbling incoherence got in the way. Stammering as I hadn't stammered since childhood, I sounded half-deranged even to my own ears, and not at all like someone to take seriously. Honestly, I couldn't blame the newspapers for their reaction.

'Let me get this straight,' replied a journalist with an incredulous laugh after I'd made my feeble pitch. 'You want us to give you money for this, er... *story*? Um, I don't think so.'

Afterwards, feeling deflated, I slouched on. Who was I kidding? My journey was an ordinary thing, something anyone with two feet could do if they wanted. Stories far more newsworthy than mine went unreported every day.

I had to face up to it: I'd run out of funds, and by early May I'd have to stop. It was inevitable. And, yet, I still couldn't see myself failing. The final day at the North Cape was so clear in my mind that I *knew* it would happen exactly as I foresaw it: lone steps across a snow-covered headland above a wild northern sea. I knew I'd succeed—I was 100 per cent certain—but couldn't imagine how. For a short while my thoughts whirled in turmoil, seesawing from one extreme to another, awash with absolute certainty *and* crushing doubt.

But the doubt didn't last. Failure still lay weeks ahead, and Rømø was still fresh in my system, filling me with an optimism that couldn't be suppressed. How could I worry about the future when an uncountable number of birds were singing now, when the sea stretched west to a limitless horizon, when I faced six more weeks of absolute freedom? Despite the fundraising failure I still had everything I wanted *right now*, and that was what counted.

I marched north along the coast, sometimes in crisp sunlight, sometimes in drizzle, always blasted by the wind—but always singing. I found myself laughing at small things: at locals who walked their dogs by car, sitting in the driver's seat holding a leash while poor Fido trotted along outside. I laughed at the gulls: frequently and spectacularly accurate with their droppings. (I was sure they did it on purpose.) And most of all I laughed at myself. Early one morning I almost lost the tent. I pulled out the pegs, turned away to bag them, and at that moment an opportunistic gust whooshed in from nowhere and rolled my home west toward the North Sea like an out-of-control tumbleweed. The chase was desperate—but how could I not laugh at it?

Despite the physical effort of walking into a constant headwind I felt curiously at ease. Each day's twenty-or-so miles still left me tired, but the aches seemed irrelevant, as though happening to someone else. And it wasn't just a physical feeling of ease, but of mental ease, too. I felt relaxed about daily decisions, such as my route. For over 4,000 miles, navigation had been something I'd had to pay close attention to, but here, I simply stuck to the coastal dyke and let the miles unroll of their own accord. With the sea as my handrail there was no getting lost. I walked entranced, not knowing what lay ahead, but always eager to find out. My long-term future may have been uncertain, but if anything it made the present feel even more remarkable. I savoured every step I took.

At day's end on March 18 I finally met my first unhelpful Dane. I stepped inland from the exposed coast to seek a place for camp, and when I saw a man outside a farmhouse I approached him respectfully. The farmer listened as I began my usual spiel, but said nothing, his expression dour. Undeterred, I stammered on, trying to prompt a response until, eventually, I ground to a halt and simply asked: 'Yes or no?'

'No,' the farmer said grimly, but I could see the cost. There was conflict in his eyes, as though a small part of him wanted to help. For his sake I wished he'd answered differently. People who said yes were always so much happier for saying it.

At a second farmhouse a short way down the road I had more luck.

'Yes,' replied a lady in a blue tracksuit who answered the door. 'You can camp.' She looked flustered, but I could see her rising above whatever had caused it. She paused and looked out at the cold, grey evening. The wind was increasing and spots of rain were splattering down. 'You know what?' she said, reconsidering her offer. 'I don't think you can camp.' For a moment, my spirits plummeted, but then the lady lifted them straight back up. 'How about you come in and sleep in the spare room instead?'

And so I met Anne.

Anne led me into her home; it was warm and calm inside, a glorious sanctuary from the wind. Anne paused in a hallway, and looked at me apologetically.

'I'm sorry if I seemed unwelcoming. I'm an occupational therapist. At least, I have been all my working life. But recently, I reached a point where I'd had enough. I'm just… burnt out, you know? So I'm changing career. I was having problems with the computer-programming course I'm doing, and then my little dog Phia started barking and peeing on the floor, and then the phone rang… and then you came knocking on my door asking to camp!' She laughed. 'Everything happened at once!'

Anne showed me to the spare room, turning in the doorway. 'It's odd,' she observed, as much to herself as to me, 'how I don't feel I have to be scared of you.' She shrugged her shoulders and laughed. 'I live alone, and here I am inviting a strange man from another country into my house. I don't know how you do it, but you do it well!'

Anne left me to sort myself out and shower. Deeply grateful, I was careful to leave the bathroom exactly as I'd found it. I spent longer cleaning the shower after I'd used it than I spent cleaning myself. Afterwards, I joined Anne for dinner, and the following six hours seemed to pass like a snap of the fingers.

At first, we talked about Denmark and the Danes. Anne confirmed what I'd already noticed—that most Danes were open and friendly, and far less serious than their neighbours to the south.

'We have a word that sums us up as a people,' Anne explained. 'It is *hygge*.' The word sounded a little like she was clearing her throat. 'I am not sure I can translate it into English,' she continued, 'but it kind of means warmth, cosiness, getting together and sharing the good things in life. *Hygge* is… being with family and friends. It is… drinking wine together, having a picnic, going on a bike ride. It is easy companionship beside the fire on a cold winter's night. It is sitting down in comfort at the kitchen table to discuss life… like we are doing!' Anne laughed. 'Here you are, taking part in *hygge*. You could almost be a Dane!'

We talked about the landscape, about the living ocean, about Rømø. 'It is a wonderful place,' Anne agreed. 'But I don't like it so much in summer. You'd think everyone in the world was there!'

We talked about travel, maps, music, friends, family. The conversation flowed, and the ease of it was extraordinary. Part of me looked on with astonishment at how I was sitting in a stranger's kitchen in a country not my own, chatting without stammering as though Anne were an old friend. The remarkable thing was how normal it seemed; in truth it was a rare experience that my life could easily have lacked. These encounters were a side of solo travel I hadn't given much thought to prior to starting The Walk, but they'd become a treasured side, increasing in value the longer the journey went on.

Inevitably, we discussed my journey, too.

'You are on *two* journeys, you know…' Anne observed perceptively, after listening to some of my tales. 'There is the walk itself *and* the journey inside. You may not realise it, but you are clearly on a spiritual quest. It must have changed you?'

She was right—I *was* on a quest. A quest to move forward as a person. I'd quite forgotten! I'd become so wrapped up in the small details, the hour-by-hour pleasures and challenges, that I'd given little thought to the big picture.

For most of the time I simply bimbled along, happy with my freedom, but beneath the surface I *was* still engaged in a quest that was transforming who I was and what I believed. Sitting there, I compared myself to the youth who'd taken his first step in Calabria, and saw that I wasn't remotely the same person. At its most basic level, I'd achieved a state of ease and happiness beyond anything I'd imagined. Or perhaps that wasn't a basic level. Happiness is such an overused and misunderstood word. In its truest form, the state of happiness can be so powerful there aren't even words to describe it. So perhaps finding true happiness was the whole point. *Was that what I'm moving toward?*

'Of course it's changed me,' I joked, ironically too happy to take the subject seriously. 'How could it not? My legs are shorter, my feet are lumpier, and I suspect I'm going to smell bad for the rest of my life!' Anne laughed.

The hours flew by, until eventually we noticed with surprise that it was 1.30 a.m., a time I rarely saw.

'Well!' Anne exclaimed, eyebrows raised. 'One of those days when there aren't enough hours!' Reluctantly, we brought the evening to a close.

Anne sent me on my way early the next morning with a hearty breakfast and a parting hug. But, as with every single experience since Calabria, she came along with me as part of who I now was, adding yet another layer to all the layers already in place.

As I marched into the new day the sky seemed improbably blue, the restless North Sea supernaturally alluring, the space around me a manifestation of freedom itself. I forgot to pay heed to the miles; instead I simply celebrated each breath and step. The March day was cold and breezy—just another ordinary windswept day. But it wasn't ordinary to me. My Italian brother, Flavio, would have summed it up perfectly. '*Straordinario!*' he'd have exclaimed, if he'd been here with me. In a way, he was.

The wind—the damp and salty wind—blew. Goodness how it blew! It was cold, fierce, unrelenting. For the next 200 miles it became the main feature of my life. Sure, sand featured too, and water, forever curling in waves to my left, but the wind had the greatest impact, transforming spring-warmth into winter-cold, gentle drizzle into stinging bullets, flat terrain into taxing

Windswept sand dunes beside the North Sea, March 20, 1998.

uphill, forward momentum into near standstill.

Miles that should have been easy became wearing. Days that should have been pleasurable became unpleasant. So fierce was the blast that I sometimes retreated from the beautiful but exposed coast and walked inland instead. But even far from the sea there was little shelter—the flat landscape gave the wind space to rush unimpeded. I'd pictured Denmark providing a carefree month, and I'd hoped to reach Norway rejuvenated, but thanks to the wind I was beginning to feel that I'd arrive on the verge of exhaustion.

North of Esbjerg the coast became wilder. Timidly, or perhaps wisely, civilisation kept itself far back from the sea's raging edge, and soon I found myself walking upon surfaces that might never have known human feet. The beach stretched ahead to a moisture-blurred horizon, unchanging mile after mile, waves on one side, dunes on the other, birds wheeling overhead, white sand underfoot. Only occasional paths through the dunes, and junk washed up by high tide, hinted that civilisation still existed.

Like the wind, the waves never ceased. They rolled in every few seconds, curling into tubes, exploding into foam and froth, then sucking sand and shells back into the depths. Sometimes I had to stop and watch, and often found myself screaming with excitement at the drama of it. The thunder of surf accompanied me all day long; it filled my dreams, too. When I camped in the dunes I couldn't escape the surf's roar. It merged with the wind, with the hiss of sandy spindrift striking the tent, with the cry of gulls. It became hard to imagine an existence that didn't include the roar of pounding surf.

Occasionally, the beach's surface changed to shingle, pebbles, masses of slimy seaweed, but never to a surface that was easy to traverse. The beach was as taxing to walk across as fresh snow. Whenever it became too taxing I turned inland. Large dunes—curling like waves themselves, tufted with grass, rippled with texture, tracked with bird prints—gave way to heathlands and stunted pinewoods. Progress here wasn't any faster, but it was at least different. And when this grew too much I returned to the endless beach and sank into bare sand once again. Emptying sand from my boots became an hourly task.

And still the wind blew.

The wind, I decided, was blowing for a reason, probing me to see how deep my hard-earned happiness went. It was testing me to see how much I really had learnt. It was one thing to feel happy when life was going well —the real trick lay in staying happy when it wasn't. And so I worked hard at holding on to happiness, searching for pleasure in the gruelling miles, for meaning in the wind, for gratitude in everything I had. I was partially successful, but my happiness was more brittle than I'd hoped. It didn't take much to crack it.

It wasn't wind or terrain that most cracked it, but the people I met. Although I spent most of my time alone, I still encountered more people each day than at any other point of the journey. I met anglers and dog walkers on the beach, farmers in fields, cyclists on heathland trails, shop keepers in villages. Frustratingly, I discovered that my emotions had become tied to whomever I meet. When someone smiled or offered help my mood soared; if they were cold or refused help my mood plummeted. It had started back in Germany when my friend Charles had hung up on me. The rejection had been hard to shake. When the mean campsite owner had turned me away I'd become angry. But when the friendly woodcutter,

Kurt, had invited me in I'd soared again.

What, I wondered, *was going on?*

On March 20, a campsite owner near Oksbøl sucked away my happiness. We chatted for a while when I checked in, but he had nothing good to say.

'Denmark has become too crowded,' he told me grimly. 'There are five million citizens—a million too many. And it isn't as friendly as it used to be.' He stared glumly outside, at trees shaking in the wind. 'The weather is growing worse every year. There used to be more seabirds. It's because the sea is more polluted.' He paused, then droned on. 'Why are you going to Norway anyway? It's full of nationalistic, religious fanatics. The people are unwelcoming. They're standoffish, rude. And it *always* rains there. Listen, Norway is a grim place filled with grim people. You should go to Sweden. In the Swedish woods you'll find real wilderness. Although there are too many mosquitoes. But Norway's fjords and mountains? Overrated.'

Afterwards, as I set up my tent, I felt drained and depressed. I slept badly.

But at the next campsite a lovely old lady restored my mood. She was so eager to please that she broke into a run toward me when I arrived, and in her enthusiasm to help kept forgetting to speak English, rolling through Danish, German, English and French in turn, laughing at herself, making me laugh too. When I set off the following morning she rushed forward again—she'd left her front door open just so she could wish me well. 'Bon voyage!' she bubbled cheerily. 'Viel Glück. I mean... good luck!'

I left, laughing. But I felt confused, too. I was like a small boat that was being tossed about on waves made by other people. Why couldn't I simply cut through the waves and stay happy regardless?

On March 22, in heavy fog, I reached Henne Strand, a small resort set back from the dunes. In the cheerless weather it looked sad and neglected. Its main street was lined with run-down cafés. There were shops selling cheap clothes and plastic junk. It was Sunday, and heavily muffled visitors were wandering about, most looking lost and bored. I was here to buy food, and perhaps sleep at the resort's campsite—if it was open. The site looked promising at first glance; the barrier across its entrance was raised, and when I rang the office doorbell a middle-aged lady promptly appeared. But her welcome was as cold as the wind. 'No, we are closed. We open in fourteen days. Come back then.'

The door closed in my face and my spirit plummeted once again. Despondently, I marched back through town. She had every right to turn me away, this I knew. A business was a business, and closed meant closed, nothing more. But there'd been no hint of apology or empathy, no eye contact or *humanity*. The lack of it made me feel less than human too.

I returned to the beach, and a mile later turned inland again, seeking a hidden spot for camp. Three visitors standing beside their car stared at me suspiciously as I passed as though I were a zombie in an apocalypse. I stared right back at them, ugly bastards. Even a stare seemed capable of bringing me down.

It bothered me that my mood had become so linked to how others treated me. Hadn't I learnt a thing? For sure, I'd learnt that I needed people. But I *had* people now. People were the problem. What I was feeling wasn't anything like the loneliness I'd previously suffered.

'Is this part of my quest?' I asked the wind. 'Something else to over-come?' The wind didn't answer. Perhaps there was no answer. Perhaps what I was doing—spending so much time alone—was an *un*natural thing.

After all, I *was* a member of a social species—as The Walk had helped me understand. I was part of a species that had become what it is through sharing, working together and mutual support. Was it possible that my natural need for human contact had been so neglected over the last eleven months that every encounter was now taking on an exaggerated signifi-cance to compensate? If that was the case, the only solution would be to spend more time with people—a difficult thing to achieve on a solo walk.

And, of course, nature still remained essential. I was also a member of a species that was *more* than social, that didn't exist in an isolated an-thropocentric bubble but was part of a wider natural world. Yes, I needed people, but I needed nature, too.

So, how could I reconcile the two? And in the meantime—more urgently—how could I stop my moods from being tossed about by the few people I met?

I hadn't a clue.

I walked on.

The wind grew stronger. On March 26 I could only walk with a lean. North of Thorsminde, the dunes gave way to a long dyke, and the farm-land to the east of it was as flat and open as any landscape I'd ever seen.

It didn't offer a stitch of cover.

'Don't worry, it'll stay dry today,' a fisherman assured me. He pointed to a Danish flag. It whipped about frantically as it pointed north. 'It'll not rain. It never does when there's a south wind.' But predictably, by mid-afternoon, horizontal rain was stinging my face and penetrating my waterproofs as though they didn't exist. Shuddering from the onslaught, I distracted myself by imagining what I'd say to the fisherman if I met him again.

By 5 p.m. I couldn't take it any longer. I turned inland, uncertain what to do about camp. Could my tent withstand this wind? On a whim, I approached a collection of ordinary-looking farm buildings, hoping there'd be someone around who'd let me pitch my home on a building's leeward side, or, better yet, allow me a night in a barn. Mice and cow muck would be preferable to camping outside.

After dumping Ten Ton in the doorway of an open garage I walked around, calling out 'hallo', but received no reply. I rounded a corner and came to a larger building. Several cars were parked outside and a sign hung above the door: *Tûkak Teatret* it read. *Teatret?* A theatre perhaps? It seemed like an odd place for a theatre—but then again, this remote, wind-blasted coastline was an odd place for anything.

The doors were unlocked and I stepped inside. The lobby was dark but warm, and a large, shaggy dog came trotting up wagging his entire rear end, followed by a dark-haired youth with Inuit features and an open, hospitable smile.

'Welcome to the Grønland Institute,' the youth said. 'I am Eminguak, and this is Rufus. How can we help you?'

Feeling vulnerable, I explained.

'Of course, yes.' Eminguak answered without hesitation. 'We'll fix you up. Let's see… we have a small cabin. How does that sound? We'll check with Reidar.' And I thought: *how much better this is than a door closed in my face.* Tiredness vanished in an instant. Happiness exploded once again. I didn't care about my moods now. I mentally punched the air with joy.

Eminguak introduced me to Reidar, the founder of the theatre. Reidar was older, somewhere in his forties, with a tanned face and short grey hair. He was an island of calm compared to the howling elements outside. He led me through to his office, sat me down, and smiled warmly.

'I am Norwegian,' he explained. 'I come from a small village in the mountains. And here I now am—a mountain man living by the sea! When I first moved here and saw how flat it was I thought to myself: *what am I doing here? This landscape is so plain.* But it didn't take long before the sea changed me. It is... alive. Every day is different. And there is so much space. Back home, sunrises and sunsets were hidden by mountain walls, winters were long and dark, and I only ever saw lakes and rivers, never such a huge body of water. The first time I saw Oslo's fjord I thought that was the sea! But then I came here... and... well, nothing was the same afterwards!' He smiled broadly. 'I couldn't live in mountains again after this.'

Eminguak stepped back into the office and handed me a large mug of steaming tea.

'I am from a small settlement in Greenland,' Eminguak said. 'A place you can only get to by boat or plane. There is nothing to do there and the weather is *so* bad. It is still snowing there—spring hasn't even thought about starting.' He laughed. 'My friends back home don't understand why I like it here so much. But to me this is the big city!'

After I'd finished my tea Reidar and Eminguak gave me what they called the grand tour.

'Our theatre was set up in the early seventies,' Reidar explained. 'We run theatre training courses, mostly for Greenlanders, but also for other indigenous people. We keep stories and cultures alive that might otherwise be lost.'

They led me into a large barn—the theatre itself. It was painted jet black inside and had a raised stage and rows of folding seats. Beyond it was a small museum displaying wooden sculptures and masks, an ancient skin-covered sea kayak from Greenland, and historical photos of Inuit life in Greenland, Alaska and Siberia. Next came a large dining room where a group of Danish teachers sat in stockinged feet, taking a break from their five-day course. With quiet enthusiasm and obvious pride Reidar and Eminguak showed me their world, and I thought to myself: *who knew that an ordinary farm along a bleak stretch of North Sea coastline would turn out to be a rich and fascinating place where creative people were carving out an original path through life?* Once again I had to acknowledge a simple truth: there is no ordinary.

My hosts left me in the dining room for a few minutes, and I chatted with one of the teachers, a passionate woman from Aarhus who truly believed that her mission in life was to use education to make the world a better place, one student at a time. 'Every single conversation can make a difference,' she said. 'Each moment, whether planned or unplanned, whether it goes well or poorly, can be a lesson.'

Eventually, Eminguak returned. 'Your room is ready!'

The *room* was a long wooden cabin that looked like an old-time railroad caboose. It sat on the farm's edge, propped upon cinder blocks. Several thick wooden posts were braced against the sides to hold it in place. The interior was palatial, to my eyes: bright pinewood walls; tables, chairs, and a bunk; electric lights. Everything my tent was not. The cracked windows, the grime in the corners, the torn cushions, the dead flies—they bothered me not.

'Will this be okay?' Eminguak asked uncertainly.

'Oh yes!' I grinned, barely containing my happiness. If he only knew!

I settled in, spirits soaring. What a roller-coaster ride this was turning into! The cabin reminded me of 'The Bohemian Bothy', both in its ramshackle comforts and the unexpectedness of landing in it just when it was needed. And it *was* needed. That night, rain lashed against the windows as though seeking to shatter them; it hammered upon the walls and roof as though determined to beat a way through. And the wind *attacked*, surpassing even Great Arber's winds for unrestrained violence. My home swayed, shuddered and rocked, and but for the braces would likely have blown right over. But it wasn't my tent: it didn't leak or threaten to tear in half, and the rocking motion only increased my gratitude for where I was—and for where I wasn't. Soothed like a baby in a swaying crib I slept in utter contentment. Even when the storm pulled me from sleep in the middle of the night there was pleasure in being woken. *Just listen to that!* I thought in awe, as the storm tore at the world outside. I doubt that any accommodation anywhere in the world was *more* appreciated that night than 'The Rocking Bothy' was appreciated by Mad Mountain Jack.

Dawn brought sharp sunlight, colder temperatures, and only the merest whisper of a breeze—a miracle after the night's violence. I set out with enthusiasm into a world that once again seemed renewed, my mood—as always now—a reflection of the kindness I'd just received. I tried to express my gratitude to Reidar and Eminguak, but words seemed to fall short. I saw that my grin did a better job. By the time I walked away my new friends wore broad grins too. There it was again, the contagious power of a smile.

Outside 'The Rocking Bothy' the morning after the storm, March 27, 1998.

Northwards I plodded up the coastline, the landscape growing increasingly wild. To my left the untameable North Sea roared in memory of the storm, grey-green waves rolling in and smashing against the beach. Great piles of foam lay on the sea's edge, wobbling like jelly. 'Don't worry,' another fisherman assured me. 'The weather's set fair for the whole of next week. It'll feel like summer by the weekend.' The moment he finished speaking I cursed inwardly. Now he'd done it!

For a few hours, sunshine and windless air lulled me into believing that the forecast might be true. Life was temporarily idyllic. I scaled the 100-foot cliffs of Borjerg and paced along them on firm turf, skylarks exalting overhead. But it didn't last. Clouds soon rolled in, swiftly followed by smothering fog. Moisture soon beaded rough moorland grasses, and down upon the beach old World War Two fortifications loomed from the clag—ugly concrete bunkers that matched the ugly conditions. Black windows filled with staring ghosts watched as I trudged by. I camped in the dunes feeling unsettled, wishing I was back in 'The Rocking Bothy'.

The next day I reached the town of Thyborøn, and cast around hopelessly in the fog, my map not matching reality.

'Are you looking for the *mission*?' a well-meaning lady asked, taking me for a homeless tramp.

'No,' I replied with a laugh. 'Just the ferry terminal!'

Thyborøn sat at the northern end of a long peninsula, with the North Sea on one side and a broad fjord on the other. To continue north, I took a car ferry across the fjord's narrow inlet, a brief ten-minute ride through the fog. There was little to see once out on the water, so I spent the journey talking with a young cyclist from Trønder. He was in the area to visit his girlfriend, although he admitted that time in the saddle took priority. We chatted easily while gulls chased the ship, eventually discussing the fortifications littering the coast.

'The Germans built them,' the cyclist confirmed. 'Part of their Atlantic Wall. Not all were finished, and some have now been dynamited and removed. There is one in the centre of town that people have to pass every single day. Everyone wants it destroyed, blown up, but no one can figure out how to do it without blowing up the town too!'

Back on dry land I followed another long dyke, and then, for the next three days, weaved through the wildest environment I'd encountered since the Bohemian Forest: a place of untracked pinewoods, undulating heathlands and acres of grassy dunes. In the grey, windy weather the landscape felt stirringly rough and elemental. Numerous birds filled the sky, and long-legged cranes patrolled ponds and pools. Roe deer drifted through the trees. The heathlands and woods were open enough that I could travel off trail without too much difficulty, but sheltered enough that discreet wild camps were possible. I drank from clear pools, and travelled quietly and respectfully, always watching for bird nests when I placed my feet. The land felt primeval, assuredly a place to treasure, and ten years after my visit Denmark recognised this, designating it the Thy National Park, the country's first national park outside of Greenland. The designation was justly deserved.

Miles passed. March ended and April began, but it didn't arrive with spring-like weather. Instead, the wind switched to the north and whipped ferociously across the sea. I wrapped myself in every stitch of clothing I possessed but still shivered as I walked, the temperature barely above freezing, the wind chill *far* below. Feeling like an April fool I battled north, laughing ruefully at how persistently different Denmark was to how I'd originally foreseen it. A month-long holiday by the sea? A chance to relax and recoup? Forget it! Was this winter never going to end?

I woke to light snow falling on April 2, and when I resumed progress up the beach and felt the piercing thrust of the north wind I gasped aloud. Head down, I tried turning off my thoughts, practising all the coping tricks I'd spent eleven months developing—but to little effect. The miles seemed endless, and by day's end my wind-battered spirit was dragging in the sand like a heavy anchor. But another kind campsite owner revived them, letting me stay for free, even though his site wasn't yet open.

'Is this weather normal for April?' I asked the owner.

'Normal? Oh sure, sure, this is normal,' he replied with a deep, rolling laugh. 'Also normal is wind and rain, heat and sun, fog and hail, sleet and… well, you get the idea yes? We get everything here. You never can tell what comes next. But it is *all* normal.'

The 'normal' weather continued the next day, with heavy snow that smothered the landscape white. I looked around in disbelief—I might have been back in the Austrian Alps or camping along the frozen Rennsteig. Snow lay six inches deep right down to the water's edge. It didn't seem right, seeing so much winter on a beach in April. Neither did it seem fair —hadn't I left winter behind when I'd descended from the Harz? Several more inches fell overnight, pressing upon the tent, and by dawn icy water pooled upon my floor. Striking camp brought a return to unwelcome sensations I thought I'd left far behind: numb hands and feet, and searing pain once blood began to flow. *This is NOT FUN!* I roared inside.

The day that followed was the least comfortable of the entire trip until that point. It was a monotonous, chilling, sodden, head-down slugfest of a day. The miles led north-east along a slush-covered beach into a brutal headwind, and I was soon plastered in snow. With the temperature just above freezing, the snow was as soaking as heavy rain, and in no time it penetrated my waterproofs and drenched my clothes. My gloves succumbed too, quickly becoming saturated; as did my boots, doubling in weight as water soaked them.

As I trudged through the slush, I found myself thinking dark, angry thoughts. *Useless bloody waterproofs. Aren't they supposed to keep water out, not soak it up like a sponge?* I wished I were tougher, wished I could endure the conditions without complaint. I stared in frustration at the black sky,

Another walker on the beach, hunched against wind and snow, April 4, 1998.

in loathing at the snow-covered beach, and cringed as icy rivulets ran down my back. I thought about Norway again, picturing myself alone in similar conditions on wild fjells. I imagined feeling this cold and wet. Norway's maritime climate makes wind, rain and snow the dominant weather—the idea of spending weeks enduring it prompted an intense burst of anxiety. If I felt this uncomfortable up there I didn't see how I could cope. Not for days and weeks on end. And it wouldn't only be uncomfortable—it would be genuinely dangerous. Walking the length of Norway had seemed like a fantastic idea, but now it seemed like sheer madness. I pushed on miserably.

Minutes passed like hours, and I kept hypothermia at bay through motion alone. Only one detail staved off despair: the promise of a night indoors in the next town, Løkken. Anne had given me the address of a friend named Bitten who lived there. She'd promised me she'd phone him and explain I was coming, and had assured me he'd take me in for a night. The idea of it shone with beacon brightness as I pushed through the snowstorm. It was a rock of hope to cling to while my sodden clothes clung to me.

Løkken was a long time coming, but eventually it appeared from the storm: a short pier reaching into the sea, three snow-covered fishing boats stranded on the beach, and a hint of civilisation just behind the dunes. Without wasting a second I turned inland into town, and asked the first person I saw where Nørregade was, Bitten's street. The man took his time answering, and I felt myself freezing to the spot while he thought about it. Finally he replied. 'I am sorry. I don't know!' Perhaps seeing my anguish, he directed me to the tourist office, and although it was closed a street map outside showed Nørregade. Great! Things were starting to go my way.

In haste, I sloshed across town, excited that the day was nearly done. I even went so far as to smile. I didn't stop to consider what I'd do if Bitten wasn't there. The thought was too unthinkable.

Nørregade soon appeared. The street was lined with shops, restaurants and businesses, although all were closed for the season. Walking swiftly, I soon reached Bitten's home. Looking up at it, I saw a large sign. 'Rooms for Hire' it stated in Danish, German and English. *Perfect!* I grinned. Even if Bitten wasn't around I'd fork out some cash and stay indoors. Saving money seemed irrelevant. Shelter had become everything.

But a night indoors wasn't my fate, at least not in Løkken. The front door was locked, no one answered the doorbell or my pounding fist, and when I peered through a dark window I saw why: the building was deserted. Broken furniture had been pushed against walls and dust lay heavy as snow upon the floor. The place looked long abandoned. *Damn*, I thought. *Damn-damn-DAMN!*

Trying to remain positive, I told myself that perhaps Anne had simply got the house number wrong. I knocked next door, but the nervous elderly lady who answered hadn't heard of anyone named Bitten, and said she knew everyone living on the street. I tried the house on the other side— no answer—then explored a courtyard behind, rattling a few doors in desperation, calling out 'Bitten, hallo?', but eventually gave up. It was hopeless. A black mood descended upon me. It was like Christmas all over again. Only this time I was exhausted, soaked and freezing.

In despair, I turned to leave the courtyard and took a few steps. They were a mistake. I stood on something snow-covered and slick, and before I knew it my feet were higher than my head. I landed heavily on my back, and afterwards lay pinned by Ten Ton, stuck like a tortoise overturned. For a moment I lay still—soaked, numb inside, beyond caring—while huge wet flakes spiralled onto my face. Time stopped.

I felt thoroughly defeated.

Eventually, I escaped Ten Ton's embrace and looked to see what I'd slipped on. It was a new window, lying flat on the ground, buried by snow. The glass was now cracked, which served someone right.

'Damn silly place to leave a window!' I muttered aloud.

I stood still for a few seconds, replaying my own words. *I'll probably never say that again*, I thought. A unique comment for a ridiculous situation.

Suddenly, I felt a grin spread across my face. I couldn't stop it from growing. I shook my head in bemusement. *Damn silly place to leave a window?* What a comment! Laughter erupted—and for a while wouldn't stop. So what if I was cold and wet! So what if this wasn't the April I'd wanted! So what if I wasn't going to sleep indoors! So what if I'd wiped out on a window! This—the journey, the snow, *everything*—it was all suddenly too funny. Laughter overcame discomfort; it entirely defeated the storm. It was just a little *weather*, after all, nothing more!

As if realising that the contest was lost, the weather gods finally desisted and the snow ceased—although the wind still blew with penetrating cruelty. I marched onward up the beach on legs that did my bidding despite their reluctance, and an hour later turned inland to a campsite that was wonderfully, fantastically, open.

The owner, Hans, was an intimidating, blond-haired giant, but his welcome belied his fierce appearance. When he spoke his voice was full of empathy and kindness. 'Hmm… isn't it too cold for tent camping?'

'No,' I replied. 'Not too cold. I've camped in worse. Mind you,' I continued, sensing an opportunity, playing my cards carefully, 'I'd rather sleep in one of your chalets… if only I could afford it.'

It did the trick. For the price of a tent site (lowered the next morning to no price at all), Hans led me to chalet number ten. I stepped over its threshold to discover bright lights, a real bed, an electric stove, a private shower, and (best of all) warmth and dryness—glorious *liberating* dryness. After hanging all my wet gear I wallowed in the sheer luxury of it, until Mattias—Hans' thirteen-year-old son—came knocking on the door.

'*Fader* says you are to come to dinner,' Mattias informed me, which wasn't a difficult command to obey. Within a minute I was seated at a large table that groaned under a mountain of food, sharing a feast with six adults, eleven children, and three dogs. The most uncomfortable day of the walk had swiftly become one of the most memorable.

'We have owned the campsite since February,' Hans explained. 'And this is our first day open... and you are our very first customer! We are having a little celebration, and it seems right that you are with us.' He smiled hospitably. 'And so we want you to eat as much as you can!'

He didn't need to invite me twice.

———

I slept the sleep of the exhausted, and woke refreshed to a dreary, misty morning, snow still lying deep. After giving chalet number ten a thorough spring clean I returned the key to Hans.

'I slept *soooo* well,' I told him. 'Comfiest bed in four thousand miles.' I wanted to give something back, and reckoned he'd feel real pleasure if he knew *his* kindness had given *me* real pleasure. 'Best campsite in Europe,' I stated, meaning it. 'And I've seen a few.' Hans grinned with pride.

I set off up the beach through soggy, thawing snow, and laughed aloud. The day was frigid, but at least it wasn't snowing anymore, or raining— although I should have kept quiet. After 200 yards rain began sheeting down. But no matter. Nothing could get to me now.

After finding laughter in the snowstorm the day before I felt I'd turned a corner, overcome a major crux. My happiness—I suddenly saw—had nothing to do with the weather, or with my hopes and plans being met, or with other people being there to help or not help, or with any external factors at all. Anne's friend hadn't been there. I'd been cold, wet, exhausted. Conditions had been appalling. I'd fallen hard. I'd finished up lying on my back in the snow. Fate and all the gods of long-distance wanderers had conspired against me. And yet I hadn't broken. Instead, I'd laughed. And it had come from within. It was such a small thing, finding happiness inside, but the discovery felt monumental. It was like the day after Christmas all over again. I felt reborn. I sensed that The Walk would never again be the same.

As if to prove it a morning phone call to Base Camp brought fantastic news. Lowe Alpine were sending replacement waterproofs to Norway. Even better, Rex Interstock—the photo library back in London who were handling all the photos I took—had sold one of my landscape shots to an advertising agency for a whopping £600, extending the journey by almost two months. The news left me *weightless* with optimism. Perhaps I really was going to make it all the way? The gods *were* on my side!

A little rain couldn't touch me. *Rain? Pah—what rain?* Half a mile down the beach I joined two teenagers in an exuberant snowball fight, and the silliness of it had us all laughing. Afterwards, I walked along sandy cliffs that rose and fell seductively, through gusty winds, drifting fog, and pelting rain, and imagined I was on a wild *mountain* walk once again. It all felt wonderfully familiar.

Eventually, the rain stopped and I escaped my waterproofs, clearly a mistake; as soon as I packed them away the rain resumed, heavier than before. I pulled the waterproofs back on, but might as well have not bothered. Soon, I was as wet and chilled as I'd been the previous day.

Splashing on, I thought about endurance. I decided that the difference between real and wannabe adventurers is that real adventurers don't give up, ever, no matter how hard the going, or how uncomfortable they become. I was a long way from being a polar explorer or a high-altitude mountaineer, but I wasn't going to give up either. People back home had sometimes acted as though I could endure unpleasant conditions simply because I didn't feel them. They acted as though it were easy for me, which was why I could do it and they couldn't.

Well, bollocks to that, I thought as I trudged through the deluge. I felt every degree of cold, every biting gust of wind, every chilling drop of rain. My limbs ached as much as anyone's would, my feet felt as sore, my entire body as weary. This wasn't easy. It wasn't comfortable. I didn't have anything special helping me. The main difference was that I *wanted* to be here, outside in direct contact with the natural world. Wanting this changed everything. I'd also learnt three fundamental lessons. One, that no matter how unpleasant the discomforts were right now they'd one day become pleasant to look back on. Two, that they wouldn't last. Three, that they actually made life better. What would sunshine be without rain, or water without thirst, or shelter without exposure? I could endure because enduring increased the pleasures certain to follow, because enduring ultimately brought rewards. Everything increases in value when it has been earned.

Late in the morning I neared Hirtshals, a large seaport. I'd return to Hirtshals in five days to catch the ferry to Norway, but I wanted to reach the northern tip of Denmark first. For now, it was just an outpost of civil-isation along the rain-washed coast. Despite the weather there were other people on Hirtshals' beach, although the majority were hunkered down in cars that had been driven onto the sand. The occupants sat behind glass, staring blankly through swishing windshield wipers. Dry they may have been, but none of them looked as happy as I now felt.

I met one family actually outside, walking a tiny, bedraggled dog.

'Your hands,' the father asked. 'Are they supposed to be that colour?'

'Um, what?' I replied.

'Well… they are bright blue.'

I laughed, shrugged. They'd pretty much been that colour since October. My feet too. I'd grown used to it.

Leaving the beach, I splashed into town and, on a whim, called by the youth hostel. It was a gleaming five-star palace, nothing like the simple hostels the organisation had once offered. Its decorations were opulent; its restaurant was set with cleverly folded napkins and extravagant flower arrangements.

I rang the reception bell and a shortish man emerged. He didn't come over to the desk, but stayed back halfway through his office door. He looked annoyed at having been interrupted.

'Yes… I speak English,' he answered, frowning as though he didn't want to. He stared at my dripping clothes and sandy boots. A look of distaste appeared. *Here we go again*, I thought.

'Do you have any beds available?' I asked, guessing the answer.

'No.'

'Really? None at all?' I asked gently, trying to make a connection, looking the man in the eyes, appealing to the fellow *human being* within. 'You are *completely* full?'

The man shifted from foot to foot, perhaps feeling a touch of shame. But if so, it didn't last.

'Well… um… it is two hundred kroner for a room…' he said hesitantly. 'Er, no… I mean… two ninety-five.'

He remained half in the doorway, clearly wanting to retreat, confident that the quoted price was going to be too high. Which it was. I could see judgement writ on his face. *I don't want you messing up my beautiful hostel*, his expression said.

But I didn't feel any resentment or anger this time. My own happiness wasn't touched. I just felt disappointment, for his sake. I wanted to make *his* life better. I wanted to do something kind for him instead. Perhaps I could leave something lasting.

'Well, thank you anyway,' I said. I stared into his eyes and smiled. I put everything I had into a look of empathy. 'I *understand*.'

And I saw confusion spread across the man's face.

Walking away, I wondered if anything would change. Perhaps he'd give the encounter some thought. Perhaps he'd even treat the next vagabond differently. I could only hope.

After all, kindness breeds kindness. Forgiveness breeds forgiveness. Ripples spread.

Back in the rain I felt strangely elated for someone who'd just been looked at with distaste and essentially turned away. No, not elated. That wasn't even close to it. I felt free, profoundly free. I'd done it. My mood was no longer linked to how others treated me. I still needed people, but happiness itself lay in my hands, and in mine alone.

I soared. I *was* on a quest, and it *was* changing me. Even if I failed to make it to the North Cape it wouldn't matter one bit now. I'd already achieved and learnt more than I'd ever imagined.

There was more than one way of measuring a journey's success.

———

The final four days in Denmark were quieter, but definitely not anticlimactic. There were no more life-altering encounters, no more lessons learnt, and no more major obstacles to overcome. I simply plodded up the beach at an unspectacular three miles an hour, feeling at home, noticing and savouring the details, growing unexpectedly nostalgic for the sandy, breezy, watery way of life that was soon to come to an end. Norway, The Prize, was so close now I could almost taste it, but the thought of leaving the North Sea coastline prompted a throbbing ache of loss in the pit of my gut.

Day by day the snow thawed, but enough remained in sheltered corners that finding water for wild camps was easy. Temperatures stayed cold, the air damp, but finally the sun beat aside the murk and shone on a silver sea and the greening land, bringing colours to life I'd forgotten existed.

How different the place looked in sunlight; how welcoming, how alive! On April 8 I sat atop a lonely dune and watched the sun slowly sink into the sea, and the entire living land held its breath with me—then sighed with utter contentment once the sun had slipped away.

I took one final detour inland to visit Northern Europe's largest sand dune, the Råbjerg Mile: a migrating dome of sand that shone in the distance like a pale glacier. Tiny black specks upon it became people, and soon I stood at the highest point, 130 feet above sea level, surrounded by a great sweep of bare sand. I gazed east and west to *two* seas—the North Sea and the Baltic, both now in view. Jutland was narrowing; Denmark was running out of land. The very tip of it, Grenen, lay just a few miles ahead.

I reached Grenen, and the end of the walk's third stage, on April 9. Snow was flying horizontally through the air once again, clouds obscured the sun, and a fierce wind blew—but I wouldn't have wanted it any other way. The wild conditions were perfect for The Walk's third grand finale. From Skagen Nordstrand, the exposed beach at Denmark's northernmost point, I paced on to Denmark's land's end, and the final steps were half reluctant, half exuberant.

Grenen appeared. It was a long finger of sand jutting out to sea. Grenen marks the meeting point of the Skagerrak and the Kattegat, of the North and the Baltic Seas, and beyond its sandy tip the two seas were colliding in a maelstrom of water. Large waves were running into one another, clashing from a multitude of directions, erupting into white water, roaring louder than the wind. It was a thrilling spectacle—nature at its wildest—and for a moment I completely forgot why I was even there. The entire environment was in turmoil. Dark clouds swept by overhead, stinging pellets of snow flew through the air, snaking tendrils of sand-spindrift hissed across the beach, and two seas raged.

I loitered for several minutes, leaning into the wind and snow, not wanting to rush the final few yards. Ahead of me on the sandbar a bright red tourist bus was parked, along with a large tractor that had pulled it. Visitors ventured from the bus in twos and threes to snap quick photos, look around briefly, then dash back to shelter. An estimated one million people a year visit Grenen. I watched as another thirty visitors arrived in a second bus. But they didn't stay long—for everyone but Mad Mountain Jack this wasn't a day for hanging around outside.

Turbulent water at Grenen, April 9, 1998.

Eventually, I had Grenen to myself. I took my last Danish steps, storing away the sensation of boots sinking into sand, and then, there I was, alone at the top of Denmark. I'd done it! I'd walked across continental Europe from one sea to another, from the placid Mediterranean to the tumultuous waters at Grenen. Norway lay ahead, but for a fleeting moment The Prize suddenly felt like an entirely separate journey, unconnected to this. I'd been through a lot in 4,550 miles. I'd walked through forests, over mountains, across plains, and along an epic beach. I'd endured the heat of summer and the sting of winter. I'd experienced a continent of variety, and learnt a little. But all I now felt amid the crashing fury of the storm was an incredible sense of peace.

Two days later, on April 11, Easter Saturday, I caught the Color Line ferry to Norway—although I almost caught the ferry to England by mistake.

I returned to Hirtshals by bus, train, train, and bus. The journey didn't pass without incident, and it reminded me how much I preferred my simpler mode of travel, and how much I loathed being a slave to timetables. There was a missed connection through no fault of my own, a search for a well-hidden bus stop, and a scare when the final bus driver mixed up his timetables.

'When do we reach Hirtshals?' I asked, double-checking my carefully worked plan.

'Oh, two-thirty,' he replied carelessly.

My heart raced. 'What? But we're supposed to connect with the ferry, and the ferry leaves at one forty-five!'

'Oops, noooo… sorry… wait a moment,' the driver said with a laugh, unconcerned. 'I meant twelve-thirty. Silly me! Don't worry—you'll catch your boat.'

'My' boat was huge, an eight-storey blue-and-white edifice mightier than any human-made object I'd seen in almost twelve months. It stood alone at the dock, towering above all the harbour buildings, and I thought: *this is going to be travelling in style!* At the ticket office I collected my free ticket, a generous gift from Color Line who had agreed, over a year earlier, to grant me free passage both to and from Norway, although the lady behind the desk wasn't so sure about handing it over.

'Never seen one of these before,' she observed, momentarily flummoxed by the zero where the price normally lived. But a quick phone call confirmed that everything was on the up. 'What did you do to get that?' she asked, bemused.

'Well,' I said. 'First of all I fell down a mountain in Switzerland…'

Afterwards, gut churning with excitement that I really was heading to Norway, I marched up a long walkway and stepped aboard. After battling Ten Ton into a luggage locker designed for regular suitcases, not monster backpacks, I set out to explore the ship. It was impressive—clean, modern and comfortable, offering restaurants, plush carpets, and even a cinema, utterly unlike any environment I'd inhabited in months. It was also surprisingly quiet. The quietness was odd, but I didn't let it trouble me—at least not until departure neared. But with only fifteen minutes left the ship's emptiness struck me as wrong. I searched high and low, and finally tracked down another human being: a neatly uniformed Color Line employee who was walking down a corridor ticking off items on his clipboard.

'Excuse me,' I asked breathlessly. 'This *is* the one-forty-five ferry to Kristiansand, isn't it?'

'Oh no, sir,' he replied calmly. 'This is the three-thirty to Newcastle, England. You want the *other* boat. Um… you'd better hurry, sir.'

The other boat? What other boat?

I looked out a porthole and saw, sure enough, a second ferry now in view; it hadn't been there earlier.

Hell's bells! Turning on my heel, I murmured a quick: '*Tak*—thank you,' and sprinted away, my boots clomping heavily. I raced down several flights of stairs, flew down a long corridor, found the luggage lockers, but realised they were the *wrong* luggage lockers. I sprinted back up another flight of stairs, almost knocked over a janitor, dashed through an empty dining room, and finally found the right lockers. Retrieving Ten Ton was a struggle—it was wedged in place until a strap tore and it came free. Racing away, I lost a minute searching for the exit, dashed off the boat, ran down the ridiculously long walkway, crossed a stretch of concrete that seemed to elongate as I ran, thudded up another walkway that shook until I feared it might collapse, and finally reached the correct ferry's entrance just as the ticket inspector was easing its heavy metal door shut. Happily, she saw me and paused.

Gasping, sweating, flustered, I handed over my ticket.

'Um, this is a *bus* ticket sir…' the lady said, handing it back.

'Oh, sorry. Sorry, hang on a mo.' I rummaged through my pockets, spilling out old receipts, the lady all but tapping her foot as I held up departure. Finally, I found the correct ticket.

'Er, welcome aboard.' The lady smiled, although she didn't seem certain about letting me on.

But I'd done it. *Norway, here I come.*

It's just as well, I thought later, once I'd squashed Ten Ton into another locker, *just as well that most of my journey is by foot.* If I'd tried crossing Europe by any other means it would *never* have worked. I'd have probably ended up in Africa.

My footprints along the endless beach, April 8, 1998.

PART V
NORWAY

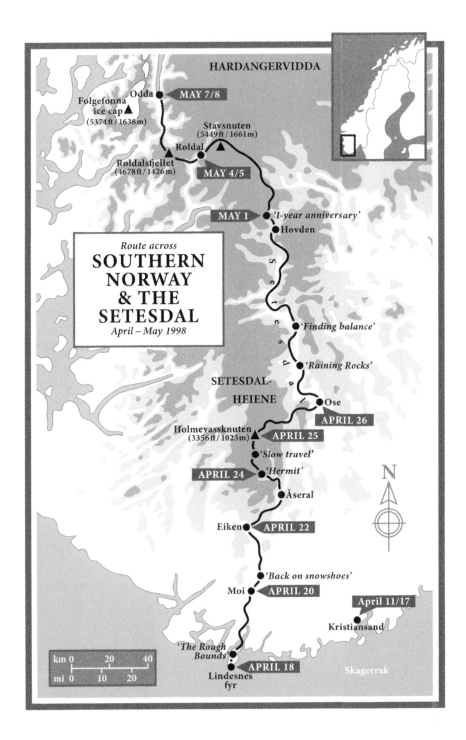

Route across
SOUTHERN NORWAY & THE SETESDAL
April – May 1998

HARDANGERVIDDA

Odda ● MAY 7/8

Følgefonna ice cap ▲ (5374 ft / 1638 m)

Stavsnuten (5449 ft / 1661 m)

Røldal ●

Røldalsfjellet (4678 ft / 1426 m)

MAY 4/5

MAY 1 ● '1-year anniversary'

● Hovden

S e t e s d a l

● 'Finding balance'

● 'Raining Rocks'

SETESDAL-HEIENE

● Ose

APRIL 26

Holmevassknuten (3356 ft / 1023 m) ▲ APRIL 25

● 'Slow travel'

APRIL 24 ● 'Hermit'

● Åseral

Eiken ● APRIL 22

● 'Back on snowshoes'

Moi ● APRIL 20

April 11/17

Kristiansand ●

'The Rough Bounds' ● APRIL 18

Lindesnes fyr

Skagerrak

N

km 0   20   40
mi 0   10   20

KRISTIANSAND
Chapter 1

IT WAS SNOWING in Norway, of course—snowing as though winter would never relinquish its grip on the land.

Land! Norway! Norge! It appeared after four and a half hours upon the choppy Skagerrak. Suddenly, the waters stilled as they came under land's influence, the ferry ceased pitching, and I stepped outside onto the sun deck into conditions that were definitely not sunny. Under charcoal-grey skies, and in curtains of falling snow, I watched reefs sweep by, the skerries guarding Kristiansand's sheltered harbour. Dark and jagged, the rocks loomed like half-submerged beasts. This wasn't soft and sandy Denmark but a harder, fiercer and older place. A land with its bones on display. I wouldn't have been surprised to see an ancient Norse monster standing upon a headland, glaring wildly at the passing ferry. First glance at Norway and already I could believe its ancient legends. First glance, and already it was tugging on my emotions. First glance, and already The Prize had me captivated.

The sun deck was deserted, and so I yelled at the top of my voice like a Viking returning home after months at sea. Some emotions need airing.

After a few minutes, the mainland came into view. Forested hills covered in snow rose from the sea, their summits lost in cloud. After so many months crossing flat landscapes the hills looked like mountains, although they were insignificant compared to everything that lay beyond. I felt a shiver of trepidation. I faced 2,500 miles of snowy wilderness. The rivers would soon be roaring in flood as spring set in, the lakes would rest dangerously hidden beneath softening snow, the terrain would be steep and rough, and odds were high that the weather would be windy and wet. With Norway no longer an abstract dream but a real place the idea of walking alone through it to the North Cape suddenly seemed utterly preposterous.

But then I let loose another battle cry, pushing the doubts aside. *The doubts are natural*, I told myself; *fear is part of why I've come*. Norway was going to be special *because* it was big, wild and scary. This was what I wanted—a land that put me in my place. The challenge was to see if even Norway could eventually come to feel like home.

Kristiansand, Norway's fifth-largest city, home to 85,000 residents at the time of The Walk, eventually came into view, calming my nerves. I planned to spend a week in Kristiansand, which meant that the wilderness wasn't an immediate concern. My body needed time off, and there were chores to do, reports to write to prompt donations for the homeless, gear to mend and replace, maps to buy and supplies to pack. I'd be starting the journey fifty miles west of Kristiansand at Lindesnes fyr, Norway's southernmost point, but I wasn't going to rush there. With snow falling heavily there was little point rushing anywhere.

After disembarking, I tramped across slush-covered streets to Kristiansand's tourist information office, seeking information on cheap places to stay, but the office was closed. Back at the Color Line terminal, a helpful receptionist handed over a map to a hotel that might suit my budget, and also gave directions to a campsite in case the hotel didn't work out. The hotel didn't—it too was closed—so I sploshed for eight wet miles to the campsite. Soon, water was seeping through my coat, but I tried to ignore it. Walking through precipitation and feeling damp was something I was going to have to get used to. Some things in Norway are inevitable.

The campsite sat on the shore of a broad saltwater inlet, the Topalsfjorden. Technically, the site was still closed for the winter, but an outhouse had been left open and a sign showed where tents could be pitched. I settled in. Aside from occasional planes thundering into the nearby airport, it was a quiet and beautiful spot. The best part was the cost. The site was free.

The week off passed productively. I took a bus into the city each day, and by week's end the drivers recognised me as a regular. From Kristiansand's post office I collected a large pile of letters, as well as a bulky gear parcel from Base Camp. Inside it were the snowshoes I'd bought in the Alpine village of Mayrhofen, as well as replacement waterproofs from Lowe Alpine. I put the waterproofs to instant use, and how novel it seemed to own rainwear that actually kept rain at bay! From the offices of the Norwegian national mapping authority, Kartverket, I bought a great pile of maps that covered the length of the country, optimistically believing that I would find the funds to complete the journey. I sorted the maps into parcels and posted most of them ahead. In outdoor gear stores I sought advice and suggestions; at a launderette I washed all my clothes and discussed the weather with locals; at a barber shop I had my medusa locks tamed; and at various food shops I made careful selections from the disturbingly expensive food. A day's food in Norway, I quickly discovered, cost the same as a week's food in Calabria. Still, the week off was all about preparing for the wild, and how better to prepare than by eating? I bought masses of food, and set to the task of dispatching it with great enthusiasm.

As the days passed I grew to know Kristiansand's citizens a little better. They were reserved at first, but opened up dramatically when I outlined my plans. I learnt that it was going to be a long, hot summer. I also learnt that it was going to be a cold, wet summer, because the previous summer had been good, and two good summers one after the other never occurred. I learnt that there was an exceptionally deep mountain snowpack this year, but also far less snow than normal. I learnt that it would thaw early, but also that it probably wouldn't thaw at all. The conflicting opinions didn't fill me with confidence.

For the first three days snow kept falling. Soon, it lay a foot deep. In town, ploughs pushed up mountainous piles beside roads, while inches of slush swamped walkways. Eventually, the flakes turned back to rain, and the snow began to thaw and sink into the sodden earth. I'd hoped to relax outside at least some of the time during the week, but instead spent endless hours stormbound inside the tent. Rain hammered, and my shelter was soon leaking worse than ever. Puddles spread across the floor just as they'd been doing since the Alps. To keep the flood at bay I stuffed socks into corners to sponge it up. When the socks were saturated I wrung them dry just outside the entrance, then stuffed them back in place. During the heaviest downpours I had to wring them out every thirty minutes—I felt I was bailing a sinking ship. Permanently wet inside, my squalid little home

Not quite the week off I'd hoped for. Deep snow in Kristiansand, April 15, 1998.

soon acquired a brand-new name: Auld Leakie. Leaking was what it did best. It wasn't an ideal tent for six months in Norway, but a new tent was beyond my means.

According to information gleaned from locals, Kristiansand is Norway's sunniest city. Several residents offered this useful snippet while they stared out at the unrelenting rain, their expressions deadpan. It was wonderfully ironic how the Norwegian sense of humour appeared to be so impressively *dry*.

The days passed. Still the rain fell. As I hid in Auld Leakie I made up my own words to 'Norwegian Wood', a favourite Beatles tune:

'I once took a walk, or should I say, it once took me?

It led me up north, going insane, Norwegian rain…'

The week's highlight came when I visited the offices of Den Norske Turistforening, or DNT for short. The DNT—the Norwegian Trekking Association—is a venerable organisation that maintains over 12,000 miles of summer hiking trails, marks 4,300 miles of winter skiing routes, and oversees the management of some 500 mountain huts. Spread the length of the country, the huts were of particular interest to me—I had no doubt there'd be times over the next six months when a night indoors would be appealing—so I joined the DNT without hesitation. For a small deposit, a key that unlocked *all* the huts was handed over, and I regarded it with delight. But that wasn't the highlight. The highlight was the reaction of a DNT volunteer when I answered her question about *where*, exactly, was I heading.

'Well, pretty much *everywhere*,' I explained. 'I'm planning to walk from Lindesnes to Nordkapp.'

The volunteer was a middle-aged lady: dark hair woven in a bun, motherly smile. No doubt, as a DNT member, and, even more than that, as a Norwegian, she spent a great deal of time in the mountains, and likely knew them well—which made her response somewhat *concerning*.

'*Nei*,' she said gently, shaking her head, frowning. '*Nei-nei-nei*. It is far too early. There is too much snow. You need to wait until July. At the moment, skiing is okay, but soon the thaw will make travel too difficult. Honestly, what you are planning is not a good idea.'

She paused for a moment to make certain she had my full attention. Then, she looked me hard in the eyes, and uttered one of the most memorable lines of the entire journey.

'You WILL NOT get through,' she stated with absolute finality.

LINDESNES FYR
Chapter 2

ON SATURDAY APRIL 18 I made my way to Lindesnes fyr, Norway's southernmost point.

To my surprise and joy the morning dawned with sunshine, not rain. Packing away my ice-stiffened shelter was an all-too familiar battle, but better than striking camp in a deluge. What did numb fingers matter anyway? I was about to begin the most adventurous six months of my life, and the sun was shining. If ever there were a good omen this was it.

In Kristiansand's bus terminal the ticket clerk grew animated when he heard my plans. He hastily phoned a local newspaper, but no journalists showed up—a shock to my new friend—but unsurprising to me after the reaction I'd received from Denmark's press. Soon, the bus whisked me away.

For the next hour the journey was ridiculously easy. A twisting road ran beside lakes and fjords, crags and forests, and all I had to do to enjoy the scenery was sit back and stare out of a window. I'd intended to read, but couldn't look away from the rugged landscape outside. It looked beautiful and accessible, but also slightly unreal, as though it were a one-dimensional painted backdrop. I realised that this was how many people saw Norway—through a car, bus or train window. Sitting within a vehicle was also how most visitors travelled long distances. The ease of it made choosing to travel by foot feel like an odd, masochistic choice—which it was, in some regards. But I also knew that walking was so much more than that. From within the bus I merely saw the landscape passing swiftly. On foot I was deeply immersed in it, and *all* my senses were used to their fullest.

I changed buses in Mandal, took a second bus to the small village of Vigeland, then stuck out a thumb to hitch the final eighteen miles to Lindesnes fyr. The fifth vehicle stopped—a van driven by a bearded local. He didn't get out, but gestured for me to push Ten Ton into the back beside his wheelchair. The man drove me to Spangereid, a village halfway to my destination, and en route barely spoke a word. My questions were answered with grunts, and he asked none of his own—he simply drove as though helping someone was a normal part of everyday life. But I finally won a burst of emotion from him when we swerved around a large clump of turf that must have fallen off the back of a gardener's truck. It sat in the middle of the road and was bristling with long, vibrantly green grass. 'Ah...' I joked, 'Troll lost his toupee.' The man guffawed loudly, then chuckled appreciatively for the rest of the drive. I felt I'd paid for the ride.

The next driver was more talkative and even more willing to help. He hadn't planned to drive as far as Lindesnes fyr but took me there anyway. Over the final miles he quizzed me about my journey, but not for his own interest. He wanted to make certain I understood what I was getting myself into.

'Travel is worse than difficult away from the roads,' he explained. When he dropped me off his final comment was urgently given. 'Be a coward,' he commanded.

He drove off, then screeched to a halt, backed up.

'You have your map?' he asked, leaning out the window. 'And emergency food?'

'Yes, and spare socks,' I added, grinning. 'It's okay,' I said. 'I'll take care.'

Only partially reassured, he finally drove away.

Lindesnes fyr was now before me. It was a staggeringly beautiful place, a treeless rockscape of headlands, inlets, knolls and shimmering sea. Several wooden buildings sat upon the headland, along with Norway's most famous lighthouse, a whitewashed tower topped by a bright red lantern room. It wasn't especially tall, but it rose proudly above the headland and looked as though it offered a commanding view. The twenty-kroner entrance fee was a justifiable extravagance, given the occasion, and within moments I was up on the viewing platform, surveying the jagged coastline first, then the panorama inland, thinking about all that lay ahead.

The treeless rockscape at Lindesnes fyr, April 18, 1998.

Down below, a group of light-hearted scuba divers were prepping for immersion in the sea—squeezing into drysuits, pulling on air tanks, donning flippers.

'How cold is the water?' I asked when I joined them.

'Hum,' one huffed deeply, breathing in. 'Cold enough to raise your voice at least four octaves!' He finished his reply with a high-pitched squeak.

'Actually... it is about two Celsius,' (thirty-six Fahrenheit), another explained. 'It is not so cold.'

'Two degrees?' I shuddered. 'You must be crazy.'

The scuba divers laughed at that, every one of them.

'Look who is talking,' one of them teased, pointing to Ten Ton.

We bantered for a while, then pulled out cameras. The divers wanted a picture of the mad English hiker standing in their midst.

'We'll put it in our club magazine. The caption will be: guess which one is going to Nordkapp!'

'You know, hundreds of people have made the *tur* north,' one of them explained. 'We call it *Norge på langs*. Norway lengthwise.' The others nodded.

'Yes,' another said, 'there were two British men on skis a few years ago… they started right here on roller skis!'

'Three girls did it last year…'

'I know a lady who did it when she was sixty-five…'

'And I have a friend who has a friend who did it inside two months…'

This was all very well, but I knew it wasn't going to be quite the stroll they made out. And anyway, I had no intention of following a quick straight line.

Before plunging into the chilling waters one of the frogmen kindly took a photo with my camera: of myself standing beneath a signpost that pointed north. According to the sign Nordkapp was 2,518 kilometres distant, or 1,564 miles, which I assumed was the distance by road. Even if one could travel in a dead straight line the distance was still 1,089 miles. Norway is a *long* country. At Lindesnes I was still closer to the Mediterranean than Nordkapp, a thought-provoking fact.

I left the frogmen and picked my way south across exposed rock to land's end, then sat beside the sea for half an hour, just as I'd done at Melito di Porto Salvo almost a year earlier. With warm sunlight on my face, and lulling waves washing Norway's granite edge, it was a peaceful spot. But I wasn't at peace. My stomach churned with excitement. My mind spun with emotion. This was another moment to savour, to pull in deep, to store away for the rest of my life. I still couldn't take for granted that I was here, living my dream—even after so long underway. I felt nerves too, and exhilaration —and ultimately the exhilaration won out. If the laws of nature could have been changed to match my mood I'd have been soaring and swooping through the air like one of the exuberant seagulls.

I felt an urge to jump up and race north, but instead held myself in check. After all, I thought: *what's the hurry?*

As I stared at the sparkling sea I decided that 'what's the hurry?' would be the motto for the rest of the journey. Whether my funds ran out in two months, or whether I made it all the way to the North Cape in six, not hurrying would define my approach.

Eventually, I stood up and turned away from the sea. I resolved to treasure every single step.

'Guess which one is going to Nordkapp?' Lindesnes fyr, April 18, 1998.

THE ROUGH BOUNDS
Chapter 3

YEARS EARLIER, BACK in Britain, I'd taken several week-long walks across a wild part of Scotland's west coast: Knoydart. Mountainous and remote, accessible only by boat or a long walk, Knoydart is famous—or perhaps infamous—for the roughness of its terrain and weather. So challenging is Knoydart by British standards that a visit is almost a rite of passage for the nation's mountain-going folk. Visitors afterwards can hold their heads high. 'Yes,' they might declare with pride to folk who haven't yet braved the region, 'I've crossed the *Rough Bounds* of Knoydart.'

But, compared to the Rough Bounds of Lindesnes, Knoydart is a manicured park.

On the first afternoon I covered all of three miles, not the ten planned. At that rate, I worked out with amusement, I'd reach the North Cape in… three years! I finished the day scratched, muddied and weary. It was exactly as I'd been warned. Travel was worse than difficult.

The landscape was a natural obstacle course, littered with impediments to travel. There were crags, boulder fields, gullies, ankle-wrenching tussocks, tight thickets, bogs and pools. There was no path, no easy line to follow. Even the weather was rough. It was chillier, damper and darker than back at the sea's edge. There, the sky remained clear, but here, it was smothered by dark clouds. It felt like something from a legend: the Wilderness Where the Sun Doesn't Shine. Civilisation and sunlight clung to the coast, but neither dared venture inland.

And yet, it was exactly what I wanted. It was entertainingly inconvenient, an antidote to all the flat miles I'd crossed since mid-February. It was land as land was supposed to be, rich and varied, showing no sign it had ever been touched. It demanded respect and humility. It forced me to change my perspective, turned me into just another creature crawling across the surface. Here, I couldn't expect to get where I wanted when I wanted. I might get there, or I might not. It reminded me of the *sottobosco*, where I'd learnt my lessons well. This time, I didn't try to bludgeon my way across the land, giving my all to get *there*. This time I slowed my pace and focused on *here*. I'd been dreaming of here for months.

And *here* was beautiful. It was intricate, multi-textured, fascinating. Each turn presented something new. It wasn't epic in scale—it was small and hemmed in—but it eclipsed everything I'd so far seen. The thrusting Gran Sasso, the ice-age Mandron glaciers, the glowing Dolomites, October's moonlit cloud seas, the frosted wonderland along the Rennsteig, Rømø's sandy heaths… these places all suddenly paled. Perhaps it was merely because I was here, not there. But whatever the reason, I couldn't imagine a more thrilling place. Yes, I'd learnt that I could find the wild in a tree stump, but *this* was what I'd *really* come for. The rocky knolls and moss-covered boulder fields, the birch woods and sucking bogs, the silent lakes and tumbling streams, the damp scents and clean air—they touched my senses and stirred my emotions.

Here, truly, was the *other* Europe, underfoot already just steps from the coast. And I wasn't even close to the mountains. I grinned with delight at finding wildness so soon.

Norway, like the rest of Europe, has been inhabited for millennia. But Norway, unlike the rest of Europe, offers large areas that have never been overrun or visibly altered. Its landscape is simply too mountainous, its climate too testing. Only three per cent has been cultivated; ninety per cent remains undeveloped. Norway's 4.5 million inhabitants are spread thinly.[2] The majority live around Norway's mild, gulf-stream-warmed edges, close to fjord and sea. A smaller number live inland, often isolated by miles of forest and *fjell* (the Norwegian word for mountain). The wild land/developed land ratio is the exact reverse of the ratio found in my own country.

---

2. The population at the time of my visit. By 2020 the population was nearing 5.5 million.

Back in England, pockets of wild land are like small islands surrounded by a vast sea of agriculture and urban development. But in Norway it is civilisation that forms the islands. In Norway, it is incredibly easy to leave the human world behind, as was blatantly clear from the first step I took.

Onward I walked through this unpeopled land, although I'm not sure 'walking' fully describes it. Yes I walked, but I also scrambled, jumped, ducked, weaved, stretched, grabbed, pulled and pushed. But I did it without haste, determined to work with the land, not fight against it. My grin broadened with each step, but I felt doubt, too—doubt at the practicalities of travelling this way for six months. Even unhurried progress sapped my strength and energy, and I suspected that even rougher terrain waited in the mountains. Could I really cross it all? But I pushed the doubt aside—worrying about the future wouldn't achieve anything. Better, for now, to simply enjoy where I was.

Progress came to an end when I reached an island-studded lake, a location so soul-stirringly scenic I felt incredulous that I could have it all to myself. I'd aimed to go further, but couldn't walk past this. Finding a flat spot for camp took time—the ground was either too rocky, too tussocky, too steep or too wet. But eventually I tracked down a workable patch of earth, and settled in. The 'Rough Bounds of Lindesnes' campsite sloped, but it overlooked the lake, and the view was so beguiling I couldn't complain. I had a job getting to sleep, not because of the slope, but because I had to keep peering from Auld Leakie to check that the view really was there.

___

Day two began with more of the same: snail-slow progress across unrelentingly rough terrain. A soaking drizzle increased the rough atmosphere, and I pulled on my new waterproofs, well aware that it wouldn't be for the last time. The coat was lime green and neon bright, the overtrousers a mismatched navy blue. They weren't colours I'd have chosen, and they made quite the fashion statement. I wondered if they'd reduce my odds of seeing wildlife. Elk[3] and deer would either spot me long before I saw them and flee in fear, or they'd fall to the ground clutching their sides with laughter.

---

3. Eurasian elk are known as moose in North America.

189

But the waterproofs worked, and for that I was hugely grateful.

With moisture blurring distant views the land felt wilder than it had on the first day, but I reached its northern edge eventually, coming to an unpaved road. The road led back to Spangereid, and once there I sheltered within a fjordside boathouse, considering the best course of action. I may not have been hurrying, I may have been treasuring every step, but I already felt as though I'd walked 100 Norwegian miles, not eight.

When I continued, I adopted a more practical approach, alternating short wilderness stretches with spells along quiet roads. On the third day, sunshine blazed, and with the land rising into rounded mountains I could barely contain my joy. I bought extra provisions when I reached the tiny village of Moi, and while packing them into Ten Ton outside the supermarket I could hear the owner inside telling customers about my journey. One of them, a pale, old, wispy-haired man, stepped outside and gave me two large chocolate bars.

'Here,' he said, offering them up, 'I bought these for you.'

On the road from Moi I had to turn down three rides. A middle-aged lady offered the third. 'Us Norwegians,' she explained, 'we just like to help. It's simply what we do.'

By late afternoon I was 1,000 feet above sea level, alone in a forest, with snow underfoot once again. Warm evening sunlight spilled through the trees, releasing intoxicating, pine-laden scents. As I settled into camp I couldn't stop smiling at how the journey was unfolding. To reach camp I'd covered the final quarter of a mile by snowshoe, and compared to snowshoeing back in the Alps progress was easy. There, my snowshoes had sunk deep in early winter's light and powdery snows. But here, the snow was old, dense and heavy, and my snowshoes only sank a few inches. I hadn't been certain they'd work, and the discovery filled me with optimism. I'd prove the DNT lady wrong. I *would* get through.

On the fourth day heavy rain fell, and the snowpack rapidly softened. The first hour of snowshoeing through it was a reality check that taxed muscle and spirit far more than I'd expected. The deteriorating surface sucked at my snowshoes and added pounds of weight to each step. Better-designed snowshoes might have helped, but I didn't know that better snowshoes existed. Even if I had known, I wouldn't have been able to afford them. My old Mayrhofen snowshoes were heavy and simple. They lacked

Snowshoeing to camp, April 20, 1998.

crampons and a snow-shedding design, and their bindings held my entire foot fixed in place. They made progress feel unnatural, like an exaggerated, flat-footed pantomime of walking.

Step by step my legs tired and my doubts returned. After two hours I slumped against a tree for the umpteenth rest and gazed upward, wondering: *have I made a mistake? Is Norway going to be impossible?* A flock of geese flew by, honking noisily. I'd noticed a similar flock the previous day, heading north through blue skies. But today's geese were retreating south. With the temperature close to freezing, and winter still burying the land, I thoroughly understood their change of heart.

Desperate to continue in good style I pushed on, but after another hour sank into submission. I didn't mind challenging terrain that I could get my teeth into, but this 'sloppy-porridge snow' was too much. I thought about why I was here: to embrace the land, not battle it. Grinding myself into exhaustion when the best of Norway lay weeks ahead seemed foolish. It was a sign of someone out of tune with nature, not in tune. Or so I told myself. Trying to convince myself that I wasn't merely taking the easy option, I turned for the valley.

For the next two days I stuck to quiet roads and weaved north without struggle. The scenery was glorious: pastoral farmland in flat valley bottoms, forested mountains all around, lakes still covered in ice, masses of roadside snow. I became hypnotised by the rhythm of walking, by the way my legs ticked along with minimal effort. No longer did I have to consider every step. I was free to enjoy the scenery and cover miles almost without effort. I pushed my doubts about the future to the back of my mind, and ignored the inner voice of dissent that claimed I was cheating.

Rain fell often—heavy showers between short-lived patches of blue. With each passing hour the snow thawed a little more. Tree limbs pinged up as I strode by, the diminishing snow no longer heavy enough to weigh them down. There were puddles, pools, babbling brooks and cascading waterfalls. But the snow wasn't thawing fast enough. Ahead, the first real mountains swept upward into clouds. Coming from Lindesnes, there was no easy route through them or around them—the valleys all dead-ended. The mountains formed a barrier that I'd have to cross.

On April 25, seven days from Lindesnes, I restocked in a small lakeside community, phoned Base Camp to assure them all was well, stuffed six days' food into Ten Ton, and then, with a gulp of trepidation, climbed into the mountains.

It began promisingly, with a good trail that switchbacked uphill toward a lake. The trail was covered in snow but it had been firmly packed by a long winter of skier and skidoo use. I didn't need snowshoes. My boots barely left a mark. The gradient was as relentless as the falling rain, but the firm surface made the ascent manageable.

It was different at the lake. Instead of skirting around it the snow trail cut straight across the middle. The lake was still snow-covered, and the corrugated tracks left by skidoos were still evident, but they were fading tracks, made—from the look of it—*many* weeks earlier. I examined the lake nervously. In places, the surface was cracked. A few sections gleamed with a beautiful but menacing glacial-blue. If I broke through with Ten Ton on my back I'd sink like a rock.

I paused, staring ahead. Beyond the lake a snow slope rose into fog. I could see a few isolated trees and rocks, but nothing else. It felt immense, void-like.

This was the Norway I'd come for, The Prize that I'd sought, the *other*

Europe I'd walked 4,650 miles to find. But now that I was here I wasn't certain I wanted to be. The emptiness was profoundly unsettling. The effort I'd have to make intimidated me. *Am I capable of this?* I asked, doubting that I was. *Should I commit?* I wanted to… but also longed for a reason not to.

I stood for several minutes in the rain, catastrophising. So much could go wrong. I imagined breaking through snow into a hidden lake, or being swept away by a swollen river, or being caught in a snow slide on steep ground, or simply losing my way in the immensity of the fjells, then running out of energy and food.

This wasn't a forest with firm ground underfoot. It wasn't a single mountain with a settlement a short distance below. It was a snowy wilderness that stretched north for almost forty miles. When I stepped into it I'd be 100 per cent on my own. Part of me wanted to turn about and flee.

I made my decision.

Cursing myself for what I was choosing to do, I strapped on my snowshoes and shuffled forward.

Progress was gruelling from the start. I sunk a foot deep with each step. Walking taxed every muscle. From the look of the trench-tracks I came upon, the local elk and deer populations were having an equally torrid time. As an experiment, to see if the snowshoes were part of the problem, I tried walking without them, but that was worse. I sank waist deep and escaping the hole was almost impossible. I restrapped the snowshoes and wallowed on, and once around the lake began climbing into the fog. I moved almost in slow motion. Not hurrying here wasn't a choice, it was forced upon me. *I can do this,* I kept telling myself, *it's no big deal.* I tried pushing from mind the blankness of the land ahead, and the immense effort required to cross it. But such realities were hard to push aside. Doubt kept growing.

And yet, at the same time, I was also leaping about inside like an excited Arctic fox. *Just look where I am!* I thought with amazement. *I'm in Norway! I'm really doing this!* It struck me as utterly inexplicable, how wonder and anxiety could exist side by side.

For the next four hours I worked harder than I'd worked since Melito. But all I had to show for it were three miles gained. When five isolated cabins appeared unexpectedly through the fog I decided that enough was enough. The cabins were probably locked, but a rare patch of snow-free ground lay beyond them—a gift too inviting to resist. Just being near the cabins brought comfort. Despite all the lessons I'd learnt, and all the wild places I'd passed through, and everything I believed I wanted, I still wasn't ready for *this* level of wild. I clung to the cabins the way a lost child might cling to a familiar blanket.

I approached the rust-red buildings and checked the doors in case any had been left unlocked, but all were securely fastened. I peered through one of the windows and saw simple furniture, colourful rugs, and brightly varnished wood—all the comforts of home. I looked in at them with longing while rain beat upon my shoulders.

Norwegians, in general, don't like to suffer unnecessarily in their mountains. They see nothing heroic in discomfort—most would far rather choose a cabin over a tent. Which isn't to say that Norwegians aren't hardy, mountain-going people. Far from it. Being active in the fjells, engaging in *friluftsliv*, is built into a Norwegian's DNA. *Friluftsliv* means 'outdoor living', and it is part national pastime, part national philosophy. *Friluftsliv* is to Norwegians what *hygge* is to Danes. It is a way of living that is passed from generation to generation—some Norwegian children learn to ski only months after they've learnt to walk. *Friluftsliv* is a reflection of both the abundance of untrammelled nature in Norway and its accessibility. Whether skiing in winter, hiking in summer, or sailing and fishing year round, many Norwegians will be engaged in outdoor living. *Friluftsliv* is as Norwegian as rain, snow and fish.

Nearly a quarter of all Norwegian families own a second home; many of them are remote mountain huts. Skiing to the family *hytte* in winter, stopping in the middle of nowhere, then digging down to find the doorway, is a common activity. For those without their own cabins there are clubs offering one, as well as businesses that make the company *hytte* available to employees. Then there is the DNT, with the largest hut network of all.

Unfortunately for me, none of these cabins belonged to the DNT. I stood with my back to them and stared out across the snowscape into rain and fog. It was easy to understand why Norwegians chose cabins. I had to laugh at myself. *Just think, I'm camping in this for fun!*

Reluctantly, I stepped away—but then stopped. I caught a familiar scent in the air, a whiff of smoke! How could I have missed it? Smoke was curling from the chimney of the first cabin I'd tried. Barely daring to hope,

I snowshoed back to it.

It took surprisingly long for the occupant to answer my knock, as though whoever lived inside had to make their way through a huge mansion. But eventually I heard footsteps, followed by the jangle of keys, then the sound of one lock being dealt with, then another—which seemed odd, given the cabin's remote location. Finally, the door opened, and a short, bearded, elderly man stood in its place. He looked at me with a faraway glaze in his eyes, showing no surprise at receiving a visitor. Thrown by his expression, I struggled to think of what to say. It couldn't be every day a stranger called by. When last had he seen someone? It might have been months.

Finally, I spoke, but the hermit shook his head, held up a hand to stop me.

'Nei Engelsk,' he murmured softly, and I ground to a halt. He was the first Norwegian I'd met who didn't speak English as though born to it.

Feeling awkward, I tried two simple words that were almost universal, and hoped the hermit would see that what I was asking was clearly silly. I hoped he'd notice my soaked clothes and take pity on me instead. 'Camping?' I asked, pointing out into the sopping-wet wild. 'Okay?'

But there was no pity: the hermit didn't care what I did. He merely shrugged his shoulders, gave a faint nod, then closed the door gently. I couldn't help but smile. What else would I expect? Anyone living alone out here clearly wasn't going to invite in company if they could help it.

I trudged away and camped in the rain, surrounded by miles of snowy nothingness. But I drew comfort from knowing there was another human just 100 yards away. It helped considerably.

———

At dawn rain was still falling, which was all the excuse I needed to roll over and reclaim sleep. Happily, the delaying tactic worked, and by the time I roused myself the rain had ceased. As I rolled up Auld Leakie, squeezing as much water from it as I could, I looked towards the cabins, searching for signs of life, but couldn't spot any. No movement behind windows, no lights, no curl of smoke. Perhaps the old man was sleeping late too—a perk of being a hermit.

I strapped on snowshoes, set off, and within minutes the rain resumed. *Ah well*, I thought, *this IS Norway*.

Heading up. Fog soon completely smothered the view. April 26, 1998.

For the next eight hours I toiled across a landscape that had very little land to it. It was more a *water*scape, an environment offering water in every possible form. It was all 'porridge snow' and rain-soaked slush, rushing river and ice-covered lake, dense fog and pelting rain. Every surface was wet to the touch. Everything dripped. The sound of rushing water filled my ears; swirling fog filled my vision. Boots were soon soaked. Socks squelched with each step. And, despite the new waterproofs, my clothes were soon cold and clammy beneath them, clinging as uncomfortably as they had back on the Danish beach. After two hours I was so drenched from sweat I reckoned jumping into a river would make little difference. The immense, snow-covered, watery wilderness had me out of my comfort zone in more ways than one. Nothing about it was comfortable.

Moving incredibly slowly, I laboured uphill, referring to my map and compass every few seconds. Never before had I navigated with such concentration and precision, making certain I knew *exactly* where I was at all times. I followed compass bearings without deviation, counted steps to estimate distances, matched minor details on the map with subtle changes underfoot. With fog blurring land into sky I was practically in a void, and even a small mistake could get me lost. Getting lost was something I desperately wanted to avoid.

I worried about falling over cliffs without seeing them, and stepping onto hidden lakes and breaking through. Norway is home to over 450,000 freshwater lakes. According to my map a large number lay along my route. Even if I chose a different route, there'd be lakes along it. Large and small, they waited like traps, hidden beneath mushy snow. Based on all my experiences with maps, I wasn't even taking it for granted that every lake was marked. I picked a route that avoided everything flat that could be a lake, and anything steep that might avalanche.

Time slowed. But I made progress, and—reassuringly—lakes appeared where they should. As did rivers, another challenge to overcome. The first river was free of snow and I forded it through shin-deep water. The second was in spate from rainfall and snowmelt, but short stretches were bridged by snow, and one of them granted passage—although my pulse leapt halfway across when a section collapsed behind me. Further rivers and lakes came and went, recognisable on the map, but the longer I walked the more disconnected from reality I came to feel. Soon, it seemed inconceivable that a more solid world existed elsewhere. I'd never felt so far out on a limb. Not even when I'd been lost for two days in the Aspromonte. It was a precarious feeling, as though the limb could snap at any moment, as though something was about to go horribly wrong.

With each step, anxiety increased. It was soon worse than it had been in the Aspromonte. Here, the dangers were real. A lake *could* swallow me if I made a mistake. An entire snow slope *could* give way—whether I made a mistake or not. The scale of the wilderness was on a whole other level. Having a detailed map only proved it. I was surrounded by a *huge* landscape—nothing but fjells, snow, and lakes. Awareness of it pressed upon me with colossal weight.

Back in the Aspromonte, anxiety had overwhelmed me. I'd travelled in a panic, rushing to get to the far side. But since then I'd learnt enough to maintain control, just. My inner voice screamed for flight, but I battled it with reason. *Look*, I argued, *I CAN cross this land. I AM crossing it!* I told myself that rushing would lead to mistakes, but if I kept going slowly I'd get there eventually. I compared the landscape with other places I'd successfully traversed: snowbound Alpine passes and the frozen Rennsteig.

I compared it with the Aspromonte, reminding myself that what I'd feared there had ultimately come to feel like home. I told myself that I knew the risks, that there weren't any unknowns. I told myself: *you want to be here.* And it worked, to a degree—but only enough to keep a lid on the panic, not to remove it. Fear still boiled beneath the surface, ready to erupt at any moment.

The trouble was, I couldn't ignore reality. No one knew where I was. I was solely responsible for my safety. I couldn't ignore that under sopping-wet snow ten feet deep this landscape could never be the home I wanted all wild places to be. And I couldn't ignore the truth of everything my father had been saying for years. *Andrew, your choices are dangerous and unnecessary. Life is already risky enough.* He was right, I now saw. But it was worse than dangerous and unnecessary; choosing to be here was also unnatural. Natural behaviour was the avoidance of risk, not deliberately choosing it.

Earlier in the journey, civilisation had rarely been more than a few hours away. When I'd entered the wild, both commitment and consequences had been lower. But now, viewed from the perspective of this bigger, emptier landscape, I saw that I'd only been playing. This wasn't a small wilderness where escape was easy. This was the real thing. And it was proving to be more than I could physically and psychologically handle.

Early in the afternoon I came to the day's largest lake, and from it began climbing a broad ridge, straining from the effort. Resetting my compass bearing every minute to match the hidden twists of the ridge, and still counting paces, I gained altitude, closing in on 3,000 feet for the first time since the Brocken. I reached the summit in a brisk wind, and I whooped at the sight of it. Unexpectedly, it offered the first patch of bare ground since camp: windswept rock stripped of snow, an island that I stepped onto with gratitude. But I couldn't stay long. I was too wet to remain motionless. Within minutes I was chilled and shaking.

With gravity on my side the descent should have been easier, but it wasn't. The angle was steeper than the map suggested and I floundered down it fearful of setting loose the entire slope. I frequently sank thigh-deep. The effort felt Herculean. Halfway down I recalled the memorable words: 'you won't get through'. Well, I *was* getting through—but at a cost. Much as I didn't want to accept it the DNT lady had been right, and much as I wanted to complete a high-level route across Norway I could see it wasn't realistic. Not for me anyway, not on these snowshoes, and not in this snow. I couldn't do this for weeks on end. I could barely do it for a day.

This wasn't merely entertainingly inconvenient, as the rough ground near Lindesnes had been. It was inconveniently impossible. I'd have to adapt, change my route. It was the only answer.

The angle eventually eased. Nervously, I crossed a sagging snow bridge over a torrent, reached flatter terrain, then slogged on. I made for a track marked on the map, but when I reached the location all I found was deep snow. Another river held me up an hour later. Twenty feet wide, slow and dark, it twisted languidly through the snowscape. After scouting possible crossing points I picked my spot. I waded across with peat-stained water to my crotch. It didn't help me feel any dryer.

The final few hours dragged as though time had stopped. I wallowed wearily through a nothingness of rain, fog and snow. The entire world seemed lifeless and forgotten. No creatures stirred—no insects, birds, or mammals. I stopped for camp when I reached the first sign of life since morning, a line of stunted birch: black skeletons against the snow. They called to me like old friends. In eight hours I'd covered seven miles and I was done. I couldn't imagine taking another step.

Sleep at 'Camp Nowhere' was so deep I didn't hear the solitary elk that must have visited during the night. I was probably dreaming of a sun-dappled Apennine beech wood when it passed just six feet from the tent. Dawn revealed massive hoofprints in the snow that hadn't been there the evening before.

The third day in the snow was even harder. Harder because my body had little left to give; harder because the sun came out and the snow softened even further; harder because conditions convinced me I wasn't physically capable of enduring the high-level good-style route I wanted; and harder most of all because discovering that I came up short wasn't an easy thing to live with.

And I *had* come up short—of that I had no doubt. From The Walk's start I'd truly believed that I was someone who could keep moving forward no matter the terrain, someone who—when it came down to it—could face the wild without fear.

I'd come to Norway wanting nature to put me in my place, and I'd believed with all my heart that it would be a place of belonging. The idea that I belonged within nature was the fundamental belief that had underpinned the entire journey. And I'd found belonging. I'd found it in a great range of different environments. But nature had now shown me that belonging only went so far.

As I turned east toward the nearest valley, not north and onward into the wild, my anxiety diminished. I wasn't heading toward more toil, but toward manageable travel. Perhaps because of this, and perhaps also because I could now see where I was going, the wild felt friendlier. Under clear skies, smooth white fjells rolled away to a boundless horizon. I stared in awe as I toiled, wonderstruck by Norway's scale. *At least I have this*, I thought. *At least I'm here now.* And in any case, it was only a short-term tactical withdrawal. I'd return to the high fjells soon enough, when they once again blocked the way.

Although not too soon, I hoped.

Late in the afternoon, heavy with tiredness, I finally reached snowline. The twisting Setesdal valley appeared below: a granite-walled, flat-bottomed, snow-free corridor. I continued toward it, stepping off the snow. The earth underfoot supported my feet. It was reliable, familiar, living. It was where I belonged.

CHASING SPRING
Chapter 4

OF ALL NORWAY'S landscapes, the most famous are its fjords. Deep and narrow, carved by glaciers, hemmed between mountain walls, the fjords offer a rare kind of scenery that is genuinely and unarguably breathtaking.

The Setesdal provided the first taste of fjord scenery—albeit without an actual fjord. In place of saltwater the Setesdal offered a flat valley floor. It was patchworked with fields and forests, with small farms and settlements, and with a broad, meandering river, but the effect was the same as though a fjord were there—scenic drama to drop the jaw. With 2,000-foot granite slabs rearing abruptly to snow-covered peaks, and neck-craning views around every turn, it wasn't merely the most impressive valley I'd visited since the Alps; it was the most impressive valley I'd visited on the entire journey. Or so it felt as I strode through it.

The Setesdal twists north for ninety miles, running from the village of Evje towards the Hardangervidda plateau. Where I joined the valley it was rural, but the wild never felt far away. It was constantly in sight, always accessible via a quick sideways step into a forest. The cultivated land was a narrow ribbon—and all the more beautiful for it. After everything I'd been through, the Setesdal was exactly what I needed. It was Norway on a manageable scale. For the next five days it offered a snow-free route north.

My first stop was the small community of Ose where I found a food shop-cum-restaurant-cum-bar. I eased myself onto a stool and ordered a platter of fish and chips. An amiable, talkative local wandered over and eased down beside me. He avoided small talk, went straight to local facts.

'Lynx,' he told me. 'We have a lot of lynx here. Look…'

The man was in his late fifties. He was pale and balding, with a large belly that tsunamied over his belt, which made him the least-fit looking Norwegian I'd so far met. He reached up to a shelf and pulled down a dog-eared photo album. It contained numerous images of camouflage-clad hunters standing beside recently deceased lynx.

'Two hundred sheep a year,' he explained. 'That's how many they kill. We have to keep them in check. And we have bears here now, more every year. Some of them are huge—two hundred and fifty kilograms. They kill sheep too. They're becoming a problem.'

By this point, my mouth was too full of food to respond, which was probably just as well. But the man didn't care. Impressing visitors with dramatic information was his task, and he was fully committed to it.

'Many of our glaciers are advancing,' he announced. 'They have been for seven years. No other mountains in Europe can offer that.'

This fact *did* impress me, and I hoped it were true. Let all the glaciers advance! I'd get to see for myself soon enough.

The man—Tomas—finally moved beyond hyperbole. He told me that he had been born in the Setesdal on a small farm, back when Norway was a 'quieter and bigger place'. Opportunities for work had been limited in his youth, so he'd done what his Viking ancestors had done 1,000 years earlier: he'd left home for the North Sea.

'I worked on an oil rig. Forty days on, forty off. It was hard manual work in appalling weather… but I could never have earned the same wage back on the farm. North Sea oil changed my life.'

North Sea oil had changed Norway, too. Discovered in 1969, petroleum and natural gas brought the kind of wealth to Norway that Vikings could never have dreamed of. Within a few years, Norway went from being an average nation with an average standard of living to an uncommonly rich nation with a standard of living few other countries could match. There was irony in it, of course, that a country which took such great care of its own local environment should found its wealth on an industry that polluted the entire planet, but perhaps there was precedent. After all, the Norwegian raiders who descended so savagely upon Lindisfarne in 793, kicking off the Viking Age, hadn't worried about the damage they were causing overseas.

So long as they brought wealth home.

For his part, Tomas looked as though he'd benefited rather too well from Norway's wealth. Ironically, he wasn't impressed by the fitness of his neighbours, either.

'People here don't ski anymore,' he lamented. 'They all own skidoos. They've all become so unfit. Winter used to be peaceful, with folk quietly touring on skis, but now there's always a skidoo roaring and whining somewhere. And to think, we pretty much invented skiing.'

Which wasn't far off the truth. Although archaeological evidence suggests that people in China were skiing as early as 10,000 BCE, there's little argument that Scandinavians refined the pursuit. For thousands of years people skied during Norway's long winters simply to get about, but everything changed in the mid-1800s when a farmer from the Telemark region saw that skiing could be so much more than shuffling around on planks. Neglecting his agricultural duties, the farmer—Sondre Norheim —put all his energy into redesigning the ski, and then 'playing' on it. He introduced new bindings, experimented with shorter lengths, reshaped the ski, included jumps and slaloms while out skiing, and ultimately won people over with his unmatched mastery over snow. Norheim lived in Morgedal, a valley forty-five miles north-east of Setesdal, and it was from there that modern skiing spread to the world.

'Not that people would be skiing this late in April,' Tomas continued. 'March is prime ski season, early April if spring holds off, but once spring hits… well… you can't ski.'

'Or snowshoe?' I asked.

Tomas grimaced. 'You'll be alright up on the Hardangervidda. Spring comes late up there. The snow doesn't usually melt until July.'

Which wasn't what I wanted to hear.

———

I followed the Setesdal north, hunting for signs of spring. I'd been on the hunt since February, and there *had* been signs, but the trouble was I kept leaving them behind. Even though I was only moving north at three miles an hour, spring hadn't been able to keep up. Here, tree buds weren't open and the valley floor was still winter-yellow. Spring growth hadn't begun.

But there *were* signs, for those paying attention, which I most certainly was. The snow had thawed from the valley floor, rivers were swollen, waterfalls were cascading, and rocks were tumbling from above as ice released them. From a campsite I named 'Raining Rocks' I listened in awe to volley after volley of crashing rock. The thunder of it rumbled across the valley, echoing from wall to wall. It was easy to imagine why people had once believed in trolls.

There were signs of spring in emerging insect life; in spiders and foraging wood ants that visited camp, as well as in the first mosquitoes. The first Norwegian *mygg*—and what a misleadingly small and innocuous name is *mygg*—was twice the size of a typical Apennine mosquito. It was armed with an oversized needle, and it homed in with a deep, menacing drone. I quickly repelled it, but it brought to mind the trillions destined to emerge up on the wet Norwegian tundra. If they were all this big, summer wasn't going to be quite as pleasant as I'd hoped.

There were further signs of spring in the lengthening days. The sun now rose before I did, and set after I'd gone to sleep. It was shining now, raising the temperature into the upper fifties—and that was the surest sign of spring of all. The warmth felt so gloriously unfamiliar on my face and arms that I abandoned forward momentum for several hours and basked like a marmot upon a sun-warmed granite slab, shirtless for the first time since September. Sighing away my cares, I relaxed as I hadn't been able to in seven months. After a long winter, feeling the sun's warmth sink deep and banish the cold and damp was indescribable.

When I bimbled leisurely on I felt like a new man on a new journey. Life suddenly seemed easier. A short way on, a farmer stopped his vehicle to offer a ride. A few minutes later, a van driver did the same. A family I passed mid-afternoon called out from their home as I ambled by, wondering if I wanted a bed for the night. I was sorely tempted, but the Setesdal was too magical—sleeping *inside* would have been a waste. Happily, the open-hearted family understood. They sent me on my way with a bag of fruit and a cheerful wish for a '*god tur*'.

'Touring' on, I recalled the Mezzogiorno where I could have done with such unsought kindness. Back there, I'd wanted to prove that I could stand on my own two feet. I hadn't sought help, and for the most part help hadn't come. Here, where I no longer needed it, help was regularly offered. For making it this far, for everything endured, I felt as though I was finally reaping the reward. The designation—The Prize—felt more apt with each step.

Norway, I was coming to see, was The Place—the land I'd been searching for all along, even with its impossible-to-cross uplands. It wasn't only the quality and extent of the wild, or the *friluftsliv* lifestyle, or the kindness of its people, or the evident prosperity of a functioning society. There was something else too, something deeper and even more appealing.

I mulled over it for the rest of the day and then, while resting in camp in late evening twilight, the answer finally came.

It was *balance*—that was the thing. Norway had balance. There was balance in the way people approached one another, with quiet respect at first, hospitality later. There was balance in the way rural Norwegians appeared perfectly capable of looking after themselves, but didn't hesitate to step forward and offer help to others. Most of all there was balance in the way the modern human world seemed to nestle into the natural world without subjugating or destroying it. Homes and farms didn't sit *on* the land—they sat *in* it. Their turf roofs and wooden walls had been constructed in humble sympathy, not in dominating arrogance. Developed land existed in perfect proportion to land *un*developed. One could find civilisation while crossing Norway, but not too much of it. Whether by accident or design, civilisation and the wild seemed to coexist in Norway without either being diminished.

This balance was a joy to behold. It suggested that humanity *was* capable of sharing the planet, not just exploiting it. Obviously, balance with nature was far easier to achieve here than in a crowded city. But that didn't mean it was impossible elsewhere. All it would take was a shift in outlook. We could welcome nature instead of chasing it away. We could let it fill in the gaps, give it opportunities: rooftop wildflower meadows, green walls, wild margins, more trees, more nesting sites, more ponds, less concrete. Norway's balance demonstrated that civilisation and the wild didn't have to be mutually exclusive.

The following morning, Norway's balance showed up in the weather: steady rain to counter the previous day's sun. Mist drifted about the mountains; raindrops speckled the river; waterfalls streamed down crags that had previously been dry. The conditions made the Setesdal's ribbon of civilisation appear narrower and the surrounding fjells wilder, and the change thrilled me; it was like travelling through an entirely different landscape.

The River Otra speckled by rain, Setesdal, April 28, 1998.

Kept dry by my waterproofs, and maintaining a slow pace to avoid sweating, I found myself comparing the Setesdal with rural valleys in the southern Apennines. The Setesdal had the same tranquillity, but it balanced the Mezzogiorno's dryness with dampness, its spikiness with softness, its heat with coolness. Here, there was no roadside trash, no farmland given over to brambly jungle, no roaming packs of flea-bitten dogs. The surrounding forests were accessible, not closed off like the *sottobosco*; and they offered unlimited scope for outdoor living, with water a-plenty and soft mulchy earth to sleep upon. I'd fallen in love with the Apennines, but there was no doubt the Setesdal better met my needs.

Farmland and forest, civilisation and wildness, sunshine and rain: the balanced valley offered it all. London's suburbs were where I'd come from, but I found myself thinking that I wouldn't have minded coming from here.

May 1 arrived. The Walk became one year old.

Walking was now my life. It was what I did, it was who I was, it was what I'd been doing for twelve full months, and it was what I'd be doing for the foreseeable future. Forget running out of funds, or reaching the North Cape—I couldn't imagine ever stopping. This unshackled life was all there was to existence. Waking to birdsong, to the symphony of a rushing river, to wind whispering through trees; packing up and moving gently on, the day ahead a blank slate; immersing myself within intimate details and epic panoramas; thinking small thoughts about basic needs and grand ideas about life's ultimate meanings; being surprised by every twist and turn, forever finding out what lay ahead; choosing yet another site in a million for camp, then whiling away evening hours just looking, just being: this was my life. It was simple and complex, filled with motion and stillness, a thing of introspection and infinite expansiveness. Gratitude for everything The Walk had become washed through me.

As with May 1 a year earlier, the day began with sunshine—but finished with rain and fog. And as with the start, I began by knowing where I was—but finished with only a vague idea. This time, though, not knowing didn't matter. My Setesdal detour had merely taken me east of all my detailed maps, but I'd return to them in due course. And in any case, I could still *see* and *feel* where I was, and that was *here*, in a mountain kingdom beyond compare.

It was as the wise Calabrian shepherd had once said when I'd wanted to know where we were: 'We are here.' He'd pushed aside my map, gesturing around at the surrounding landscape instead. I hadn't seen the wisdom at the time, but I did now.

I was here. And here was everything. It was why so many places now felt like the Best Place Ever.

The rain and fog didn't dampen the anniversary. It was balance again, the quality I'd come to cherish. I even cherished the rain when it teased me—ceasing when I pulled on waterproofs, resuming when I took them off. This was merely the mountain gods' way of keeping me in my place. Not that I could forget my place now, not after my struggle in the snow. Because of it, I knew who I really was. The high fjells had revealed the truth. You can't hide from yourself in certain wild places, or be what you're not, or achieve the unachievable. Dreams and fantasies count for little. Self-delusions are soon shattered. Walk alone into mountains like Norway's in early spring and you'll eventually come face to face with yourself, and you'll likely become a humbler person for it.

Humbler, and better balanced. The Setesdal wasn't where I'd planned to be, but I'd benefited from it. It had broadened my perspective on Norway, on myself, on life. What had begun with disappointment—that I wasn't capable of following a high-level route—had given way to acceptance, and finally appreciation. Back on the fjells I'd learnt some fundamental truths about who I was and, more importantly, who I wasn't. In the days since, I'd realised that I could torment myself because of those truths—wishing I'd been strong enough to keep slogging away up high—or I could embrace them and move on. Once again it was all about *balance*. Yes, I was here for wild mountains, but it didn't have to be *all* mountains. There was as much to be gained beneath them as there was atop them. That Mad Mountain Jack could even think such a sacrilegious thought revealed how far I'd come.

The one-year anniversary passed in laughter, at my own choices mostly, especially my choice for camp. At day's end I trudged far into the wild to find a suitable anniversary site when I could easily have camped near the road. I'd reached the northern end of the Setesdal, and snow once again buried the landscape. Crossing it was as taxing as ever. Soon wet, soon fatigued, I ridiculed myself for choosing to walk miles further than necessary. But such pointless miles were appropriate for the anniversary— they were symbolic of The Walk as a whole.

In truth, The Walk wasn't a necessity. Even I could see that. To an observer, it probably looked worse than merely unnecessary—it probably resembled an excessive amount of suffering for no obvious gain. It could even be called an exercise in futility, and I laughed at the idea of it. *Yes*, I thought in delight as I snowshoed through sloppy snow that I didn't have to snowshoe through, *that's what I'm doing. I'm engaged in a magnificent exercise in futility. And I'm loving every ludicrous step of it!*

I set up camp upon the only snow-free ground for miles: a stony spur above a tumultuous river. The location was soul-stirringly wild, although not ideal for practical reasons. Tent pegs barely dented the ground, and large water drops fell from pine trees overhead, shaken loose with each gust of wind. Rain was soon falling too, and I considered delaying camp, waiting for the shower to pass, but decided to begin, convinced the rain was set for the night. For once, I struggled to pitch Auld Leakie. Poles refused to slide into sleeves that normally welcomed them, pegs bent, and before long the tent was soaked outside and in. Anyone watching would have thought I'd never set up camp before, and I couldn't resist laughing at my ineptitude. *A year underway, and still Mad Jack can't pitch a tent!* Success came eventually, just as the rain stopped, which prompted the day's loudest laugh of all. I should have waited!

The Walk wasn't ever going to let me have it easy—and it was better for it.

Camp two days later made up for it; balance, yet again. Instead of stony ground I had a springy mattress of peat and wild grass; instead of an exposed spur I had shelter beside a granite knoll; instead of rain I had clear skies and a wide panorama across mountain after mountain.

It was sheer bloody perfection, and I sat back and wallowed in it.

I'd returned to the high fjells, to the southern edge of the immense Hardangervidda. Rising above camp were 5,000-foot mountains with wild-sounding Norse names: Haukelifjell, Stavsnuten, Sveigen. Snow still buried their flanks, but spring had opened small patches of ground beneath them, precious spots like the one I'd chosen for the 'Mountain Mattress' camp. A mile away, a road cut over the plateau, but it was out of sight, sound, and entirely out of mind. There was barely any traffic at this time of year anyway. All I could hear was wind playing over rocks, a nearby stream gurgling softly, and occasional croaks from ptarmigan. And all I could see was a snowy mountain kingdom glowing with golden evening sunlight.

I was ready for the fjells again, recharged after the week of easy walking. I possessed a new mindset—and more realistic expectations. Weeks crossing snow were probably beyond my capabilities, but I hoped I could manage two days. I wanted to head west and reach Norway's fjords, and two mountains barred my way. Road tunnels passed beneath both, but a route across the tops looked possible. I was ready to give it my best shot.

I began early the following morning, long before sunlight lit the valley. With snowshoes strapped in place I turned uphill—and made a wonderful discovery. Expecting the 'quicksand snow' I'd encountered just days earlier I found 'concrete snow' instead: snow that had frozen solid overnight. I grinned, scarcely able to believe my good fortune. Feeling only the smallest

Back in the fjells, May 4, 1998.

stirring of anxiety I pushed up a silent valley rimmed by dark crags, aiming for a high pass. Clear evidence of recent avalanches fanned steep slopes either side, and threatening cornices hung overhead, but everything appeared to be locked in place by the short night's freeze. I moved steadily, not wasting time, but not rushing either. Being back in the fjells was a dream come true, and also a vindication. I'd shown respect to the fjells a week earlier by retreating, and this gift of easy passage felt like respect repaid.

The snow softened once sunlight hit, and the snowshoes were soon essential, but I made it across the pass before conditions became dangerous. Soon, I was beneath snowline again, following a trail—an actual mountain trail, the first in many moons—downhill through a tantalisingly familiar landscape of rocks, heather, rushing streams and drystone walls. For a few miles, I could have been back in England, descending from a Pennine fell. I even had familiar British weather: grey skies and a squall of stinging hail. The twenty-mile day finished in a plunging U-shaped valley, at the village of Røldal, in an empty campsite near Røldal's stave church. A hint of green edged the trees and the subtlest scent of blossom hung in the air, thrilling suggestions that the long hunt for spring was almost at its end.

210

Røldal was the perfect place for a day off, and I didn't skip the opportunity. The following morning I slept straight through until noon.

———

May 6—the walk's 371st day—finally delivered what I'd so long been waiting for. Few days have been more memorable.

It began with the longest sustained climb since the Austrian Alps—a 3,000-foot haul into the mountains of the Røldalsfjellet. Dawn came with alpine clarity, with intense blue skies and air crisp and sharp. Dew beaded every pine needle, every stem of grass. By the time I'd climbed above tree line the day was heating fast, and I did something I hadn't been able to do since early October: I changed into shorts. Walking bare legged was such a small thing, but after all I'd been through it felt momentous.

With my trusty Excalibur in hand I switchbacked uphill. An ever-expanding panorama had me feeling I could fly, but I held myself in check, conserving energy for the mountains ahead. A narrow pass cut through them, but I didn't like the look of the heavily burdened cornices that hung above it. Plus, today wasn't a day for passes. It was a day for summits!

When I reached snowline I strapped on snowshoes and the real work began. Soon, sweat was flowing, my sunglasses steamed over, and my muscles strained. But I kept on climbing until the angle eased and the entire world opened wide.

Whoa, I thought, coming to an abrupt halt. *Whoa!* I stared around in surprise. *Was the world really this big?*

The summit I'd reached was only 4,511 feet above sea level. It was a minor summit, similar to thousands across Norway, entirely modest by the numbers, but the view wasn't modest—it stretched immodestly in every direction. It offered none of the spikiness of the Alps, none of the forested variety of the Apennines, but it was immense: a vast white expanse that rolled away without apparent end. Most eye-catching was a massive white dome fifteen miles north: the Folgefonna ice cap, known as the White Maiden of Hardanger—at eighty square miles the third-largest ice cap in Norway. Seductively unblemished, it shone with startling brightness, looking unworldly and untouchable. There, indeed, was the *other* Europe—a wilderness that put the human animal firmly in its place.

The mountains of Norway have a different *feel* to mountains elsewhere in Europe. Part of this is down to the moist climate and soft northern light —and to the atmosphere of mystery this creates. Part is due to the eroded appearance of the mountains, to a powerful ambience of unimaginable age, to an awareness that what had been Himalayan in height 450 million years ago has since been worn down to this. But the biggest difference comes from knowing that the mountains haven't been overrun by people. Look across the Alps, Apennines or Pyrenees and you'll know there are thousands of people among them. But look across Norway and you'll know that people are spread thin. This makes all the difference in the world.

I stared at the view for a long while, captivated by the emptiness. For all I could tell, I was the only person left on the planet. But eventually the urge to make progress won out. According to my map, the best route lay north-west—five miles across an undulating plateau. The distance was short compared with the uplands I'd retreated from ten days earlier, and nothing compared to the Hardangervidda I'd have to cross in a few days, but I still felt a burst of anxiety. *Would I fail again?*

Energised by the views, I set out, determined to succeed. As before, hidden lakes studded the plateau, and I proceeded with caution, weaving around all flat areas, leaving behind a snaking trail that looked like the wanderings of a drunkard. Clouds were now building upon surrounding fjells, growing in the warm air into dark-bellied cumulonimbus, threatening the kind of electrical weather I hadn't experienced since the Apennines. But oddly, there were no clouds above my plateau, as though the mountain gods were granting me safe passage. It was uncanny how good conditions were. I whispered my heartfelt thanks.

The snow was soft, but far more supportive than it had previously been. My snowshoes only sank six inches. Progress was steady, although by no means easy. But I relished the effort—the sensation of muscles working and sweat flowing, of lungs expanding and heart pounding. And I began to relish the situation even more. Here I finally was, doing exactly what I'd come to Norway to do, walking alone across the country's high fjells. Before long, elation replaced anxiety. I stared around as I walked, still awestruck by Norway's immense space. I thought about how far I'd come. *You've earned this*, I told myself. *A year of effort, and this is the pay-off.* There was nowhere else in the world I would rather have been.

My weaving snowshoe tracks across the Røldalsfjellet, May 6, 1998.

I felt as if Norway's high places had been unlocked. *If I can cross this mountain, why not every mountain?* All things suddenly seemed possible.

The miles passed, too swiftly by the end. When I reached the plateau's far side I was tempted to turn about, retrace my steps, and enjoy the plateau all over again. Ahead now were plunging snow slopes, treacherously steep, but I only paused long enough to remove my snowshoes. The steep snow was perfect for kicking steps, and although a slip would have been catastrophic I proceeded down gullies, ramps and between crags with confidence, high on life from the elevating traverse above. It was only when safely down and staring back at what I'd just descended that I felt any doubt. But by then it didn't matter—it was all behind. I felt childishly proud of myself for successfully negotiating such difficult terrain.

Now back beneath snowline, the solid earth gave me a burst of energy. I paced down a deepening valley, the Oddadalen, with a broad grin spreading across my face. I strode beneath walls of rock, past foaming waterfalls, heading toward sea level—an altitude I'd not visited since Lindesnes eighteen days earlier. And when finally I reached it after twenty-four miles of effort I stopped abruptly, rubbed my eyes with disbelief, and then began laughing and twirling like a man who'd just found water in the desert after endless days of desperate heat and thirst.

Everything had changed!

Trees were in full leaf. Bracken fronds had unfurled. Rejuvenating scents of blossom filled the air, wildflowers decorated the ground, and the grass was long, lush and *outrageously* green. I'd barely seen a flower, leaf or green blade of grass in eight months. Since last I'd been at sea level an explosion of growth had occurred. I'd stepped straight from a plateau buried in snow into full-on spring, and the intensity of so much growth and new life was almost an affront to the senses. Was such a green even possible? Surely my eyes were playing tricks!

Forgetting myself entirely, I rejoiced in the spring as only someone who has lived outside all winter can.

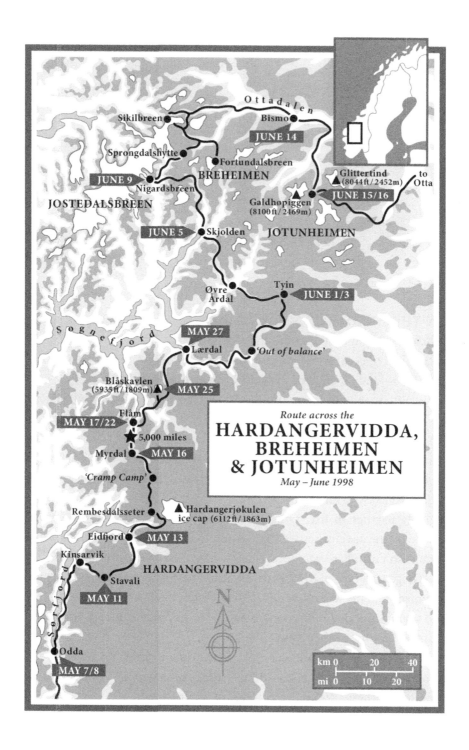

Sikilbreen

Bismo

Ottadalen

JUNE 14

Sprongdalshytte

Fortundalsbreen

Glittertind
(8044ft / 2452m)

to Otta

JUNE 9

BREHEIMEN

Nigardsbreen

JUNE 15/16

JOSTEDALSBREEN

Galdhøpiggen
(8100ft / 2469m)

JUNE 5

Skjolden

JOTUNHEIMEN

Øvre
Årdal

Tyin

JUNE 1/3

S o g n e f j o r d

MAY 27

Lærdal

'Out of balance'

Blåskavlen
(5935ft / 1809m)

MAY 25

Flåm

MAY 17/22

5,000 miles

Myrdal

MAY 16

'Cramp Camp'

Rembesdalsseter

Hardangerjøkulen
ice cap (6112ft / 1863m)

Eidfjord

MAY 13

Kinsarvik

HARDANGERVIDDA

Stavali

MAY 11

S ø r f j o r d

Odda

MAY 7/8

Route across the
**HARDANGERVIDDA,
BREHEIMEN
& JOTUNHEIMEN**
May – June 1998

N

km 0   20   40
mi 0   10   20

215

THE HARDANGERVIDDA
Chapter 5

ON THE SHORE of the Sørfjord, beneath the immense Hardangervidda plateau, I met my first fellow tourists since September, and I regarded them with mild concern. For eight months I'd been the only visitor—so far as I could tell—and I'd enjoyed my status, especially when locals reacted with hospitality as though I were unique. Would the hospitality continue once I was just another face in a sea of passing faces?

The first tourist was a New Zealander, Greg, a cheerful, straw-haired man about my age. He was weaving north in a rusty car of considerable vintage, and strapped to its roof was a battered kayak that looked as though it had argued with far too many mid-river rocks.

'My partner in life,' Greg joked, affectionately thumping his boat. 'Shared some adventures we have. And bloody useful to have in Norway. It rains so much here you never know when a boat'll come in handy!'

Greg was a typical Kiwi, easy-going and positively determined to laugh at himself and the world. He hoped to reach the North Cape in three weeks, and spend time 'paddling round beneath the midnight sun', but was aware that fate may have other ideas.

'This old car of mine is crook. Every time it starts up it's a bloody miracle. But it wouldn't matter if I got stuck in the boonies. Wherever you are out here there's some sweet stretch of water to paddle.'

Exploring Norway by water was an entirely different way of experiencing the country, and the idea appealed. It made me wonder if I was missing out by travelling only on foot. But Greg didn't give me time to consider it for long. 'Here, mate,' he said, delving into his car's boot, 'want a stubbie?'

A stubbie, it turned out, was a beer, and I downed two over the next hour. Greg soon had me bent over in silent laughter, telling the kind of self-detrimental stories most people keep back solely for close friends.

'You know, you might want to tramp across New Zealand next,' he observed finally, 'when you're done here. I reckon you must be several coals short of a full barbie to be doing what you're doing. You'd fit right in!'

The second tourist, a fit-looking cyclist from Munich, had a very different approach. He was riding from Bavaria to the top of Norway and back, and doing it as swiftly he could.

'My shortest day was one hundred kilometres,' he told me, 'but that was into a headwind. Usually I ride twice that.' In a hurry, he wasn't keen to stop for long, but he had enough time spare to disparage my ultimate destination.

'You are going to Nordkapp?' he asked. 'That place is for *tourists*. I am going somewhere far better...' And away he rode toward it in haste, not letting on where it was. But I didn't mind. North Cape was good enough for me, and reaching it as quickly as possible was definitely not the point.

I took a day off near Odda, a town at the head of the Sørfjord. It was an unexpectedly industrial place. A hundred years earlier, Odda had been one of Norway's most-visited tourist destinations, but the tourists began staying away when hydropower plants and smelters were built above and even within the town. Odda's fjord-head location was spectacular, but the factories looked dismal to my eyes, and the industrial hum emanating from them all night disturbed my dreams. I felt disheartened that Norway wasn't entirely immune from heavy industry. Thousands of locals might have gained employment over the decades, but the cost was high. Despite its incredible beauty, the Sørfjord has become one of the most polluted fjords in the world.

From Odda's post office I collected my latest resupply parcel and a stack of mail, redirected from a town further south. Sauda had been the original collection point, but my ever-evolving route had taken me far from it. Back in Italy, this would have meant never seeing my post again, but such logistical hiccups were easily overcome in Norway.

'Yes... our Sauda office will forward your post,' a clerk in Røldal's post office had assured me three days earlier. 'Do not worry—it will reach Odda before you.' Unlike the postal officials back in the Mezzogiorno, it was almost as though he wanted me to receive my mail. How strange!

From Odda, I walked north beside the Sørfjord, and soon the landscape on display became the Norway from travel brochures. Down at fjordside the land was green and beguilingly pleasant. There were apple and cherry orchards filled with trees softened by white and pink blossom. There were fields of lush grass being grazed by hundreds of sheep, small wooden farmhouses looking spick and span, and even small vineyards that might have been plucked straight from Tuscany. Tanned farmers worked in rolled-up sleeves, and flowers grew en masse along uncut banks. The feeling was pastoral and wonderfully southern. If I hadn't known better, I would have guessed I was beside the Mediterranean Sea, not a Norwegian fjord.

The orchards and vineyards clung to a narrow strip of land directly beside the fjord, but above them the environment looked more appropriately northern. Where cultivation ended pine forests began, and they continued steeply uphill toward a world of eternal snow. The Sørfjord is twenty-three miles long and rarely more than a mile and half wide, and the mountains rearing from it don't waste time gaining 5,000 feet of altitude. As I continued north, I gazed with appreciation at the precipitous topography, enjoying the contrast between the tamed and untamed environments. It was Norwegian balance again, and as far as I was concerned it was perfect. *The Best Place Ever*, I thought, mocking myself for thinking it yet again.

Every so often, the Folgefonna ice cap came into view far above, looking as unblemished as ever. I'd seen an especially impressive view south of Odda, where a crevassed tongue of ice plunged rudely into a side valley, the Buardalen. Information gathered in Odda confirmed that this outlet glacier, the Buarbreen, was advancing, just as the talkative Setesdal local had claimed. The Folgefonna receives some of the heaviest precipitation in Norway, an estimated 196 inches a year at the ice cap's south-western corner—an incredible sixteen feet of water. Although the Folgefonna's outlet glaciers had been in retreat since the Little Ice Age of the 1700s, heavier than normal snowfalls in the early 1980s had reversed the trend. By my visit, the sheer mass of snow pressing on the ice cap was pushing outlet glaciers back into the valleys. Measurements from aerial photos taken in 1959 and 1997 revealed that the Buarbreen had advanced 360 feet. Another outlet glacier on the Folgefonna's southern side had gained

Blustery day along the Sørfjord, May 10, 1998.

almost 600. Impressive as these advances were, they didn't match the gains made by glaciers further north. The Briksdalsbreen, an outlet arm of mainland Norway's greatest ice cap, the Jostedalsbreen, had surged 1,056 feet in five years—on average more than half a foot a day. The knowledge that Norway was bucking the global trend of glacial retreat made my day.[4]

Despite blustery weather, I took my time walking alongside the Sørfjord. Sometimes on the quiet main road close to water's edge, more often up on hillside tracks, I weaved north. There were many pauses. I lost time to photography, waiting for sunlight to fall exactly where I wanted, and I spent hours sitting, savouring the location. The southern ambiance and the green flush of spring were too soothing to rush, but I reached the northern end of the fjord eventually, and late on May 10 camped near the small village of Kinsarvik. My site overlooked the Hardangerfjord, a fjord famous for its snow-white spring blossoms. But all I could think about now were the snow-white fjells above. My chosen route led away from sea level and uphill into one of Europe's greatest wild places: the Hardangervidda.

---

4. Since the year 2000, however, the advances have ceased, and ever-warmer summers have begun melting Norway's glaciers faster than at any time in recorded history.

The Hardangervidda is Europe's largest mountain plateau. Covering 2,500 square miles, the vidda is a great expanse of rolling tundra and high fjell, pretty much all above tree line. The Hardangervidda is high and wet enough to hold several glaciers, among them the Hardangerjøkulen ice cap —at twenty-eight square miles the sixth largest in Norway, and at 6,112 feet the highest summit above the plateau.

The vidda's cold upland climate provides a suitable environment for many animal and plant species rarely found further south, such as Arctic foxes, as well as a creature that once roamed much of northern Europe: reindeer. Norway's largest herd of wild reindeer—an estimated 15,000 at the time of my visit—live upon the vidda. Every year they migrate east to west across the plateau, heading from winter grazing lands to higher-altitude calving grounds. Much of the plateau is enveloped within the borders of the Hardangervidda National Park, Norway's largest national park, and the reindeer are carefully protected. According to a lady in Kinsarvik's tourist office, if I wanted to see reindeer living as nature intended, and if I wanted to experience 'Old Norway'—the Norway from thousands of years past—the Hardangervidda was the place to be. 'Up there,' she explained, 'it's impossible to miss them. Especially on the route you're following. You'll see hundreds.'

Despite feeling that I'd unlocked the fjells with my traverse of the Røldalsfjellet, I still felt nervous. Instead of a plateau crossable in two hours, the Hardangervidda could potentially require a full week's toil. Aside from one solitary road there was nothing up there but snow, lakes, rivers, and more snow. Travel would be open to the elements the entire way, and it would be physically draining, even in ideal conditions. Under a deep spring snowpack, it wasn't a wilderness I could take lightly.

To make the crossing manageable I decided to break it into two stages. The first would take me onto the plateau for three days, but then off it again and back down to sea level at Eidfjord. The second stage would be longer: it would lead past the Hardangerjøkulen and then north-west into a formidably vast mountain wilderness. It was exactly the kind of challenge and environment I'd come to Norway for, and I couldn't wait to get to grips with it, but I still suffered doubts. The Røldalsfjellet had shown me what was possible, but so had the soggy Setesdal fjells. Would I find firm snow, or soft; would I struggle, or find elation?

Wild scenery in the Husedalen, May 11, 1998.

On the morning of May 11 I left Kinsarvik and tramped up a deep valley, the Husedalen. Within two miles, the orchards fell behind, as did the colours and scents of spring. A narrow path twisted up the valley through birch woods, still un-leafed and skeletal, and into the upper Husedalen. It was a stark, glacier-scratched place of dark slabs, sparse vegetation and rushing water. Snowmelt gushed from the mountains, and the Kinso River in the valley's centre was swollen and foaming, plunging over several water-falls. The largest of them—the Søtefossen—soon appeared ahead, falling over slabs into a cauldron of spray. As a gateway to the Hardangervidda, the Husedalen was thrillingly theatrical.

Climbing steeply, I came across a small red T painted onto a prominent rock: my first Den Norske Turistforening waymark. The splash of paint looked garish and intrusive, but it did help to identify the route. Over the following weeks, the waymarks would become a familiar sight, and I soon got over my initial reaction. The Ts were insignificant in such an immense landscape, and later, on foul-weather days of slanting rain and thick fog, they became reassuring navigational aids. After the trip was done, I'd only need to look at a picture of a red T painted onto a lonely rock to find myself transported to Norway, to feel my pulse raised once again by the prospect of following a path into wild northern fjells.

On this first encounter, I leapfrogged upward from T to T, spending more time on bare rock than the official trail. Snow streaked the mountain above 2,000 feet, but through devious rocky detours I avoided it, until reaching 3,000 feet. Above that, drifts barred the way, and after sinking thigh-deep into the first I accepted that snowshoes were needed once again.

In sunshine and squally showers I snowshoed across a minor pass. A broad snowfield lay below it, but beyond that the landscape was neither snow-covered nor snow-free—it was striped like a zebra, half brown, half white. Snowshoes were necessary for the drifts, but awkward for snow-free ground, and potentially damaging to vegetation. For the rest of the day I spent as much time stooped over, fastening and unfastening snowshoe straps, as I did actually making progress.

Following the Ts I descended to a river and found it running high and fast with snowmelt. My map showed a bridge, but like many mountain footbridges in Norway it had been deconstructed for the winter and sat unhelpfully on the far bank. A careful fording followed, with powerful water above my knees. Spring travel in Norway, I was coming to see, was neither fast nor straightforward. But at least I had my first DNT hut to look forward to—the Stavali Hut. An affordable night indoors? A simple rustic cabin? A wood-burning stove to sit beside? What more could a homeless mountain vagabond want?

The DNT offers three levels of huts. First, there are large, fully staffed lodges similar to Alpine refuges, many with electricity, showers, restaurants and saunas. Next, there are unstaffed self-service cabins equipped with everything visitors need for cooking and sleeping, including pantries stocked with food. Finally, there are small no-service cabins that don't offer provisions. Users of all the unstaffed huts are asked to leave payment behind for their stay and for any food they've taken—a system of trust that says everything that needs to be said about the kind of place Norway is.

The Stavali belonged to the self-service category of hut. It was a three-storey wooden lodge painted rust red, and I approached it with excitement, even happier for shelter now that a snowstorm was nipping at my heels. I pulled out my treasured DNT key and opened my first hut door. After removing my boots I explored the spacious interior, and was instantly impressed by the cleanliness, and by the large number of bunks on offer: sixty-two all told. The only thing lacking was ambience. The air inside was cold and stale, and the empty rooms gave the hut an abandoned feel. It wasn't the rustic little cabin I'd imagined, but I wasn't about to complain. I settled happily in.

A cold wind howled all night, testing the sturdiness of the hut's walls. At 2 a.m. the front door blew open with a crash and several doors within the hut slammed shut. I sprung bolt upright in bed. Feeling childishly spooked, I padded down dark corridors and relatched the front door. I wasn't used to being alone in a large empty building. I wasn't even used to being indoors. It felt unnatural.

The morning made up for it. Packing Ten Ton was significantly easier than usual with no tent to fold away and no wetness or cold to fight. And outside it *was* cold. After sweeping the hut clean and depositing my payment I stepped outdoors into icy conditions. Puddles were glassed over, frost sparkled on rocks, and an unclouded sky domed over the blinding-white Hardangervidda. I set out with a howl of joy, thankful beyond expression to have received such an astoundingly perfect day.

Conditions, I soon discovered, were even better than I'd realised. They were better, even, than the Røldalsfjellet had been. The plateau above Stavali was completely snow-covered, but the snow had frozen solid overnight, and it remained frozen the entire day. Snowshoes weren't needed, and I strode into the heart of the vidda without struggle. Enjoying every step, I covered mile after snowy mile, and eventually reached a place so remote and snowbound it was hard to imagine that orchard-lined fjords existed anywhere, let alone ten miles away. The snowy plateau rolled away in all directions, and I celebrated my incredible situation with every easily taken step. *This* was the Norway I'd dreamt of.

According to the map, a trail crossed the vidda in roughly the direction I wanted, but it was hidden beneath the snow. Not that I needed a trail in such clear conditions. I could see vast distances and avoid the snow-buried lakes with ease. The snow was crunchy underfoot and slightly rough. My boots gripped it without slipping. It made the plateau the easiest landscape to cross of the entire journey.

Despite the great visibility, I spotted no reindeer, nor any prints they might have left. 'It's impossible to miss them,' the lady had said. I smiled

The Hardangervidda and the prominent peak of Hårteigen, May 12, 1998.

at the memory. How wonderful—I was achieving the impossible! But I did come upon several ptarmigan, standing out against the snow in highly visible *summer* plumage. A ptarmigan's feathers alter to match the season —they whiten in winter, become mottled-brown in summer—but something had clearly gone wrong here. Were their brown feathers a sign, I wondered, that the snow was lingering later than usual? Or did the ptarmigan change too early every year? I was pondering these questions when I almost stepped upon a ptarmigan that *hadn't* yet lost its white camouflage. Without warning, it exploded skywards from my feet with madly flapping wings and a raucous cry. Startled, I stepped backwards, tripped, and fell over. I had no answer to my questions, but had no doubt which colour of ptarmigan I preferred.

I reached the plateau's far side late afternoon, *far* sooner than expected. After setting up 'The Sunburn Camp' I hid within Auld Leakie to escape the sun. I hadn't been able to buy sunscreen yet—this was Norway, after all, not known as the sunniest of nations—and my face and neck were roasted. But the discomfort couldn't dent my happiness or my relief. I'd crossed the first stretch of vidda in a single day, not the three I'd anticipated.

If conditions stayed like this the Hardangervidda traverse wasn't going to be the gruelling slogfest I'd feared.

The following day dawned cloudless, but this time without a hard frost. By the time I broke camp the temperature had climbed to heights not reached since September in Italy, and when I descended below snowline into a deep valley, the Hjølmadalen, I wilted in seventy-degree heat, imagining myself back in the Mezzogiorno. The scenery, as I tramped toward Eidfjord, was stupendous—sheer-sided granite walls, lush summer foliage, and enough waterfalls to make it look as though the mountains were melting. But the blue skies now felt like a dubious gift. Though beautiful, they spelled deteriorating conditions on the vidda. The deep snow would surely be degrading into barely crossable slush.

I set out early the next morning, hoping to beat the heat. I paced quickly uphill from Eidfjord, but by the time I reached the head of the Simadal valley and began a relentless 3,000-foot ascent the temperature had climbed to a will-sapping level. The snow turned out to be every bit as soft as I'd feared. It was identical to the slop that had defeated me weeks earlier, only this time I had enervating heat to deal with as well. But I strapped on my snowshoes and proceeded, determined to take each step as it came.

Progress was slow, but just about manageable. My chosen route led along a broad ridge then descended below an outlet arm of the Hardangerjøkulen glacier. The arm—the Rembesdalsskåka—pushed between two ridges, filling a valley with pale blue ice. The glacier looked like a massive river in flood that ancient magic had frozen into sudden stillness. Staring at it, I could easily picture a time 10,000 years earlier when much of Europe had been overrun by ice. The picture was thrilling, but I was under no illusions about the glacier being a welcoming place. It was different from the vidda, which had potential to become welcoming when the snow finally thawed. The glacier could never be home, even in the height of summer. But that was why it appealed—for the absolute wildness it represented.

From the look of its tapered edge, the glacier was retreating, not advancing like the Folgefonna. I wished the opposite. I wanted all of Europe's glaciers to surge forward. Of course, most were thawing into oblivion, and I ached from knowing there was nothing I could do to reverse the trend. To me, diminishing glaciers represented Europe's diminishing wildernesses. They represented the diminishing connection my own species has with

Beneath the Rembesdalsskåka, May 14, 1998.

nature and all the attendant problems this lost connection has led to. I hated all these diminishments to my core. But at least I had the Rembesdalsskåka before me right now, a vision from an older time. Here was the ice age *and* wild Europe living on, despite everything. It was a sight to celebrate.

Snowshoeing on, I passed beneath the glacier, although not easily, or safely. The wild here wasn't merely an abstract concept—it was an actual physical obstacle. First, there were unstable snow slopes to descend. On occasions, snow shifted as I crossed it, and three times I came upon gaping black cracks that forced long detours. Staying in control in the slush, not sliding downhill too fast on my smooth-bottomed snowshoes, took all my energy, all my concentration. The valley below the glacier was a hard-won goal.

Once down, passage grew even more precarious. To proceed I had to cross a river that flooded from the Rembesdalsskåka's snout. It was a discouraging sight. The heat had thawed a great mass of snow and much of the meltwater was now raging across my path. I approached the river nervously, choosing my crossing spot with care. Trying to ford it was unthinkable—I'd be swept away in an instant. Fortunately, a series of snow bridges spanned the torrent. Although they had softened in the heat they looked large enough to offer support.

I reached the first snow bridge via a granite slab. The slab, covered in lichen and drenched by spray, was almost my undoing. The moment I stepped onto it with my snowshoes I almost skidded straight off. It would have been the end of the journey. If I hadn't drowned in the violent river I surely would have in the ice-covered lake it fed. Arms waving, I kept my balance—just. Heart pounding, I moved carefully on. I reached the snow bridge then inched across. My snowshoes sank far into the sagging snow, but the bridge held.

The second bridge was narrower, and a feeling similar to vertigo overcame me halfway across. The raging river pulled my focus off balance. By the time I reached the far side my stomach was churning with fear. I paused a long while before the third and final bridge. *Can't I just stay where I am? I wondered. Wait until summer has melted all the snow and revealed the human-made bridge on my map?* The answer, of course, was no. I pushed on before completely losing my nerve.

The final snow bridge was broader. It hid the river from view. But it *felt* all the more dangerous. As I crossed it, every instinct screamed: *NO! RETREAT!* I could sense the river's power, hear its thunderous roar, feel it through the shuddering snow. The passage felt so touch and go that by the time I reached the far side I knew I could never cross back again, not even if my life depended upon it.

Afterwards, I stood for long minutes, breathless and shaking. It didn't matter that I was safely across. I was now committed. There was no going back the way I'd come. I was completely beyond help, far out on a limb, and the only possible route was the one ahead: a wilderness of thawing snow.

I pushed on, sinking knee deep, struggling to lift the snowshoes free to take each step. The second DNT hut of The Walk—the Rembesdalsseter —lay a mile further, but it took well over an hour to reach. The snow was diabolical, the heat purgatorial, and I laboured in a stupor, too exhausted to find any real pleasure in the landscape. It was extraordinary—I could see that. But I wanted the day done.

The Rembesdalsseter was far smaller than the Stavali Hut, and it matched exactly my idea of what a wilderness cabin should be. But I couldn't enjoy it. I was too aware of my isolation, and too awed by the effort that still lay ahead. I barely slept from anticipating it. I tossed and turned, picturing endless miles of thawing white plateau, hoping for a cold night, for a biting frost, for a surface that I could skip lightly across. But my hopes weren't met.

I left early, before the sun was above the horizon. Breakfast had been inedible—my stomach refused food. My legs felt weak and shaky. As I began making tracks I wished the day were already done.

Legs and lungs began protesting after the first quarter-mile. After half a mile I seriously considered turning back. But there was little to gain from retreat. Summer was clearly here and there might not be another frost for months. At least I could see where I was going. As elsewhere, a large number of lakes lay along my route, but being able to see flat snow made avoidance easier. Crossing the vidda in poor weather, in thick fog, would be even worse. *What if the weather changes?* The thought increased my anxiety, added to a growing sense of urgency. Feeling grateful for clear conditions, but cursing the heat, I pushed on, across a wilderness of white that stretched as far as could be seen.

Despite the anxiety, I still felt some pleasure—at first. The plateau's immensity prompted awe, and even a touch of pride that I was attempting to cross it. But as the sun rose higher into the sky, as the snow softened, and as the effort increased, my focus narrowed. Soon, all I could think about was the strain of making progress. There wasn't room for anything else.

Time slowed until it had practically stopped. By mid-morning the vidda had become an arena of light, heat, sweat and toil. It seemed extra-ordinary, that a landscape so deeply buried in snow could feel so furnace hot. The air shimmered from heat—I saw desert mirages above plains of white. Sunlight rebounded from the snow. Sweat poured from my body. My T-shirt was soon clinging-wet, my sunglasses steamed over. I drank what seemed like gallons each time I stopped, which was often. I aimed, whenever possible, for small ridges of snow-free tundra, but they only ever helped for short distances. Within a few steps I was always back on snow, struggling through it, my muscles screaming.

I forced my body on, examining my options. One option was to stop and camp, breaking the effort into shorter stages. But the idea tormented me. It made sense, but I couldn't bring myself to do it. I felt too anxious to reach the vidda's far side while I had good weather. And I felt too anxious

A wilderness of white, May 15, 1998.

to bring the effort to an end. The snow was too gruelling—I simply wanted to be done with it.

The landscape made me anxious, too. It was astonishingly blank and open, and I felt exposed upon it—too exposed to stop and sleep. The vidda after Stavali had shown me that I *could* feel comfortable on a snowbound plateau, but not when the fjells were buried in slop.

The slop was the main issue. It was just horrible. And what if it grew even worse? What if I camped and woke to conditions that genuinely were uncrossable? It was unlikely, but was it worth the risk? The thought of being stranded raised my anxiety to its highest level yet. The need to get off the vidda almost overwhelmed me.

Calling upon everything I'd learnt, I kept my pace slow and focused on each step. But by late afternoon, with the end almost within reach, the urgency to reach the far side finally overtook me. Desperate to have the day done I let my control slip, and it led, arguably, to the worst route-making decision I'd ever made.

The decision was made at a lake—a final obstacle after a day that had felt like one continuous obstacle. The lake was long and narrow, and it blocked access to a pass and the vidda's end. When choosing my route I'd planned to detour around it, but the extra distance suddenly seemed unthinkably far. A mile before the lake I'd finally chanced upon firm snow—old tracks packed down by heavy skidoos. On any other occasion I might have resented such intrusive evidence of machines in the wild, but here I was overjoyed. *Three cheers for all drivers of skidoos!* But there was a problem. The tracks didn't skirt the lake but arrowed directly across it, offering an enticing shortcut toward the day's end. All of a sudden, I found it impossible to resist. Too exhausted for rational thought, too impatient to consider the consequences, I did what I'd so carefully avoided doing on every upland stretch so far: I stepped out onto a snow-covered lake.

After five days of heat it could have ended right then, or at any time over the next quarter-mile. One soft patch of snow, crack in the ice, weak spot along my route, or misstep off the packed skidoo trail, and I could have broken straight through. It wasn't until I was halfway across that I came to my senses. Suddenly, I awoke with a jolt, with an incredible feeling of disbelief, with a surge of anger at myself and a shocking rush of adrenaline, but by then there was little point turning back. Moving delicately, entirely focused on the ambiguous surface underfoot, I snowshoed on, unbuckling Ten Ton's waist strap as I went. If time had run slowly before, now it all but ceased. Like something from a nightmare, the far shoreline appeared to recede even as I willed it closer. The minutes stretched into an eternity of doubt.

Of course, I made it across—but I stood on the far side fully aware that I might not have. I made a promise to never make such a decision again, no matter how tired I became, or how desperately I wanted to get to where I was going. The lesson had been seared into my memory.

The climb to the pass, then the descent, took me further into exhaustion than I had ever been taken. But I kept on going, discovering once again that I was capable of far more than I'd ever imagined. Soon, the vidda's edge appeared below. It was marked by the Bergen to Oslo railway track— a black line curving across the snow—and, as with the skidoo tracks, I was overjoyed to see it. As it drew closer my anxiety faded. Soon a different kind of churning sensation grew in my stomach—relief. It finally boiled over when I reached a small patch of snow-free grass. I stepped onto it, whooping with joy. It felt like the greatest patch of grass on the planet.

I camped right there, a quarter of a mile from the railway. As I hid from the blazing evening sun my legs rebelled and tied themselves into agonising knots of cramp, a testament to the demands I'd made of them. But with the plateau crossed, and the Greatest Effort Ever over and done with, I no longer cared.

As always, the rewards of travel—the emotions of success—were proportional to the effort expended and difficulties faced, which on this occasion meant they could barely be contained. The 'Cramp Camp' became a camp of soaring euphoria.

The image of my lone snowshoe trail weaving across the Hardanger-vidda would stay with me for a *long*, long time.

Evening at the 'Cramp Camp', May 15, 1998.

IN GOOD COMPANY
Chapter 6

TWO DAYS LATER I was back at sea level, wallowing in idleness not snow, reclining on a campsite lawn that was softer than a plush carpet. A turquoise fjord sparkled nearby. Birds sang, green-leafed branches hung overhead, and delicate petals of apple blossom floated through the air like confetti.

Honestly, life wasn't so bad.

I'd reached Flåm, a tiny village beside the Aurlandsfjord, an arm of Norway's longest fjord, the Sognefjord. Flåm boasts a population of just 350, but it can find itself overrun by tens of thousands of tourists in high summer—most delivered by town-sized cruise ships, others by the Flåmsbana railway. But in mid-May it seemed sleepy, and inexpressibly idyllic.

Best Place Ever, I thought, laughing inside.

It had taken two days to descend to Flåm. The first had involved miles more through untracked snow, tackled with a body that felt creaky and abused; but the second had been easier, a gravity-assisted descent into the Flåmsdalen, a valley of emerald light, a return to the land of the living. I'd descended from winter to summer several times now, but the experience wasn't lessened by repetition. If anything, the rebirth grew more glorious each time.

I'd made my descent along the Rallarvegen: the Navvies' Road, a temporary road created in 1904 during construction of the Oslo–Bergen railway line, but built so well that hikers could still use it. I shared the route with other mountain walkers, the first I'd seen since the Brocken. My fellow pedestrians gave me uncertain looks, perhaps wondering why I carried so large a pack when theirs merely contained lunch. Or, possibly, the looks were of concern—after my adventure on the vidda I was burnt to a crisp, wilder in appearance than your average troll, and probably smelled like a musk ox. It might have explained why an elderly Norwegian couple reacted the way they did when I stopped to talk.

'Oh, um, er...' the man stammered as his wife tucked herself behind him. 'Er... Flåm *that* way,' he gestured quickly, 'Myrdal *that* way.' And the couple hastened off.

Really? I thought, laughing. *Do I really look as though I don't know which way Flåm is?* All I'd wanted was a quick chat. I hadn't spoken to anyone in five days.

Fortunately, the campsite owner down in Flåm was as talkative as he was welcoming. Scratching his black beard, he laughed when I told him I'd just crossed the Hardangervidda without seeing a single reindeer.

'What? None at all? That's some feat,' he joked. 'If I were you I'd phone the *Guinness Book of Records!*'

Instead, after phoning Base Camp to reassure them of my continued survival, and the charities to check on fundraising, I settled comfortably into camp. Hours of hard-earned relaxation followed, then, late in the afternoon, I wandered into town. It was May 17—Norway's national holiday. The celebrations were shortly to begin.

Norway's granite bones might be ancient, but the nation has only existed as an independent state since 1905. Once a realm of Viking chiefdoms strung along the rugged coastline, Norway took its time becoming a unified self-governing nation. For 800 years, Denmark and Sweden tossed ownership of Norway back and forth in a game of international pass the parcel. The human history of the period reads much like the rest of Europe's: a sordid tale of powerful minorities squabbling, bullying and murdering one another for dominion over a powerless majority. It wasn't until May 17, 1814, that Norway finally stood up and declared independence, adopting its own constitution. But even then Sweden wouldn't completely let go. Before long, Sweden's king was once again king of Norway. True independence finally arrived in September 1905 following an almost unanimous vote by Norwegians. At last, one of Europe's most peaceful and fair-minded nations had full control of its own destiny.

Constitution Day parade through Flåm, May 17, 1998.

Given the length of time Norway was governed from elsewhere, and given that it was overrun in 1940 by Nazis—still recent history for some at the time of my visit—it's easy to understand why Norwegians so appreciate self-rule. From my very first step, I'd been impressed by the patriotism on display, and by the pride Norwegians felt in their country. When I complimented them on their hospitality, on their scenery, on how clean everything was, on how well everything worked, they merely shrugged with inoffensive superiority, as if to say: 'Well, this is Norway; what else would one expect?'

When I reached Flåm's village centre I found it bustling with activity. Locals were milling about cheerfully, many wearing their *Bunad*, the traditional national dress. A small brass band was gathering, its members ranging from small children to an ancient trumpeter who might even have remembered Norway's independence in 1905. Soon, the band struck up a boisterous tune and begun marching across town. A flag-bearer proudly led the way, and everyone else fell in behind, small flags in hand.

When the band reached an open area in front of Flåm's town hall they formed two lines. Everyone else settled into chairs. Short speeches followed, then more music. The highlight, for me, was a small girl who crept away from her parents and stood directly beside the band. Pumping her right arm in and out, wiggling her fingers, puffing her cheeks, she accompanied the band on an imaginary trombone, her face turning bright red with effort. After the band had blasted out its last note she rushed back to her parents, her face alight with satisfaction at a job well done.

Remembering my journey across the Hardangervidda, I knew exactly how she felt.

I lazed the following two days away in Flåm's campsite—except it wasn't lazing, merely balance. The hot weather continued, but it was far easier to tolerate down in a green valley while resting in camp. Evening shade and coolness came hours earlier than up on the exposed vidda. Towering valley walls blocked out the sun long before it set. A farmer inside Flåm's grocery store explained that this could make life hard in winter.

'We go four months without direct sunlight,' he said, then paused a moment, a bleak look entering his eyes. 'It can seem like a long time.'

So good had the weather become that I began wondering if rain was now a thing of the past. Twelve days earlier in Odda, I'd bought seam sealer for Auld Leakie's leaky seams, the first time it had been available. But since applying it there'd been no opportunity to see if it worked—I'd experienced nothing but blue skies. I laughed at the irony, then laughed again at a sudden idea. If I kept applying it, would the sun shine all summer?

I stayed up until midnight each evening swapping travellers' tales with three fellow campers. The companionship was a tonic, but it was only a taste of what lay ahead. On May 20 I bought a train ticket to Norway's second city, Bergen, spent a day trying to make myself presentable, and the following morning met up with two visitors from England who'd flown out to share a week of my Norwegian life.

Tanya and Richard climbed from the airport bus and strode up to me outside Bergen's railway station, large smiles spread across their faces. Richard, an officer in the British Army, was carrying his dull green army rucksack, or bergen, as British Army personnel called their packs.

'This is great,' Richard exclaimed. 'I've always wanted to bring my bergen to Bergen!'

Both Tanya and Richard were members of the KRAP Club, a mountain-eering club I'd joined by invitation three years earlier. The club had been formed by a close-knit group of graduates from King's College, London. I'd first heard of the club from one of its members, Robin, met by chance in Zermatt during my six-month traverse of the Alps. Robin and I had shared several evenings in camp, had climbed a glacial peak, and after the trip we'd become friends. A couple of months after finishing my Alpine walk he'd invited me to join the club.

Up until that point pretty much all my adventures had been solitary. At my own college in Derby I'd kept to myself, going to great lengths to hide my stammer and social awkwardness. Although I'd been a member of Derby's mountaineering club I'd only used it as a means to get to the hills. As soon as the college minibus reached its destination off I'd always gone on my own. Joining the KRAP Club had given me an unexpected second chance for a college-like experience, a chance I knew I shouldn't waste. At first, the weekend trips took me far beyond my social comfort zone, but sharing the outdoors with like-minded individuals soon added an extra dimension to the hills. It boosted my confidence, and greatly increased my tiny circle of friends.

The acronym KRAP stood for 'King's Rock and Plod'. At the club's founding someone had suggested the name to the president, Ingrid, and she'd thought it perfect, not noticing what the acronym spelled. But it was perfect—it matched the group and their sense of humour to a T. As I soon discovered, the club members didn't merely head for the hills to climb, cave and walk—they also went to laugh. The club was full of characters; legends were forged; no moment was ever dull. As the club T-shirt stated: 'There are good weekends, bad weekends... and KRAP weekends!' The memories, laughter and friendships will last a lifetime.

As well as Tanya and Richard, my friend Robin had also planned to fly out, but his job had forced him to postpone his visit until June. I knew Tanya and Richard less well, although I'd shared several weekend trips with them. But conversation was easy from the start—Norway saw to that. The train ride back to Flåm was spectacular, especially the descent down the incomparable Flåmsbana. As the train lurched into tunnels and swept around turns, one moment on one side of the valley above a sheer drop, the next moment on the other side, Tanya and Richard exclaimed their delight. The Flåmsbana is one of the world's steepest rail journeys. In just 12.6 miles the line descends 2,841 feet. As an introduction to Norway no other route could compete. I'd ridden it to reach Bergen, and had loved every second, but sharing it with Tanya and Richard added an extra layer of pleasure. Their enthusiasm increased my own.

Back in Flåm, I guided my companions to the campsite. At the first opportunity, Tanya pulled me aside. 'Andrew...' she began, hesitantly, 'do you mind if I sleep in your tent, not Richard's?'

The request caught me off guard, not because sharing tents was unusual on mountain trips—it wasn't, it was normal practice regardless of gender, it led to not everyone having to carry a tent—but because it hadn't crossed my mind that either Tanya or Richard would ask to share a tent with me.

'Richard snores,' Tanya continued. 'If I share a tent with him I probably won't sleep all week.'

It was a fair point—and a detail I'd forgotten. On KRAP trips, the entire club had often slept in single dormitory rooms, and I'd lost sleep myself. Richard wasn't the only snorer.

I understood Tanya's request but felt instantly awkward. Although I'd slept in mixed dormitories a few times, I'd never shared my tent with anyone, let alone with a girl. It meant absolutely nothing—it was simply a shared shelter—but it made me uncomfortable. In truth, even talking to a girl made me uncomfortable and awkward.

But the most embarrassing aspect was the tent itself: it stank to high heaven. It could just as accurately be called Auld Reekie as Auld Leakie. The stench would probably keep Tanya from sleep far more effectively than snoring ever could. But how could I refuse?

'Of course,' I mumbled, behaving as I always did in social situations, trying to hide my embarrassment. I hoped the tent's aroma wasn't as offensive as I feared.

Happily, Tanya survived her first night inside Auld Leakie without complaint, and sharing the tent wasn't as uncomfortable as I'd feared. Tanya was considerate, kept her gear contained, and made the small space work. As far as I could tell, she didn't even notice my awkwardness.

Soon, the three of us were climbing into the fjells. The perfect weather had finally given way to cool, grey, drizzly conditions, but progress uphill seemed unusually easy. Richard was a natural storyteller—he had a great feel for the small details that bring tales to life, and as we weaved uphill he shared a few of his military adventures. Tanya had stories of her own, plus a knack for asking great questions. She kept the conversation flowing. The talk and laughter continued even when the trail steepened and drizzle began falling. I barely noticed the effort—a clear benefit of backpacking in company.

Soon, the views broadened and snow-capped fjells appeared across the valley. Richard and Tanya hadn't been to Norway before and were suitably impressed.

'It's like Scotland,' Richard said.

'But bigger,' Tanya added, and we all agreed. The watery atmosphere felt identical to the Highlands, the pine trees and heather were exactly the same, and the mountains had been sculpted in similar ways. But the scale was strikingly different—an exaggerated fantasy version of Scotland.

Seeing Norway through their eyes was another benefit of company. In addition, three sets of eyes spotted more than one set ever could.

'Is that... an eagle?' Richard suddenly pointed, and Tanya and I caught a fleeting glimpse of a large bird of prey right before it disappeared behind a ridge. I wondered how much I'd missed from always being on my own.

Mid-afternoon, we stopped near a waterfall and set up camp. The drizzle eased and Richard rustled up a hearty stew. 'Why don't we take turns cooking dinner each evening?' Tanya had suggested earlier in the day, an idea we'd adopted. It was a win for me, but of dubious benefit to my companions, given the quality of my standard eat-it-if-you-dare stew.

As we tucked into Richard's dinner I thought to myself: *yet another benefit of company.* I'd grown used to cooking every night, but this was better. Taking turns meant an easing of the workload for everyone. Mutual support, mutual benefit—an approach humans have been practising for millennia, to huge evolutionary advantage. It made my solitary approach feel like a laughable choice, an evolutionary step backwards.

The second day took us through shifting clouds, the surrounding fjells only half seen. We made camp at tree line on a heathery ridge 3,000 feet above the waters of the Aurlandsfjord.

'This is *amazing!*' Tanya said. 'Perhaps we could camp here for two nights, not just one?' Richard and I promptly agreed. I'd spotted the location on my map, and had suspected it would make for a standout camp. It felt satisfying to get it right.

We stayed up late, drinking whisky from the Isle of Skye, swapping yarns, waiting for daylight to fade. Heavy wet clouds rested upon the mountains, but true darkness was a long time coming, and when midnight arrived we gave up waiting and turned in. Those solitary, endlessly black camps during the long winter seemed to belong to another lifetime.

Familiar conditions greeted us in the morning: low clouds, grey hues, dampness—reminiscent of many a day back in the British fells. Leaving camp pitched we angled uphill with light packs and were soon above snowline, heading towards the 5,935-foot summit of Blåskavlen, the highest peak in the area. The snow yielded an inch or two beneath our boots, but in the chill air it was nothing like the slop I'd negotiated a week earlier. We didn't need snowshoes, which was just as well—the message to bring them hadn't reached Richard and Tanya. The ascent felt easy, and not just because of firmer snow. Company played a significant part. We took turns breaking trail, swapping out when the leader grew tired. Once again, it was mutual support, mutual benefit. I found myself wishing Tanya and Richard had been around for the previous week's wallow across the Hardangervidda.

For a long while we saw nothing but fog and snow, but Richard and Tanya were soon smiling. 'Now *this* is how I imagined Norway,' Richard said. Careful compass work led us to the highest point, a broad snow dome perched above cloud-hidden glaciers. We hunkered down to snack, three insignificant specks in a white void.

The magic began on the way down. Imperceptibly at first, but then with increasing speed, the fog thinned, broke apart, and soon the sun was shining with dazzling brightness upon the snowy fjells. Blåskavlen was the highest elevation I'd reached since the Austrian Alps, and the view extended far. For Tanya and Richard, it was their first real glimpse of Norway's vastness. It had impact, prompting colourful language from Richard and a radiant smile from Tanya. 'What a day!' she exclaimed. 'What a place!' We glissaded back down in high spirits, the smiles as thrilling to me as the fjells.

Richard and Tanya on Blåskavlen, May 25, 1998.

I marvelled at that—at how smiles had come to mean so much. Back in London, they'd been a common part of life; noticed, of course, but never fully appreciated. But since Calabria, smiles had become something rare that I craved. A simple smile from a passing stranger had lifted my morale more times than I could say. As I'd realised in northern Germany, a smile could make the world a better place, and it had become a daily goal, to share my own whenever I could. Tanya and Richard's smiles held even more power than a stranger's, perhaps because they were now familiar. Their smiles felt like unspoken dialogue, messages of friendship and connection, and knowing that I could cause them raised their worth even further. I'd suggested climbing Blåskavlen, and it had led to real joy. Bringing joy to other people made the entire day worth living. It was something my normal days lacked.

We made it back to camp mid-afternoon, and the hours that followed would be hard to beat. We talked and laughed, feasted on Tanya's spaghetti dinner, then feasted on the spectacular view. Three quarters of a mile below us, the Aurlandsfjord sparkled with diamond light. Toy-sized boats travelled the fjord, leaving behind V-shaped wakes, their engines silent to us so far above. Sunlit slopes soared from the fjord; waterfalls cascaded down ravines. By late evening, the entire landscape took on a rich, golden hue, and all three of us stared in silence, utterly consumed by the majesty of it. Norway had never been better—*and how much better still*, I thought, *was sharing it.*

Later, tucked in to our sleeping bags, Tanya and I spoke about everything we'd seen. It was soon clear that Tanya loved mountains with a passion, for reasons I could relate to. She even understood my journey with a depth few others had shown. Her questions were thoughtful, her observations insightful, and her enthusiasm was a joy to behold and feed off. Somehow, Tanya made talking easy, and I forgot I'd ever been a stammerer. For her, it was probably an ordinary conversation, but for me, after a long year alone, and a lifetime of shyness, it was an extraordinary event.

Afterwards, I lay awake for hours, reliving the day, feeling awe at my own part in it. *I'm with other people*, I thought, *and for once I'm making it work!* Yes, I'd made it work elsewhere, but only for short periods, a few hours at a time, and the uniqueness of The Walk had always helped. But here, I was spending days with two people I hadn't known well, and the company had become comfortable, fulfilling and *natural.*

Is this what I've been going without for so many years? I asked myself, feeling incredulous at the choices I'd made. Lying within Auld Leakie, near a girl who also loved mountains, I found myself dwelling on *all* the things I was missing. I could manage alone, but was that *really* what I wanted?

The following day was tougher: seventeen miles over a snowbound plateau toward Lærdal, the next valley. The plateau was lower than Blåskavlen, but the snowpack was far softer, and without snowshoes we couldn't cross it. Fortunately, an upland road went the way I needed, and Tanya and Richard were up for following it. The road was only open a few months each year, and had only recently been cleared of snow. In places, it cut through drifts fifteen feet deep, creating impressive, white-walled canyons. The view from the road was heartbreakingly wild, but we all felt cut off from the landscape, and the hard pavement soon began taking its toll. Tanya's feet, especially, soon began to suffer.

View from camp above the Aurlandsfjord, May 25, 1998.

As always, company eased the miles—mutual support, mutual benefit. But when Tanya began limping, Officer Richard called a temporary halt to the march. Inspection of her feet revealed three angry blisters. Richard expertly administered on-the-spot medical care, puncturing, draining and dressing the wounds, but for the rest of the day Tanya walked in great discomfort. And yet she didn't complain, not once. She pushed on with a smile, determined to find enjoyment in the miles. I felt terrible for my part in her torment, for leading her and Richard onto a road. And I could empathise—I knew all too well the pain she was feeling. But I was blown away by her positive attitude and grit. Richard was doing his part, too. Road walking wasn't what he'd come to Norway for, but he didn't complain either, and found energy to deliver distracting stories for the benefit of all.

We reached Lærdal one camp and another morning's effort later; and for the final day of the visit, to spare Tanya's feet further abuse, we rented bicycles for a ride alongside the Sognefjord. The miles were sunny, carefree and filled with laughter. We saw seals, mountains and glaciers. But at the back of my mind was the awareness, once again, that I'd soon be alone. The visit had added another rich layer to my journey, but as with visits from

242

my brother Paul and Base Camp it had reminded me of the company I was going without.

And this time, there was an extra element, a reminder of something I'd managed to repress my entire adult life: a desire for more than just company, but also for a meaningful relationship. A deep, natural, innate need for reciprocated love.

And what had I expected? I was a young man, no different from any other, suffering the usual biological and emotional needs that are hard-wired into the majority of the human race. Prior to The Walk, I'd buried these needs even deeper than I'd buried my need for company. Burying them was a way to survive my abnormal shyness and solitary existence, but sharing a tent had brought them right to the surface. After a year of solitary living, I'd suddenly found myself spending time with a remarkable woman who was thoughtful, kind, enthusiastic and stunningly beautiful—what chance did I have of surviving unscathed?

Back in Calabria, I'd been certain that spending eighteen months alone in nature was what I wanted. Solitude was the only solution that I could imagine—it was the only way I could truly be me. But since then, The Walk had re-educated me, shown me another solution. Yes, I *could* spend time alone, and yes, happiness lay within, regardless of outside influences. But that didn't mean I had to ignore one of the most fundamental human needs.

Ignoring it was unnatural. Spending *all* my time alone was unnatural. And doing something unnatural was the opposite of everything I was walking for. It was an evolutionary step backwards.

The final evening with Richard and Tanya was light-hearted—on the surface. Richard told more stories. Tanya skilfully guided the conversation. And for my part I tried making the best of it, following Tanya and Richard's positive examples from back on the road. But once again I was in turmoil underneath. My stammer returned.

The final night was even worse, sharing the tent with Tanya one last time. She had a boyfriend, and probably saw me as someone she'd shared a tent with, nothing more. But I could now imagine a very different reality. Dawn came after a sleepless age, but it still came too soon for me. And then there was the farewell, and a bus, whisking my companions away, and I thought: *oh shit, here we go again.*

BALANCE
Chapter 7

ON MY OWN, I faced the fjells, or what little of them I could see. Dark clouds smothered the tops and rain swept through in veils. I wasn't surprised. The weather often matched my mood.

I felt hollow inside, and distressingly unsettled. It wasn't loneliness or anxiety. It wasn't the black pit of despair I'd fallen into at Christmas. It wasn't 'the end of the walk as we know it'. But it wasn't a whole bundle of laughs, either.

I paced from Lærdal along a minor road, then east up a valley that conditions had turned into a gloomy tunnel. My next major destination was the mighty Jotunheimen range, but I felt no excitement. The range lay five days ahead, and I'd aimed to reach it via several high passes, but I couldn't summon the motivation to return to the fjells. Masses of snow still buried them, and I simply couldn't face more snowshoeing. Instead, I slogged miserably along the valley. The miles were monotonous, and the purpose for walking them seemed unfathomable. I was moving forward physically, but seemed to be slipping backwards inside.

I felt confused, knocked off kilter. I couldn't reconcile the journey I loved with the reality that I couldn't now ignore: that, deep down, I craved a partner. The idea of sharing life's ups and downs, of mutual support and mutual benefit, gnawed at me. I'd just experienced companionship in a way I never had before. I'd found so much pleasure from sharing my small tent and my wandering life. There'd been so many benefits, practical and emotional. Shared cooking, shared trail-breaking, shared ideas, shared laughter. Mutual support was such a normal part of life for most people. It was our evolutionary advantage. Company made so much sense, and a partner would make even more. Without partners there wouldn't even be a human race. It was nature, pure and simple.

But it wasn't what I'd chosen. I was out of whack with nature—a huge problem that I couldn't brush aside. The Walk had taught me to treasure balance, but as I trudged up the valley, utterly alone, I saw that balance wasn't what I had.

I reached Lake Tyin on the southern edge of the Jotunheimen on June 1 and set up 'Camp Dreary'. The lake was frozen, the landscape midwinter white, the atmosphere chill and damp. For a while, falling snow filled the air. Would winter never end?

A track skirting the lake's eastern shore offered a straightforward route into the Jotunheimen, but snow still buried it. When I took a few explorative steps a horrible 'soup snow' swallowed my snowshoes. I retreated, too weary to proceed. I desperately wanted to explore the Jotunheimen, but hadn't the desire or strength to struggle through any more snow.

Not alone, anyway.

The Jotunheimen was supposed to be one of the highlights of the entire walk. The name means 'Home of the Giants', and it's an accurate name. Norway's highest summits rise in the range, including Galdhøpiggen and Glittertind, the two Norwegian mountains I most wanted to climb. At 8,100 feet, Galdhøpiggen is Norway's highest peak, although in periods of exceptional snow cover Glittertind's summit can surpass it. Glaciers pour forth across the Jotunheimen, deep valleys run between peaks, fjord-like lakes nestle beneath crags, and I yearned to see it all, knowing the journey would be incomplete if I didn't.

But I didn't have the energy. Not even to reach the range, let alone climb to the top of it.

I sat inside Auld Leakie, staring out at the snow. Once upon a time I'd have screamed with delight at such a wild place, but all I felt now was emptiness. What I *really needed* was someone special to share it with, and not having someone left a gaping hole. What made it worse was being unable to imagine ever having someone. What did I have to offer? Where would I even start?

Heavy falling snow at Lake Tyin, and a rare island of bare ground, June 1, 1998.

If I could connect with nature again I was certain I'd be okay. But with snow burying the fjells I couldn't even manage that. The snow was cold and lifeless. It was a barrier that separated me from my precious earth. The living soil was down there somewhere, a rich surface to sink my fingers into and walk upon gently, but it was out of reach. Happiness was buried too. It was still there, deep within, and I *knew* with absolute certainty that it *could* be found regardless of external factors—I just didn't know how. What I'd understood at the top of Denmark had been real, even if my current mood contradicted it. I couldn't move toward happiness and I couldn't move forward in the snow. Moving forward was too damn hard.

The following day, June 2, was the fifth anniversary of my Hohtürli fall. But I didn't notice. I woke to winter, and indecision consumed me. *Push on into the Jotunheimen?* I desperately wanted to, but couldn't make it happen. A planning error made my predicament even worse. My latest resupply parcel lay twenty miles in the wrong direction, down at sea level in the town of Øvre Årdal. I attempted to hitch a ride there and back, standing in sleet for three unpleasant hours, but few cars appeared and none stopped. The cold eventually drove me back to camp.

A car finally pulled over the following morning, but when I told the driver where I was heading he explained that it would be a waste of time. 'It's a holiday today—didn't you know? The post office won't be open.'

I wondered if fate was trying to tell me something.

After a third night above Lake Tyin I settled upon a plan: if I couldn't thumb a ride to Øvre Årdal I'd bloody well walk there. I'd skip the Jotunheimen—for now. But I could still attempt Galdhøpiggen in two weeks' time if I looped into the Jotunheimen from the north. I'd let fate decide. It would all depend on whether or not the gods of desperate hitchhikers granted me a ride.

They didn't. In rain, sleet and dense fog only eight cars appeared the following morning, and they all flew by in clouds of spray. And so I turned my back on the Jotunheimen and trudged west and downhill, not north and up. It was only a change of route, something I'd done many times, but it felt like a crushing defeat.

───

For the next week the weather remained exceptionally Norwegian: soggy clouds, water everywhere. When I laboured over a pass directly beneath some of Norway's most jagged mountains, the Hurrungane range, I saw nothing of them. Below 3,000 feet rain was teeming; above it I encountered fog and heavy falling snow. I could only imagine the conditions in the Jotunheimen. A *Jotun* is a frost giant—'one who devours'—and it wasn't hard to picture a Jotunheimen snowstorm doing some devouring. Perhaps it was just as well I'd taken a different route.

The only time the sun shone was when I descended to low valleys and walked along roads. Each time I turned back to the mountains the weather shut me out. I soon felt out of sync with the land *and* the weather, out of balance with everything The Walk was supposed to be. I kept on walking, but the journey itself seemed to be falling apart around me.

The state of The Walk was summed up with spectacular accuracy three days after Lake Tyin. A man saw me passing his home, and with typical Norwegian hospitality invited me in for a hot drink and cake. The valley

I was following was temporarily taking me south, and when the man heard about my ultimate destination he raised his eyebrows in confusion. 'Nordkapp? But you must have lost your way!'

He had it right, exactly. But not in the way he thought.

Determined to salvage some pride, I forced myself back into the fjells on June 6. Heading north from Skjolden, a saltwater village an astonishing 130 miles from the open sea, I splashed up trails that gushed like rivers, aiming for a rugged corner of the Breheimen range that I couldn't (and never would) actually see, even though I'd pass right through it. My boots and socks were soon soaked, my clothes damp, my waterproofs no longer waterproof after two months of use, but I felt a flicker of excitement to be away from the valley—a burst of optimism that all was not entirely lost. I climbed through a grey-brown landscape of birch and willow, passed glacier-scratched slabs, craggy knolls and countless foaming torrents, and shook off with each step a little of the malaise that had afflicted me.

I spent the night in a DNT hut—a dry haven from the deluge. When I woke to rain still sheeting down I rolled over and treated myself to a rest day, and it raised my morale another notch. I spent most of it perched beside a large window, warmed by the hut's wood-burning stove, drinking endless cups of tea, staring out at huge banks of snow that stretched into foggy oblivion. Hour by hour, the wildness of the location began sinking in. Soon I felt the old euphoria rising. Time slowed, as it always does in nature, until events from just a few days earlier seemed distant and less relevant—and far easier to accept. It struck me as pitiful that connection with nature was returning while I was sheltering from it, but for the first time in a week my own contradictions brought a smile, not a frown.

To make amends, the next day was an honest adventure, a trudge on snowshoes over a high pass. It involved a stiff scramble up a greasy crag, a leg-taxing ascent up saturated snow, careful route finding across several miles of white nothingness, two forded rivers, a great deal of sweat, and soaked legs and feet. But there was a reward: for a few hours I completely forgot that I had other needs that weren't being met. By the time I descended, those needs barely even seemed essential.

The day ended in the depths of the Jostedal, a valley of such epic proportions it felt like a landscape from a Tolkien legend. Dark mountains reared into threatening clouds, curtains of rain swept by, and when I

Crossing the Breheimen, June 8, 1998.

rounded a corner and the Nigardsbreen glacier appeared, I ground to a halt in awe. When I lay in camp that night I reckoned that, this time, the euphoria had been earned.

The Nigardsbreen is an outlet arm of the Jostedalsbreen, mainland Norway's largest ice cap. Thirty-seven miles long, 2,000 feet thick, and covering 188 square miles, the ice cap is an impressive chunk of ice. As I'd learnt back in Odda, many of the Jostedalsbreen's outlet glaciers were advancing, and the Nigardsbreen was one of them. It curved down a canyon of naked rock toward a silt-filled lake—a remnant of the ice age thrust into a valley where flowers grew.

I hiked to the glacier's snout the following morning, sharing the approach with fellow tourists, but I left them behind after strapping on crampons. I'd carried the spikes since Kristiansand without using them once, but their weight was finally justified. The crampons let me do more than just look—they turned the glacier from scenery into something real that I could engage with. As I stepped onto the ice I felt familiar emotions stir: nerves, doubt, excitement, anticipation, and they were *all* welcome.

With emotions churning, I no longer felt hollow inside.

At first, the glacier was bare ice, and relatively safe to travel. Though severely contorted and cracked, there were no major crevasses to plunge into, or unstable seracs that could fall and crush me. My crampons bit deep and felt secure—progress was nothing like wading through snow. Picking a careful route, I spiked upward through an environment utterly unlike any other place I'd been. Even the glaciers I'd stepped onto back in the Alps hadn't been like this. The Nigardsbreen was spectacular—it was tinted a piercing blue and shone as though lit from within, even on this day of leaden skies and drizzle. And it spoke, too, creaking and groaning as the great mass of it scraped downhill. Every step upon it felt worth taking.

I ventured as far as felt safe, finally halting where snow hid crevasses. They were like the lakes up on the vidda—I didn't want to step on one and break through. After taking a few photos I sought an elevated vantage point, and spotted a bulging ridge of ice. Reaching its summit was precarious, but my spikes helped, and Excalibur was finally put to the use it was designed for. I swung its sharp pick into the ice, pulled myself up, and finally reached the top. Carefully, I eased myself upright, wobbled, almost fell, but stamped down my spikes, spread my arms wide, and found stability. I stood still, above the blue ice, surrounded by the Norwegian wild.

Well, I thought, *I guess I'm back in balance*, and I almost laughed myself right out of it again.

But it was true. I *was* back in balance—and in more ways than one, even though I was clearly out of place. The glacier could never be home, and being upon it was unnatural. But that didn't mean I couldn't visit and enjoy it. And being alone for months was also unnatural, but that didn't mean I couldn't do it and enjoy that too. Neither did it mean I'd never find someone to share life with. I might, or I might not. Knowing that I wanted to, and being open to it, that was what counted.

There was nothing confusing any longer, nothing to reconcile. The reasons for walking were once again clear.

I balanced on the icy ridge for several minutes, truly appreciating *everything* I could now see.

Balance, it seemed, was like everything else. It was like water, shelter, friends, snow-free ground, smiles. To truly, *truly* value it, you have to go without it first.

Contorted ice on the Nigardsbreen, June 9, 1998.

It was raining. Again. Nothing new there. I was deep in the Breheimen, surrounded by fjells, and as usual I could barely see them. But I didn't mind. Behind layers of drifting cloud they looked dark, foreboding and Himalayan in scale. *Just perfect*, I thought. *Intimidating, but perfect.*

I trekked up the valley, sometimes snowshoeing across wet snow, sometimes placing my boots gently on patches of revealed earth. There wasn't much open ground, but there was enough now that I felt connected to it. Hours passed. I met no people, but that didn't surprise me. Conditions were downright unpleasant, the snow was still demanding to cross, and only masochists would likely be out on foot. Since Lindesnes I'd only seen people away from roads twice—beneath the Nigardsbreen and above Flåm, both easy places to get to. But in the fjells? Never. Perhaps Norwegians didn't venture into their mountains as much as I'd been told. Perhaps Norway was too big to run into other people. Or perhaps Norwegians simply had too much sense to be out on foot in conditions like this? Whatever the reason, I had the fjells to myself, and I didn't mind it one bit.

Except I didn't have them entirely to myself. Entering a deep valley, the Sprongdalen, I met some of the locals: reindeer—finally! Eight of them came into sight as I rounded a bluff, digging at snowdrifts in search of food. Their heads jerked up at my arrival and they quickly sprung away, taking their velvet-covered antlers from sight. But over the next four days I saw many more. After failing to see reindeer where they were impossible to miss I now started stumbling upon them where they were supposed to be elusive. The encounters were brief—they appeared to fear lone humans—but I treasured each sighting. Wild reindeer! Now *this* was the Norway *I'd* imagined.

I stopped for the night beneath another DNT roof, the Sprongdalshytte. I'd planned to walk further, but, just as I was genetically incapable of passing by a perfect spot for camp, so I couldn't pass by a perfectly sited DNT hut. After miles of 'porridge snow' and rain, after another day with sodden feet and damp clothes, after another night in a leaky tent (alas, the seam sealer hadn't worked), how could I pass up a night indoors? The hut provided amenities I'd once taken for granted: a dry space to stand, a heating source, chairs, a soft mattress. In my advanced state of homelessness the hut became a home within minutes. But moving on the following morning was a battle. The Sprongdalshytte was another Best Place Ever. Its comforts were hard to give up.

Another wet mountain day passed, then another. I explored side valleys, cramponned onto two further glacial snouts, felt myself falling hard for every nook and cranny. I spent longer in the Breheimen than I'd intended—five wilderness days—but it wasn't time enough. The more I saw the more I realised the range deserved a lifetime's attention, just as the Abruzzo, Dolomites and a thousand other places deserved it. All I was doing was passing through, scratching the surface, missing more than I was seeing. In the Breheimen I found wild perfection that made me want to stop walking for good. *Why keep walking when I've found what I'm looking for?* But then I wondered if leaving might be part of what made these places special. Perhaps it was like life itself, more valuable for being a place we inevitably have to leave behind, and more meaningful when we finally accept the truth of that.

On June 13 I descended with reluctance into a low valley, and for three days the journey was entirely different. Sunshine replaced rain, warmth replaced cold, pavement replaced snow. It was balance, I supposed, although

Midnight at the Sprongdalshytte, June 11, 1998.

I'd rather have been back in the mountains. But I was here for a reason: I faced a deadline, a rare thing on The Walk. My friend Robin would be arriving in a week's time far to the east in the Rondane National Park, and I had a lot of ground to cover if I wanted to make it in time.

Plus, I had a rescheduled date with the Jotunheimen. The range was back within reach and I desperately wanted to climb into it while the sun shone.

Since I'd last been at lower elevations the vegetation had grown by a staggering amount. Grass now stood three feet high, wildflowers blazed everywhere, and mosquitoes whined. Looking back toward the Breheimen I could finally see the peaks. *So that's what they look like!* Why did the sun only shine when I left the mountains? But perhaps this time the clear weather would last.

I reached the base of Galdhøpiggen late on the evening of June 15 and set up camp in a mozzie-haunted birch wood. Conditions were cool but gloriously clear. Finally, two weeks after being on the southern edge of the Jotunheimen, I'd reached the northern edge. My feet and legs ached from three long road days, but every paved step now seemed worthwhile. I spent long twilight hours examining my Jotunheimen map, then struggled to sleep because of the excitement the map caused. But who needed sleep! I wouldn't see much of the range—I could only linger for two days before I had to leave for the Rondane—but from the summit of Galdhøpiggen I'd see enough. The hypnotic mantra of *the summit of Norway, tomorrow... the summit of Norway, tomorrow...* finally lulled me to sleep.

But, once again, Norway had other ideas. Dawn arrived, and I wasn't sure if it was my alarm that woke me or the sudden onslaught of rain. Raising my head I listened in horror to a wild tattoo pelting Auld Leakie's thin walls. My thermometer read a chill forty Fahrenheit, four Celsius, and I could only imagine conditions 5,000 feet higher on Galdhøpiggen's summit. The ascent route crossed snowfields, a broad glacier and a narrow ridge—a dangerous proposition in a blizzard. Galdhøpiggen wasn't a small mountain like Great Arber, and I knew in an instant I wasn't going. I extinguished my alarm. If only the rain could be turned off as easily.

I barely left the tent all day, saving energy for a Galdhøpiggen ascent on the next. But again it wasn't to be. The second dawn announced itself with driving sleet, and with great reluctance I gave up on my summit dream. Until now, I'd reached the highest summit of every range visited, but it wasn't going to happen here. I was out of time. But I'd be back. I swore it. One day I'd return to see all the mountains that had been hidden and climb all the peaks I hadn't climbed. Well, perhaps—*if* the mountains allowed it. As I was coming to see, Norway's mountains always have the final say.

Leaving 'Basecamp Galdhøpiggen' I wandered east over a broad pass beneath Glittertind, loving the wild solitude I found. It was my one and only full day in the Jotunheimen National Park, but all I saw was fog and snow, which looked much the same as fog and snow everywhere. But at least I'd sensed something of these mountains, something of their vastness. I could definitely *feel* how great they were.

At day's end I reached a collection of buildings at Glitterheim, the first fully staffed DNT hut along my route. The refuge was preparing for the summer and looked like a construction site: workmen hammered and drilled, building materials lay in piles, two white vans were parked with engines running and music blaring, and a diesel generator killed whatever peace remained. It was notably different from the huts I'd grown used to. I camped in quiet solitude two miles on.

And then the next day I was out of the mountains, walking across forested hills and through rich farmland, and—of course—the moment the Jotunheimen fell behind the sun came out and the clouds rolled off the summits.

But I had to laugh—what else could I do? I was back in balance with The Walk, but clearly still out of balance with the weather, and it was all my fault. Back in May I'd applied seam sealer; ten days of sunshine had followed. But I'd caused all the rain since. It was obvious now! An item purchased in Flåm had done it. When I'd picked it up I should have thrown it back onto the shelf and fled the store. Damn sunscreen! Who needed sunscreen in Norway anyway?

I jettisoned this bad-luck charm at the very next opportunity.

'It's Supposed to be Summer Camp' high in the Breheimen, June 12, 1998.

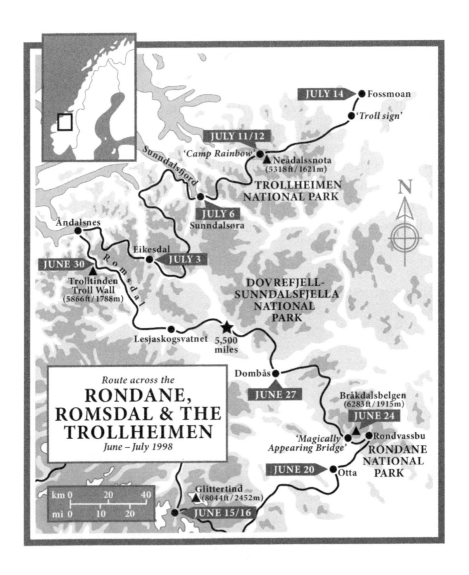

Route across the
RONDANE,
ROMSDAL & THE
TROLLHEIMEN
June – July 1998

JULY 14 — Fossmoan
'Troll sign'

JULY 11/12
'Camp Rainbow' — Neàdalssnota
(5318 ft / 1621 m)

TROLLHEIMEN
NATIONAL PARK

Sunndalsfjord

JULY 6
Sunndalsøra

Àndalsnes

Eikesdal — JULY 3

JUNE 30
Trolltinden
Troll Wall
(5866 ft / 1788 m)

Romsdal

DOVREFJELL-
SUNNDALSFJELLA
NATIONAL
PARK

Lesjaskogsvatnet   5,500
miles

Dombås

JUNE 27

Bràkdalsbelgen
(6283 ft / 1915 m)
JUNE 24

'Magically
Appearing Bridge'   Rondvassbu

RONDANE
NATIONAL
PARK

JUNE 20   Otta

Glittertind
(8044 ft / 2452 m)

km 0   20   40
mi 0   10   20

JUNE 15/16

N

AND SOMETIMES IT RAINS
Chapter 8

ROBIN, FRESH FROM London, wasn't happy. Oh, he was happy to be in Norway, and happy to be camping in the wild, but decidedly *un*happy about the mosquitoes. They were eating him alive.

'This isn't fair,' he observed, waving his arms about. 'Why aren't they attacking you?'

He was right, it wasn't fair. Since climbing into the Rondane National Park the growing numbers of *mygg* had lost interest in me. Why they'd transferred their affections to Robin so completely wasn't something I could explain, although 5,500 miles of congealed long-distance hiker grime might have had something to do with it. Perhaps mosquitoes preferred their flesh clean.

I'd met Robin in the town of Otta four days previously. He'd stepped off the train from Oslo mid-evening and I'd steered him directly to the nearest watering hole for a beer, a huge pizza, and to experience a room full of frustrated Norwegian football fans. The World Cup finals were in full swing and Norway was facing elimination.

'Another tie…' an uncharacteristically depressed Norwegian lamented as the final whistle blew. 'To go through we must now win our next game.' He held his hands up in despair. 'And we face… Brazil! We are finished!'

Ah, the anguish of the sports fan, emotions tied to events beyond his control—not dissimilar to the anguish of the long-distance walker, emotions tied to *weather* events beyond his control. The comparison gave me pause for thought, and the answer was the same in both instances: one had to care and not care simultaneously; one had to lose oneself in the moment but then accept fate and let hopes and expectations go. Easily said, harder to do. I'd been trying to make peace with conditions beyond my control since Melito.

The following morning, Robin and I walked into the Rondane. Thick fog hid the mountains, swirling across the path, but the wild was a tangible thing, pressing upon us from all sides. Straight from a busy London life, Robin was instantly captivated.

'I feel like I'm on the edge of a great empty nowhere,' he observed. 'I can't see anything, but I feel as though the mountains stretch for hundreds of miles.' It wasn't far off the truth.

Rondane National Park is Norway's oldest, and fulfils its purpose well, protecting an accessible group of mountains that might otherwise have been overdeveloped. At one time Norwegians saw little reason to set land aside for preservation. Their mountains were vast—how could they ever be spoiled? Fortunately, a few far-sighted individuals recognised that size was no guarantee of safety, as events in other countries have proved. These individuals included leading members of the DNT, and in 1904 they began campaigning for wild-land protection. Convincing the Norwegian government took decades of effort, but persistence eventually paid off in 1962 when the Rondane National Park was established. Legislation drew a line across the fjells, beyond which the construction of vacation homes, roads and other forms of 'progress' couldn't march. Further parks followed—in increasing number as the twentieth century rolled by. This was the right kind of progress.

Unlike in many other national parks around the world, where regulations limit a visitor's freedom to fully immerse themselves in nature, Norway grants visitors the right to roam and camp in unrestricted freedom. Known as *allemannsretten*—or 'every man's right'—the right of access to all uncultivated land across Norway has existed for centuries. *Allemannsretten* is as much a part of Norwegian DNA as is the *friluftsliv* lifestyle. Indeed, *allemannsretten* and *friluftsliv* belong together, and both are based not on taking advantage of the land but on travelling gently and treating it with respect. Although *allemannsretten* existed long before it was codified into law, it was raised to a whole new level when made a legal right in 1957.

As far as I was concerned, few other laws are as enlightened. The right to roam in self-regulating freedom across wild land is a natural and moral right that reflects our ancient relationship with nature. With a change in cultural attitudes, and a *huge* amount of leave-no-trace education, it could work right across Europe.

Robin and I spent our first night in the Rondane camping free and wild, and the second at the fully staffed Rondvassbu DNT hut, one of the few buildings allowed within the park. Rondvassbu welcomed us with a smile. We were shown to a clean dormitory that we had to ourselves, then shared the dining area with fifteen fellow hikers, evidence (at last) that Norwegians *were* out in their fjells—or at least visiting their DNT huts. Rondvassbu is one of the busiest huts in the DNT network. It sits beneath the Rondane's highest peaks—massive mountains with sharp arêtes and scooped-out cirques. Ringed by plateaux, and isolated from other ranges, the Rondane is all about space—or so I'd been told. With fog smothering the fjells I wondered if Robin and I would simply have to take everyone else's word for it.

But then, on Robin's fourth day, June 24, we woke to clear skies.

'Don't blink,' I said. 'This may be the only sunny day for months.'

To make the most of it, we strode briskly from Rondvassbu and set up camp late in the morning beneath a climbable mountain, Bråkdalsbelgen. Mosquitoes attacked, but we were soon heading uphill, leaving Robin's tormentors behind.

Space, it quickly became apparent, *was* the thing here. The higher we climbed the more extraordinarily open the surrounding landscape became. Progress felt extraordinary, too, for how straightforward and easy it was. The trail up Bråkdalsbelgen was entirely free of snow to within fifty feet of the summit. Travelling without snowshoes to 6,000 feet, climbing to a summit with ease, seeing 100 miles, basking beneath blue skies—Robin didn't know how fortunate he was. But a broad grin revealed his appreciation all the same. And on the summit there wasn't a mosquito in sight.

After a two-hour stay on top we descended, passing a Norwegian pair hiking up—the first fellow travellers I'd encountered on a high mountain since the Dolomites in October. Crowds, by Norwegian standards!

The clear weather persisted into evening, a treat that I couldn't take for granted. Three days earlier, rain had turned the summer solstice into an event

Robin on the summit of Bråkdalsbelgen (6,283 feet), June 24, 1998.

to shelter from, but at last I had a chance to fully experience a Norwegian summer night. Robin, tiring of his tormentors, retreated into Auld Leakie early and was soon asleep, leaving me alone outside. Oddly, the mosquitoes vanished as soon as Robin disappeared. Wrapped in my sleeping bag I settled down comfortably, ready to savour the short northern night.

Sunset at this latitude—almost sixty-two degrees north—came a few minutes before 11 p.m. It wasn't dramatic and full of colour but gentle and soft-edged. Scent-laden breezes drifted up from the valley, cuckoos and curlews called from distant slopes, and all the struggles from recent months fell away. I let my thoughts drift along peacefully like the few wispy clouds overhead. *This* was why I was here: for slow living in a slow place. Midnight eventually arrived, but not darkness. I could see details on the mountains clearly, the sky was too bright for stars, and the northern horizon glowed with reassuring warmth. It wasn't quite the midnight sun —I wasn't far enough north for that—but it was close enough.

As I lay quietly, an astonishingly powerful feeling of needing absolutely nothing, of utter completeness, flooded my body and mind. It was profoundly peaceful—a total removal of *all* cares. The surrounding land played a huge part in it. I felt embraced by it, accepted, comforted, connected. *You are*

260

home, it seemed to communicate, although not in words. *Everything is okay.* And I knew, deep down, that it was, and always would be, even when future situations might have me feeling otherwise.

I lay in a state of fulfilment for several hours, not even needing sleep.

Sunrise arrived at 2.30 a.m.: a sudden flash of red, a brief glimpse of fire, but then clouds swallowed the horizon. Finally, a deep, contented, dreamless sleep claimed me, and I woke where I lay six hours later to Robin emerging from Auld Leakie. He eased himself upright, stretched, gazed around at thick fog.

'Did I miss anything?' he asked.

To make progress from camp we faced a challenging obstacle: a wild river, urgent with snowmelt. According to my map, the river shouldn't even have been an obstacle. The map marked a bridge 100 yards from camp, out of sight of our tents, but when we'd inspected the location the previous morning the bridge had lain in deconstructed pieces on the far bank.

'Well, that's not very helpful,' Robin had observed, scratching his head.

'Tell me about it,' I'd replied. 'This isn't the first time.'

The river ran through a ravine. The ravine wasn't especially deep—only twelve or so feet—but its walls were sheer and the river was raging. The only option was to head upstream until a safe fording point could be found.

We set out the following morning, and it took a mile before we found a spot, which meant we had to walk another mile back down the river bank to return to the trail. Two miles of rough off-trail effort, soaked legs and boots from crossing the river, and finally there was our camping spot, less than twenty yards away. But at least we were over the river.

'Funny game, this,' Robin said, 'walking two miles to gain twenty yards!'

We continued downstream, heading for the trail, and soon the game became even funnier.

We both stopped dead when we reached the location of the bridge.

'Oh...' I said.

Robin looked as confused as I felt. 'What the...?'

'But how...?'

'That's just plain... *wrong*!' Robin exclaimed, laughing.

261

The bridge was now there. It had been built, perhaps while we'd been climbing Bråkdalsbelgen the previous afternoon. It spanned the ravine as though it had never *not* spanned it. We dumped our packs and crossed the damn thing several times just to make sure our eyes weren't playing tricks on us.

'Was it *really* not here yesterday?' Robin asked.

'Absolutely,' I confirmed. 'You saw what I saw.'

'Well...' Robin said, 'I quite like Norway... but it's not perfect, is it?'

We pulled on our packs and set off along the trail, thoroughly entertained.

'Anyway,' Robin said, 'it's not *all* bad. I didn't like to mention it, Andrew, but your feet did need a splash of water.'

———

From the 'Magically Appearing Bridge' Robin and I crossed spacious moorland and eventually descended into a leafy valley. We took the miles at a measured pace, and there were fewer of them each day than I'd grown used to, but that was fine—companionship and laughter had more value than distance. Despite blisters and mosquito bites Robin remained in good spirits. He continuously amused himself with quips about the ridiculous size of Ten Ton, and made light-hearted observations about the so-called food I cooked and ate each night.

'You've been eating *that* for how long?'

'Um...' I did a little mental arithmetic. 'About four hundred and twenty days. Give or take.'

'Honestly, you're tougher than you look. Being able to eat that each night is far more impressive than walking here from Italy!'

At our final wild camp he ushered me aside and took control of my dinner. First, he fried garlic and onions in the pot-lid skillet that I hadn't ever fully utilised; next, he stirred in chopped carrots, diced red pepper, and chunks of salami; then he mixed it with pasta sauce, and finished by stirring the result into a bowl of perfectly boiled tortellini. It was delicious, the tastiest camp meal since... well, since forever.

'Robin, this is amazing! I'll be cooking *this* for the rest of the trip now, not my other stew.'

Robin laughed, shook his head in despair. 'You could try varying it.'

We reached the town of Dombås on June 27, the penultimate day of Robin's visit. As with Tanya and Richard, the final day was all about sparing my guest his blisters. This time, instead of renting bicycles, we jumped aboard a train for an out-and-back trip to the fjordside village of Åndalsnes, sixty-five miles north-west. The scenery along the route was stupendous, especially when we clattered through the Romsdal valley where mountains reared with a spikiness not seen since the Dolomites. Gaping upward I knew in an instant that, just as my evening stew had been altered irrevocably by Robin's visit, so too had my planned route. From Dombås I'd originally aimed to cut through the Dovrefjell and head north at full speed. Time was getting on—it was almost July, but I was barely a quarter of the way up the country. But now that I'd seen Romsdal I had to include one final lengthy detour. The Romsdal Alps were irresistible.

And in any case, my funds were almost blown.

When I pulled cash from an ATM in Dombås I saw with horror that I only had enough money left to cover two weeks' food. If no further funds came through, if I were to fail because of it, it would be far better to fail amid some of the steepest mountains in Europe than upon the broad Dovrefjell.

Robin departed early the next morning, at 1.30 a.m.. This time, wonderful as the companionship had been, there wasn't even a slight loss of balance. Instead, energy coursed. I strode swiftly from the station, hungry for the wild, determined to make every second count. After Richard and Tanya's departure the purpose for being on The Walk had blurred, but now it was startlingly clear. I knew what I wanted, what I was in Norway for, what I was *alive* for: to live each moment to the full. I knew in which direction my path through life was supposed to head: forward. Suddenly, I found myself awash with freedom, blindingly aware that I—and I alone—was in control of my life's journey, even if this particular physical journey, The Walk, was nearly done. A thought struck that I could so easily have missed this. I could have gone through life unaware that I had control. But I hadn't missed it. I had everything I needed right here with me, and the greatest thing was I'd still have it even back in London. I didn't want to run out of funds, but if I did it wouldn't be the end of the world.

I paced into the new day, celebrating all the lessons I'd learnt.

Three days and eighty miles later I was back in Romsdal, as engrossed in The Walk as I'd ever been, although ever conscious of its rapidly approaching end.

The push to Romsdal had mostly involved low-level miles. I'd tried crossing a corner of the Dovrefjell, hoping to see its most famous residents —musk oxen, Europe's most prehistoric-looking animal—but fog and rain had hidden all. Forest tracks had followed, then sandy Rømø-like heathlands, then tarmac. But the roads hadn't been busy, especially during Norway's World Cup match against Brazil. For two hours I had the road entirely to myself, until a car pulled level and its driver leaned out of the window with a grin as wide as the sky.

'We did it,' he exclaimed, desperate to share the news. 'The unthinkable! Two zero! We beat Brazil!' And pressing his horn in jubilation he sped off.

Norwegians are mad about sport—madder, quite possibly, than most nations. For a country with such a small population it frequently punches above its weight, especially in the Winter Olympics. Four years prior to my visit, Norway had hosted the 1994 games in Lillehammer, winning more medals than any other nation, further extending their lead at the top of the all-time medals table. But perhaps it wasn't surprising—after all, Norway had invented many of the winter sports. Without doubt, Norwegians are an active race; they don't just *watch* sport, they *take part*. They play football, fish, run, ski and hike. It was revealing that not one single Norwegian had asked me why I was walking. The question had come often elsewhere, but Norwegians didn't need to ask. They already knew.

The answer was certainly clear to me when I reached Romsdal. Standing in the valley bottom I looked up at the tallest and steepest cliffs of the entire journey, fearsome rock faces that firmly put me in my place. The greatest precipice was the Trollveggen—the Troll Wall—the tallest vertical rock face in Europe. The wall is so steep that if an angry troll were to drop a rock off the top it would freefall for 3,600 feet and land 160 feet out from the wall's base. Camping beneath it (but respectfully back), I spent long hours gaping upwards, losing count of the rocks I heard crashing down. The Troll Wall had an aura of menace—an inhospitable darkness. If trolls lived anywhere, they lived up there.

Such a wall, of course, was irresistible to certain adventurous souls. Fittingly, it was a Norwegian climbing team who scaled the Trollveggen first, in 1965, beating British climbers to the top by a single day. Eventually,

The Troll Wall above Romsdal, June 30, 1998.

climbing the wall wasn't enough and some people took to jumping off it. The late 1970s and early 1980s saw the growth of a new sport, BASE jumping, and few locations in the world excited BASE jumpers more than the empty spaces beneath the Troll Wall. Even though BASE jumping was banned from the wall in 1986 following several tragic deaths, jumpers continued to come. Craning my head backwards so that I could see the jagged needles topping the wall a vertical mile above, I tried to imagine the self-assurance needed to launch into the void. But I failed. I even struggled to imagine the guts needed to climb on the wall's lower tiers. My adventure seemed extremely tame in comparison.

Norway has produced more than its fair share of adventurers: Fridtjof Nansen, nineteenth-century polar explorer; Roald Amundsen, who in 1911 famously beat British explorer Captain Scott to the South Pole; Thor Heyerdahl, of *Kon-Tiki* fame; Erik the Red, tenth-century discover of Greenland; and his son, Leif Erikson, who sailed west and became the first known European to step onto North American soil, beating Christopher Columbus to the continent by over 400 years. And there were all the other Vikings who sailed far and wide, not just across the North and Baltic Seas but also into the Mediterranean as far as Constantinople. Norwegians have never been a race to stay meekly at home.

Ironically, it was an Englishman, William Cecil Slingsby, who introduced the idea of mountain climbing to Norwegians. Slingsby was a Yorkshire-born climber who fell in love with Norway during his first visit in 1872, and returned repeatedly for decades after. He travelled all over the country, exploring and climbing, making friends, teaching and inspiring locals to climb. His love for Norway and his enthusiasm for climbing took a hold in others, who inspired others still, and he eventually became known as the father of Norwegian mountaineering. Slingsby made numerous first ascents, including Norway's third-highest peak, the jagged Store Skagast-ølstind, a mountain Norwegians of the time considered unclimbable. In 1904 Slingsby wrote a book about his adventures—*Norway: the Northern Playground*—a classic of mountaineering literature that remains in print to this day. Towards the end of the book there's a chapter set in Romsdal, and in it Slingsby describes outings on the surrounding peaks with undisguised affection. He also mentions the capricious weather, and I found that reassuring: if conditions could thwart the plans of adventurers like Slingsby, I shouldn't feel so bad when they thwarted my more modest plans.

I woke beneath the Trollveggen on July 1 to typical fjord-region weather. Its wetness moved me on. I climbed from Romsdal without regret, grateful to have seen the Troll Wall. My maps showed other dramatic mountains nearby: stabbing peaks like the Romsdalshorn, rugged giants like Store Venjetinden, but all I saw was hints, suggestions, fleeting silhouettes—a snatch of pinnacle here, a glimpse of buttress there, a vanishing ridge over yonder. And clouds. I saw lots of clouds, and rain, and fog.

For the following five days I crossed the grain of the land, climbing from wet valleys to dripping forests to fogbound passes, then back down to even wetter valleys.

The days were filled with moisture; with seeping, squelching peat; with mist, drizzle and rain; with ever-shifting clouds and pressing fog; with bogs and puddles; with endless streams gurgling and splashing; with rivers roaring and frothing; with waterfalls crashing; with water beading every stem of grass, pine needle and leaf. It was impossible to remain dry. My socks were perpetually sodden, my boots heavy with water, my trousers clinging-wet, my so-called waterproofs clammy, my hair plastered to my head.

Wet weather above Eikesdal, July 6, 1998.

When I reached the Eikesdal valley I picked up a local tourist brochure and sheltered at a bus stop to read it. '*Welcome,*' the cheery title said. '*The Eikesdal Valley is one of the area's natural pearls. The village is well protected between high mountains, and has a special climate with noticeably less downfall than in surrounding areas, in fact about half as much downfall as these.*' I laughed aloud at that. If the unceasing rain here was less 'downfall' than elsewhere then I was surprised that Norwegians elsewhere hadn't evolved fins and gills.

A shopkeeper smiled when I asked him if the weather was always as wet as this.

'On no,' he replied, peering outside. 'This is nothing. Sometimes it *really* rains!'

I took to looking at postcards to see what I was missing, and the missing would once have been hard to take—except that the watery atmosphere was now getting under my skin. Where once I'd pulled forests tight around me like a blanket I now began pulling the Norwegian weather. There was a softness to the clouds that calmed, a secretiveness within fog that comforted, a gentleness to steady rain that lulled. I wouldn't have complained if the landscape had been revealed, but I discovered to my surprise that I could manage without seeing it. There was deep magic on tap in the Norwegian fjells. Actually seeing them had little to do with it.

On July 6 I camped beside a tarn in a glacier-carved cirque, the 'Chair of the Mountain Gods' camp. The cirque only sat 2,000 feet above sea level, but the tarn was still frozen and masses of snow still lay above it. Here, winter *still* hadn't thawed. It looked exactly like the Norway from two months earlier, but I wouldn't have wanted it any other way. I suspected I'd one day look back at this watery stretch with immense affection, although I also wondered if I was only enjoying it because I knew my time here was nearly up.

Uncomfortable as the rain could be, there *were* some benefits. One was the way it vanquished mosquitoes; another was how it cleaned my cookware. By accident I discovered that if I left my dirty dishes outside at an angle for a few hours the elements washed them clean. It was a eureka moment. *Ah-ha!* I thought, *Norway: the world's largest automatic dishwasher!* It became a labour-saving trick.

There were occasional moments of visibility, a few brief episodes of drama. The most memorable occurred at the end of a long climb. I crested a pass, and with incredible timing the clouds parted, sunbeams burst through, and a huge bird swooped by. It was a white-tailed eagle, also known as a sea eagle—sometimes poetically called the 'eagle of rain'. It tore through the air directly ahead of me, wind rushing through its feathers. The wingspan was huge—easily eight feet, the widest of any species of eagle—and its brown and white feathers were ragged and unkempt, quivering from the power of the eagle's dive. The bird passed within twenty feet. I reached quickly for my camera without looking away, but already it was too late. The eagle spiralled up the valley toward distant mountains without flapping its wings—a supreme master of air currents that were unseen and unfelt by mere earthbound mortals such as myself. Too soon it was a black speck against grey mountains, then it was gone. But the memory remained, and it seemed worth all the rain for such an indelible moment of drama.

When Eikesdal fell behind I fancied a change, and descended to sea level. It put a road beneath my feet, but the Sunndalsfjord made up for it. The fjord shimmered like mercury, mountains rose into wreathes of mist, beams of sunlight strobed through clouds. After several miles I spotted movement in the fjord: dark fins, then unmistakable curves—dolphins, cutting through the water. I stopped to watch. Progress wasn't everything.

After a while a car pulled over and a lady stepped out.

'*Hei-hei*—I'm Sidsel,' she said. 'I work for the local newspaper. Every issue I write a short feature on a tourist in the area. May I ask some questions?' She paused for a moment. 'I'm always on the lookout for unusual visitors.'

'Unusual?' I asked, pretending to be offended.

'Yes,' Sidsel replied, laughing, pointing to Ten Ton. 'With *that* on your back you definitely look unusual!'

Sidsel had already driven past once but returned for a second look. Over the years, I soon learned, she'd interviewed a great many visitors and had listened to some wonderful travellers' tales, but mine stopped her dead.

'*What* did you say?' she exclaimed. 'You have walked from *where*?'

The feature Sidsel wrote was published two days later. I was sitting in a campsite near the town of Sunndalsøra, finally drying out beneath clearing skies, when the site's owner wandered over.

'I've just seen this in the paper,' she said, pointing to an embarrassingly large photo and five columns of text. 'Here, please… have the campsite fee back and also… here's a little extra to pass on to the homeless.'

I didn't know what to say, merely thanked her.

'Well,' she said, looking down at the paper. 'I felt I had to.'

If only, I wished, *everyone who heard about The Walk back home was moved to help the homeless in a similar way.*

———

I took a well-earned day off in Sunndalsøra, then returned to the fjells, acutely aware that they would be the very last of The Walk. Base Camp had offered their commiserations when I'd phoned home.

'There's nothing to report, I'm afraid,' my father said gently. 'Every payment you're owed has been paid.'

Banishing disappointment, I walked into the wild as though The Walk had months remaining, not days. Since leaving Dombås ten days earlier it had been hard to accept reality. I'd still believed that something would happen, that funds would come from somewhere, that the gods of long-distance hikers would bestow a reward for everything I'd done.

For over fifteen months I'd been able to picture The Walk's final day at the North Cape with astounding clarity. Even now I still could. My mind couldn't accept not reaching it.

Determined to live in the moment, I climbed into the Trollheimen, the 'Home of the Trolls'. Sharp to the west, rolling to the east, the Troll-heimen were the last big mountains of southern Norway. North of them were lower fjells for hundreds of miles, the land only rising again nearer the Arctic Circle. Not that I'd experience those Arctic mountains now. I consoled myself by focusing on everything that I had already experienced. I reminded myself that I still had the Trollheimen to enjoy, that I was still in Norway *right now*. The funds were beyond my control, but the next few days weren't. I wasn't going to rush them but finish in style.

Once I'd entered the Trollheimen it soon became clear it wasn't trolls I'd find but people. The July hiking season was now underway and the fjells were finally free enough of snow to appeal to all, not just masochistic long-distance vagabonds. I encountered families out for day hikes, small groups heading toward DNT huts, and anglers aiming for trout-filled lakes. For fifteen months I'd had the mountains of 'over-crowded' Europe to myself, which made the edge of the Trollheimen feel busy. But it wasn't a bad thing. Smiles were freely given, conversations started easily, encouragement came often. It was an uplifting experience to feel part of an extended mountain-travelling community. Out here we were all essentially doing the same thing, all answering the same call whether or not that call was understood or even acknowledged. It was as if the walls people often hid behind back in civilisation had fallen away the instant they'd stepped into the wall-less wild, as if they could now be the open-hearted easy-going community-minded creatures nature had intended all along. It felt like an appropriate way to celebrate everything The Walk had been, sharing its final miles with a mountain-loving family.

Despite the increase in people the wild wasn't overrun. The Trollheimen was huge and hours often passed between encounters. But what was funny was how badly timed some of them were. The first was an American behind a rock, his pants around his ankles answering nature's call. 'Oops!' he cried, hastily tugging his trousers up. Next, I stumbled upon a couple who were loudly doing something else that was perfectly natural in so beautiful a place. They were far too focused to notice my approach, so I retreated respectfully, waited awhile, made noise of my own—whistling, singing, coughing—then waited several minutes more. Certain they'd had plenty of time to finish I re-emerged, but finished they hadn't. *Ah well*, I thought, *to hell with it*, and I marched by, eyes averted. The woman shrieked and the man laughed. Both frantically disengaged and reached for discarded clothes.

There were other memorable encounters. I met an angler in her early twenties wearing spotless white tennis shoes and a rainbow-hued shell suit. Jewellery hung from her ears and neck; her face was painted with make-up; hairspray held her hair in voluminous waves. It was a striking change from the camouflage most Norwegian anglers appeared to prefer.

I met three cyclists from the Czech Republic, carrying road bikes over their shoulders across bony ground. They told me they were heading to the Trollheimshytte DNT hut, and from what I could see they were going to have to carry their bikes a hell of a distance to get there. 'These rocks aren't good for the tyres,' they explained. Clearly, I wasn't the only odd one about.

Most memorable was the girl I believe I saw in the middle of a sun-dappled birch wood. She was an absolute vision: a golden-haired bronze-skinned athletically muscled goddess in not much of a bikini. She appeared ahead on the trail and skipped barefoot into the woods with a haunting smile and laugh, quickly disappearing from view. I stopped dead, wondering if my eyes had deceived me. Perhaps I *had* been underway too long. Maybe it was a good thing I was out of funds and soon heading home.

On July 11 I walked up a deepening valley, the Naustådalen, following a narrow path into the heart of the Trollheimen. There was no one else about now. The surrounding fjells were wild and rugged, ribbed with rock, streaked with snow. Brooks tumbled and rock pools gleamed. Delicate pink flowers speckled the tundra, clouds rolled off summits, and patches of sunlight surfed across open slopes. Early in the afternoon I reached the head of the valley, and it was too close to my idea of wilderness perfection to keep on going. I stopped early and made camp, aiming to enjoy the location to the full.

At first I sat and relaxed, attempting to read, but reading was impossible—I couldn't take my eyes off the landscape. A fair amount of snow still lay in drifts, but open ground balanced it. It was a landscape of contrasts: grass and snow, earth and rock, rushing stream and motionless pool. The temperature felt comfortable and the air smelled heavenly with its scents of plant growth and sun-warmed soil. The sound of running water accompanied the songs from numerous birds. Soon, even sitting was impossible. I stood up and began wandering—but without real purpose. I took step by slow step, stopping repeatedly to take it all in.

With each breath exhilaration grew, along with a profound sense of peace and well-being. Slowly, the feelings strengthened. Soon, they filled me to my core, then expanded beyond my own borders. A sensation of extraordinary completion overcame me, as though every aspect of life was exactly the way it was meant to be. It was like being connected to something incomprehensibly immense that was utterly without limits, but not only connected—also welcomed, accepted, merged. There were no doubts left now, no anxieties, no fears. I was still fully aware that I was alone in a remote Norwegian wilderness, but being here suddenly felt like the most comfortable and natural thing in the world.

This—exactly this—was what I'd been striving for all along. Nowhere else in Norway had I felt more at home or more exuberantly content. And not just nowhere else in Norway—nowhere else *anywhere*. I may not have reached the North Cape, but I *had* achieved my goal.

Showers swept through early in the evening, chased by rainbows. At 8 p.m. crisp sunlight returned, and on the spur of the moment I scrambled to a rocky peak 1,500 feet above camp. The elation I experienced on the summit is something I'll never forget. The golden evening light; the 360-degree panorama; a lingering rainbow to the north; the taste and touch of cold, clean air; the liberating space and soothing quietness; the sheer perfection of an untrammelled snow-streaked mountain wilderness spread in every direction: it transported me to another plane of existence. If I could have merged into the rocks and soil at my feet and become one with the mountains for all time I would have without a second's hesitation. In a way, I felt that I already had.

I couldn't have wanted a better way to finish The Walk.

At home in the Trollheimen, July 11, 1998.

I stayed a second day in 'Camp Rainbow', surrounded by soft mist, lost to the peace and beauty of the place, soaring from the connection I'd found.

Out of food, I walked away the day after, although with great reluctance. Emotions welled as I trekked from the Trollheimen: gratitude and joy mixed with a sudden, gut-churning sensation of loss. In 5,680 miles I'd seen, experienced and learnt more than I could have ever hoped for. I was fortunate beyond words, but suddenly it wasn't enough.

How could I leave, now that I'd finally arrived, now that I was finally at home in the wild?

How could I end now, and let down The Passage and the Cardinal Hume Centre? It would mean far lower donations for the homeless. It felt like a broken promise. The sense of failure to the charities felt devastating.

What of my dream to walk in the Arctic? And what of the North Cape? Hadn't I always been able to picture the end? Hadn't I known all along I was going to make it? Ending here didn't make sense.

The journey had become my life. I'd thought I had so much time. But then, suddenly—boom—here we were, and the time was all used up.

Leaving was going to tear me apart.

But sometimes it just rains, I told myself, *and you simply have to accept it.*

It was true. Whatever happens, happens. And perhaps there were lessons in it. Was leaving now and learning to deal with it The Walk's final lesson? Was *this* my journey's greatest test? *Well, if it is,* I decided, *I'm damn well going to pass it.* I may have failed to reach the North Cape but I wasn't going to fail this.

I walked on, reaching for positives. My walk had done some good for the charities. Not as much as I'd hoped, but more than if I'd done nothing. And Norway would still be here. I could work hard over the winter, save up, return to finish the journey. It wouldn't be the same, it wouldn't feel like a continuous journey, but it would be something.

But oh how I wished I didn't have to leave!

My mood lightened on the edge of the Trollheimen, and it was a sign that did it. The sign sat at the entrance to a ravine overhung by mossy rocks and gnarled trees. It was triangular and bordered with red, like a road sign warning motorists of elk, ice, or falling rocks. But this sign sat far from any road, and it featured a hazard not usually encountered by motorists—at least not during daylight hours. Pictured was a distinctive silhouette from Norse mythology: a massive, hairy, large-nosed being. *Be warned,* the sign declared, *trolls ahead!*

The moment I saw it I burst into laughter. The comedic brilliance broke my mood.

Thank you, I thought, *whoever you are. Thank you for placing the sign. You made an unbearable day bearable.*

I was still chuckling appreciatively five miles later when I reached civilisation.

Idyllic farmland stretched ahead: small fields and turf-roofed cabins nestling beneath wild fjells. *What a country Norway is,* I thought, *and how fortunate I am to have walked across so much of it.* I'd take it with me when I left, whatever happened in the future. The truth of this was suddenly clear. Everything that had happened since Calabria was now a part of who I was. I'd take it all with me.

And I wasn't only ending a journey—I was also starting one. I was about to travel back toward family and friends, and also to future friends, people I hadn't yet met. Who knew what, and *who*, lay ahead. It was merely a different kind of journey—a journey into a world of people, a world that I didn't have to run from any longer. Going home didn't have to be a step backward. It could still be an adventure.

It bloody well will be an adventure, I promised myself.

And I WILL return to Norway. I'd come back in June, return to 'Camp Rainbow', then push north. I *would* make it to the North Cape.

Feeling the significance of the act, I stepped from my treasured earth back onto unnatural pavement, and I did it with gratitude.

It was okay. The Walk was done, but I was okay with that.

And I almost convinced myself that I was.

'Camp Rainbow', July 11, 1998.

BASE CAMP
Chapter 9

I FOUND A phone box in the small village of Fossmoan and dialled Base Camp—although I knew I wouldn't be calling them that for much longer.

After five rings my mother answered, and I waited while she fetched my father. I could picture the phone perfectly, nestling in a corner of the kitchen, a brown china tea pot and knitted tea cosy right beside it. The image took me straight back to childhood and to the feelings of love and security that had filled it. It really had been a happy time. It didn't matter that it had taken place far from wild nature—I hadn't missed what I hadn't known. My parents had created a home where my three brothers and I could be children, safely sheltered from the realities of an often unjust world. We'd been treated firmly but always fairly, we'd been pushed to be the best versions of ourselves we could be, and from an early age we'd been taught right from wrong. Most fundamentally, we'd grown up without ever once doubting we were loved. This love had been ever-present. It had underpinned every moment of our existence.

I heard it now as my parents came back on the line.

'Andrew,' my mother said softly, expressing a thousand comforting words simply through the way she said my name.

It was difficult not to choke with emotion as I described The Walk's final miles. I tried to sound positive, but wasn't sure I was succeeding.

'Anyway. Time to head home,' I finished. 'Bergen first, then...'

But my father interrupted. 'Just a moment.' He took a long breath, then spoke slowly and thoughtfully. 'We've been talking, your mum and I. We can't bear to see your walk end now, not after everything. Not before it's supposed to.' He paused a long while, then continued. 'We've made a decision.'

He stopped again, and I found myself holding my breath. I wondered what was coming.

'We'll need it paid back,' my father finally said. 'But… we'll lend you the money you need.'

And everything stopped. My thoughts whirled.

You'll do WHAT? Had I heard that right? You'll lend me the money?

My father had always been careful with money. He'd worked hard all his life and he managed his affairs with a considered and thoroughly long-sighted regard for the future. I could have and arguably should have learnt a great deal from him, but the rational and practical approach wasn't in my nature—and probably never would be, not when there were mountains and forests to explore.

The offer said everything that needed saying about the kind of parents Base Camp were. My father had made his opinion of my journeys clear long ago. 'Andrew, I think you're completely mad.' How many times had he said that? His words were always with me, reminding me that I didn't quite measure up. And yet, both he and my mother had stood behind me regardless. They'd gone above and beyond to help, posting out resupply parcels, making certain that sponsors fulfilled promises, chasing payments for photos and stories, updating the charities on progress. Without their work the journey would have floundered months earlier. I wouldn't have reached Norway.

But I couldn't get my head around their offer. The knowledge that I didn't have the funds to reach the North Cape had been with me every step. I'd coexisted with it so long that it didn't seem possible I could travel without it.

Insanely, something within even resisted. It wasn't supposed to be like this: *Bold Mountain Explorer Bailed Out By Parents!* Wasn't that a bit lame? I bet Slingsby managed without his mum and dad's help! Wasn't I an adult, supposed to stand on my own two feet? Wouldn't I learn more by pushing on regardless? What about fate, destiny, the will of the mountain gods? Wasn't there supposed to be a reward for all the faith I'd shown? Surely *something* would turn up?

But then I saw that something had: Base Camp! They were part of the journey too. I wasn't walking in a vacuum. I wasn't out here alone. I never had been.

'Dad...' I said.

'How much do you need?'

After some thought I suggested the absolute minimum I could get by on. The lower it was the sooner I'd be able to pay it back, and the better I'd feel about it. I'd grown used to living frugally, making do without excessive comforts. Anything else would have felt like cheating. It would have gone against the spirit of The Walk.

'Thank you,' I said, trying to express the enormity of my gratitude through tone of voice, but knowing I fell far short. How could I adequately express it, not only for this but for everything my parents had done over the decades, for all their sacrifices, for all the mundane chores, for the example they'd set, for living their lives with such integrity and honesty? How could I express gratitude for the unconditional love they'd given—and even for the gift of life itself? Words could never do it.

Afterwards, when I left the phone box, my feet didn't touch the ground. When I pulled on Ten Ton it seemed as though it were filled with feathers.

I felt fortunate and privileged beyond measure. I finally understood as I hadn't during childhood just how much I was loved. It was one of The Walk's greatest and most enduring gifts.

I turned north.

So *that* was why I'd always been able to picture reaching the end.

BØRGEFJELL

Majavatnet ●

Entrance to North Norway ●

AUGUST 1

6,000 miles ★

● 'Fast-paced road walking'

Medjå ●

'Sottoboggo' ● ◄ JULY 25

Route across
CENTRAL NORWAY
July – August 1998

N

NORWAY

GRESSÅMOEN
NATIONAL PARK

Snasåvatnet ●

JULY 22 ► ● 'Evening with the Eriksens'

JULY 21 ► ● Verdalsøra

● Movatnet

Trondheim Fjord

SWEDEN

JULY 19 ► ● 'Camp Aquavit'

● Trondheim

Reinsfjell
(5318 ft / 914m) ▲ ● Mebonden

JULY 17 ► ● 'Troll attack'

● Fossmoan
JULY 14

km 0   20   40   60
mi 0   10   20   30

THE BIG PUSH NORTH
Chapter 10

TIME WAS GETTING on. Or was it running out?

It was July 15, almost three months since I'd left Lindesnes, but I was only a quarter of the way up the country. The previous winter still hadn't fully thawed from the high fjells, but the first snows of the next could realistically fall in six weeks. I still had 1,000 miles to walk and Arctic weather could potentially stop me walking them. Unsure about the future, I'd been dilly-dallying in the south, but it was now time to cover some ground.

Time for the big push north.

With 300 miles of lower fjells ahead I lightened my load. I posted my snow gear, thermals and winter sleeping bag ahead, collected a summer bag that Base Camp had posted from home, and bade permanent farewell to my snowshoes. Ah, my snowshoes: what adventures we'd shared! What places we'd been! Would I miss them? Not for a damn second.

Light of heart, free as the wind, I paced onto the mountains of Central Norway. Although snow patches still lingered in gullies, there were no more extensive snowfields to cross, no frozen lakes to skirt, no swollen rivers to ford. The mountains were low, broad and rolling, but they weren't dull or tame. They were still rough underfoot, still remote, and still very Norwegian. Reindeer and ptarmigan lived upon them, wolverine and elk in the valleys beneath them. The views were endless. The fjells promised uninterrupted wilderness walking, and they'd be my home for the next three weeks. I hoped to cover twenty-plus miles a day and make steady northward progress. It was going to be a glorious stretch.

Except I'd forgotten one thing.

Trolls!

Trolls, of course, don't exist; not the trolls of Norse folklore. But trolls of another kind inhabit the Norwegian wild, and they are far more fearsome than any beast human imagination could ever conjure into existence.

I'd first met them months earlier in the Setesdal, and in many places since, including in the Trollheimen, but it wasn't until I crossed the Reinsfjell that they revealed their true nature.

They emerged after a long sweaty climb on a sunny, windless day. I paused for a break, easing Ten Ton to the ground. The temperature was mild, the air still, and the view expansive across fjells and forests to the distant blue spread of Trondheim Fjord. Life was good. But then I noticed a strange droning sound. It was low, vibrating and barely perceptible at first, but it increased steadily in volume, soon had me looking around in confusion, and then, when its cause arrived, had me packing Ten Ton as swiftly as I could and getting the hell out of there.

The trolls pounced, thousands of them: huge mosquito-trolls desperate for blood; tiny midge-trolls desiring only to bite, bite and bite some more. They attacked in thick swirling clouds, and they pursued me across the Reinsfjell with Terminator-like determination. The Terror Flies from the northern Apennines suddenly seemed like mild-mannered butterflies in comparison.

What is the collective noun for mosquitoes and midges? I wondered as I fled across the fjell. It couldn't be a swarm—too mild. Was it a mist of midges? Still too mild. A menace of midges? Better. A marauding mob of midges? A monstrous maddening murder of midges? A malicious moronic malevolence of mosquitoes?

No, I had it. It was simpler. It was a misery of midges. And a mayhem of mosquitoes. That sounded right. Misery and mayhem!

For the rest of the day it wasn't possible to stop without being attacked. I needed to stop so that I could apply repellent, and change into long trousers and a long-sleeved shirt to protect bare skin. And I needed to stop to rest, drink and eat. But I couldn't. Not for a second. I couldn't even slow. My only defence was to keep moving at practically a run.

The miles should have been idyllic, unhurried and free. I had wild fjells

Troll country. View across Reinsfjell to Trondheim Fjord, July 17, 1998.

in every direction, and I saw reindeer, mountain hares and countless birds. But life wasn't idyllic—it was hell, with misery and mayhem hounding me without mercy.

Setting up camp was the single most horrible experience of the entire journey. There was a moment during it when I thought: *I'm going to go insane.* But somehow I got the tent pitched and water collected and the entrance zipped shut with sanity just about maintained. I cooked dinner inside the inner tent, something I'd never before done, taking great care not to spill food, set anything alight or poison myself with fumes. It filled the tent's interior with stifling Mezzogiorno heat—an unpleasant blast from the past, but cooking outside was out of the question.

Dawn brought a moment of relief. The air was cool and rain was falling —I could hear it pattering upon Auld Leakie's walls. Except... it wasn't rain. It was mosquitoes and midges in uncountable numbers. They were in a frenzy, unhinged by nearness to a feast they'd been failing to reach all night. They were falling upon the tent like torrential rain, like a monsoon.

That was it: a *monsoon* of mosquitoes.

In biblical proportions.

Where was Robin, my mosquito magnet, when I needed him?

I doubt I've ever packed away a camp as quickly as I packed the 'Troll Hell' camp. I discovered that my repellent—a brand recommended by a local—merely made the buggers bite harder. For protection, I pulled on my waterproof coat and trousers, my gloves and balaclava, but I couldn't protect my face. I tore Auld Leakie down and sprinted away at high speed, staying in my layers despite hot sunshine. Perhaps it would have been better to have run out of funds after all.

Rushing on, sweating horribly, I considered the future. Weeks of this didn't bear thinking about. Was the Arctic tundra, with its perfect mosquito and midge environment of endless bogs and pools resting atop permafrost, going to be even worse? But I had to laugh. Just when all was well—when I had the funds, when I had open country to stride across, when I'd finally found myself at home—something else had to get in the way. It was typical!

I had to make a decision. I couldn't handle weeks of troll assault. There was only one solution: retreat. I turned for the valley. *Roll on winter*, I thought, and laughed again. I'd spent the best part of ten months looking forward to summer, but now it was here all I wanted was for the first insect-killing frost to arrive.

There were far fewer trolls down in the valley. As forest replaced open fjell the monsoon clouds thinned, and soon they gave chase only in small groups. I removed my protective layers and slowed. The relief was overwhelming.

And so the big push north became a valley walk—but I chose to accept it. It wasn't what I'd had in mind, but I was still walking. Altering the route was merely evolution at work. After all, in nature adaptation is everything. Species that don't adapt don't survive.

For two weeks I powered north, choosing paths, tracks and unmade roads where I could, but occasionally having no realistic alternative but pavement. I made one attempted return to the fjells when I couldn't stand roads any longer, but the 'misery and monsoon' atop the Gressåmoen

National Park[5] prompted another hasty retreat. I was here for the wild, but not *that* kind of wild.

But there were rewards a-plenty down in the valleys. I found a well-balanced landscape of forests and farms. I made swift progress. And most of all I found people—the hospitable Norwegians I'd otherwise have missed. On the very first evening after fleeing the Reinsfjell, down in a valley campsite, I was invited to dinner by a group of fellow campers. They'd caught several trout that day and wanted to share their good fortune. The fish were seasoned, placed alongside vegetables, wrapped in foil, buried in the hot embers of a campfire, served sizzling hot.

'Oh my!' I raved. 'This is sensational! What do you call this dish?' I expected some fancy Norwegian name.

'Well,' the cook murmured, waving away the praise—to him it was nothing out of the ordinary. 'It's only fish in a bag.'

Three nights later I was treated to another Norwegian delicacy—and it left me in a delicate state. The notoriously high price of alcohol in Norway prompts some people to distil their own alcoholic drinks, and my hosts —Olav and his friends—had done exactly that. Olav was the manager of one of Norway's largest water-treatment plants, but he assured me with a grin that nothing unsavoury had found its way from sewage plant into his home-brewed concoction.

'It is aquavit,' he explained proudly. 'Our national drink! You cannot walk the length of our country without drinking aquavit!'

He poured a generous measure. 'The name comes from Latin,' he explained. '*Aqua vitae*. It means water of life.' He and his friends raised their glasses high. '*Skål!*' they shouted. 'To life!'

It wasn't a smooth brew. On my first dram I nearly choked. But I battled on, not wishing to cause offence, and by the fourth glass it tasted fine. After that, my new friends and I had quite the merry evening.

I regretted it the next morning. It wasn't so much a hangover as a 'crushed under'. It was like waking to discover a Viking battle axe embedded in the side of my head.

'You must take some with you,' Olav suggested jovially when he saw me emerge from my tent at noon, the earliest I could get myself into motion.

---

5. The Gressåmoen National Park has been expanded and renamed since my visit. In its place is the larger Blåfjella–Skjækerfjella National Park.

'Here, make room for two bottles...'

Saying no was impossible, but I didn't carry them far. They were transferred to a bin half a mile down the road. But I carried the pounding headache for two days, and it wasn't eased by a thunderstorm that erupted that evening; the first 'KER-RACK' nearly split my head in two. It was ironic: I'd survived everything the mountains could throw at me, but it was Norwegian hospitality that almost brought Mad Mountain Jack to his knees.

Thankfully, time healed the headache, and happily, the hospitality continued. How wrong I'd been months earlier to worry that an increase in tourists would reduce Norwegian friendliness. Sure, there were a few notable exceptions, but these people no longer had any power over me, and they were few and far between. The vast majority proved that Norwegians are born with open-hearted genes.

There was a campsite owner who drove a hard bargain:

'Normally it is fifty kroner to camp,' she said. 'But, hmm... for you I think, let's say forty kroner. Or... twenty would be better, don't you think? But no, actually... I think you will stay for free!'

Another campsite owner busied himself near my camping spot while I was away showering, surprising me on my return with a lit fire and a tidy stack of firewood. He let me stay for free, too. After asking how far I was walking he replied: 'Oh, in that case... you will be my guest! Call it my walking-to-Nordkapp discount!'

There was a businessman who stopped to talk as though he had all the time in the world, and before leaving offered me use of his mobile phone (a far rarer item in 1998) so that I could call home. There were numerous offers of lifts, and there was a family who beckoned me over late one afternoon as I trekked by their russet-hued farmhouse. They invited me in for home-made blackberry juice, then offered cake, and then a bed for the night.

And what a night it was. The Eriksens treated me like royalty, not like a passing tramp. They provided dinner—fish, of course—a shower, a warm bed, and a long evening's conversation. It was everything life on the troll-haunted fjells wouldn't have been. The husband, Harald, was a gentle-mannered giant with a soft voice. He told me he'd lived his entire life in the valley on the family farm. Making a living from farming alone was near impossible, he explained, even with government subsidies, and to make ends meet he took other jobs whenever he could. He also received government money for any sheep lost to predators.

'But not for the first six killed,' he explained. 'According to the government, farms lose that many sheep every year to natural causes, and so they don't count them. But not me. Until four years ago there weren't any wolverine here, and I never lost any sheep. But last year I lost twenty-two during the summer. Twenty-two from my flock of a hundred and seven! So I am very angry with *mister* wolverine. I always carry my gun with me now—it's not illegal to shoot them.'

Harald described how there were also wolves and bears in the valley. 'I saw a bear two weeks ago through my binoculars, a long way off across the valley. A man was mauled over in Sweden recently.'

I was delighted to hear that bears roamed the landscape—it made the surrounding forests wilder. But Harald mistook my expression for fear. 'Don't worry,' he said. 'They're still very rare.'

'We also have a lot of elk,' he added. 'They appear every evening on the edge of the forest. You must have seen lots?'

He laughed when I admitted I hadn't, even after three months in elk country.

'Well, you will,' he said. 'Keep your eyes open at dawn and dusk. The government and various conservation organisations want more big animals in our forests. But, honestly, I'd prefer less. It's good we have a few, but they *are* a problem to farmers.'

Harald brought up another problem many Norwegian farmers faced: fallout from the Chernobyl meltdown in 1986. The radioactive cloud had travelled from the Ukraine to Norway and contaminated several regions, including the Breheimen and Jotunheimen. 'But not here,' he explained. 'Out west farmers still put salt crystals on the grass in spring to draw out caesium before letting their sheep graze. Perhaps you saw it?' I had indeed —I'd wondered why masses of salt had been spread across fields. I'd also wondered if drinking from Norway's mountain streams was likely to give me health problems decades into the future.

'You should be okay,' Harald said. 'We've been told the worst risk is long-term exposure to people like the Sámi who live off reindeer meat. Reindeer eat a lot of lichen, and lichen soaks up and concentrates the radiation.'

Traditional turf-roofed cabin, Trollheimen, July 13, 1998.

'So, if I get hungry I shouldn't catch and eat too many reindeer then?' I joked.

Harald laughed. 'No, and don't eat too much lichen either!'

Despite the many challenges that came with running a small farm Harald seemed incredibly content.

'Some people might want an *easier* way of life than the one we have,' he said, late into the evening, staring into the fire. 'But I cannot believe there is a *better* way. This land is in our blood. If we weren't living in contact with it I'm not sure we would really be… well… living.'

'I think I know what you mean,' I said.

My feet ticked along—one small step at a time, but the steps added up. They delivered valleys, forests, farms, villages and people into my life, then removed them. How could something as simple and slow as walking bring so much change? I still couldn't take it for granted.

287

I walked from gentle farmland to rough upper valleys, weaved across forested hills, skirted lakes, returned to farmland. The fabled Arctic Circle neared each day, but the landscape remained improbably green and lush—so idyllically pastoral at times that it resembled a landscape from far to the south, from Tuscany perhaps. I camped one night beside the Trondheim Fjord. The air was warm and humid, laden with all the scents of summer as well as the salty tang of the sea. I imagined myself back beside the Mediterranean. Broad-leafed trees swayed in a warm evening breeze, birds sang, and I thought: *is this really Norway?*

'Some visitors expect Norway to be a land of perpetual snow with ice bears walking down the street,' a local commented. 'And then they find this. I actually think some people are disappointed!'

'Well, not me,' I replied. 'After all I've been through, disappointment is the very last thing I'm feeling.'

But the land still had its moments. On July 25 I took a shortcut to connect two valleys, and discovered a Norwegian version of the *sottobosco* —the *sottoboggo*, I labelled it—a hard-to-cross wilderness of swamps and tangled growth that slowed progress to a crawl. It made a mockery of the concept 'shortcut'. Such forest swamps were part of the taiga, the immense boreal forest that wraps itself around the Northern Hemisphere. Taiga is pronounced the same as tiger, and the fierceness of the word felt appropriate. Living in it, I discovered, were the most carnivorous and fiercest trolls of all.

Happily, the July weather was friendlier—most of the time. It served up sparkling dawn dews and warm sunshine, brief cleansing showers and daily rainbows—conditions reminiscent of a mild British summer. A few thunderstorms even rumbled through, reminding me of the Apennines. But the long daylight hours were like nothing I'd experienced further south. The days were so long that I could start walking at noon, cover twenty-six miles, and still finish long before sunset. Even when I finished late I rarely saw the sun go down. I was usually too tired to stay awake late enough.

But the main theme of the big push north wasn't the southern weather, soft landscapes or welcoming people, but the sheer volume of miles that filled my days. I walked and walked and walked; for a while life seemed to involve little else. The Arctic was calling, pulling me on, and I couldn't now hold back. In two and a half weeks I covered 350 miles, and at that

Low fjells and wild forests—the backdrop to the miles, Lurudalen, July 27, 1998.

speed I was soon closing in on the mountains of the north. But the gains came at a cost: legs that began to feel old and creaky, and the first blisters since the Val Padana. Toward the end of one particularly long day an area above my groin erupted into sudden searing pain. I cried out and came to an abrupt halt, fearful that I'd done something irreparable. Somehow, I was able to get going again, though I couldn't continue with a normal stride. For the rest of the day I could only manage short half-steps. A nightmare that night featured a veterinarian-sized syringe being plunged into my groin and wiggled about sadistically, causing pain beyond excruciating. The same dream recurred every night for the rest of the big push north, and occasionally afterwards. It was so painful I began dreading sleep. The pain from it lingered into daylight hours.

But I pushed through it, through all the aches and pains, through extreme end-of-day weariness, and I did so marvelling at the body's ability to endure. After so many miles I'd learnt how to switch off pain. I acknowledged it, separated myself from it, then focused instead on the freedom I was living, on the details of the land, and on the mountains ahead. I stared into the distance hungrily, wondering when the north's first big range, the Børgefjell, would appear.

The momentous event occurred on August 1. The day began with torrents of rain, and puddles inside Auld Leakie. I considered taking the day off, but when the rain ceased my excuse went with it, and away I splashed, back onto the shoulder of the main road that I'd been following for four days—the loathsome 'Route That Everyone Follows', although most travellers were following it south, a detail I found mildly concerning.

But being on a road wasn't all bad. Soon, it wasn't bad at all. The land-scape evolved, gathering itself into growing folds, and at noon mountains appeared ahead. They were bald, grey, massive, patched with old snow, and at the sight of them *everything* was suddenly okay.

I stopped, savouring the moment. In my imagination, the wind sud-denly felt colder, the clouds darker. And it wasn't my imagination that the mosquitoes had vanished. A shiver of excitement ran through me. *It's autumn now,* the environment seemed to murmur. *Autumn!* And although it seemed crazy that August's first day could herald the end of summer I couldn't shake the feeling that something fundamental had changed. I couldn't pin down exactly what it was, but didn't mind the feeling one bit. It kindled energy not felt in weeks. *Time to move on,* an inner instinct murmured. *Time running out.*

I pushed on happily, pulled forward by the Børgefjell. Shortly before 5 p.m. I came to a striking archway across the road—an artistic represen-tation of the Northern Lights, with the name *Nord-Norge* (North Norway) hanging beneath it. To one side was a visitor centre. On a whim I turned toward it. The interior featured the usual interpretive signs and brochures, and also a woman behind a desk. She looked up expectantly when I appeared as though really glad to see another person.

'There aren't any tourists stopping,' she complained. 'It's been so quiet. We get Germans in June, Italians in July, and Norwegians in August... but the Norwegians all know where they're going and don't need my help!'

Sensing an opportunity to give purpose to a few minutes of her day, I asked several questions, and was soon glad I had. Aside from the satisfac-tion of witnessing her smile appear and enthusiasm emerge, her answers raised a smile of my own; her response to my question about midges and mosquitoes was greatly encouraging.

'They're dying out now up on the fjells. We're getting colder nights and the first frosts will occur any day. It will finish them. July is always the worst, August never as bad.'

I walked on afterwards barely daring to hope. Was the Arctic going to be manageable after all? Was the 'monsoon' nearly done?

I camped in an official site beside a large lake, the Majavatnet, finding a spot for Auld Leakie a few steps from the water's edge. Sitting in the entrance, I watched waves lapping upon a pebble beach, and stared across the lake to the looming, cloud-capped Børgefjell. A cold wind blew and there wasn't a single troll in sight. A churning sensation began deep within my belly—a feeling of anticipation and excitement that reminded me of another night spent camped beside a pebble beach, a night that now lay over 6,000 miles in my past.

I couldn't get to sleep. The anticipation acted like excessive caffeine and my heart pounded. With the first fjells of the north now before me I felt as though I was about to start a whole new journey.

An Arctic journey.

View from camp across the Majavatnet to the Børgefjell, August 1, 1998.

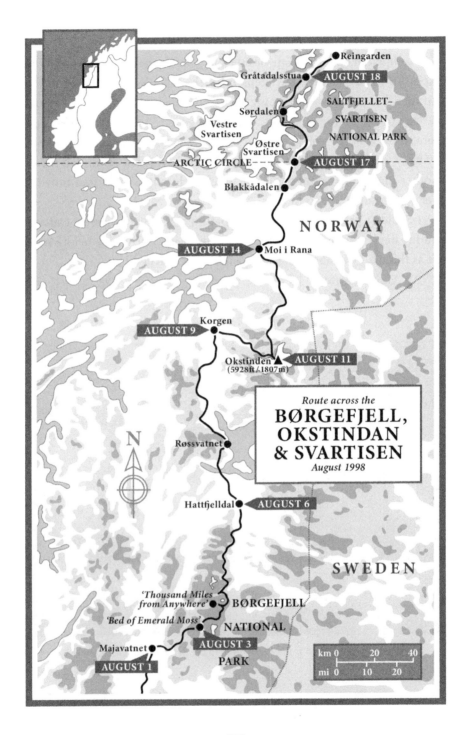

Reingarden
Gråtadalsstua AUGUST 18
SALTFJELLET–
Sørdalen SVARTISEN
Vestre NATIONAL PARK
Svartisen
Østre
Svartisen
ARCTIC CIRCLE AUGUST 17
Blakkådalen

NORWAY

AUGUST 14 Moi i Rana

Korgen
AUGUST 9
Okstinden AUGUST 11
(5928ft/1807m)

Route across the
**BØRGEFJELL,
OKSTINDAN
& SVARTISEN**
August 1998

Røssvatnet

N

Hattfjelldal AUGUST 6

SWEDEN

'Thousand Miles
from Anywhere' BØRGEFJELL
'Bed of Emerald Moss'
NATIONAL
Majavatnet AUGUST 3
AUGUST 1 PARK

km 0   20   40
mi 0   10   20

RETURN TO THE WILD
Chapter 11

STRICTLY SPEAKING, THE Børgefjell isn't an Arctic range—it lies 100 miles *south* of the Arctic Circle. But location isn't everything. What counts more are the defining characteristics of a place—the climate, the plant and animal species that live there, the composition of rock and soil, the interplay of water and ice, the amount of daylight in summer and darkness in winter. By those measures the Børgefjell is unquestionably Arctic. Once you step onto it, there's no doubt at all.

My Arctic journey began early on August 3. From camp, the fjells looked enormous, somehow *heavier* than other mountains, as though they contained more mass than narrower, sheerer-sided peaks. The Børgefjell is built from 1.7-billion-year-old granite, and reaches its apex on 5,574-foot Kvigtinden. The surrounding fjells are all massive and blunt. Some still sport glaciers. All offer great expanses of exposed rock and scree. The Børgefjell is a rugged but surprisingly simple place; an open land without secrets. It exists entirely without people. It doesn't need them, and has never really known them, except in passing. But it's also a land a few people have come to love and protect.

On August 9, 1963, the Børgefjell National Park was created, becoming —after the Rondane—Norway's second national park. As early as 1932 the DNT had suggested the Børgefjell should be preserved as wilderness, a place without cabins or marked paths, and when finally the park was born its founders agreed, stating it would 'retain a large natural area virtually free of technical intervention'. The Børgefjell is described as an 'undeveloped' park, and as a result has never become popular. This sounded ideal to me. 'Undeveloped' is the best form of development there is.

The sky was infinitely blue when I set out, and the temperature was so pleasantly mild, that the idea of being near the Arctic was laughable. I'd been warned that rain was on the way, but that didn't worry me. If anything, its approach added extra brilliance to the morning. And anyway, in Norway rain is *always* on the way.

Beneath clouds, the Børgefjell had looked intimidating, but under clear skies it was bright and accessible, as welcoming as a mountain wilderness could be. In ways that I couldn't fathom the rising land called to me as no other wild land had. I pushed forward eagerly, following a gravel trail into the birch forests that encircle the range. Three miles passed quickly, but then I suddenly ground to a halt. On the periphery of vision I saw movement; something ahead in the forest. Something black, massive and alive.

For a heartbeat or two I wondered if I'd imagined it, but instinct kept me frozen, and instinct is usually right. Trying to see past the distinctive white trunks of birch I peered into the undergrowth and, slowly, a shape took form. There's a trick to spotting wildlife in wild places. One has to soften one's vision and look at everything in general rather than one thing in particular. And then, if there *is* something to see, it will be seen. A shape out of place, movement, a fellow citizen of the planet.

An elk.

Welcome to the north, I thought!

The elk—or more correctly, the Eurasian elk—was huge, the largest mammal I'd seen on the journey. It took a few steps forward into a clearing fifty yards ahead and came into full view, sideways on, unaware it was being watched. Or maybe it knew and didn't care. Elk are powerful beasts. The males can weigh 1,000 pounds and stand seven feet tall at the shoulder. Their huge shoulder humps are all muscle, and their broad antlers can weigh fifty pounds. If a bull elk were to charge at top speed, thirty-five miles an hour, and hit with those antlers, one would know it.

Aware that charges do occasionally take place, but not feeling any threat of it, I stood still, attempting to blend into the landscape. The elk was magnificent, but there was also a hint of comedy. The legs looked too thin to support the massive body, the knees excessively knobbly, the posture awkward, the antlers like massive extra hands, and the bulbous nose clown-like. It looked like a creature put together from the unwanted parts of several other creatures, as though natural selection had been having a laugh. But, of course, natural selection knew what it was doing. An estimated 120,000 elk live in Norway, and to maintain so large a population in so harsh a place suggests the creature had been put together just right.

What seemed like an age passed, although probably it was only seconds. I gazed appreciatively upon a sight I'd been waiting months to see. Here was another of Europe's great treasures, and in its presence I felt transported to an older continent. It was the perfect way to begin my Arctic journey.

The elk finally noticed me, perhaps catching my scent. It looked my way, locked eyes, then turned and fled with surprising nimbleness and silence. It clearly knew what kind of predatory species I belonged to. Elk are hunted in Norway—an incredible 30,000 are shot in some years. Reported-ly, the meat tastes similar to venison, or grass-fed beef. Not that I wanted to find out. My preferred elk could be found wandering the woods in freedom, living the life it was born to live. Feeling regret at the fear I'd caused, but energised by the encounter, I walked on. I found myself longing for a world where creatures didn't flee the moment I appeared, a world where animal behaviour hadn't been negatively altered by other humans. To neither fear the wild, nor be feared *by* the wild—wouldn't that be a fine thing?

The next encounter was with two of my own species: a German couple. Happily, they didn't run away the moment they smelled me, although I wouldn't have blamed them. They were camping in an open glade beside a stream, and had made themselves at home. Clothes lines stretched between trees, paths had been trampled in vegetation, a large pile of cut branches rested in a pile, and a fire smouldered between a large ring of soot-blackened rocks.

'We've been here a week,' they told me. 'It's too perfect—too unspoiled to move on.'

Well, it might have been once, I thought, but didn't say it, not wishing to leave negativity in my wake or carry any with me, although I felt cowardly for not speaking up at the mess they'd made. This was not leave-no-trace camping.

Instead, I asked if midges and mosquitoes had been bad, and their reply was moderately reassuring.

'The evenings when there's no wind: very bad,' they answered. 'But during the day: no problem.'

'No problem' turned out to be a trifle optimistic, but then again, it was all relative. Sweating hard, I soon attracted a small cloud, but it was nothing compared to the monsoon and misery I'd previously experienced.

The gravel track eventually dead-ended at the national park border. Ahead now were birch woods. My map showed a path through them, but it wasn't obvious on the ground, and I didn't stop long to search. Who needed a path, anyway? I'd experienced an entire continent of forests, and they put these woods into perspective. Soon, I was weaving through willowy undergrowth that might once have tested my patience but now seemed open and easily negotiated. Plus, the woods didn't extend far. Back in the southern Apennines, tree line was at 6,600 feet, but here the trees ended at 1,500 feet. After a short distance I burst free into the sparse open space of Arctic tundra.

Much of the Børgefjell is tundra, an environment notable for its year-round permafrost—permanently frozen ground that exists just inches beneath the surface. Because of it, tundra features a lot of standing water that cannot drain away, and thin, acidic soil. Plants like lichen, moss, sedge, and bilberry grow upon the surface, rarely rising more than an inch or two. Fierce winds regularly scour the land, and temperatures remain milder right against the earth. Most Arctic plants grow low to survive.

The tundra captivated me from the very first step. It was unexpectedly and luminously green, there were thousands of tiny flowers, and there was very little grass: the ground cover was made up almost exclusively from low-growing shrubs. The diminutive size of the plants made them seem more precious than plants in less harsh environments. Each one looked tough—it had to be to survive—but also fragile. The tundra was an austere place, but the vegetation added incredible richness to it. I vowed to tread with care.

But most captivating of all was the space—the shocking *excess* of space. The landscape felt wider and emptier than any other environment I'd visited.

Moving slowly—from appreciation, not weariness—I crossed rising slopes and entered a valley, the Storelvdalen. The higher I climbed the wilder the atmosphere grew. A sense of peace descended. The only sounds came from birds, the wind and rushing water. *Ah, the song of water, the omnipresent soundtrack to the Norwegian wild!* Fjells rose all around, but I didn't feel threatened or hemmed in as I had before. The sense of space remained extraordinary. Space, I saw, was the defining characteristic. Although the Børgefjell was smaller in area and lower in altitude than many ranges I'd visited, it felt far bigger and wilder. And yet it still called, as though being here was right. Soon, the emotions of connection and completeness that I'd experienced in the Trollheimen came flooding back as though the intervening weeks hadn't occurred. The pain I'd put myself through to get here suddenly felt justified.

Early in the afternoon I reached a tarn at 3,000 feet, unnamed on the map. I'd planned to camp beside it, but the surrounding ground was covered by shattered rock. Broad snowfields lay upon surrounding fjells, and plates of ice still floated on the lake—winter lingering on even in August. In bright sunlight it was heartachingly beautiful, but not suitable for camp. I moved on with great reluctance.

Two miles further and several hundred feet lower I reached a more suitable location: a moss-softened patch of ground beside a sparkling stream. The view reached across a long lake, the Søre Bisseggvatnet, to the slopes of the Børgefjell's highest peak. It was perfect. For the rest of the day I sat on a bed of emerald moss with my back to a rock, losing myself within the landscape, thinking less with each passing minute, *feeling* more. This was an uncluttered place and it prompted an uncluttered mind. It also seemed to sharpen my senses. Soon, I felt as though I could see further, and more sharply; smell more, and more discernibly; hear more, and more discriminately; feel more, and more acutely; and even *sense* more, as though a whole host of forgotten senses had been brought back to life. As time passed I felt a change occur, as though I could now reach into the land beyond its surface to know it in a way that couldn't be articulated but was real nonetheless.

I sat in stillness, considering my place in this land. More than ever, I sensed that here—outdoors in nature, not just here in the Børgefjell—was where we as a species fit best. We weren't meant to live behind walls with soft carpet underfoot and electricity keeping us comfortable. Yes, we still needed shelter, but not *all* the time. We needed this so-called 'wild' as much, if not more. It was our original home, after all.

'Bed of Emerald Moss' camp in the Børgefjell, August 3, 1998.

Perhaps once, long before cities and extensive human-dominated landscapes existed, there hadn't even been a word for the wild. The natural world was merely the environment we lived within. But when cultivation began, a description for what we had control of, and what we didn't, was probably useful. This distinction may well have been where our separation from nature began.

Prior to that, nature had been an integral part of human existence. It constantly touched us, shaping us into what we now are. Environmental factors great and small sculpted our physical traits, abilities, senses, instincts and minds. Undoubtedly, life during this evolution was frequently hard. Almost certainly, there was no golden era when humans lived in perfect harmony with the land, and no time without tragedy, famine, danger and sudden death. But, as functioning ecosystems around the world demonstrate, plants and animals *can* coexist in relative stability. For humans to have developed into what we now are, it seems likely that there were settled periods when we fitted into nature without it excessively harming us, or us excessively harming it. Periods when nature was essentially *home*.

Since then, of course, as we've grown in cleverness, we have stepped away from that home. In the last 3,000 years, and even more in the last 300, we have separated ourselves from nature with a completeness never before achieved. We have built protective barriers against it—for understandable reasons, and with some benefits. We have remade the world and reinvented our own place in it, but we haven't been able to remake what we fundamentally are.

No matter how advanced we have become, our brains and bodies are still hard-wired to respond to and benefit from an immense range of stimuli that nature provides. Chemical compounds that plants send into the air; patterns and shapes only found in nature; sounds that prompt beneficial reactions within our brains; environmental stresses that keep our bodies strong, healthy and balanced—the human animal still requires them all, and frequently suffers negative consequences without them, as scientific research is only now starting to reveal. The senses, instincts and abilities that we once relied upon still exist within us—they are the foundation that supports us. Many of these human traits are now woefully neglected. A few may even have been lost. But many remain, waiting to be nudged awake.

This was what I was feeling: a reawakening of senses and instincts that had been asleep; a reawakening of an essential part of what our species had evolved to be. It didn't mean I had to go and live in a cave now, take a step backwards. The reawakening was a step forward to a fuller existence, a filling in of missing pieces—and it felt great. No, greater than great. It felt euphoric.

As the minutes passed my euphoria grew. It wasn't a jump-up-and-down feeling of excitement—it went deeper and filled me with an extraordinary sense of peace. It felt comfortable and ancient, as though it were an emotion I'd known far in my past.

In visiting these northern fjells I saw that I hadn't merely stepped *into* the wild, I'd *returned* to it. And I wasn't merely *at* home here—I was *back* home. As I sat alone in the Børgefjell peaceful euphoria enveloped me.

Clouds rolled across the fjells early in the evening. Soon, wind and rain rattled my shelter. From my new vantage point, it wasn't *bad* weather, and the tent didn't feel like a betrayal of my place in nature. I needed and benefited from the wild, and I needed and benefited from appropriate shelter, too. I didn't have to reject either. Getting the balance right was the thing.

I lay within Auld Leakie, the entrance half open, and cheered the storm on. Later, the rain ceased and the flame of sunset lit the fjells. Later still, in the twilight that was as dark as the night would get, sixteen reindeer ambled by. They passed twenty feet from camp and looked in my direction, but weren't troubled by my presence the way the elk had been. Here in the national park, they behaved how I wanted all my fellow citizens of the wild to behave, as though I were just another creature and this was a home we shared. At that, the day felt complete.

I had a strong suspicion that my time in Arctic Norway was not going to be the worst two months of The Walk.

I spent three days in the Børgefjell, clearly not time enough. On, on, always moving on—the long-distance hiker's eternal curse! But the days delivered more than I could have hoped for. The second brought fog, harrying winds and cold rain—conditions befitting the Arctic—and I only covered six miles. I settled into the 'Thousand Miles from Anywhere' camp early, and spent a fine afternoon sheltering behind the tent's bucking walls. The site sat near a high tarn and felt adventurously remote. The emotions experienced the day before grew stronger.

The third day was quieter, longer, but just as emotional. I walked beneath cloud-capped fjells and glaciers, across green tundra, over two passes, along a broad U-shaped valley, and around several lakes. The terrain underfoot was rough, with endless bogs, rocks, snowfields, un-bridged rivers and hummocky ground to negotiate, but it was exactly what I wanted. There were no signs that others had visited. Mosquitoes and midges were entirely absent. The miles couldn't have been better.

By day's end I left the Børgefjell and descended into birch woods. At first they felt strange and unfamiliar, as though I'd been away on the tundra for months. The vibrant colours of woodland flowers caught me by surprise after the less showy tundra hues. They seemed garish and not what I craved. All I desired now was tundra, with its rich austerity, desert-simple lines and extended horizons. It was almost as if I'd fallen in love.

On August 6 I called into Hattfjelldal, a town of 1,500 people. The post office held my latest resupply parcel, letters from home, and also a couple of surprises. The first was a bad one. A package that I'd sent to myself was missing two essential maps that I could have sworn I'd placed within it: a map of the next range, the Okstindan, and a map of the immense Padjelanta and Sarek national parks over the border in Sweden. Padjelanta and Sarek were the remotest wilderness regions I'd face on the entire journey—'The Crux' as I saw it. Crossing the area would take two full weeks and I couldn't imagine doing it without a map. In desperation, I searched Hattfjelldal for replacement maps, but none were to be found.

The second surprise was a good one, and it said a great deal about the kind of country Norway is. Among my post was an unexpected extra package, and within it a familiar possession: a little red notebook that contained all the names and addresses of people I'd met since Calabria, as well as vital logistical details like the addresses of my mail pickup points. I'd thought the notebook was safely stowed in Ten Ton; it was confounding to unwrap it in Hattfjelldal's post office! How the hell had it turned up here? The answer came when I read an attached letter, in English, anonymously written: *Found this in a telephone box. Thought you might need it!*

From Hattfjelldal, I skirted the eighty-four-square-mile Røssvatnet reservoir, detouring toward another village, Korgen, in hopes I'd find replacement maps there. Shimmering water, forested islands and mountain reflections formed a fine backdrop to some easy miles. I made my camps on wild hillsides covered by purple heather, often near birch trees with twisted trunks. The camp on August 7 was especially memorable. Mist smothered the hills and a soft rain fell. I was sheltering inside Auld Leakie when I heard bells outside, as though Apennine sheep or Alpine cattle were approaching. Accompanying the bells were throaty coughs and breathy snorts, sounds I'd not heard elsewhere, although wild boar came close. Intrigued, I peered out, and discovered a large herd of domesticated reindeer. They were flowing around the tent like a river, appearing from the mist, then vanishing again. The sight was evocatively northern.

I reached Korgen late on August 9, and at first it failed to supply the maps I needed. The only map available was of the immediate area, and I already owned that. The tourist information office seemed like the best bet, but it had closed the day before—for the rest of the year, apparently.

'The summer season is over,' a receptionist at a nearby hotel announced, but after hearing my tale he revealed that he could help. Fortunately in possession of a key to the tourist office, he led me over and opened up.

'Let's see...' he mumbled, rummaging through stacks of leaflets and brochures, riffling through drawers and boxes. 'I don't know what they've got in here. No, no, no... ah! What about this?' He pulled out a detailed hiking map of the Okstindan range, exactly what I needed, and shrugged when I asked the price. 'I don't know. Actually, I don't give a shit! Here, just take it,' and he handed it over. If only Calabria had been so easy!

The map unlocked the route into the Okstindan, and the following morning I tramped along it, singing with gusto. Rich farmland gave way to a steep-sided valley, then to mist-enveloped forests, then to a rugged cirque—a landscape notably different from the Børgefjell's. Instead of wide-open tundra it was an amphitheatre of torn rock, a savage arena that still bore the toothmarks of glacial carnage. Falling rain and shifting clouds added to the wild ambience, and occasional gaps in the clouds teased with brief glimpses of a glacier far above, its icy fangs still gnawing on bedrock. The first sight of the Okstindan range wasn't a disappointment.

Like the Børgefjell, the Okstindan is Arctic in character. The main focus is a single massive mountain, and upon it a broad ice cap: the Okstindbreen, mainland Norway's eighth largest. Rising from the ice cap are several rock peaks, including 5,928-foot Okstinden, a peak that looked temptingly climbable on my map.

Instead of pitching Auld Leakie I settled into a tiny cabin below the ice cap—Steinbua, the Stone Cottage. It was hidden away in a cliff-lined cirque, nestling against a house-sized boulder. The unorthodox building was so cramped that I couldn't stand upright inside or stretch out fully in bed. Constructed from metal, wood and stone, it looked as though an abstract artist had clamped several large boxes together in a burst of creative inspiration—only for it to have deserted him at the very last moment. But it fulfilled its purpose: it kept off heavy rain that beat a frenzied tattoo on the metal roof. Outside, through wandering mist, I occasionally glimpsed towering seracs of pale blue ice. They hung precariously on the lip of a black crag, and the relentless force of the glacier behind intermittently pushed them over the edge like giant lemmings. The thunder of falling ice echoed far and wide.

I drank too much tea that evening, but it led to an unexpected benefit the following morning. Needing to answer nature's call, I stepped outside at 4.50 a.m., a time of day I hadn't planned on seeing. But I was soon glad I saw it. Rain had been forecast to continue, but instead the clouds were dispersing, the sun had freshly risen, and the cliffs and seracs rising above Steinbua were glowing with intense yellow light. A great howl of appreciation escaped my lips without warning. A few seconds later it echoed right back—nature's call of another kind.

By the time I was underway, dawn's finger-nipping air had become rolled-up-sleeves warm. From the cabin I climbed to an open fjell—a glorious, spacious, unmarred place[6]—then descended to a wide tarn, the Okstindjønna. The scenery was beyond spectacular; it set me gaping and grinning with joy. To my right the mountain was smothered by the ice cap, a mass of snow and ice that gleamed beneath an azure sky. Sharp summits rose above it, dark triangles of rock wreathed in shifting fog, and much-crevassed arms plunged from it, reaching right down to the Okstindjønna's turquoise waters. The tarn was mirror-still and highly reflective, afloat with icebergs cast off from the glacier. I sat beside the tarn on a sun-warmed rock feeling wonderstruck by the scenic drama, awestruck by the wildness I'd wandered into, and grateful for the day I'd been given. If this were the Alps there'd have been thousands of people alongside me—and the crowds would have been justified. But this was northern Norway and I had it entirely to myself. It was wild Europe at its absolute best, and there wasn't even a trail leading to it.

It wasn't a day for rushing, or for covering long distances; it was a day for stopping and staring. With reindeer and ptarmigan for company, I picked a leisurely path eastward across rough ground, and stopped for camp early, pitching my shelter on a verdant patch of mossy tundra. Beside camp was a shallow pool of crystal water, a perfect mirror for the surrounding fjells. I lay shirtless beside it and basked, as happy in my solitude as I'd ever been.

I set out again early in the evening, leaving camp pitched and most of my gear behind. I clambered uphill with Excalibur in hand and soon had my crampons strapped to my boots. Loving their bite, I balanced up steep snow and reached the Okstindbreen. Onward progress now involved risks. Soft snow covered the ice cap, and dips in the surface hinted at crevasses.

6. Upon which a large modern hut, the Rabothytta, has since been built, with a prominence that completely alters the landscape.

The Okstindan, August 11, 1998.

A rising wind was whipping west with real Arctic bite, and clouds were moving in from Sweden. They'd already consumed the highest summit in the area, 6,286-foot Oksskolten a mile to the east, and were approaching fast. But for once the risks seemed justifiable and I pushed on regardless, delicately traversing the ice cap for a short distance before scrambling onto rock. I reached the summit a few minutes too late, arriving second place to the clouds, losing the views I'd climbed for, but somehow gaining more from the thrilling remoteness. Okstinden wasn't a place to linger, but I lingered anyway, relishing the wild perch.

By the time I descended below the clouds the Okstindbreen was glowing orange from the setting sun, and although the wind had become an unpleasant bully I paused again, too taken by the glacial landscape to leave it. Standing in such a location brought bittersweet emotions: elation to be present in so extraordinary a place, but also painful awareness that this moment, like life, couldn't last. Surprisingly, the sense of imminent loss added to the moment, rendering it all the more precious, all the more intense. The knowledge that a moment—or a life—*has* to eventually end doesn't have to be a negative thing. Instead, it can focus the mind and profoundly increase appreciation, as it did for me on the Okstindbreen. Staring across the glacier I ached at how beautiful and fleeting it all was.

The wind eventually chased me down the mountain with gusts that occasionally pushed me into a run. By the time I'd regained camp the entire Okstindan range was hidden within clouds and the wind was raging. I repitched Auld Leakie, turning its lowest end directly into the gale, then settled in for a wild ride.

A long night followed. Avalanches of air poured off the ice cap and smashed into my home. But it wasn't only the wind that pulled me from my dreams but the dreams themselves. They were so funny, so appallingly happy, and so fantastically reflective of my state of mind, that I woke laughing from them several times, just as I had back in the northern Apennines.

The Børgefjell had exceeded my expectations, and then the Okstindan had surpassed the Børgefjell. I wondered if the next range, the Svartisen, would do the same.

———

The Svartisen began with rain—the kind of straight-through-your-waterproofs downpour I'd expected from Norway all along. Hurled sideways by a fierce wind, the deluge wasn't remotely pleasant, but it didn't dampen my spirits. If anything, it raised them. What could be better for an epic northern realm than epic northern weather?

And Svartisen is epic. Located on the western half of the Saltfjellet mountains, Svartisen is the collective name for two ice caps: the Vestre (western) Svartisen—the second-largest ice cap on Norway's mainland—and the Østre (eastern) Svartisen, the fourth largest. Together, the two ice caps hold 142 square miles of Norway firmly locked within the ice age. Svartisen means 'Black Ice', perhaps a confusing name for a glacier, but it suited the entire range. Reaching down to coastal fjords on its western side, Svartisen's closeness to the sea means that storms are frequent. When they barrel inland Svartisen's valleys become dark tunnels beneath dark fjells, and at those times the name feels entirely appropriate.

Svartisen sits within the Saltfjellet–Svartisen National Park, a park established in 1989 to protect 846 square miles of wilderness. A few outlying areas, such as the low-reaching snout of the Engabreen glacier, are well visited, but great stretches of the park's interior go weeks, months, or even years without experiencing human footfall. Svartisen's inclement conditions and untamed landscapes aren't what most people are looking for when they visit northern Norway. Svartisen's treasures are many, but they are not easily earned.

One other important detail sums up Svartisen: a certain latitudinal line—approximately 66°33' North—bisects the range. At this line the sun shines for twenty-four hours on midsummer's day each year and disappears for twenty-four hours in midwinter, and north of it is a fabled land that imaginative suburban schoolchildren read about in awe and dream of one day exploring. The line of latitude is the Arctic Circle, and it makes Svartisen most assuredly an Arctic range.

I reached Svartisen on August 15, seventy-five miles and five days after leaving the Okstindan. In between had been lower fjells, a generous measure of rain, and a short break in the town of Mo i Rana. From my unusual perspective, Mo was an ugly metropolis. I'd entered it cheerfully, singing joyfully, but the noise, traffic, concrete, graffiti and industrial hum of the city temporarily deflated my mood. I'd stayed in a managed campsite, and it had been full of young Norwegians and Swedes visiting for a music festival. There'd been drinking, fights, policemen called, and loud music all night long. Added to that was Mo's inability to supply the desperately needed map for The Crux—a disappointment and a growing concern. Mo i Rana was home to 18,000 people, more than any town I'd visited since Bergen, but it was the opposite of home to me. I wasn't sorry to leave.

I approached the Svartisen from the south, walking up the Blakkådalen valley. After a first day of low clouds and drizzle, and a soggy camp, I only covered nine miles on the second day. But what miles they were—more like swimming than hiking. By the end I was starting to think I should have purchased scuba gear in Mo, not just food. Tiny rivulets trickling down the fjells became raging torrents that required care to cross. Clothes were soon clinging-wet beneath my waterproofs. My boots and socks were soon heavy with water. Toward the day's end I reached a DNT hut, the Blakkådalshytta, but for once did the unthinkable and passed it by. I wanted to feel worthy of Svartisen, to prove to myself that I could cope with it even in appalling weather. The night that followed wasn't comfortable—Auld Leakie's floor was soon awash—but attention to detail kept my sleeping bag and a few essentials dry, and by dawn I felt I'd earned the right to continue deeper into the range.

As if in reward, drier conditions prevailed by the time I set out. The weather was still cloudy, the air chill and damp, but rain was holding off—a gift from the gods after the previous day's deluge. In high spirits, I paced cross-country up the Blakkådalen over open slopes of bilberry, willow and a few stunted birch, pausing every so often to gorge on cloudberries. Cloudberries are a golden-orange fruit that grow close to the earth near tundra marshes. I'd noticed a man picking them in a valley north of the Okstindan, and after explaining what they were he'd generously passed over a handful. One taste and I was an instant convert. Norwegians harvest cloudberries for use in jams, tarts, juices and even as an ingredient in aquavit. Rich in vitamin C, they became a useful addition to my backpacker's diet, and I feasted whenever I saw them. Not only did they taste good, foraging for them *felt* good. It wasn't exactly living off the land, but it was satisfying to take a small step closer to it.

On I walked. The fjells grew steeper and craggier. My map marked a trail up the valley's centre, but it was so little used and easily lost that ignoring it and picking my own route felt easier. Compared to figuring out a path through the tangled hills of the Mezzogiorno, navigation up a massive, wide-open valley was child's play. Getting lost here was practically impossible.

As the miles passed my excitement grew; the Arctic Circle lay right ahead. Crossing it would be a milestone to celebrate. I'd been dreaming about the Arctic since childhood, and walking toward it for fifteen and a half months. Back in Mo, I'd bought a small bottle of Highland whisky to mark the occasion—an expensive but justifiable extravagance. My only concern was making sure I celebrated at the correct location, but where *exactly* the Arctic Circle ran was hard to tell.

Attempting to figure it out, I stopped frequently, lining up features on the ground with my map. Looking around, I noticed the trail 100 feet below me, clearer here than it had earlier been. It weaved up the valley and passed beneath a small wooden arch. *An arch? Could it be?* I descended quickly, joined the trail, approached the arch, and laughed aloud when I read the

The Arctic Circle, August 17, 1998.

single word that had been carved onto it: '*Polarsirkel*'. I hadn't expected to find a physical gateway to the Arctic in the middle of nowhere!

Savouring the moment, paying attention to all the details, I stepped slowly through—and crossed into the Arctic for the first time in my life. *How far from Calabria I now am!* Back in the Aspromonte I'd walked in fear, unsettled by the wild. But now, here in the Svartisen, two days from the nearest road, I felt the complete opposite. *The polar opposite!*

Discarding Ten Ton, grinning inanely as though all my dreams had come true, I sat beneath the arch. Then came the long dram of whisky, and in that location—a windswept *Arctic* wilderness—it went down as well as any whisky ever had.

The Arctic had been special to me since childhood. My impressions had been shaped by adventure stories, by school history lessons about Arctic explorers, by television documentaries, by all the Arctic photographs I'd ever seen, and most completely by the rare bursts of winter weather that British newspapers called 'Arctic blasts'. The magical transformation that snow brought to my suburban home confirmed what I imagined about the Arctic: that it was as different from Pinner as any place could be. Over time it had become a promised land for me: a mythical realm, the pinnacle of all wild places. Once I started backpacking, I measured Britain's mountains against it, often subconsciously. The more Arctic they'd felt the more I'd valued them. The 6,280 miles I'd walked since Melito had shown me that other kinds of wild places, both tiny and immense, *all* had extraordinary value, but the deeply ingrained idea that the Arctic was the ultimate wild place remained. It was why I'd chosen to walk from south to north—because the Arctic was the supreme wilderness destination that I aspired to reach.

And now I was finally here.

So much of what we feel in the wild is based upon what we expect to feel. So much of what we take away is based upon what we bring. The moment I crossed the *Polarsirkel* the landscape felt bigger and emptier, the wilderness more *real*. I knew that the landscape hadn't really changed, and yet, because of everything I brought with me, it truly had.

What is and isn't wilderness, and what is and isn't an adventure, is entirely subjective. A place like Svartisen might feel remote and wild to some, or accessible and tame to others. And entering the Arctic alone and on foot might seem adventurous to some, or a walk in the park to others. But that's the great thing about mountains and wild places, how they give each visitor a chance to forge their own experiences, especially when visiting alone. Out here I was completely free to be myself, free to react without being influenced by other people's reactions, free to create my own reality—and the reality of entering the Arctic lifted The Walk to another level.

Overcome by excitement, I continued up the valley, and a mile further came upon a change that wasn't only in the mind. Two side valleys opened up to reveal the Svartisen ice cap spilling downward from the plateau. Gouging through one of the valleys was a broad outlet arm, the Fingerbreen, a pale blue glacier wrinkled and textured with crevasses. At the sight of so much glacial ice the land's scale and wildness increased even further. I stood taking it in, awestruck by the surroundings, awestruck also by my good fortune. *I'm really here*, I thought in celebration. *I'm really walking in the Arctic! The ARCTIC for goodness' sake!* I couldn't quite believe it was true.

The terrain grew appropriately rougher as the day went on. A slippery descent led to a silt-thick river, and fording its swift waters demanded concentration and respect. A mile on and 1,000 feet higher my planned

Overlooking the Fingerbreen, Svartisen, August 17, 1998.

route crossed the river again, but up here it was narrow and foaming, totally uncrossable, and it forced me into a long detour across rocky ground patched with snow. The detour took me south of a narrow lake and deposited me below another arm of the Svartisen. All of a sudden I felt an urge to change plans and climb the glacier, to find out what lay on its far side. It was five in the afternoon, too late to be heading uphill onto an Arctic ice cap, but the idea suddenly felt irresistible.

As if in reward, progress turned out to be as easy and safe as glacial travel could be. The glacial arm—unnamed on the map—was free of snow, easy angled, and entirely without crevasses. Like the Nigardsbreen months earlier, the ice was intensely blue and seemed to glow from within. Compressed glacial ice absorbs light at the red, orange, yellow and green end of the visible colour spectrum and reflects back the shorter wavelengths at the blue end, and even under scowling clouds the process was at work, making the glacier shine like the waters of a tropical lagoon. In comparison, the surrounding fjells appeared almost black. The name Svartisen, Black Ice, seemed hopelessly inaccurate.

The climb topped out at a broad 3,000-foot pass. Wind blasted across it, but the view removed its sting. A glacial wilderness stretched ahead: a sweeping ice-age kingdom entirely removed from the Europe most people knew. Dark rock peaks rose like islands above the ice cap, and I climbed them in my imagination, knowing this was as far as I dared go alone. The limitations from being solo could have brought frustration, but the benefits were greater. Company might have unlocked the upper ice cap, but it would also have removed the powerful thrill of isolation. Once again, a great wave of awe swamped me, raising goosebumps. I felt my senses sharpen, and the entire environment suddenly seemed extraordinarily vivid. *How muted life would be*, I thought, *without moments like this. A life without awe is a life only half lived.*

A dangerously crevassed glacier plunged away on the pass's far side, but beside it an ice-free slope offered a manageable route down. Clambering over slabs, loose boulders and old patches of snow, I made my way into the next valley, the Sørdalen. Hemmed between mountains and glaciers, it echoed to the roar of rushing water and the moan of a scouring wind. I wandered down it, legs weary but spirit soaring, searching for a spot for camp. The pleasure from being present in such a place was intense— I didn't want the moment to end. The pull of the land seemed magnetic. I felt absorbed by it—and absorbed *into* it. I was shocked by how *at* home I felt, even though I knew it could never be home. This wasn't a place for permanent settlements. Even if park regulations allowed me to live here I doubted I had the skills required for surviving in such a harsh place. And even if I had the skills it would be wrong to use them. A home built here in Svartisen's untrammelled heart would destroy it just as Count Ernst had destroyed his beloved summit of the Brocken. No, this was a different kind of home, a home for the heart but not the body. A home for the imagination. This was a place to visit but never stay; a place to cherish and always carry inside. This wild corner of Arctic Norway was an *idea of home*, a spiritual home that could underpin life elsewhere. Just to have been here this once, to have merged with it so completely, and to know forever after that it existed—that was enough.

The night that followed was memorably and appropriately wild. Arctic winds tore at my shelter, and lashing rain came after midnight, more than Auld Leakie could shrug off. By dawn the floor inside the tent was awash, but it was no big deal. This was the Arctic and I wouldn't have changed a thing.

I only walked three hours the next day—three sodden hours down a waterlogged valley, assaulted continuously by wind and rain. The terrain underfoot was as rough as any I'd ever crossed; a muscle-testing, balance-challenging, ankle-threatening obstacle course of rocks, hummocks, and bogs. Swollen rivers poured down the fjells. I had to ford them all. Within ten minutes I was wet to the skin, waterproofs thoroughly defeated, and I had to pause often to empty my boots and wring out my socks. But I found nothing but pleasure in it. Physical discomforts were barely noticed amid so much wild grandeur. Blue skies and sunshine might have granted easier passage, but easy passage would have been to miss out on what this place truly was. The Svartisen and fierce conditions belonged together, and I celebrated their union, revelling in the turmoil and wildness.

All the same, when the familiar red Ts of a DNT-marked route led to two modest huts right on the edge of the wilderness I didn't, this time, walk by. Three hours had been time enough to enjoy the elements at their worst, but one *could* have too much of a good thing.

There were two huts at Gråtadalsstua, one with a lock my key couldn't open, a second that was unlocked already, and into it I moved. As usual, I had the comforts all to myself, and I made the most of them, using every square inch to dry clothes and gear. The seventy-five-kroner fee seemed a small price to pay for such a clean palace. Listening to rain hosing the windows that night, feeling the hut shudder in the wind, demonstrated with absolute clarity *why* the human animal had distanced itself from the wild all those millennia ago. Of course, I'd known why all along, and I understood it. But it was a crying shame we hadn't known when to stop.

I walked out of Svartisen the next day. I crossed a broad fjell, descended several thousand feet, and reached a small outpost of civilisation, Reingarden, late in the afternoon. The valley was impossibly lush after the high fjells—a reminder of how warm Arctic Norway is compared to similar latitudes elsewhere. A woman was working outside her home in shirtsleeves, tending an immaculate lawn that looked like something from the English shires. She looked up when I appeared, and I realised she was the first person I'd seen in five days. But I didn't pause to talk, merely waved cheerily. Just 100 yards ahead another trail climbed back into the Saltfjellet, and I made straight for it.

Arctic fjells were calling, and they couldn't wait.

Emptying water from my boots after another river crossing, Svartisen, August 18, 1998.

SEPTEMBER 8

Frostisen Ice Cap
(5656ft/1724m)

Skjomen

Unnamed peak
(4724ft/1440m)

Paurohytte

SEPTEMBER 5/6

'Cloudberry Land' ★ 6,500 miles

'Bear
Bothy'

SEPTEMBER 2

'Leave the
Nordkalottleden'

Akkajaure

SWEDEN

Route across

PADJELANTA
NATIONAL PARK
& LAPONIA

August – September 1998

PADJELANTA

AUGUST 31

Viribaure

Máhttoajvve
(4780ft/1457m)

SAREK

NORWAY

NATIONAL

NATIONAL

Fauske

Blåmannsisen
Ice Cap
(5120ft/1560m)

PARK

Staloluokta
'Ten Ton weighed'

PARK

Sulitjelma

AUGUST 22/26

AUGUST 28

'Begin following
the Nordkalottleden'

N

AUGUST 19

'Burning map'

Bjellåvasstua

SALTFJELLET-
SVARTISEN
NATIONAL PARK

km 0   20   40
mi 0   10   20

THE GREATEST FORTNIGHT EVER
Chapter 12

FINALLY, AFTER MONTHS of having DNT huts entirely to myself, I reached one already occupied.

The hut, Bjellåvasstua, sat in the middle of the Saltfjellet, down in a valley beside a lake. It was a modest wooden shelter—an outpost of civilisation that gave scale to the surrounding wilderness instead of ruining it. Or perhaps there was ruin, but I couldn't now see it. Once, the very idea of a cabin in such a wild landscape would have dismayed me. But my views had mellowed. After so many hut nights I'd grown to love the simple comforts they offered. I still believed they didn't belong in places like the Svartisen or the Børgefjell, or any location where they were built prominently, but here, where the wild was marginally softer, and where shelters could be tucked away, they felt appropriate.

I saw our place in the wild differently now. A wilderness without people was as unnatural as a human-dominated landscape without any wild. Small settlements dotted across the land—this was becoming my idea of natural perfection, especially if the settlements could only be reached on foot.

The tundra leading to Bjellåvasstua was so idyllically spacious that by the time I reached the hut I was floating on contentment. Arrival only increased the contentment further. A dry cabin after a day of rain: a vagabond's idea of heaven! I'd grown so used to having shelters to myself that it didn't cross my mind someone might have beaten me to it, which is why I stared in momentary confusion at the scene I discovered inside:

a wood-burning stove already crackling with fire, a woman and teenage boy bustling about the kitchen, and a huge white dog with a tail wagging in friendship. *What?* I thought, followed by: *damn!* Shamefully, my initial reaction was resentment, but I overcame it quickly.

'Hei-hei!' I sang, a cheerful Norwegian hello, before continuing in English. 'Is there room for one more?'

There was, of course, no question about it—and would I like a hot drink? In moments a mug of steaming apple cider was in my hands, and I thought: *perhaps sharing isn't going to be so bad!*

The cabin had two bedrooms and I settled into mine, then joined my fellow residents for dinner. There were four: the woman and boy I'd already met, plus the woman's husband and a daughter in her early twenties. The latter two had been out fishing when I'd arrived and had succeeded in their task. The frying of fresh trout soon filled the hut with far finer aromas than I usually brought to such places.

To my surprise, the evening that followed was deeply relaxing. The Pierson family approached conversation slowly and easily, and the periods of silence were unusually comfortable. I'd feared sharing a cabin partly because I'd feared losing my connection with the wild, but there was no loss here, only gain. So peaceful were my companions that the hours spent with them increased my contentment further.

I awoke the following morning to the tantalising aroma of bacon, and wished my breakfasts consisted of more than cereal and powdered milk. When I stepped from my room I saw the Piersons near the front door, lacing their boots, preparing to leave. They looked up and smiled—a wonderful gift to receive first thing in the morning, and a rare treat on my walk. While I'd slumbered late the family had cooked and eaten their breakfast, swabbed the floors, straightened the furniture, and readied their packs for departure, somehow doing it all without making a sound. With incredible kindness, they'd also saved a plate of bacon and eggs for me, leaving it on the stove to keep warm.

As the family turned to go, the husband, who bore the wonderful name of Odd, wished me a '*god tur*', and confirmed what we'd agreed the evening before: that we'd meet down in the Saltdalen valley. 'Nine p.m.,' Odd said. 'The Kro Café, near the Nordnes Campsite.' It was there that he would present me with an item I so desperately needed: a map of The Crux.

During dinner, when he'd learnt that I hadn't been able to track down a map of Padjelanta and Sarek, Odd had generously offered me use of his.

'I crossed that area forty years ago,' he'd explained. 'I still have the map.' He gazed wistfully into the distance, reliving the past. 'Ah, I treasure that map. It holds many special memories. It was a magical place, as you will see. But if you take care of it, and promise to post it back afterwards, you can borrow my map.'

After another idyllic day crossing open tundra, we met as planned. Odd and his family had walked a more direct route to the valley, driven twenty miles to their home, then Odd had driven back. All to lend a complete stranger a map he clearly cherished.

The Kro Café was dark, rustic and atmospheric, decorated with reindeer antlers, old skis and ancient snowshoes. Fishing nets hung from a beamed ceiling, and the wooden tables were set with tea lights; their flames flickered within hollowed-out river stones, partly hidden from view. Unfortunately, as it turned out, the candles were so well hidden I didn't notice them until it was too late.

I bought Odd a coffee and we talked awhile about long walks and wilderness adventures, before Odd pulled out his map. It was a beautiful sheet, full of colour and character. Published in 1952, it was printed upon heavy, woven paper and was practically a historical artefact. I was impressed and humbled that Odd was willing to lend it. Incredibly, it looked good as new. It had clearly been taken care of.

Keen to examine the details of The Crux, I spread the map across the table and traced my finger excitedly over the remotest terrain of the entire walk. For a few seconds all was well—but then it happened. The centre of the map, the very heart of the Sarek National Park, suddenly and inexplicably began changing colour. First it turned brown, then black, and as the darkness blossomed and spread I couldn't, for a moment, grasp what was going on. But when a flame appeared, as though Sarek had become a volcano, the cause was suddenly clear: *hell*, I thought, *the map: it's on fire!*

'FIRE!' I yelled.

Odd reacted more quickly than I did. While I puffed ineffectively at the spreading wildfire Odd jerked the map off the candle, off the table, and hastily beat at the flames. In a second the fire was extinguished, but the damage had been done—the treasured map was no longer good as new. It bore a six-inch-wide hole in its centre, edged by brittle, charred, blackened paper.

There was a moment's silence. The scent of smoke hung in the air.

Horrified, I apologised repeatedly—as embarrassed as I'd ever been. But Odd, although visibly upset for a few seconds, swiftly gained control of himself and waved my apologies away. 'It is nothing,' he murmured calmly, shrugging.

And then he saw the humour of it, and began laughing, and for a while couldn't stop. Eventually, he looked up, and spoke with a generous, good-natured smile.

'So,' he said, 'I hope the map will be of use to you. At least... what is left of it!'

The Crux was due to begin at Sulitjelma, a town half a day's walk from the Swedish border. First, however, came two more days of Norwegian tundra: two more days of glorious solitude upon rolling Arctic fjells. So good was the stretch that I couldn't imagine ever experiencing better walking. The Arctic was the promised land, and it turned me into somebody new, somebody more fulfilled than I'd thought possible—and I had no idea that this was merely the start.

After so much unmarred beauty, Sulitjelma was a shock when first I saw it. It was an old mining town, and it had clearly been built for functionality, not beauty. With old mine tailings above it, rain falling upon it from grey skies, deserted streets, boarded-up stores, and rusting machinery decaying back into the earth, it looked industrial and down at heel. The town campsite sat too far from Sulitjelma's centre to be of any use, so I set up camp ten minutes above town in a birch wood. I'd planned to pause for two days—time off before The Crux—but now that I'd seen the town I wasn't sure I'd stick to the plan.

I returned to town the following morning, aiming to purchase supplies and collect my latest resupply parcel, but had little success. The town's two food stores were spartanly stocked and didn't offer the kind of lightweight produce I needed, nor even fuel for my stove. For The Crux I'd have to carry food for two full weeks—far more than I'd ever carried. For once, fresh produce would have to be limited. Powdered and dehydrated food would take precedence. The canned goods Sulitjelma offered wouldn't do at all; they'd likely break my back.

Sulitjelma's post office didn't meet my needs either. The clerk hunted for my parcel, but came up blank. It wasn't her fault, and I thanked her for looking and told her not to worry, but as I trudged back to camp I cursed Sulitjelma as an ugly, useless, end-of-the-world place. Even the phones didn't work. Calling Base Camp was impossible.

I was up early the next morning, waiting for the bus to Fauske, a larger town twenty-seven miles west that would hopefully offer better-stocked stores. According to the bus timetable and the post office clerk there were two buses to Fauske each day, a 7.30 morning bus and a 3.30 afternoon bus. To be safe, I reached the bus stop twenty minutes early.

Time always runs slower at bus stops, especially on cold, drizzly mornings in the Arctic. For what seemed like hours I paced backwards and forwards, flapping my arms for warmth, discovering with surprise that I could see my expelled breath. Back on the Saltfjellet, there'd been bursts of red in the bilberry and yellow in the birch, and above 3,000 feet the tundra had been copper hued, no longer verdant green. I wondered when the first snows would whiten the tops, and when the nights would darken enough to reveal stars. At dawn now the sun clung to the horizon for hours where once it had hurried into the sky. It was still August, but autumn was coming on fast.

Unlike the bus.

After a cold age, 7.30 arrived, but no bus arrived with it. Another age followed, and at 8 a.m. a bus finally appeared, but it was rattling toward Sulitjelma, not away. Seeing me standing at the stop the driver brought his vehicle to a halt and leaned out of his window.

'Waiting for the Fauske bus?' he asked. 'There isn't one until three-thirty, you know!'

'But what about the seven-thirty morning bus?' I asked desperately.

'Sorry,' the driver said. 'There's no such bus. There was one at *seven*.' With an apologetic shrug he drove away.

Cursing Sulitjelma even more vehemently, I prepared to hitch.

Traffic was sparse—in thirty minutes only two cars appeared. But happily, the second car stopped, and once underway my fortunes began improving. The driver, Robert, cranked up the heat to thaw my frozen body, and quickly offered to not only take me to Fauske but also drive me back again once my shopping was done. As if to confirm the change in fortune, the sun burst out the moment Sulitjelma fell behind.

With all my chores completed the return ride was a celebration. And there was even more to celebrate back in Sulitjelma when the post office clerk chased after me as I walked by.

'Your package! It arrived!'

Improving matters further was the appearance of a café that I could have sworn hadn't existed the day before. And then there was the weather, miraculously transformed to warm and sunny. As I lounged in camp that evening, stuffed with hearty café food, surrounded by the sights, sounds and scents of nature, I reconsidered my previous opinion of the town. A few hours earlier, I'd wanted to damn the place. *If ever I write about my trip*, I'd thought, *I'll get my revenge. I'll describe Sulitjelma as the grimmest town in Europe.* But now, with all my needs met, I realised how negative that would have been. During the return drive Robert had told me a little of Sulitjelma's history, how it had gone from a bustling town of over 3,000 residents to a fading community of fewer than 900.

'When the lease on the copper mines expired in 1989 the government took over running them, and concluded they weren't economically viable. So they shut them down. The workers all moved away, the railway closed, shops closed, and our school is on the verge of closing. Young people don't stay—there's nothing for them to do here. If it wasn't for out-of-town visitors Sulitjelma wouldn't have a future.'

There was a useful lesson in that, I realised: a lesson in not kicking a place—or a person—when it was down. Sulitjelma needed a boost, not con-demnation. Most likely, if ever I wrote about the town my words wouldn't make the slightest difference, but that wasn't the point. The point was that *friendly* Sulitjelma had much to offer; *beautiful* Sulitjelma showed that beauty came in many forms; *resilient* Sulitjelma had much it could teach. For example, it taught that first impressions aren't always right, and that knee-jerk first responses aren't good responses to act upon.

And it taught that if one looked hard enough positives can *always* be found.

Cotton grass and glaciers above Sulitjelma, August 26, 1998.

I left Sulitjelma on August 26, shouldering the heftiest load of my backpacking life. Somehow, I squeezed two weeks' food into Ten Ton. As I staggered uphill the earth trembled beneath my feet. I worried about falling over. If Ten Ton landed on top of me I'd never get up.

A hot sun beat down and sweat beaded within minutes. My stomach churned from nerves and excitement—the wilderness ahead was as daunting as any I'd faced. It was the scale, the sense of the unknown, and the rough weather I'd likely face. It was the rivers I'd have to ford, one of which looked massive, and the challenge of off-trail route finding across The Walk's most difficult miles. Most of all it was the utter commitment required: the knowledge that if something went wrong no one would be able to help. The anxiety felt all too familiar. I thought I'd left it behind, but perhaps never would. And perhaps I didn't want to, I realised, on reflection. If anxiety was a sign that I was pushing beyond my comfort zone then it was a welcome emotion. If I didn't push my boundaries, if there wasn't discomfort, how could I keep moving forward?

The first few miles were a steady slog up an old mining road, but soon I was back on the tundra, following a narrow path. Glaciers and rugged fjells rose above, but the atmosphere felt welcoming; bright sunlight shone on flowers, cotton grass swayed in the breeze. Away to the north I glimpsed Norway's fifth-largest ice cap, Blåmannsisen, and I crossed extensive snow patches that were practically glaciers themselves. Above 3,000 feet some were so large I began wondering if I'd find crevasses, and the moment I thought it there crevasses were: black slits blocking the route. But I didn't pause, even with Ten Ton on my back. I picked up speed and launched myself over, an exhilarating start to Europe's greatest wilderness.

I camped beside a glacier-blue lake, and the temperature that night delivered a clear reminder that the seasons were rapidly changing. By midnight, a glitter of ice coated Auld Leakie's walls. When I stepped out to pee at 1 a.m. I stared into the heavens at the first stars I'd seen since April. They sparkled as though alive, as though communicating some deep eternal message, and it took hours afterwards to reclaim sleep, with awe and excitement coursing through my veins. Approaching the Swedish border the next day, I noticed fresh snow dusting the fjells. My excitement jumped another notch. Winter's first blast! No plot was ever more thrilling than the changing of seasons in the Arctic.

I reached Sweden early in the afternoon on August 27. The border was marked by a pile of rocks and a small yellow sign: 'Norge' on one side, 'Sverige' on the other. I paused, wishing there'd been room in my pack for whisky—The Walk's eighth country deserved a toast. Instead, I took a long dram of ice-cold water from the nearest stream, and decided it was better than whisky anyway, better than any drink I'd ever tasted. Suddenly, everything seemed better: the sky bluer, the air cleaner, the future brighter. I strode into Sweden barely noticing the weight pressing upon my shoulders.

The Swedish landscape instantly *felt* different. Arctic Norway had been spacious, but Sweden's space surpassed it. The wilderness stretched ahead to apparent infinity, offering nothing but mountains, valleys, lakes and forests. There was no hint it was part of a continent overrun by half a billion people. The idea of roads and villages, factories and cities seemed nonsensical. They might have been a million miles away.

Losing altitude, I followed a shallow valley to a milky-blue lake, and after a couple of hours reached a small cabin. Managed by the Swedish equivalent of the DNT—the Svenska Turistföreningen, or STF—the cabin was occupied by two Swedish women. I guessed they were in their late sixties.

'How long have you been out?' I asked, imagining it had taken them several days to reach such a remote spot.

'Oh, three hours,' they said. 'We began after lunch!'

My mind boggled. 'What, did you *run* here?'

They laughed. 'A helicopter dropped us off five kilometres away. It'll collect us again on Monday.'

It was my turn to laugh; clearly things were done differently in Sweden! But it was also an indication of the land's scale. A landscape so big that people had to be helicoptered into it was clearly a big place.

Two hours later I reached a second cabin, this one unoccupied, and I decided to stay the night. It would keep off the rain I sensed coming. Two fair-weather days since Sulitjelma were surely as many as I could hope from The Crux. Sure enough, by midnight, drumming rain pulled me from sleep.

But by dawn the skies were clear!

It was a sparkling miracle. Unable to believe my good fortune, I paced north, knowing that such conditions couldn't possibly last. This was the Arctic, for goodness' sake! It was supposed to be the journey's crux, the most challenging fortnight, not the easiest.

Incredibly, the challenges eased even further when I joined the clearest trail I'd walked since the Alps. Odd had reminisced about rough paths that petered out, but his beta and map were forty years out of date. Unknowingly, I'd landed on the well-blazed Nordkalottleden—the Arctic Trail—a 487-mile-long path opened five years earlier in 1993. The Nordkalottleden weaved from Norway to Finland through Sweden's remotest landscapes. It was easy to follow, but still an unpretentious mountain path, and a secret to most hikers—as it was to me until I caught up with two Germans who happily explained everything.

'Not many people know about the trail yet,' Erhardt and Brock told me. 'But it must be quite the happy surprise for you, yes? We've spent a fortune for only ten days on it... and you've stumbled upon it by chance! You must have been born under a lucky star!'

It certainly felt lucky. But then again, maybe it was earned. I'd put some work into getting here, and perhaps the Nordkalottleden was the reward, or part of it. The Crux itself was beginning to feel like one huge prize. Maybe it was even *The* Prize!

I walked with Erhardt and Brock for three enjoyable miles. The two

Germans had suffered high winds, zero visibility and falling snow during their trek. This was their final day, and they were delighted to see the sun. Their stories were entertaining, and made progress feel easy-paced, until they asked me to slow down. Apparently, even beneath Ten Ton, I was walking too fast.

Before long we came to the edge of an immense lake: Virihaure, supposedly Sweden's most beautiful. Staring across calm waters to distant, cloud-wreathed mountains, I found the accolade easy to believe. With birch leaves dancing in a mild breeze, and sunlight warming the tundra, it felt like the most benign place on the planet. Life was beginning to feel ridiculously carefree.

I parted company with Erhardt and Brock at another STF cabin, but not before they'd talked me into weighing Ten Ton on the cabin scale.

'Aren't you interested?' they asked. 'We certainly are!'

In truth, I wasn't sure I was, but I soon found out. It took two of us to hoist Ten Ton onto a hook, and the result was soon in: a deeply embarrassing thirty-nine kilos, eighty-six pounds.

'Scheisse!' my new friends swore. 'You *are* earning your luck!'

Leaving Erhardt and Brock waiting for the helicopter that would whisk them back to civilisation, I sauntered quietly along the Nordkalottleden. The trail angled across the shoulder of a broad fjell, revealing Virihaure in all its glory—the view was too special to pass. I made camp in a soft-edged hollow above the lake, sheltered by dwarf birch. The hollow had been used before: a stack of firewood sat beside a large stone fire ring, but I quickly dispersed the wood, rocks and old ashes, returning the location to a more pristine state. A small boulder rested nearby, with nothing special about it, but someone had lovingly decorated it with wildflowers and sprigs of heather, as though in offering. When twilight developed I understood why they might have been placed. From a distance, the rock gave off an unusual, ethereal blue light. When I stepped closer the light faded; when I stepped away it returned. *Oooo,* I thought, *an enchanted rock!* It was strange and inexplicable, and hauntingly beautiful. I stood and contemplated the rock for some time, but eventually gave up trying to figure it out. Better to accept the mystery, I decided, and merely look on in wonder.

'The Enchanted Rock Camp' became one of the most elevating of The Walk. With Virihaure a mirror, evening sunlight spilling through birch trees,

Evening calm beside Virihaure near 'The Enchanted Rock Camp', August 30, 1998.

a gentle breeze whispering its many secrets, and the Enchanted Rock emit-
ting its otherworldly glow, the entire area soon felt enchanted. It filled me
with peace, and I slept the kind of deep and rejuvenating sleep I hadn't
managed since childhood.

This was some wilderness I'd wandered into.

I woke to another sparkling dawn, another gift from the wilderness gods.
I was now in the heart of the Padjelanta National Park, at 766 square miles
Sweden's largest. Established in 1963, the name comes from a Sámi word—
Badjelánnda, or Higher Land. A region of lakes, tundra, grassy plains and
rolling fjells, Padjelanta is surrounded by even higher mountains: those of
coastal Norway to the west and the giants of the Sarek National Park to the
east. As elsewhere in the Arctic, space was Padjelanta's defining feature. It
stretched in every direction, reached to every horizon. Nowhere in Sweden
lies further from a road than here, and no other region exists in a more
natural state.

Padjelanta's scale is impressive, but the park is only one part of a larger protected area, Laponia. A World Heritage Site since 1996, Laponia covers some 3,600 square miles, encompassing not just Padjelanta but also the neighbouring national parks of Sarek, Muddus, and Stora Sjöfallet, as well as several nature reserves. In Laponia, elk, reindeer, Arctic fox, lynx and even brown bears go about their business in freedom. Here, Europe's only indigenous people, the Sámi, can practise traditions that stretch back to the last ice age. Here, long-distance vagabonds seeking the *other* Europe can know—with absolute certainty—that they have found it.

Besotted by everything I'd found, I set out early from 'The Enchanted Rock Camp', unwilling to waste a second of what, *surely*, would be the last clear day. Back down to serene Virihaure I tramped, around its shore I walked, and on into the water I splashed, for a cleansing, if numbing, swim. Afterwards, the trail weaved across the tundra to a high pass. I hid Ten Ton amid boulders, then continued uphill across untracked ground, finally summiting a modest fjell, Máhttoajvve. Away to the east the larger fjells of the Sarek National Park crowded the horizon. Hung with clouds and glaciers, Sarek's mighty fjells dwarfed my modest summit, and yet my perch, surrounded by immense space, probably gave a grander view. Easing myself down, I revelled in the location, staying so long I quite forgot where I'd hidden my pack. Reclaiming it took half an hour of head-scratching and laughter while I quartered the slope, but it was worth it for an Arctic summit where time seemed to stand still.

Back on the Nordkalottleden I met more walkers, all following the trail from hut to hut. I hadn't anticipated meeting anyone during The Crux, but welcomed the encounters. Meeting others added to my own growing happiness; sharing my feelings only increased their power; leaving strangers laughing made me laugh all the more. Among the hikers were a Dutch couple I'd encountered the previous day. They'd needed assistance with navigation and were delighted to see me again.

'YESSS!' they shouted when they saw me. 'We found you!' Grinning, they handed over a small bottle of whisky. 'We bought it from the last hut,' they explained, 'a thank you for your help. But it's not only for saving us from heading to who-knows-where... it's your trip, too. We really feel you've earned it!'

Dutch hikers, mountain gods—they were all giving gifts, and the gifts

On the summit of Máhttoajvve, August 31, 1998.

continued, for the rest of the day, the day after, and the day after that. I walked across fjell, valley and tundra, appreciating my gifts with each step, unable to believe I'd received so many. Being here was a gift; I still couldn't take it for granted. And the weather was a gift, one I'd never have dared hope for. A single good day might have been expected at some point, but an entire week of sunshine up here in the Arctic? Impossible! And yet it continued day after day. Even when dark clouds rolled in one night and rain threatened, the next day still arrived clear. I had dawns that sparkled and sunsets that glowed, and uninterrupted 100-mile views, and midday skies unsullied by even a wisp of cloud. The Crux was beginning to remind me of the previous year's 'Endless Summer'—except it felt even more extraordinary.

The Nordkalottleden was a gift too: a perfect trail that led exactly where I wanted. And the wild camps were gifts, each with a great sense of place, each as view-drenched and comfortable as the best that had gone before. Even the land gave gifts: cloudberries and bilberries to feast upon, and the sweetest water imaginable to drink.

This wasn't The Crux any longer. It was the opposite—it was the easiest and most glorious stretch I'd ever walked.

I felt astonishment at just how easy everything was. Navigation, walking, camping—all easy! Even staying physically comfortable was easy. Other hikers looked sunburnt and trail-weary, but I felt as though I were living in luxury. This wasn't the Mezzogiorno, hot and tangled; or the Central European winter, cold, dark and perpetually wet; or southern Norway, snow-buried, rain-lashed and mosquito-bedevilled. Conditions had *never* been gentler, not even back in the comfortable suburbs of London. I was never hot, cold, hungry or thirsty. I didn't even feel tired. My energy felt limitless.

Travelling in such ease, I was free to focus on the land instead of my own physical needs, free to lose myself in the intimate and the expansive, in the sights close at hand and those far away.

I saw free-roaming, velvet-antlered reindeer. I listened to thousands of birds singing. I swam with darting fish in mountain lakes. I spied ptarmigan with breasts turning white, already preparing for winter. I passed bogs edged by white-tufted cotton grass, and skirted numerous tarns, some shimmering with sunlight, some perfect mirrors. I paused to watch mountain grasses dancing in the breeze, their seeded heads gleaming like flecks of gold. I marvelled at the colours and patterns of lichen—works of art all—and at the endless expanses of bilberry, now torched into blazing scarlet by the approaching autumn. I breathed deep the scents of sun-warmed peat, splashed my face in cleansing rivers, and threw my arms wide to embrace the monumental space. I pulled it all in, the entire wonderful wild, and leapt about inside, as intoxicated and happy as a drunkard.

And day after day the happiness kept building.

September arrived with a hard frost that silvered the landscape, followed by sunlight that transformed the frost into steam. Geese heading south honked in flight, but why were they leaving? Why would anyone leave an Eden like this? On the forested shores of another lake, Akkajaure, I stopped to pass the time of day with a hut warden who'd spent three months on site; she wasn't sure about leaving either, although she'd have to when the hut closed for the season in a week's time.

'It gets under your skin, doesn't it?' she observed. 'The peace and space of the Arctic.'

The wide spaces of Padjelanta, September 2, 1998.

It clearly *had* got under her skin. When I'd approached she'd been sitting outside on a stool, looking as peaceful as anyone I'd ever seen. 'Welcome,' she'd said simply, but there'd been such heartfelt warmth within the single word it spoke like ten thousand.

Her name was Eva, and she told me she'd travelled far and wide over the years, but after her summer here she now preferred 'travelling in one spot'.

'It's been so unexpected,' she said, 'how I've seen more here, staying in one place, than I ever saw during fifteen years of travel. When you get to know a place, I mean *really know it*, every rock and plant and patch of earth, it changes completely. There's a sense of attachment. Belonging. Security.' She laughed. 'I'm not sure I can really describe it!' She paused a while. 'Of course, it's the Arctic too. The Arctic changes everything.'

That was for sure.

Eva asked if I'd seen the Northern Lights yet, saying she'd noticed them two nights earlier. I told her I'd watch out. She also mentioned 'the bear' that lived up the valley, pretty much where I'd planned to camp that night. I replied I'd watch out for that also.

'I haven't seen it,' she admitted. 'But lots of hikers have. Two groups claim it followed them. But I *have* seen the bear shit! So keep your eyes open.'

My eyes were wide open as I pushed into a forest along an overgrown trail, no longer following the Nordkalottleden. Sensing an *edge* to the wild not sensed before, I walked miles further than originally planned, heading through twilight shadows to a small cabin that Eva had mentioned. On this occasion, four solid walls felt like a more sensible choice than a flimsy tent.

I reached the 'Bear Bothy' shortly after eight, with darkness gathering. Small and rustic, but clean and well maintained, it sat amid forests and fjells so vast it was conceivable that human feet hadn't explored them all. I collected water from a nearby lake, and howled my delight at pink alpenglow lingering on Sarek's highest tops. Later, with a crescent moon hanging in the frosty night sky, more howls rang out, and they weren't my own.

Wolves, perhaps?

This really was some wilderness I'd wandered into.

I found a pile of bear scat on the trail the following morning soon after leaving the cabin. It was an impressive mound, a dark and fibrous dollop filled with half-digested berries, and when I held my hand near it gave off heat—although it might possibly have been heat from the morning sun.

It was the seventh day out from Sulitjelma, and the start of a two-day stretch that I'd originally considered 'the crux of The Crux'. My planned route led far from any path, but the miles weren't remotely difficult and route finding was as simple as it had ever been. I barely needed the map; the land itself was an open book. I climbed from forest to spacious tundra, and the tundra—'Cloudberry Land' as I now called it—showed the way.

Broad hills capped by rocky knolls, tarns sparkling silver, burbling brooks, gold-tinged birch, vibrant red bilberry, an intense blue sky, snow-streaked fjells, and everywhere space—it exceeded everything I'd ever hoped the wild could be. My journey had always been about finding Europe's special places, locations that felt like the centre of the universe. There'd been many over the miles, but they'd all been relatively small in scale and swiftly left behind. But here, every patch of ground felt like the centre of the universe. No matter where I walked, rested or slept I remained in the centre. It made the world beyond seem even more irrelevant than usual.

It stopped my thoughts from reaching behind or ahead. My nearness to the North Cape, and the end of this extraordinary way of life—only six weeks off now—didn't trouble me. I didn't even consider it. I hadn't suspected I could feel so consumed by a place or absorbed by an experience. I hadn't known I could become so deliriously happy.

I'd been happy on The Walk before, of course. In a few places I'd truly soared. But the soaring here didn't last for mere minutes or hours. It kept building, mile after mile, day after day. It was becoming a crescendo of happiness, and each time I thought I'd reached the pinnacle of what was possible I discovered that another pinnacle rose above it. I was reaching levels of happiness so enhanced I was starting to wonder if I was losing it. But perhaps the highest level of happiness *was* a kind of insanity?

'Happiness' didn't even feel like the right word. It certainly wasn't happiness as I'd ever understood it, or had felt it, or had seen it described. It wasn't euphoria, or elation, contentment, joy, exhilaration, fulfilment, ecstasy, rapture or any other descriptive word I could think of. It was a sense of infinite well-being entirely new to me—a state of being I hadn't known existed.

Possibly, there wasn't even a word for it. Words didn't fit.

Whatever it was, it extended from having *all* my needs met. Being physically comfortable was merely the foundation. Feeling safe played a part—there wasn't a single aspect of the surrounding wild I now feared. I had no concerns of any kind, no anxieties that I'd lose my way, suffer an injury, or require help that wouldn't come. I had no worries about funds running out, or angst at my ability to live up to my own lofty ideals. The future didn't matter. Neither did the past. Cares were simply gone—I'd been released from them all.

There was meaning and purpose in every step, in every moment. I was living my dream, doing what I *knew* I was meant to be doing, and doing it with a lightness I'd never before achieved. I had no doubts about The Walk, just belief and pride in it. The journey was *right*, pure and simple; fully formed and complete. I was fulfilling other purposes too: fundraising for the charities, and sharing happiness with fellow hikers along the trail. There was purpose in simple physical motion, in keeping every throbbing sense and instinct alive. And there was purpose in being still, in travelling in one spot, in feeling the wind, hearing every bird call, noticing every detail.

There was meaning in every rock, leaf and patch of ground. Meaning and purpose were everywhere.

But the happiness found its deepest source in the belonging I now felt. The connection I'd experienced in the Trollheimen—the merging with something incomprehensibly benign and infinitely vast—had expanded to a point where it felt unbreakable. It pulled me beyond my own limited boundaries and made me feel embraced and supported; an invaluable part of an unlimited, all-encompassing whole. Disconnection and loneliness were unimaginable. The need for human connection was no longer a separate need. The connection with nature encompassed people—it encompassed everything. It felt like a meaningful connection with existence itself.

For sixteen months I'd been on a quest, pursuing an elusive goal that I hadn't been able to name, giving my all to reach it. I'd been close, several times, only to have it slip away. I'd even reached it—or so I'd thought back in Paradise Glade, on the summit of Corno Grande, in the Trollheimen, and in numerous other locations. But those moments, great as they'd been, were fleeting imitations of what I'd now found.

The Walk had achieved its full potential, and the extraordinary happiness that came with it—the Padjelanta Happiness—was The Prize I'd been walking for. It was greater than I could have ever imagined.

<hr>

Happily insane, or insanely happy, I trekked on across the tundra, singing and laughing like a madman. But how else was *Mad* Mountain Jack supposed to behave? It was probably just as well I went the next five days without meeting anyone.

On September 3 I came to the river that had intimidated me in planning. It ran swift and cold and reached to my upper thighs, but fording it was a piece of cake. Afterwards, happily insane, I camped in the remotest location I'd ever been, and felt laughably at home. Insanely happy, I crossed back into Norway the following day with the 'the crux of The Crux' successfully completed. No miles I'd walked anywhere had been easier than The Walk's 'most difficult' miles.

Norway, with its steeper fjells and narrower valleys, felt less spacious than Sweden, but it was familiar—an old friend. A sea eagle welcomed me back. It passed directly overhead, eyeing me as if in curiosity, head tilted for a better view. Once again, there wasn't time to grab the camera, and once again I didn't care. The experience was better lived than photographed.

On September 5 I neared my first DNT hut in several weeks, the Pauro-hytte, although reaching it wasn't straightforward. The hut was situated beside a long lake, and—according to Odd's map—approached across the lake itself. The trail led onto a peninsula that jutted into the lake, somehow jumped across open water, then continued on the far shore. Was there a bridge? Or was the lake shallow enough to wade?

The truth, it turned out, was neither. When I reached the lake I discovered a small aluminium boat. It was attached to a rope that was also attached to both sides of the lake. To get across one had to pull on the rope hand-over-hand. *Simple*, I thought.

Ah, if only it had been.

After taking off Ten Ton I picked up the rope and began pulling, then heaving. Nothing happened. Whoever had last used the boat had stranded it high and dry on the opposite bank. Dislodging it took everything I had, but finally, just as I was beginning to feel I was engaged in an unwinnable tug of war, the boat slid free with a loud metallic groan. *Great! Now it'll be easy!*

Ah, if only it had been.

Once the boat was in the water I pulled it slowly toward me. But then it stopped, forty feet from reach, and wouldn't budge another inch. I pulled and strained, and finally admitted defeat. When I stared to the far bank I saw the reason: the rope had been looped around a large boulder and couldn't feed out as intended. Whoever had last used the boat had a lot to answer for.

Amused by the problem, I stripped, waded into the numbing lake until I was chest deep, and swam the final few yards. Climbing into the little boat was entertaining—I almost capsized it. Once in, I pulled it to the far bank, freed the snagged rope, then pulled the boat over to Ten Ton. After drying myself, I dressed, loaded Ten Ton, then pulled the boat back across the lake one final time. It was the strangest 150 feet of the entire journey!

I stepped into the Paurohytte shivering from my swim, feeling as though I'd truly earned my stay. Ahead of schedule after Padjelanta's easy miles, I decided to stop for two nights. I spent the following morning

Scrambling above the Paurohytte, September 6, 1998.

in stillness, but balanced it with an adventure early in the afternoon. The highest peak in the area rose nearby. It didn't have a name on my map or a trail up it, but I couldn't resist. The ascent was made via a dry glacier and a careful scramble along an exposed granite ridge, and I felt nothing but delight at each difficult step. My Hohtürli fall was long forgotten. The summit panorama was magical, reaching from Sweden's highest mountains to the rock needles of the Lofoten Islands. Even the rock at my feet seemed magical, sparkling with mineral flecks. Later, back at the Paurohytte, the sunset was the fieriest of the year. It turned Arctic ice caps red.

I walked on the following day as though in a dream, through fjells that kept on growing in beauty, and reached the end of The Greatest Fortnight Ever the day after that.

The return to civilisation didn't dent the Padjelanta Happiness—the power of it had become self-sustaining. The happiness continued as I crossed a final pass, descended to sea level, and reached the first paved road since Sulitjelma. The tangy scent of salt and seaweed reached me half a mile from the water's edge. Before long, I was trekking alongside Skjomen, a fjord that seemed more beautiful than any I'd previously seen, although my state of mind may have been an influence. Granite walls curved upwards from water that looked like polished metal, silver mists hung about the fjells, and the large Frostisen ice cap shone above, fiercely white beneath a greying sky. Soon, I reached gentle farmhouses, green fields, and birch woods that glowed with iridescent light—and the emotions I felt, emotions born not just from the past two weeks but from *all* the weeks, and from all the lows as well as the highs, spilled over as though from a bottomless well, and there truly aren't words to fit the happiness that consumed me.

I walked on feet not touching the ground, my face hurting from the broadness of my grin, repeating the exclamation my Italian brother Flavio had spoken back in the Dolomites.

'*Straordinario! Straordinario!*'

And it *was* extraordinary, this life I was living, and this discovery I'd made: that happiness, simple happiness, could be boundless, could keep on growing, and could have no upper limit.

Skjomen fjord, shimmering with light, September 8, 1998.

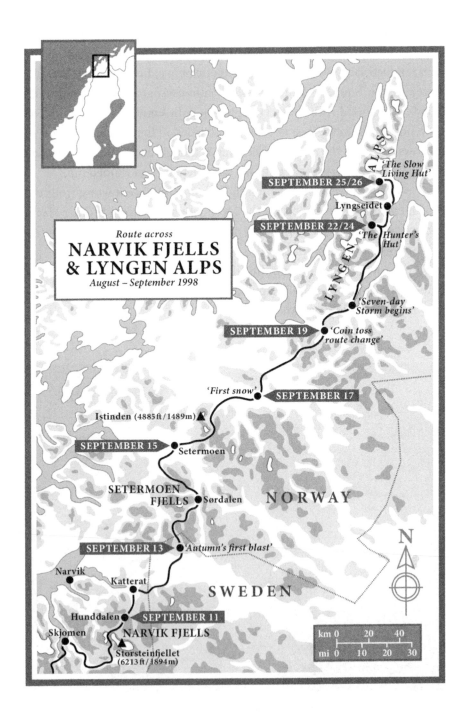

Route across
NARVIK FJELLS & LYNGEN ALPS
August – September 1998

'The Slow Living Hut'

SEPTEMBER 25/26

Lyngseidet

SEPTEMBER 22/24

'The Hunter's Hut'

LYNGEN ALPS

'Seven-day Storm begins'

SEPTEMBER 19 · 'Coin toss route change'

'First snow' · SEPTEMBER 17

Istinden (4885 ft / 1489 m) ▲

SEPTEMBER 15 · Setermoen

SETERMOEN FJELLS · Sørdalen

NORWAY

SEPTEMBER 13 · 'Autumn's first blast'

Narvik

Katterat

SWEDEN

Hunddalen · SEPTEMBER 11

Skjomen · NARVIK FJELLS

▲ Storsteinfjellet (6213 ft / 1894 m)

N

km 0   20   40
mi 0   10   20   30

ON SACRED GROUND
Chapter 13

DAY BY DAY the Arctic was changing.

Burning flame colours were spreading across fjell and forest with astonishing speed, banishing summer's greens, altering the land beyond recognition. Sharp and clean smells were becoming soft and mulchy; life-laden scents were evolving into scents that suggested end-of-life transition. The atmosphere was moistening and thickening, the light becoming subdued and melancholy. Long distances were becoming harder to see. Sunrise was arriving later and sunset earlier—each day was eight minutes shorter than the day before. An hour of daylight lost every week. Daylight, quite literally, running out.

And the temperatures were steadily falling.

Walking on, I felt as though I'd crossed another boundary, entered a new land 1,000 miles from where I'd just been. A week earlier I'd been living in high summer. I'd danced across Sweden in shorts and T-shirt; I'd swum in mountain lakes and had basked beneath the life-giving sun. But now, I wrapped myself in waterproofs, fleeces, hat and gloves. On September 13, the first gale of the season swept through and it had me cowering. I walked with my head down, leaning into thuggish gusts, wearying quickly from the struggle. The wind howled a warning: *not long now*, it seemed to say. *Leave while you still can.*

But despite the discomforts, the Padjelanta Happiness remained. Perhaps because of it, colours seemed more intense than any I'd previously witnessed.

Possibly, they *were* more intense—maybe the Arctic autumn was always like this. The golden birch and russet rowans down in the valleys were glorious enough, but it was the tundra that stole the show: a great flaming expanse, a carpet of red and orange spread across the fjells. Wasn't tundra supposed to be barren? It was yet another secret, another side of Europe most people missed. Who knew the Arctic could be Europe's most colourful environment?

Still soaring from The Greatest Fortnight Ever, I weaved north through the Narvik Fjells feeling gratitude and awe. Was *all* this really possible? Dark mountains rose tall and jagged, glaciers tearing at them, erosion hard at work. From a pass, while standing upon a rubble-strewn glacier, I witnessed an avalanche of granite—a car-sized boulder tumbling down a gully, dislodging other rocks, creating a din like rolling thunder, before eventually coming to rest, followed by pulsating silence as though the entire world was holding its breath. Further down the valley, I came upon house-sized boulders deposited by glaciers long-since thawed. They were surrounded by tundra that looked like a glacier itself—a glacier of scarlet, ochre and gold. I had to stop and throw my arms wide. *What a place this is.*

A sacred place.

In recent weeks, everything had changed. Not just the season or the landscape or my perception of it but who I fundamentally was. A walk is such an ordinary thing, something that the majority of humans do every day. Even backpacking is relatively ordinary—thousands do it every weekend. But for me, repetition had transformed it. Waking in the wild, wandering all day in freedom, immersed in nature, settling somewhere new at day's end, making the earth itself home, then doing it all again the next day, and then again—ten times more, a hundred times more, then another hundred, and then another…

The length of the journey, the sheer amount of repetition, had taken it beyond ordinary. Repetition had transformed a simple activity into a way of living that was shot through with meaning and reward. A journey that may have seemed like endless discomfort and dulling routine to some had been alchemised into something potent and intense, an existence of pure bliss.

No longer was I in competition with myself while I walked, debating ideas about good style, agonising when I had to choose a lower route or

At home in the Arctic, Narvik Fjells, September 16, 1998.

when it differed from my expectations. The Walk, now, was *exactly* what it was meant to be, whatever shape it took, wherever it led.

And no longer was I merely passing through. For thousands of miles I'd been passing through, never stopping long, but now I wasn't *passing through*—I was *part of.* I was finally *here*, wherever here happened to be.

I'd begun The Walk hoping it would become a way of life, and it had. But then it had become so much more. It was now an act of worship; no other definition fit. I worshipped the wilderness, the universe, and my existence within it. I worshipped the very ground I walked upon. It wasn't soil and rock any longer but a home to tread with absolute respect. The earth beneath my feet had become sacred—I was walking on sacred ground.

It was quite a prize, this existence that my walk had become. It felt perfectly formed, offering no loose ends, like a finished work of art, requiring no further brushstrokes or chiselling. Nothing about it could be improved.

It might have been a good place to stop. But I still had 500 miles to go.

Locations changed, days passed, each one as full and rich as any that had gone before. Norddalen, savage Storsteinfjellet, the Nihkejávri Glacier, wild Hunddalen—names on the map became a part of who I now was. When I reached Katterat I took a train to Narvik for two days of rest and chores. The break could have broken my mood, but my mood was now unbreakable. Still insanely happy, I returned to the fjells, looped into Sweden, crossed back into Norway, and began the final burst of high tundra walking. I sensed such deep wisdom in the tundra—not wisdom that could be put into words but wisdom that could only be felt. It suggested that everything was okay—and would *always* be okay, even when my journey was done and I stepped away from the wild. Even if I lost contact with the person I now was I would always know that I'd been him. I would always know he was possible—I would always know that the Padjelanta Happiness was possible—and I suspected that would be enough.

The weather cooled further, felt Octoberish, then Novemberish. On September 17, driving rain turned to sleet and the summits whitened. Progress was harder in the storm. My limbs doubled in weight and the boundless energy I'd possessed in Padjelanta dwindled away. Ten Ton started to feel heavy again. I noticed the clamminess and stink of my clothes. For the first time I thought about The End, and not with dread but a touch of longing.

Snowline dropped further the next day, and the next night the sky revealed the fabled Northern Lights for the first time, visible on the horizon through a gap in the clouds. It was a faint but luminous band of green, and it was swiftly stolen from view, but the memory lingered.

On September 19 I deviated one final time from the route I'd originally planned. As had happened before, it was a postcard in a store window that tempted me off track: an image of alpine-sharp peaks. The peaks were the Lyngsalpene—the Lyngen Alps—rearing over a mile from the fjord at their base. I hadn't known such striking peaks existed so far north, but after seeing the postcard I had to visit. There was only one drawback: they were far off route, and I'd have to take a ferry to get back onto it. *Should I go?* I decided to let fate decide, and tossed a coin, just as I'd done many times in the Apennines. Heads I go to the Lyngen Alps—and heads it was.

Winter, unfortunately, beat me to the range. It beat, with savage intensity, *against* the range. It began with clouds billowing in from the west, and

The storm begins, Lyngen Alps, September 20, 1998.

soon the first splash of rain hit. Trudging along a fjordside road I watched strengthening winds whip up white-capped waves, then grow so strong they hammered the waves flat. Soon, the wind was flinging heavy rain at my back and pushing me into a run, straining my weary legs. But at least it wasn't a headwind. Gulls and terns were attempting flight into the wind, but could make little progress. Some were even flying backwards. I laughed at that. Backwards-flying birds; whoever saw such a thing!

I camped above the small settlement of Horsenes in soggy woodland near a foaming river, and spent the evening translating the autumn fury into my journal:

The autumn wind is in the trees; the leaves are in the sky.
It won't be long 'til warmth is gone and snow will deeply lie.

The next day the storm roared with end-of-season finality. Instead of camping I aimed for a private mountain hut that a local had generously revealed. Referred to as 'The Hunter's Hut', it sat above tree line right in the heart of the Lyngen Alps. Above it were several fjells that might prove climbable if conditions relented, and the idea of standing atop one, and being granted views across sharp summits and tumbling glaciers, kept me climbing when stopping early would have made more sense.

I arrived at the hut in sideways rain and rejoiced at the unlocked door —it hadn't been guaranteed. The shelter was more rustic than a typical DNT hut, but it provided everything I needed. The roof didn't leak and the wood-burning stove radiated so much heat that Mezzogiorno warmth was soon melting my chocolate supplies. The cabin also offered company: a white mouse who stared up with surprised eyes. *What the hell are you doing?* I imagined it asking. *No one comes up here this time of year.*

I stayed three nights in 'The Hunter's Hut'—three wonderful storm-bound nights, time out from relentless forward progress. I did little but read, eat, cut firewood with an old, blunt saw, and celebrate—celebrate the thrilling isolation (or ice-olation, as soon enough it was). Outside, the storm flung wave after wave of moisture against soaring land with a savagery that befitted the northern latitude. The hut shuddered, waterfalls cascaded off the roof, and the snowline edged lower each day until eventually it reached the hut, then passed below it. It was mid-September and winter was back. *Winter! Here we go again.*

Except I didn't go anywhere. For the first two days I stayed put, 'travelling in one spot', as Eva from Padjelanta had sagely put it, and getting to know that spot well.

Sitting in 'The Hunter's Hut' I remembered two of The Walk's finest shelters—the Bohemian and Rocking Bothies. As with those shelters, the hut raised my appreciation of four walls and a roof to a whole new level. It let me appreciate the storm without having to battle it. I hadn't even seen the Lyngen Alps yet, but the detour had still paid off.

There's something about remote wilderness cabins in savage weather, I wrote in my journal as I sat before the stove, my feet stretched towards glowing embers. *And there's something about slow living,* I added, while hail rattled the window. I knew what that 'something' was. 'Slow living' and 'doing nothing' were essential pastimes. They were the balance to all the walking, the foundation of a life fully lived. 'Slow living' was when details sank deepest, when outside distractions faded away. I suspected it was the side of The Walk I'd remember most clearly and fondly when I looked back from future decades.

On the third afternoon I managed a short foray upwards, my curiosity finally getting the better of me. I battled to a lonely tarn, and was rewarded with a brief lull in the storm and a tantalising glimpse of the mountains.

A brief lull in the storm, Lyngen Alps, September 24, 1998.

But for most of the time snow fell heavily, fog clung tightly, and progress was slow and treacherous. As I stumbled and slipped on rocks hidden beneath a foot of snow I discovered that—surprise, surprise—I was still done with winter walking. I'd endured too many miles of it. The North Cape lay three weeks away, and three weeks of snowy floundering across high fjells held little appeal. I hadn't the energy or desire for it. At this stage of the journey I could only face a lower, easier route.

I left 'The Hunter's Hut' the following morning and returned to the fjordside road. It led north to the town of Lyngseidet and a modern SPAR where I restocked on food.

'When is the sun next going to appear?' I asked a woman standing at the entrance.

She stared out at the driving sleet, grimaced, shook her head.

'Maybe April,' she observed, deadpan. And then she laughed, although it was a laugh of little mirth. 'Snow's a month early. And it's still twenty Celsius down in Oslo.' This extra information didn't help.

I settled into a second private mountain hut that night, the final hut of the journey. It was sited north of Lyngseidet up a remote valley, and it gave two more days of slow living before the long trudge to the North Cape began. With snow piling up, the Lyngen Alps still hidden within warring clouds, and the wind moaning, I made the most of the shelter while I still had it—I'd soon have to go without. Here was a chance to live a quiet hermit's existence for a few hours more, and I granted myself freedom to do it guilt-free. Wanting for nothing, I savoured each passing hour, feeling calm within the storm, enjoying the uncomplicated pleasures of a seat beside a fire, a steaming-hot drink, a window to gaze through, and unmeasured time to think—or to not think. I sat mulling over what it is to be young and free of responsibility, and how fortunate I was to still be a boy when in generations past world events would have forced me to become a man. I fantasised about staying in the cabin forever, living the simplest life possible, and I carefully avoided thoughts about The End, or the huge effort required to reach it. There was no need to think such thoughts. The End—and life after it—would come soon enough, as assuredly as death and rebirth are part of nature's endless cycle.

As I stared out at the storm I fingered the five small pebbles I'd plucked from the Mediterranean Sea seventeen long months ago. They would soon be delivered to their new home.

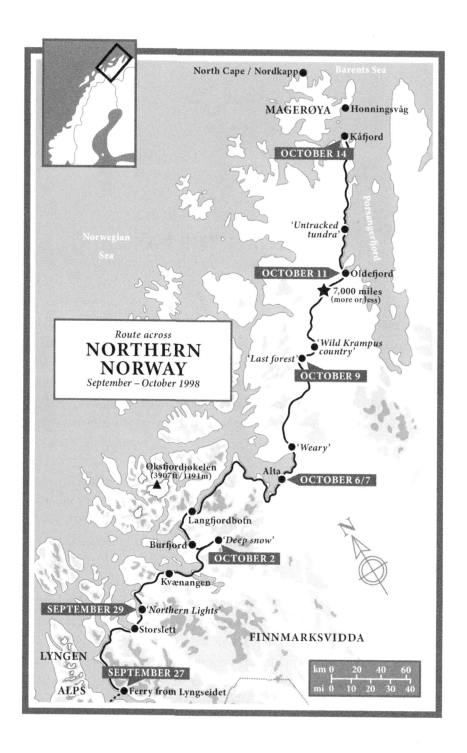

North Cape / Nordkapp•   Barents Sea

                              MAGERØYA   •Honningsvåg

                                         •Kåfjord
                              ⬤ OCTOBER 14

Norwegian   'Untracked
                                   tundra'
Sea
                    ⬤ OCTOBER 11 •Oldefjord
                              ★ 7,000 miles
                                (more or less)

        Route across   'Wild Krampus
        NORTHERN   country'
        NORWAY   'Last forest'•
        September – October 1998   ⬤ OCTOBER 9

                                •'Weary'

        Øksfjordjøkelen   Alta
        (3907ft/1191m)   •   ◀ OCTOBER 6/7
              ▲

                         •Langfjordbotn

                  Burfjord• •'Deep snow'
                              ⬤ OCTOBER 2

                  Kvænangen•

        SEPTEMBER 29 ▶ •'Northern Lights'
                      •Storslett   FINNMARKSVIDDA
        LYNGEN
        ALPS   SEPTEMBER 27 ▶
                      •Ferry from Lyngseidet

                              km 0   20   40   60
                              mi 0   10   20   30   40

345

UPHILL ALL THE WAY
Chapter 14

THE LYNGEN ALPS were revealed the day I left them. As a ferry carried me east across Lyngenfjord, the storm clouds that had battered the mountains for a full week finally began shearing apart. There was a hint of brightness, a passing snow squall, and suddenly the first patch of blue in a week appeared.

Blue sky! I thought. *I remember that!* By the time I set up camp on 'The Golden Terrace' overlooking the fjord the mighty Lyngen Alps were popping into view one by one—a grippingly theatrical emergence. I stopped what I was doing to watch. Dinner could wait.

A final inch of snow fell overnight, but dawn brought brittle-clear skies and a hard frost that turned Auld Leakie stiff as board. Clouds wreathed the Lyngen Alps once more, but dazzling winter sunlight set my fjordside home gleaming. By the time I was underway the world shone with diamond brightness.

For the next few hours I struggled to make progress. As hard as I tried to keep moving forward the landscape kept stopping me, demanding I stand and stare. The Lyngen Alps were emerging again, looking like the mightiest mountains of the entire journey. Up there, winter was fully established, but down at sea level autumn hadn't fully relinquished its hold. Birch trees still held their leaves, despite the previous week's ferocious winds. The leaves hung like splashes of paint—flaming reds, oranges and yellows, even while snow lay beneath them. It was the first time I'd seen snow on the ground before leaves had fallen, a reversal of how seasons normally unfold.

The Lyngen Alps emerge, September 28, 1998.

It reminded me of Calabria, where spring had put leaves onto beech trees before winter had thawed from the ground. The unusual back-to-front seasons had helped the Sila Range feel like an exciting new environment, and it had the same effect here.

Now back on a coastal walk, I followed a road over headlands and around fjords. There was little traffic and I barely noticed the pavement. Yellow-leafed birch woods, turquoise fjords, snow-covered fjells—the landscape had never been more colourful or better balanced. There was even a balanced amount of civilisation: farms, isolated cabins, small settlements, villages. Alongside the fjords were large A-framed structures, built from wood and draped with nets. Hanging inside them were rows of stockfish—cod mostly—all drying slowly in the cold air as fish have been dried in the Arctic for thousands of years. Close inspection revealed fish perfectly preserved, not rotting away. The local gull population didn't seem impressed. Kept from the fish by the nets, they flapped about madly, protesting their hunger and frustration with ear-numbing raucousness.

After skirting the Kvænangen Fjord I turned inland, seeking a wilder route, but waist-deep snow turned me back. Accepting my fate, I returned to

347

the road. A mere ribbon of pavement couldn't cut me off from nature—the connection I'd developed was unbreakable. The wild still surrounded me, still touched all my senses, and I still slept within it each night. I camped one night beside a boisterous river, the next on an exposed spur yards from a fjord and its lulling waves, then in a birch wood carpeted with snow and fallen leaves, and then atop a broad fjell that stretched away into a white wilderness. I felt completely at home.

The coastal landscape was full of life. I saw dolphins, their fins cutting the water; gulls swooping low to snatch up fish; cormorants perched on sun-kissed rocks with their wings spread wide. I saw explosions of fish setting calm fjords boiling, trying to escape some hidden predator. In camp, I was serenaded by birds, visited by lemmings, watched by deer. A red squirrel scampered over Auld Leakie one evening, apparently interested in my stew. It sat motionless atop the tent, staring at my pot of food, weighing up its chances of a successful snatch and run. A huge bull elk paid camp a twilight visit. Breathing steam like a dragon he paused to inspect the tent, staring down at the strange human lying within it, then moved ponderously on. The moment filled me with awe.

The road may have been easier to walk than rough ground, but the uphill stretches were starting to test my strength. Perhaps it was the cumulative effect from seventeen months of walking, or an innate natural response to the changing seasons and shortening days, or simply from knowing that the journey was nearly done—whatever the reason, my energy was waning fast. I found it harder to get going in the mornings, harder to keep going in the afternoons. It was even hard, sometimes, to stay upright, especially at high elevations where the road was covered by ice. I fell twice, arms windmilling as though in a comedy sketch, and was glad there was no one around to see it.

At the base of each icy pass were winter-closure gates. They were still open, but I wondered if they'd soon close. The road was the only realistic route north, and I didn't know if it stayed upon all year round. The North Cape is located on an island, Magerøya, and the only way to reach the island at the time of my visit was by ferry. If a winter storm closed the road would the ferry at its northern end still run? Despite my rising tiredness, I increased my pace, hoping I'd reach the ferry before it was too late.

September drew to a close and the cold intensified. My fingers struggled

A fjordside rest, September 30, 1998.

each evening with journal-writing, their dexterity reduced by frost. Darkness now exceeded daylight: a stark reminder that the far north's two-month-long polar night was rapidly approaching. But for now, the extra darkness wasn't a bad thing. It gave the Northern Lights room to shine.

There'd been no guarantee I'd see the Northern Lights again. But the mountain gods smiled, and two nights north of Lyngen they returned. The sky-stage was well set: a night without clouds and air that was cold and crisp. The lights began gently, glowing faintly on the northern horizon as though a strange green dawn were approaching. Slowly, the glow spread upward, forming into luminous green curtains banded with red. The curtains rose tier upon tier, swirling and flowing like water, forever forming and reforming, pulsating as though pure energy had sprung to life. I watched for hours, lying in the tent entrance, utterly spellbound. The Northern Lights moved as though alive—I hadn't known they *could* move. I'd only ever seen photos of the lights. *Still* photos. The way they rippled and danced across the stars held me transfixed.

They returned the following night, and the night after. The days were full of natural wonders, but it was the nights I treasured most. Each evening I lay on my back and stared up at the show, trying to etch the magic into my memory, knowing photography could never do it, especially with the 50 ASA slide film I carried. Any attempt would have been sheer futility, like trying to paint a smell, or keep an emotion in a box for future use. It couldn't be done; I couldn't capture the lights.

As free as the Northern Lights, I thought.

For five frosty nights the lights continued, only ceasing when clouds swept in. With each display I re-examined an entire continent of extraordinary sights, searching for something comparable, failing to find anything. *For sure*, I thought, *I've seen some marvels. But these Northern Lights surpass them all.*

Staring at them, it was easy to understand why people had often imbued them with supernatural beliefs. The Sámi traditionally believed that the lights were the souls of the dead, and when they shone at their brightest it was best to stay inside, behave with solemnity and respect, and above all keep children quiet. Waving at the lights to tease them could bring bad fortune, sickness, even death.

'Well, we didn't believe that,' an elderly shopkeeper told me in the village of Burfjord. 'We waved white handkerchiefs at them when we were children. We did it to speed the lights up, and sometimes I swear we succeeded, until our eyes could barely keep up. But when we started to hear crackling and hissing sounds we always lost our nerve and ran indoors. We were told that if the lights moved too fast they'd come down and take us away.' He stopped and laughed. 'We were never brave enough to find out if that was true!'

Souls of the dead, dancing animal spirits, warring warriors, harbingers of doom, loving reminders of the creator—many causes have been attributed to the aurora borealis. Science, of course, has its own explanation: the aurorae occur when charged particles emitted from the sun during solar storms penetrate the Earth's magnetic field. These particles collide with atoms and molecules in the upper atmosphere and form bursts of light. Green aurorae come from collisions with oxygen sixty miles above the earth, red from higher-altitude oxygen, blue and purple from collisions with nitrogen. The explanation was all very well, but meaningless as I watched the display. Most magic tricks lose their magic when the 'how' is revealed, but not the aurorae. As I'd discovered many times before, it's not what we *know* that affects us most strongly—it's what we *feel*.

On the fifth night I waved, just to see, but the aurorae didn't descend to Earth and whisk me away. Not physically, anyhow. But my imagination was carried far into the heavens.

———

October began, the final month of the journey, and I figured it was just as well. My spirit wanted The Walk to continue forever, but my body had other ideas—it felt more drained with each passing day. My nose ran as I walked, not from *a* cold but from *the* cold. Somehow, despite seventeen months of soakings, freezings and bakings, despite repeated spells of weariness, hunger and thirst, I hadn't caught a single cold or succumbed to a single illness. This felt like a notable achievement, but I wasn't sure it could last. In my weakened condition good health felt like a fragile state.

October 2 brought a thaw; easier on the fingers, but harder overall to cope with. It came with a steady rain—a cold spray that seeped through my waterproofs and washed away the snowpack, revealing a darker, browner land. Trudging through rain and fog I soon grew hot and clammy, but chilled rapidly each time I rested. Now that the surrounding land was free of snow again I ventured off the road, but progress across sodden, tussocky ground was exhausting. I found myself thinking about The End. It waited two weeks ahead, and all I desired now was to reach it with the minimal effort possible.

I returned to the road.

By day's end all I wanted was to stop, but there was nowhere I could— the landscape was either too rough, too exposed or too flooded for camp. Dusk was well advanced by the time I finally found a spot, but it wasn't a comfortable camp. Rain drummed down hard, penetrating Auld Leakie's seams and walls. The dampness spread across the floor and settled into my spirit. I lay awake into the small hours, too tired to sleep, even though I felt capable of sleeping for a month.

Rain was still falling at dawn—the weather gods testing Mad Mountain Jack's diminishing resolve. Lying in my sleeping bag, I barely had enough motivation to light the stove for breakfast, let alone pack away a soaked tent and walk. Accepting fate, I hid within my sleeping bag all day, not even fully leaving it to use the pee bottle. The day passed slowly, with reading, a great deal of eating, some dozing, and a fair amount of optimistic writing: the first paragraphs of the various end-of-walk articles I hoped I'd soon be able to complete. I smiled ruefully at that: writing about The Walk's end on a day when I didn't manage even a single step.

The rain turned back to snow after nightfall. It soon plastered every surface, and the tent slumped beneath the weight, but I welcomed its insulating softness. Snow seemed friendlier and warmer than rain.

I bullied myself onward the next day, refusing to listen to my tired body. Heavy snow showers came and went, trailing grey curtains to the ground, covering the road in slush. Sometimes I walked in bright sunshine, able to forget the effort, and sometimes in maelstroms of snow, noticing little but my weariness. A passing motorist took pity on me after one storm. Seeing snow on my shoulders and pack he slowed his car and offered a ride. The passenger seats were jammed with children but he was sure there would be room.

I thanked him but, as usual, politely declined.

'Strange as this may seem,' I explained, rustling up an ironic grin, 'I'm actually doing this for fun.'

The man laughed, and drove away looking wonderfully bemused.

Walking on, bolstered by the kindness, I acknowledged that I *was* still having fun, although 'fun' was too feeble a word. The emotions were more complicated and infinitely more powerful. I still felt immense happiness—it was so deep-set I reckoned it would never fade. And I felt great satisfaction in the fact that I was still walking, when walking was so hard to do. I wasn't just placing one foot before another, but practising 'will' over 'will not'. I wasn't only making progress, but stubbornly achieving what I'd set out to achieve. Each step now was a declaration of intent and a clear statement of identity. *This* was who I was—a man who moved forward—and mere exhaustion wouldn't stop me. The journey had degenerated from being a light-hearted saunter across sacred ground into a draining slog along a road—and the change seemed entirely appropriate. The greatest moments had been the greatest moments precisely because of the hard graft that had earned them, and *this* was the hardest graft of all. I had no doubt that the rewards at The End would be all the greater because of it.

Another day's hard labour took me to Alta, one of the world's north-ernmost cities. As with Mo i Rana, it wasn't the most attractive of places. It was filled with utilitarian buildings: modern, square edged and bleak. Like many northern communities in Norway, Alta had been scorched in 1944 by retreating Nazis, and what were the surviving population to do in the face of an unforgiving Arctic environment? Rebuild slowly with an eye on beauty, or put shelter and function first? In any case, who was I to pass judgement on appearances? All I needed from the town was a simple hotel room and a bed for two nights, and Alta capably provided it. Recuperation was sorely needed.

But the day off didn't help—what I now needed were *months* off. On October 8 I continued north, as weary as if I hadn't rested. The miles from Alta passed sluggishly, and I discovered two essential facts. The first was about The Walk: that at this late stage there was no such thing as easy walking, no downhill, that even downhill could feel like up. The second was about myself: that my physical energy wasn't like happiness. The hap-piness I'd found in Padjelanta was boundless. It would always be available; it couldn't be depleted. But my energy most definitely could be.

It was quite a thing to discover: that there was an upper limit to what my body could do. Youth was all I'd ever known, the vigour of it pretty much taken for granted. But now? I'd experienced a stark truth that I wouldn't be able to forget. Youth *wasn't* eternal. Old age would eventually come, with its inevitable conclusion. How appropriate that I'd come to know this during what was, essentially, the journey's old age.

But the discovery didn't feel negative. I considered it as I walked, and soon found gratitude. If I hadn't pushed so hard I'd never have known how hard I *could* push. How could self-knowledge of this kind ever be anything but empowering?

Too many people finish life without ever knowing what they are capa-ble of, and when it's too late find themselves wondering 'If only I had'.

How profoundly satisfying it would be to one day say 'I'm glad I did!'

North of Alta, in soaking rain, I entered the journey's final forest. It grew both sides of the road, patient and watchful. Soft-barked pine trees filled the air with a resin-rich scent, and the forest floor was carpeted with moss. It was too tempting to resist. I stepped away from pavement onto the gentle surface, and wandered among the evergreens with appreciation. It was like being back among old friends. Pine boughs hung heavy with silver beads of water, and I reached out to brush my fingers through them, setting thousands of tiny droplets free. Within the shelter of the forest the rain seemed less wettening, and by the time I reached the far side and climbed into open country I was floating on contentment, despite my weariness. I now found myself in an intricate landscape of crags, tarns and small birch thickets—an environment remarkably similar to the 'rough bounds' near Lindesnes. The familiarity boosted my morale further. It was a wild place —dark, sombre and earthy—perfect Krampus country, and where once it would have intimidated me now it only brought comfort. I camped early, too in love with the location to continue any further.

I'd miss these places.

I attempted more off-trail miles the following morning, but the energy-sapping terrain defeated me and I angled back to the road. For the rest of the day it led across a spacious plateau that offered Padjelanta-wide views. I walked the miles reliving The Greatest Fortnight Ever, feeling gratitude for where I was and also for everywhere I'd been. At some point I completed the journey's 7,000th mile, although it didn't seem worthy of celebration. It was experiences I celebrated now, not statistics. I couldn't even be sure the statistics were accurate. I'd been measuring distances with a tiny measuring pen that I ran over my maps, but it missed the small twists and turns. If each daily measurement since Calabria had been off by even a fraction, which seemed almost certain, the cumulative error would be significant. In any case, I didn't honestly care if this was a 6,500-mile walk, a 7,000-mile walk, or something longer. I didn't care if I'd climbed the equivalent of twenty-eight Everests, twenty-nine, or thirty. The numbers had never been the point. The point was that I'd started beside the Mediterranean and now I was walking across an Arctic landscape near the top of the continent. Put simply: I'd come a *long way*, a statistic that brought nothing but pride.

The next day I walked in a dreamlike daze of tiredness and pleasure blended together. There were no trees upon the landscape now, nor even any mountains. I'd left both behind. This was pure Arctic tundra, a high-*latitude* environment that felt like high altitude, even though it sat at sea level. It gave uninterrupted views, and also unlimited space to think. My thoughts made the most of it, roaming back across Europe's many wild places and also—for the first time—to life after The Walk. A suburban existence wouldn't work for me now, not after everything I'd seen. *Where will I settle?* I wondered. At the foot of a mountain somewhere, I decided, perhaps in the Highlands of Scotland beneath the Cairngorms, a range that closely resembled parts of Norway. *How will I make it happen?* It was impossible to say, but I'd find a way. If I could walk here from Calabria I could do anything I wanted, within reason, and a mountain home wasn't unreasonable. It would have to be somewhere I could touch the wild any time I wished, somewhere I could lose myself to find myself whenever such a thing became necessary. And from it I'd plan my next long walk—not in Europe but further afield. Perhaps I'd walk the length of the Rockies, through the United Sates, Canada and maybe even into Alaska. *Yes, that would do it: a walk to Alaska! What will I find on a journey like that?*

But then I laughed at myself, and refocused on where I was. Dreaming about the next trip when I hadn't finished this one! Focusing on where I wasn't instead of where I was! Hadn't The Walk taught me anything?

That afternoon, a fierce wind picked up, so biting it made my head throb, even with a balaclava and hood protecting it. Exhaustion deepened. The following morning, I struggled to escape my sleeping bag. Each morning was now a genuine battle to get going, far harder than it had been during the previous winter. I lay cocooned long after sunrise and thought *I'll just wait until it gets light,* well aware it never would while I hid within my sleeping bag. *Still dark,* I observed an hour later, and snuggled ever deeper, trying to forget the cold miles and uphill toil that lay ahead.

It seemed miraculous that I got myself walking each day.

Finally underway, I descended from open tundra and reached Porsangen, the last fjord. The miles alongside it were all hard won, every step seemingly uphill. The distances between rests shortened, and time spent resting lengthened. I could no longer maintain a consistent temperature. I was too warm when walking, too cold when resting. I alternated from sweat to shivers and shivers to sweat all day. I felt deplorably weak, as though the gentlest breeze could bowl me over. I sat beside the road head in my hands and trembled from tiredness. I sat as though lost in a fog, and balked at how far I still had to go.

And yet, through it all, my excitement mounted. Churning within my gut were emotions of hope and anticipation; emotions that announced at full volume the approach of a truly great event. They ricocheted about my body with uncontainable energy, even while my body sat slumped. *How is it possible*, I wondered, *to feel such powerful excitement AND such crushing exhaustion simultaneously?* The two feelings didn't belong together, but together they were.

Only a few cars passed, but most of the drivers must have guessed where I was headed. There were toots of encouragement, and thumbs up, and several offered rides. There were even wolf whistles, made from a southbound car of girls. Back in Calabria on The Walk's very first day a car full of youths had tried running me down. I preferred the wolf whistles.

Another day arrived: October 12—'*Arctober 12*', as I labelled it in my journal. The sun rose, but not high. It now sat so close to the horizon that noon was lit like sunset, and the beauty of it brought the Padjelanta Happiness back to the surface. It was always there now, waiting for a little nudge, and here there was much to nudge it: expansive tundra, sparkling bays and inlets, low headlands and plunging cliffs. When the road disappeared into a long tunnel I stumbled appreciatively across untracked tundra above it. Beside me waves surged against rocks. Gulls and ravens wheeled in the sky. Twice I walked past reindeer herds. Several reindeer wore collars with bells, and the clanging notes took me straight back to the Apennines and Alps. How easy it was to return to other places as though I were still there! Sun-dappled Calabrian beech woods, the wild Pollino, airy Abruzzi ridges, the 'Grand Finale on the High Crinale', Alpine cloud seas, ice-encased Bohemian forests, Denmark's restless sea, snowy Hardangervidda, magical Trollheimen, savage Svartisen, spacious Padjelanta—I carried all these places inside. I might one day forget the details, but I'd never forget how the places felt.

I made camp in a glacier-scooped cirque right at the sea's edge, and spent the evening staring into space, listening to an evocative soundtrack of seabirds, cackling ptarmigan, a tumbling brook and rolling waves. Tears brimmed at the surrounding beauty. For a moment, pure emotion overcame me. How could I ever leave this land? How could I say farewell to The Walk? The love I felt for everything it was, for the good and the bad, was so impossibly sweet and all-encompassing it was almost hard to take.

Long shadows on the tundra, October 13, 1998.

I'd fallen in love with something soon to end.

Another exhausting day followed—another twenty miles of endless uphill walking, another blurring of tundra and seascape, tiredness and elation, love and loss.

Late the day after that, Arctober 14, I reached Kåfjord, the end of the mainland road.

I sat alone in a cold and draughty shelter awaiting the 5.30 p.m. ferry to Magerøya. The wind whirled through gaps in the shelter's walls and my emotions whirled with it. Outside, the incoming tide raced down the fjord with the force of a river in flood, as unstoppable as time itself, while the sun slipped towards the southern horizon.

Tens of thousands of visitors also bound for the North Cape had waited on the same wooden bench, and many had left their mark. Jo Hansen had carved his name there; so too had Monsieur Henri Icsen. Heinrich Schmidt had sat here exactly one month previously, on 14/9/98. Fascinated, I read name after name, until four words stopped me. 'I LOVE A NENE' someone had declared, and in a fog of tiredness I read it in puzzlement. *A Nene?* I wondered. *What the hell is 'a nene'?* It took a while, but when I realised it

357

was just another name I began laughing, and for a long while couldn't stop.

Oh, mountain gods, I'm losing it, I wrote in my journal right there. *I think I need to go home.*

The ferry was far larger than I'd expected. It arrived in deepening twilight, dead on time.

An official beckoned me on board. He was muffled in a heavy orange weather-suit but still looked freezing cold and grim, as though he wanted nothing but to be somewhere else, somewhere warm.

'Barbados?' I asked, eyebrows raised.

His face cracked into a grin.

'Barbados, yes!' he agreed. 'All aboard for Barbados.' He looked out into the bleak night. 'Wouldn't that be bloody nice!'

Twenty minutes later the bright lights of Honningsvåg appeared across the black waters of the Magerøya Sound. The North Cape waited a mere twenty-two miles beyond it.

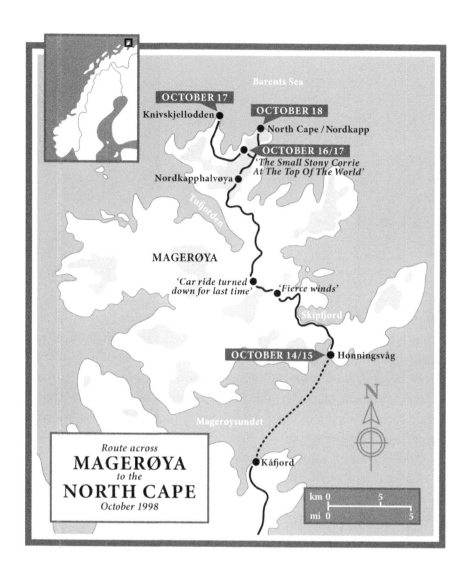

Route across
MAGERØYA
to the
NORTH CAPE
October 1998

THE NORTH CAPE
Chapter 15

FROM THE FACTS alone, the North Cape isn't anything special. It isn't Europe's tallest, steepest, or remotest sea cliff. The rock isn't rare, or unusually hard, or uniquely formed. And, contrary to much of the publicity, it isn't Europe's northernmost point, nor Norway's, nor even the island of Magerøya's. On Magerøya, the Knivskjellodden peninsula juts almost a mile further north, and 650 miles beyond that is Norway's Svalbard archipelago. One might consider the North Cape a bit of an imposter.

And yet, there *is* something about the place.

Rising sheer from the Barents Sea, the North Cape makes an emphatic statement. When seen, it is a rock that can't be ignored. And when considered, it is greater than simple facts might suggest. The North Cape might seem like just another over-publicised tourist destination, but it can mean so much more, especially when it's taken 7,000 miles to reach.

The North Cape was formed beneath the waves of the ancient Iapetus Ocean some 430 million years ago. Fine-particled clays settled in layers upon the ocean floor, and over time hardened into mudstone and shale. Eventually, the Caledonian orogeny—a landscape-transforming epoch that pushed up Norway's original Himalayan-sized mountain range—put the shale under immense pressure, brought it to the surface, then folded it over. After that, erosion got to work, whittling rock down grain by grain. Glaciers also did their bit, scouring and sculpting the North Cape plateau. The North Cape might be a mere sea cliff, but it rears like a full-fledged mountain.

History doesn't record who first discovered the North Cape, but it was most likely bold pre-Viking seafarers who travelled beyond the limits of the known world and did what the human species does so well: furthered the boundaries of knowledge. Inevitably, others followed, and the headland eventually became well-enough known to acquire a name: Knyskanes. In 1553 it was 'discovered' again, this time by an English navigator, Richard Chancellor. Taking part in an expedition to find the North-East Passage to China, Chancellor sailed past the soaring black rock, noticed that the coastline turned south after it, and gave the headland its current name.

A century later, the North Cape became a destination for the first time. It was an Italian—Catholic priest Francesco Negri—who first made the headland a goal, reaching it late in 1664 after a journey lasting several years. Negri travelled north in the name of scientific research, and wrote a book upon his return—*Viaggio Settentrionale*, Northern Journey. In it he concluded that at the North Cape—at the '*edge of the world*'—his journey was done. There was nothing more to be learned.

The North Cape's fame spread over following centuries as travellers willing to endure the hardships of the far north began bringing back tales of the continent's edge. By the late 1800s, organised tourism finally reached the headland, and increasing numbers of visitors were delivered by steamer to a nearby anchorage. Most visits were made in midsummer, the aim being to not only stand upon Europe's northern edge but to also witness the midnight sun from it. The midnight sun is visible at the North Cape from mid-May until the last day of July—two and a half months, evidence of just how far north the headland is. Such a phenomenon—blazing sunlight when the stars are supposed to shine—was quite an attraction. It still is.

During the twentieth century, access became ever easier and the North Cape's popularity grew. Nowadays, an estimated 200,000 people visit each year, the majority arriving via the road across Magerøya that was built in 1965. Because of it, the modern-day headland isn't the untrammelled place it once was. It now sports a clutter of buildings, sculptures, a parking lot, fences and signs. But the cape's wild power still resonates. The surface may have been scratched, but the dark cliffs still plunge 1,000 feet, the icy waters still clash far below, and the great expanse of empty space beyond the plateau's edge still pulls at the imagination. The frozen seas of the North Pole lie 1,300 miles north, but they don't *feel* far away. The North Cape might not be the edge of the world that Negri once considered it, but modern travellers report that it can still feel as though it is.

I wondered how it would feel to me.

———◆———

The town of Honningsvåg was barely visible in deepening twilight when I disembarked from the ferry, and yet I sensed something of its wild northern atmosphere. Clustered around a natural harbour, Honningsvåg's streets climbed steeply towards rocky hills. From what I could see, the buildings were all boxy and unembellished, with roofs steeply angled to shed snow, and sturdy walls crafted to defeat cold and wind. I couldn't see any trees. With a chill Arctober wind cutting through the darkness, Honningsvåg felt like a true northern outpost—a settlement at the end of the world.

Following the suggestion of a woman working in a brightly lit supermarket, I tramped to a small hotel overlooking town. The hotel receptionist —an elderly lady with her hair in a tight bun—refused to believe I'd walked from Calabria. She shook her head with doubt, her expression a reward in itself. To have almost completed a journey that someone couldn't believe made the closeness of completion all the more satisfying.

She was also unable to grasp that I was only travelling at three miles an hour. She explained that I could easily make it to Nordkapp and back in one day.

'And you really should,' she urged. 'You *have* to come back by Friday night for the young people's disco. They always like meeting new folk.'

Even stinky English walking trolls? I wondered.

Eventually, I made an escape and settled into my room. But I struggled to sleep; my excitement ran too high. To make amends, I grabbed plenty of rest the following day—The Walk's final rest day—spending most of it lounging on my bed, and the remainder of it eating. I ventured into Honningsvåg just once, for lunch in a small café, and shared a table with a talkative local.

'It's too quiet up here,' the man explained. He was roughly my age, and pale-skinned as though he saw very little sun. 'We are so far from everything. Our shops only have so much in them. Mostly we have to order stuff, then wait weeks for it. Order, order, order... wait, wait, wait. It can be tiresome!'

Honningsvåg, October 15, 1998.

A sailor by trade, the man had great respect for the local waters. 'The weather can be savage… the waves crazy! We often lose power and sometimes go days without electricity. My wife is from Oslo, and she doesn't like it here, especially the winter darkness.' He smiled ruefully. 'I think that if I want to stay married I will have to move south.'

That night, I lay in bed thinking about how far from everywhere this northern tip of Norway truly was. It wasn't just an edge-of-the-world feeling—it was an edge-of-the-world reality. The location made my stomach churn with excitement and achievement. Would I feel the same if I'd come by cruise ship or car? I suspected that 7,000 miles of walking had turned *my* North Cape into an entirely different place from everyone else's. It was an intriguing aspect of travel, how people visit the same places but seldom experience them the same way. The approach can change a location profoundly. I suspected it worked for life, too.

I left Honningsvåg at 10 a.m. after another fitful night's sleep. As I paced from town a flood of emotions surged—so many that I couldn't pin down how I felt. Much if it was contradictory. I felt eager but reluctant, euphoric but anguished. I wanted the journey to end, but goodness I didn't! I longed for an end to tiredness, discomfort, and the need to always trudge on. I longed to be back with my family. But I raged at the idea of ending this life of freedom and purpose where my place in the universe had become known and assured. How could this end? It would be like ending a part of myself. *Who* I was had become inseparable from *how* I was living. The love I felt for The Walk set me soaring, just as knowledge that I'd soon have to part from it threatened to crush me. The contrasting emotions swept against one another like the warring seas back at the Grenen—until the sheer effort of walking into a biting Arctic wind reduced my focus to more immediate needs.

The road to the North Cape skirted Honningsvåg's harbour, crossed an isthmus, then looped upward onto a plateau. The plateau was open and treeless, arguably a bleak place, but to me achingly beautiful. Grey skies hung above it, bursts of rain splattered onto it, and a fierce wind blasted across it, but the harsh conditions felt appropriate. They matched the occasion and provided a final physical test to justify the reward waiting ahead. I leaned into the gale and battled forward, walking without a plan. How far I made it depended on many things: on tiredness and the weather, and on what the mountain gods allowed. I hoped to camp within striking distance of the North Cape but didn't want to actually reach it. Not yet—not today. And not even the day after.

I wasn't ready.

The road carried a surprising amount of traffic—a car every ten minutes. It was a reassuring sight, raising the possibility that I wouldn't have to walk back to Honningsvåg once The Walk itself was done. At one point a police car pulled over and the officers asked where I was going. I had to laugh; where else was there to go up here but the North Cape? Generously, they offered a ride, a pleasant change from the police encounters I'd had in the Apennines and Czech Republic. As usual, they didn't understand my reasons for declining. It was likely the last time I'd have to try and explain the unexplainable.

Struggling in the wind, I paused for several long breaks: once behind a huge rock, once within sight of the sea where rolling waves erupted against land in explosions of white water, once beside a small green hut that stood isolated on the plateau. Peering through a window I saw stacks of reindeer antlers and shelves of reindeer skins—not an everyday sight. I considered camping in the lee of the hut, using it as a windbreak. The gale was now so fierce that pitching Auld Leakie in the open would be difficult, if not impossible, but in the end I pushed on. The location didn't *feel* right. Somehow, I knew I was meant to keep moving forward.

Further miles passed, Europe fast running out of land. The road, now empty of traffic, lost height, and twisted around several lakes with dark waters whipped into a frenzy, before climbing onto the spacious Nordkapp-halvøya, the 'Plateau at the Top of Europe'. The North Cape was now within reach—a fact that I couldn't fully accept. It lay fewer than five miles ahead. Two hours' walk; excruciatingly close. Once again, emotions flooded to the surface. I wasn't sure whether to laugh and dance, or break down in despair at life's cruelty, at the way everything had to eventually end.

I covered another two miles, and then, as if controlled by an outside force, stepped off the road. Instinct more than conscious choice took me north-west across bogs, stones and ankle-breaking hummocks. After a short distance the plateau swept downhill into a steep-sided valley, a location that so closely resembled a high-mountain cirque that its nearness to the sea seemed ludicrous. *Home!* I thought the moment I saw it. Best of all, the wind howling across the plateau failed to reach into it. I was able to pitch Auld Leakie with ease, and this, The Walk's final campsite—'The Small Stony Corrie At The Top Of The World'—became one of the finest campsites of the entire journey.

As I settled into familiar camp routines my emotions settled too, until calmness ruled. It was as though this wasn't the very last campsite, merely *another*, with many others still to follow. I cooked my usual evening stew, and devoured it thinking back to one of the phone calls I'd made the previous evening. I'd talked with a journalist at the *London Evening Standard* who had interviewed me before The Walk had begun.

'So, how are you going to celebrate the end?' he'd asked as a final question, to which I'd had no answer. 'Come on,' he'd insisted. 'You've had eighteen months to think about it!'

'Er...' I'd mumbled. 'Um...'

The truth was, I *hadn't* thought about it. Sure, I'd thought about *reaching* the end, but *celebrating* it? Why would I celebrate the end of something I loved so much that it physically hurt? But the journalist had pressed, and feeling that I had to come up with something all I'd managed was a feeble joke.

'Well, perhaps I'll celebrate by staying in bed the next day.'

It was only now, twenty-four hours later, that I saw what I should have said. That I didn't need to celebrate the end because the journey itself had been a celebration, every single step of it: a celebration of freedom, a celebration of the natural world, a celebration of *living*. Cringing, I laughed at my slow-wittedness. How typical, that I'd been given an opportunity to share something profound but instead had joked about staying in bed!

Sleep in 'The Small Stony Corrie At The Top Of The World' was better than it had been in Honningsvåg. The earth moulded itself to my shape; the clean Arctic air was like medicine for my lungs; the song of water and wind created a lulling pathway straight into sleep. But I still awoke several times, my dreams interrupted by laughter. The Walk was nearly over, but the Padjelanta Happiness lived on.

———

Dawn arrived with a glitter of frost and Auld Leakie's walls sagging, which could only mean one thing: winter had returned. I shrieked with delight: it was *exactly* what the Hollywood script demanded. The end I'd pictured had always included snow.

Leaving camp pitched, travelling light, I set out on The Walk's penultimate day, aiming for the Knivskjellodden peninsula, the northernmost point of Magerøya. The North Cape could wait until tomorrow. Chuckling with happiness, I tramped across a snow-dusted wilderness, forever climbing and descending. A biting north-east wind whipped across the plateau. Grey clouds swept by overhead. The Barents Sea was visible to the north, storm-tossed and savage, white-capped waves streaking across black water. Wild as it was, the landscape felt comfortingly familiar. Even though I'd never walked upon *this* stretch of earth before it was home from the very first step, and a surge of love for it filled me. I felt such deep kinship with the land; with *all* wild lands. It was so strong I wanted to cry out from the pleasure of it. I never wanted to let it go.

The miles passed slowly, but slowly was exactly the right speed. Expecting an off-trail route to Knivskjellodden I was surprised when I came across a narrow trail, and along it a familiar sight: a red 'T' painted onto a prominent rock. It transported me to all the other DNT-marked routes I'd followed, and to so many other corners of Norway. The path appeared to lead where I wanted, as if fate were helping me on my way. It curved down-hill into a shallow valley, dropped beneath snowline, and finally petered out at a wide bay. From there I continued off-trail again, across slabs of pink-hued granite. The Knivskjellodden peninsula is built from igneous granite, not metamorphic shales like the North Cape. The glacier-smoothed slabs offered solid footing for the final 200 yards.

And then I was there, as far north as I could go.

Arrival was something else, a moment to hold onto forever, not just for where it was or for how extraordinary it felt but also for what was now plainly in view. Rising across the bay was the North Cape itself: my goal for so long, a dream made real, a vision solidified, and at the sight of it I screamed and screamed my elation into the wind.

'I'm here! I'm bloody *here!*'

Huge turquoise rollers answered back, smashing into land's end, ex-ploding into towers of spray that the wind carried swiftly away.

For a long while, I simply stood and stared.

The wind, eventually, forced me to seek shelter. I picked a spot beside a boulder where I could still see the North Cape. It was now obvious why the headland was considered the 'Top of Europe'. It didn't look like just *another* place; it was clearly *the* place. It towered over the sea, intimidatingly dark, imposingly sculpted; a buttressed, gully-riven monolith of rock, immutable before the chaos of white water at its feet. Captivated, I stared for an age, loving that it still lay in my future—but excited beyond measure that it would soon be part of my past.

I'd be there tomorrow.

The return to camp was easier with the wind at my back. It began with a sighting of a sea otter—a real treat. Its fur was dark and slick, and it flowed along at water's edge with a fluidity that suggested it was made from water itself. Eventually, it merged into the waves. Carrying the vision with me I followed the DNT trail back above snowline, picked up my own footprint trail across the plateau, and followed that home.

'Auld Leakie, my trusty friend—there you are!' I exclaimed affection-ately upon arrival. 'I'm home!' And home I was, in every way possible.

The Walk's final dinner was a feast, a great pile of everything I had left over. Afterwards, with a candle flickering and the stove keeping the frost at bay, and the fluttering caress of snow now falling again outside, I penned my penultimate journal entry.

This is so perfect. Well, almost. All I need now is the Northern Lights one final time.

Two hours later the mountain gods granted my wish, breaking the clouds apart and unfurling a flickering green curtain across the stars. It was almost too much to believe—I hadn't seen the aurorae in sixteen days, and would have missed them if I hadn't peeked from the tent at that exact moment. I watched, awestruck, then gasped aloud as three shooting stars burst right through the display. They were followed by a fourth shooting star, the brightest I'd ever witnessed. It flashed into existence far to the north, for a moment lighting the night. Shockingly bright, intensely green, it arced across the horizon, visible for one, two, three seconds. It finally vanished an instant before hitting the sea, leaving a bright streak behind that hung in the blackness for long seconds. *Fireworks for the end!* I laughed, before acknowledging: *and how easily I could have missed them.*

How easily I could have missed The Walk itself.

Eventually, I zipped shut the tent and returned to my diary. *How much we must miss for not looking*, I observed, and then, a little later, added a final meek request to all the gods of mountains and weather and long-distance travellers: *please, keep the skies clear for tomorrow?*

But it was a request too far. An hour later snow was falling hard.

———

From the journey's very first step I'd been able to picture the final day perfectly. The image had always been strikingly clear: my lone figure tramping across sunlit snow to a dark headland rising above a churning Arctic sea. At no point had I ever doubted it would be any different. Some things are written in the stars.

The final day—Nordkapp Day—began with shivers. Penetrating cold pulled me from sleep. The thermometer inside the tent read fourteen Fahrenheit, minus ten Celsius—the coldest reading since February's ice-encrusted Rennsteig. Auld Leakie's walls were coated in frost. When I

All smiles on the final morning, Nordkapp Day, October 18, 1998.

brought the stove to life the frost began thawing, filling the tent with fog. The discomforts within my squalid home were significant, but I didn't care. What a thing it was to know that this was the final morning of The Walk!

I could scarcely believe my eyes when I stepped outside. It was too improbable, too Hollywood scripted, too much a fairy tale sprung to life to be true. And yet there it was, the conditions I'd always pictured: fresh snow beneath a blue sky. A scream of joy erupted without warning, the way it had many times across an entire continent. My imaginary gods *had* listened yet again. They'd breathed their approval and granted their final reward. I almost burst with gratitude at the day they'd given.

Striking camp was a battle in the extremity-numbing cold, but I'd done it before, and it was so much easier knowing I wouldn't have to do it again.

And then, with Excalibur in hand, I climbed from 'The Small Stony Corrie At The Top Of The World', as always leaving nothing behind but my deepest appreciation. Strapped to Ten Ton were reindeer antlers I'd stumbled upon the day before, and when I reached direct sunlight I grinned at the shadow they cast. *Hey look, the looming silhouette of a wild Krampus!*

Standing above 'The Small Stony Corrie At The Top Of The World', with the Knivskjellodden peninsula in the background, Nordkapp Day, October 18, 1998.

How I loved what Krampus had come to represent. It was my adopted spirit creature, a representative of the *other* Europe, the Europe I'd so often found. Here it was beneath my feet again: the untrammelled Europe, the sacred Europe, showing no sign that others of my own species had ever visited it. There were boulders and slabs, grassy tussocks and frozen peat, streaks of ice filled with bubbles, 'art snow' delicately sculpted by the wind —all arranged as nature intended. As I stepped gently I thought back to the journey's many surfaces: to sun-baked soil and mulchy woodland floors, to loose sand and unyielding rock, to piney trails and glacial ice, to grassy meadows and boulder fields, to oozing bogs and snow in its many forms. How passionately I'd come to treasure all the natural surfaces of our richly textured living earth.

What a privilege it had been to get to walk so much of it.

Up on the plateau the morning air cut more keenly, but I cared not. It was Nordkapp Day—nothing else mattered. I was too full of memories to feel any discomfort. Spindrift at my feet danced and swirled like the Northern Lights; ice crystals glittered and flashed like fireflies in the Mezzogiorno beech woods; sharp rocks cutting through snow could have been Alpine peaks piercing magical moonlit oceans of cloud. I held an entire continent within, and I could dip into it any time I wished, relive any moment I chose, revisit any place my heart desired. No treasure could ever be greater than the treasures I carried inside. Compared to it, the cold was nothing.

My route across the plateau led back to the road. A single set of tyre tracks broke the fresh snow upon it, four parallel canyons heading to the North Cape and back. Other people were about. I'd always imagined standing alone at the end, although I now realised that either alone or in company would work. Both had much to offer. Not only was I less tied to my own expectations, I was *more* tied to other people. I'd passed through many lives since Melito, experienced much generosity. I'd learnt that the world was a far friendlier place than most media sources would have me believe. I'd made friends, and I wondered about them as I set off along the road. There was Flavio, my Italian brother from the Dolomites; Carl the butcher and his hospitable East German family; Anne, Reidar and Eminguak from Denmark; Odd, who'd lent me his Padjelanta map; and so many others from so many walks of life. What were they doing now? Every single encounter had enriched my life. Even the hard-hearted souls who had turned me away had positively impacted the journey. Their actions had brought frustration and even despair, but they'd also taught lessons I'd never forget. I hoped I was a better person because of them.

The final mile began, and when I noticed how swiftly I was walking it I forced myself to slow down. Each step was now too precious to rush; each moment priceless beyond measure. But even at a snail's pace progress still came. As I'd discovered, small steps add up. Take enough of them and an entire continent can be crossed. Too soon a large blue sign appeared directly ahead. It bore a single word: 'NORDKAPP', and beyond it was the clutter of civilisation that marred the headland.

Almost there.

But I had one final detour to make first. A short distance away, jutting east from the plateau's edge, was a spur that would hopefully give a good view of the North Cape's plunging cliffs. I wanted to see the cliffs for context before standing at their top.

I set off toward the spur, happy to delay the end for a few minutes more, but was halted before I'd covered fifty yards. I heard a vehicle, and I turned to see a military jeep appear on the road. It stopped abruptly and two uniformed men leapt out. They shouted and waved their arms frantically, beckoning me back. *Well*, I laughed. *So much for freedom; so much for the perfect Hollywood ending!* I waved back, and at further shouts accepted fate. I dropped Ten Ton and sauntered casually to the road.

'Yes?' I asked innocently, when finally I stood before them. 'How can I help?'

The men identified themselves as officers of the Norwegian Navy, out on patrol. They were about my age, wore padded, dark blue uniforms, and looked very stern.

'Where were you going?' the taller of the two demanded. 'Why were you walking to the edge?'

'To take some photos,' I answered lightly. 'Is that not allowed?'

They didn't reply directly, but frowned. 'Where you were going... it is too dangerous. You might fall off.'

At that, without meaning to, I burst into laughter. I couldn't help myself.

'Look,' I said. 'I just spent a year and a half walking here from Calabria. I walked the length of four mountain ranges, in pretty much every kind of bad weather you can think of. I'll probably be okay.'

The officers looked at one another, considering what I'd said. The tall officer spoke again, but this time his voice sounded defensive. 'Tourists don't know the danger. It's easy to fall off. People do. Well, they have. Most visitors simply don't take enough care—they don't understand wild places like this. They can be unpredictable. Nordkapp is dangerous.'

I stared up at the cloudless sky, around at the flat and clearly defined plateau, taking in the sparkling beauty of a land that had, essentially, become my home. Was it wild, unpredictable, dangerous? Not anymore.

Carefully this time, I explained what it was I'd just done and who, exactly, I now was. At first, like the hotel receptionist in Honningsvåg, they point-blank refused to believe that I'd just walked across the entire continent, and I rejoiced at that. But slowly, anecdote by anecdote, I won them over, until eventually they nodded in understanding, then laughed along with me. Soon, we were on first-name terms.

'So how are you getting back?' the tall officer, Roald, finally asked.

'Not walking I bet?' guessed the other, Svein.

'Too bloody right. Never again! I'm going to burn my backpack, throw away my boots...' And they both laughed, perhaps seeing that I didn't mean it.

We parted as friends.

Once the officers had driven away I returned to my detour and soon stood on the plateau's edge. The North Cape was now revealed, and from such close proximity it looked even mightier than it had the day before. Deeply impressed, I ran through two films: photos of Knivskjellodden so small below; of the empty Barents Sea and the vast northern horizon; of the North Cape itself, towering above the waves; of myself standing in front of it, grinning inanely like the happiest fool on the planet; and of myself flat on my back as though 7,000 miles of effort had ultimately been too much.

'Well, he almost made it.' Nordkapp Day, October 18, 1998.

And then I picked up Ten Ton and took the final steps—and it was exactly as I'd always pictured: lone figure, dark headland, sunlit snow, churning sea.

The end could have been an anticlimax. But it wasn't. Not a bit. As I walked across the plateau, passed the barely noticed buildings and signs, towards the famous metal globe sculpture, a triumphant roar filled my head. It was just me up here now, alone on the headland at the top of Europe, and soon all that was required to reach its edge was ten more steps, then five, then one…

And then I was done.

What followed is probably embarrassing, but I don't care: there were jubilant animal howls, great ringing 'Yaaa-ha-haaaaas', maniacal laughter, more howls, then a mad skipping dance, round and round in crazy circles with Ten Ton still on my back.

The emotions couldn't be contained.

The moment was *straordinario*, as Flavio would have put it—truly extraordinary, almost too much to take. I grinned and grinned and grinned. My face started to ache. There had never been a moment like it.

The North Cape is no impossible-to-reach destination, no Everest or K2, no South Pole, but at that moment—to me—it was all the summits of the world rolled into one.

Afterwards, I lingered for an hour, and spent it trying to regain a modicum of dignity. The visitor centre was closed, which suited me fine, and I sheltered against it, nibbling my remaining snacks, with the view to the north tugging at my imagination. Soon, contentment, a quieter emotion, settled within. But I still couldn't stop smiling. I wouldn't be able to stop for days.

Eventually, the cold moved me on. But before heading south there was one more thing I had to do.

Reaching into my pocket, I grasped the five small pebbles I'd plucked from the Mediterranean Sea a lifetime earlier. I pulled them out, stared at them in my gloved hand. They were small and rounded; perhaps more rounded now than they'd been back at Melito di Porto Salvo. One was delightfully green, streaked with quartz; another pinkish red, embedded with crystals; another pale orange, flecked with grey; another silver-white, patterned like marble; the last charcoal-black, speckled with minerals that shone like stars. I stared, and considered what these five stones represented.

A lump rose in my throat. Tears welled in my eyes.

What places we'd been, these rocks from another land!

What love I'd found on my walk!

What a place Nordkapp was, what a day, what a journey!

And what a thing to have to let go...

Hesitantly, I walked to the edge and stood quietly, looking north.

A gust of wind blew. The Arctic air felt cold and clean against my face. Time slowed, almost stopped.

But then I drew back my arm, launched it forward, and *four* colourful pieces of Mediterranean rock spun out over the Barents Sea and were lost to sight.

The North Cape, October 18, 1998.

PART VI

EPILOGUE

ONE SMALL PEBBLE

AFTER LEAVING THE North Cape I didn't rush south. England called, but only distantly. In the end it took two weeks to return. Why rush 'home' when I was already there?

The journey south began on foot, a further six snowy miles, ending when the first car to appear pulled over. It was quite something to finally be able to say: 'Yes... thank you... I'd *love* a ride!'

Back in Honningsvåg I made a string of jubilant phone calls to Base Camp, sponsors, and the charities. The Passage and the Cardinal Hume Centre told me that the publicity had been extensive, and that the fund-raising was going well—it would eventually reach £25,000.

'You've also given everyone something to get excited about,' I was told. 'It's been such a positive thing, following your journey.'

I stayed in Honningsvåg for two nights, revelling in the strange notion that when I left it wouldn't be on foot. No longer would I have to walk on, day after day, month after month. No longer would I have to pack away a frozen camp each morning, heave on Ten Ton, and pace myself for the struggles ahead. The immense task was over, and I finally realised how completely it had dominated every action and thought. In Honningsvåg I felt released as though a great weight had been lifted.

Perhaps Ten Ton had been too heavy after all. (Okay, we all knew that already.)

For days I felt euphoric, exactly as I had after surviving my fall from the Hohtürli Pass. I was alive, and knew it; free, and felt it. The future was a thing of unlimited possibility. Only occasionally did bouts of heart-wrenching loss occur, but the pain seldom lasted long. The Walk may have ended, but my love for it endured. For much of my stay in Honningsvåg I simply grinned and grinned, overcome by the satisfaction and joy of completion.

The famous Hurtigruten coastal steamer eventually carried me south: a day's untroubled passage across silver water to the Lofoten Islands. 'Look!' I exclaimed in awe to a fellow passenger as the *MS Nordlys* approached a milder land. 'Trees!' After weeks upon the tundra, trees had never looked so extraordinary. I'd practically forgotten they existed.

The other passenger merely shrugged and looked away. But I couldn't stop staring. There was so much I'd never again take for granted.

From Lofoten a bus took me to Narvik, a train carried me south to Trondheim, then I jumped back onto the Hurtigruten for the cruise to Bergen. Mountains appeared ahead and disappeared behind, fjords came and went, forests passed, miles flew by, and I didn't have to lift a finger. Or raise a foot. It felt like cheating—and cheating felt great.

I made one final foray into the fjells before leaving Norway; a final farewell to the land I'd come to love. In a raging blizzard I battled through waist-deep powder to a remote hut perched on the edge of the Hardanger-vidda, and spent two nights immersed in slow living one final time.

And then Color Line whisked me across the North Sea at no charge, and before long I was on a train crossing my own country, then walking from a familiar station through a familiar London suburb, returning home from the hills the way I had many times before, except this time *everything* seemed different—most of all myself.

My mother practically screamed when she answered the front door. 'You're here! You made it! Andrew—you're *really* home!'

I felt my North Cape grin return. As my mother led me indoors it grew wider. Once again, my face ached from it. I was home! But in a way I'd never been before. What home meant had changed. Home was no longer restricted to a small suburban building. It now stretched across forests and meadows, mountains and valleys, plains and beaches. Home was so much bigger.

And yet this Pinner home remained special—more special, now, than it had ever been. As I'd learnt over the miles, to *truly* value something, you have to go without it first.

My father appeared. He pantomimed a face of shock, laughed, held out his arms, and we hugged. 'Well, you did it,' he said. He looked me up and down, nodding his head in what looked, to me, like approval. 'And you know what? It's *really* something.' I beamed. From my father, compliments didn't come much larger.

Hours later, once emotions had calmed, he had the final word, as usual. 'Of course, I still think you're completely mad.'

I knew he did. And I wouldn't have wanted it any other way.

———

Afterwards, I settled back into my ordinary suburban life, although when I focused on the details I saw that it wasn't ordinary at all. For a few months I couldn't have been more content. I appreciated my parents and brothers more than I ever had before, and savoured the simple comforts as though they were the height of luxury. The roof over my head was something I could never again take for granted. Plus, it was only temporary. This time I was merely passing through.

To my surprise, I even found myself enjoying Pinner, the suburb I'd so desperately wanted to escape. Its familiarity was comforting, and being greeted with smiles by people I'd known before The Walk, and now bumped into daily, took on a meaning it never had before. Plus, Pinner had changed—to my eyes at least. What had seemed like an idyllic country village throughout my childhood, and an urban prison in my early twenties, was once again doing a passable impression of a country village. Back on the North German Plain I'd discovered that wildness existed everywhere in nature—in a blackbird's song, in a rotten tree stump—and Pinner confirmed it. I found miniature wildernesses in Pinner's uncultivated margins, in nearby deciduous woods, along the little River Pinn, and in every nook and cranny where the earth had been left undisturbed. There was much about Pinner that I found ugly, noisy and outrageously wasteful—that was for sure—but the emotions that arose when I engaged with the pockets of nature were curiously similar to the emotions I'd experienced in the Arctic.

The deep weariness I'd suffered during the journey's final weeks began to fade. I started running again, loping through the woods, feeling light and free without the baggage I'd carried for so long. At the end of

November I joined the KRAP Club for a weekend in the Peak District. The gritstone crags and heather moors were a welcome sight, but I treasured the company more. The extraordinariness of being among peers was a treat beyond value.

For the first two weeks I focused on writing end-of-trip reports and sorting through the 7,000 slides I'd taken. The photographs brought immense pleasure. I was astounded by how closely the scenes matched my memories, even landscapes from Calabria, as though I'd seen them a day before, not eighteen months. With a small selection loaded in a carousel, I gave the first of several talks, hoping to boost fundraising for the Passage and the Cardinal Hume Centre. Facing a room of expectant faces, I stammered through my story, seeking inspiration from The Walk's hardest moments. If I could cross the Hardangervidda on crappy snowshoes I could damn well overcome my stammer and talk in public.

Inevitably, I returned to work, but approached it differently—creating worth from doing it to the best of my ability, from concentrating on the moment, not wishing I were somewhere else. Work was merely part of my journey now—and it too was temporary. From the moment I returned home I began planning the next long walk, a 6,000-mile trek across North America. My father threw his hands up in bemusement when I revealed the plan, but what else could I do? I was still Mad Mountain Jack, and long walks defined me. How could I ever give them up? North America's larger, grizzly-bear-inhabited wildernesses unsettled me, which was what I needed to keep moving forward. As I'd thought near the top of Norway: *a walk across the Rockies to Alaska—what will I find on a journey like that?*

What I found is a whole other story, but the short version is: far more than I expected. In July 2000, deep in the Colorado wilderness, I crossed paths with Joan, the most extraordinary woman I've ever met, and she altered my life's trajectory. My desire for more than just company, for a meaningful relationship, for mutual benefit and mutual support, for love, was finally met, and—even better—reciprocated. It was nature, pure and simple, and it turned my life upside down. I still made it to Alaska (and not without adventures along the way), but the journey after that—the shared journey with Joan—was the greatest adventure of my life. It led, ultimately, to leaving England for good, to moving to Colorado, to marriage, parenthood, and an entirely new way of life.

Family camp, Colorado, June 2013.

An existence that would have been terrifying and unachievable to the shy Pinner boy, and anathema to the freedom-loving mountain vagabond, became an existence I willingly chose and fully embraced. It wasn't a continent-spanning walk, but it was shot through with meaning and purpose. It wasn't always easy, but it sure as hell helped me grow and move forward. Choosing marriage and a new country meant giving up a great deal, but the rewards earned far exceeded what was lost, especially when I did as The Walk had taught: focused on where I was, not where I wasn't, and on what I had, not what I didn't. Mad Mountain Jack gaped at his new life in astonishment, unable to take any of it for granted. Even now, two decades later, I still can't quite believe the balance I found.

Besides, there are worst places to live than Colorado. What I'd wanted —to live at the foot of a mountain—was what I now had. I only had to step outside to find adventure, and you can be sure I stepped outside often, and still do, pretty much every day. The roots I've put down in Colorado's forests, canyons and mountains, the intricate details I've learnt, and the deep connections I've established—with people as well as the land—are all the better for not having to always walk on. As a husband and father, multi-month walks are on hold until I enter a different season in life, but with frequent nights out and daily adventures, nature remains a constant part of life. The wild is no longer a place I visit. It's simply a place I live.

For years, the only regret from The Walk was a small item I'd misplaced: the little red notebook that contained all the names and addresses of everyone I'd met between Calabria and the North Cape. I'd had it in Honningsvåg, but by Pinner it had gone, and this time it wasn't found and anonymously returned. In the year following The Walk I wrote several letters, attempting to track down some of the people, but I received no replies. Social media didn't exist, internet searches were limited, and eventually my life moved on.

From time to time, I wondered about my friends spread across Europe. I thought about Flavio, my Italian brother, the most. When we'd parted he'd given me a small camping knife so that I'd remember him, and remember him I did every single time I used his knife when cooking dinner in camp over the next two decades. Flavio's brother, Andrew, had died of a sudden brain haemorrhage at forty-four. His father had died the same way at a similar age. When I'd met him, Flavio was soon to turn forty-four himself. He faced an uncertain future. Each time I thought of him I wondered: *is he still alive?*

Finally, in 2020, with the publication of *The Earth Beneath My Feet* approaching, I began searching. I emailed the Italian Alpine Club, wondering if they could ask their members to help with the search, but as before I received no reply. But then, two months later, an Italian approached me on social media, explaining that he'd just read about my search in an Italian Alpine Club magazine. The magazine had shared the picture I'd sent of Flavio, the story of our meeting, and an impassioned plea from the editor. The man thought he knew who Flavio was.

He did. They were close friends.

The man, Bepi, put us in touch. Bepi told me that Flavio cried when he learnt by phone that I was looking for him, and tears of joy rose to my eyes when I learnt that he was alive and well. Finally, Flavio and I reconnected, twenty-three years after we'd met—and like the original meeting in the Dolomites, it was *straordinario*, one of life's greatest and sweetest moments.

Even two decades on, The Walk was still giving rewards.

Twenty-three years have now passed since I stood at the North Cape, although it still seems like yesterday. I am no longer the same person I was back then, and yet, in everything that matters, I haven't changed at all.

From the moment I finished The Walk I wanted to share the story, but when I tried writing it I struggled. To begin with I was too close and couldn't articulate what it meant. Then life got in the way: the journey to Alaska, marriage, children, a new Colorado home. How could I spend time writing about the past when *right now* was where The Walk had taught me to live?

But slowly, working in fits and starts, I made progress, deciphering the ten journals I'd filled, studying the photographs, reliving memories so vivid they might have been formed days earlier, not years. The more I wrote, the more I realised that I *did* hold an entire continent within, exactly as I'd thought on 'Nordkapp Day'. Even now, I can return without effort to the sanctuary of 'Paradise Glade' in Calabria, where a tiny silver brook meanders beneath a canopy of shimmering beech leaves; to the summit of Monte Mulaz in the Dolomites, where pinnacles of rock are glowing as though lit from within; to the windswept North Sea coast, where a million seabirds fill the sky with motion and sound; to the wild heart of Svartisen, where swollen rivers cascade down rugged fjells and rain pelts sideways. I can return to an uncountable number of places and moments—and the sights, sounds and scents of them, and what they meant to me, is all still there.

It was perhaps the greatest discovery I made while writing, that when The Walk ended it hadn't ended at all. All the experiences, all the lessons, all the emotions, all the rewards—every meaningful aspect of the journey —still lived within. I needn't have feared losing The Walk because it couldn't have been lost. It had become an indelible part of who I was. I couldn't have let it go even if I'd tried.

And I didn't try. For sure, I lived in the present exactly as The Walk had taught, but I did all I could to apply the lessons from the past. Perseverance, patience and optimism; self-reliance and self-belief; the wisdom of being still; the dynamism of action; the immense power of gratitude; the release of letting go; the knowledge that I can choose my own path—these lessons became guiding principles underpinning everyday existence.

From The Walk's hardest moments I learnt that life isn't always comfortable, that it doesn't always go to plan, that change is inevitable, and security an illusion. But I also learnt that storms pass, that life's snowy wildernesses with their hidden lakes can be navigated if care is taken, and that changing direction can be an essential part of moving forward. I learnt that life's anxious situations and uphill struggles serve a purpose: for the self-knowledge they can teach and the strength they can build. And from everything I went without—much of it previously taken for granted—I learnt true value. Hot water from a tap still astonishes me. A smile will always remain a prized gift.

From being judged with contempt and disgust; from being turned away; from passing by brightly lit windows and feeling cut off; from the panic attacks of loneliness; from receiving help when help was truly needed —from all this I learnt how much a single act of kindness could mean. I learnt that the world can be improved one encounter at a time. This has become something I try my absolute damnedest to practise every single day.

From The Walk's failures I learnt that I don't always live up to my own lofty ideals. But I also learnt that I can try again, that each morning I get yet another chance to be the very best version of myself I can possibly be. Yet Another Chance has become an empowering daily mantra.

From 7,000 miles of motion I learnt the true value of stillness. From stillness I learnt how to pay attention, and from paying attention I learnt that there is no such thing as ordinary, that *extraordinary* is always present, often hiding in plain view. And from learning that there is no ordinary I finally learnt to see past expectations and fully appreciate where I am and what I have. It took far longer than it should have, but I finally learnt *gratitude*, a state of mind so powerful that its benefits cannot be overstated.

From starting when I hadn't the means to finish, and from overcoming challenges that I wanted to retreat from, I learnt to trust my instincts and never let anyone—most of all myself—tell me that something is impossible. I learnt to follow my own path through life, even when it runs contrary to how others live—and to how others argue I should live. I learnt that I have unlimited choices, and that even when events occur that are beyond my control—life's inevitable blizzards—I can still choose how I react to them. Choosing control, instead of choosing to passively let the winds of fate blow me wherever they will, has profoundly altered life's journey.

From wandering far I learnt how to find my way home. I learnt that home isn't a place at all but a state of mind, a state of *being*. I learnt I could find home wherever I was: in the suburbs, at work, in a stranger's smile, in clouds sailing by overhead, and of course in the wild. Before The Walk, whenever I returned to the wild, it would take weeks before I fully sloughed off civilisation and felt connected. But afterwards, the connection remained whether I was in the wild or not. I brought it back to civilisation with me.

As it turns out, most of what I learnt on The Walk doesn't only apply to mountains and the wilderness—it applies *everywhere*.

Of course, I also learnt that I'm only human, that I'm forgetful, flawed and make mistakes, that tangled forests will often set me back, and that some lessons will have to be relearned over and over. Moving forward is a never-ending journey.

Perhaps the greatest lesson learnt, however, will never need relearning: the Padjelanta Happiness. To have experienced it the way I did is to know it is possible, and knowing it is possible underpins life. I may never physically return to Padjelanta, but what I found there I still carry inside. Because of it, I'm still travelling in freedom and optimism, still beginning each new day as though it is a blank slate, still open to detours, still chomping at the bit to get going and find out what lies ahead.

It is why the journey to the North Cape will never end.

In writing about the *other* Europe, I've come to see that my perception of the continent might be profoundly different from most other people's. Instead of it being a continent of towns and cities, farms and factories, roads and rail routes, my Europe is also a land of mountains and valleys, forests and meadows, narrow paths and untrammelled space. Instead of it being an overcrowded continent of endless noise, my Europe is also an uncrowded continent of soothing peace. Instead of it being limited by rules and restrictions, my Europe is also a land of freedom. The continent I know is a land where nature can still be found, a land that offers endless possibilities for solitude and adventure—and while there obviously isn't as much nature left as there was 10,000 years ago it is most assuredly still there. I saw it, experienced it, lived within it. But many people have no idea it exists.

A great deal has changed within Europe since my journey took place. A few of the changes are good. Forests are more extensive; some 6,500 square miles of new forest have grown and a third of the continent is now covered by trees. There are many new national parks and nature reserves; twenty per cent of Europe's surface now enjoys some form of legislated protection. And many threatened species have received help: European bison and wolf populations are growing, chamois are spreading back through the Apennines, brown bears have returned to the Alps.

Of course, countering it are changes that haven't been made, and changes that *shouldn't* have been made. The human population continues to grow, and our unsustainable way of consuming continues. The pressures on wild lands only increase, and fragmentation of natural environments only worsens. Our climate is in flux: storms are more intense, extremes more extreme, averages dangerously altered. Plant and animal species living within specialised ecological niches are finding their existence ever more precarious, and many are not surviving. Our wildest rivers run heavier with pollutants, our air is more contaminated, our food contains ever-greater concentrations of poison. We've come so far but appear to have forgotten where we've come from. Nature is the foundation that our very existence is built upon, but we are chipping away at it beneath our feet.

And yet, because of everything I saw during The Walk, I still feel optimism. When I think about all the work done, all the people who take action, all the enlightened individuals who show restraint, all the organisations that fight for species and environments that can't fight for themselves, all the people who try to live *alongside* nature, and all the landscapes that have escaped the trampling death of progress—then I feel immense hope.

And when I remember that individual steps count, that every single day provides yet another chance to be the very best version of ourselves we can be, that the world *can* be improved one tiny act at a time, that change is *always* possible—then I feel immense hope.

Yes, a great deal has changed within Europe since my walk. But does the Europe I saw still exist? Is the kind of adventure I had still possible?

As I see it, the answer is easy: go find out for yourself.

Lace up a comfortable pair of shoes, place a few essential items in a backpack, and throw the pack onto your shoulders. Turn your back on the human world for a month, a week, or even a single day, and begin placing one foot gently before the other. Cast aside all timetables, forget all plans, avoid the shortest and most obvious path. Let distractions distract, let the smallest details enthral. Don't cower from the elements—open yourself to them. Breathe deeply, listen carefully, touch every surface, taste what you can. Look around; look within. Work your body hard, but be still, often. Laugh—at yourself. And don't ever be afraid to get lost.

I promise you this: if you go in search of the *other* Europe—and the *other* world—if you walk with the earth beneath your feet, you won't ever regret it.

I don't.

As I write these final lines, I hold in my hand one tiny pebble. It is small, rounded, pale orange, flecked with grey. It is a tiny memento from an extraordinary time, and when it came down to it I couldn't let it go.

I'm glad I didn't. As I hold it now I feel as though I have the entire journey, and the entire universe, in one hand. It provides perspective. And that perspective fills me with unlimited hope.

Auld Leakie still in frequent use, Colorado, 2021.

ACKNOWLEDGEMENTS

A LONG TIME ago in a mountain range far, far away... a young backpacker plodded north with several curious ideas circulating within his head. Among them was the muddled notion that he didn't need other people, and that he was proving it with every step. Conveniently, he'd pushed from mind all the help he'd already received. Instead, he focused on what he wanted to believe. *I'm alone*, he argued. *I'm doing this all myself.*

Happily, the journey that followed helped him see more clearly. By the end he fully understood that he *did* need other people. He understood that needing others was a natural, precious and beautiful part of life.

As I now know, neither my walk nor my books would have been possible without help. I owe a huge debt to a great many people. I feel incredibly fortunate that this is the case.

First and foremost I need to acknowledge my parents, Valerie and Ken—Base Camp. Without their behind-the-scenes toil I might have failed to even reach Germany, let alone the top of Norway. Unfortunately, there hasn't been space in my books to describe even a fraction of the support they gave, just as there isn't room in these acknowledgements to express the full depth of my gratitude for it. But I hope they know just how much they are appreciated, valued, and above all loved.

Starting with funds for only a third of the journey was a huge leap of faith. But I wouldn't have been able to leap (and keep on leaping) if the following individuals and businesses hadn't provided support. In alphabetical order, my gratitude goes to: Bridgedale, for donating twenty-four pairs of hiking socks; Color Line, for granting me free ferry passage to and from Norway; the Cotswold Outdoor store in Shepherd's Bush, London, for offering a discount on backpacking gear; First Ascent, for donating two Therm-a-Rest sleeping pads; Fuji Film, for twice donating 200 rolls of Fuji Velvia slide film (first for my Europe walk, then for my journey up the Rockies three years later); the National Map Centre for donating

390

many of the maps I needed; Lowe Alpine, for donating two rucksacks, two sets of waterproofs, and an entire wardrobe of backpacking clothes; Paul Brown and Dan Thory from Rex Interstock Photo Library (now Shutterstock), for processing for free all my photos, cataloguing them, and forwarding them to media outlets as needed; the late Robert Saunders, a pioneer of lightweight backpacking tents, who twice gave me Jetpacker tents for my long walks; Steve Roberts from the Scarpa Mountain Boot Company Ltd, for donating three pairs of Manta boots for my walk up Europe, and further pairs for the walks that followed.

I remain indebted to Philip Barnett, for funding my 6,000-mile journey up the Rockies through his business, Radical Ltd. Would I have met Joan, started a family, and now live in Colorado, without that support? On such generous acts do entire lives change.

My mission to raise funds for the homeless would have been far harder, if not impossible, without the publicity The Walk was given by a great many newspapers, magazines and publications. No one *had* to print a word, and my gratitude goes to every writer, journalist and editor who chose to. I especially want to acknowledge Ian McMaster from *Spotlight Verlag* magazine, the travel editors at the *Daily Express* and *Express on Sunday*, and the team at the travel website *TravelDex* (no longer operating). These three media outlets published regular trail reports, helping me reach a far wider audience than I otherwise would have. *Spotlight Verlag* and the *Express* paid for these reports, significantly boosting my limited funds. My gratitude for this is immense.

My gratitude goes to the staff and volunteers at the Cardinal Hume Centre and The Passage. Their dedication to London's homeless was (and still is) inspiring, and their encouragement was unexpected but hugely appreciated. My gratitude also goes to everyone who donated to these two charities. The majority of donations came from private individuals, none of whom *had* to give. But they chose to—and through giving made a real difference to real lives.

My gratitude goes to all the friends and strangers who wrote to me while I was walking. Again, no one had to write—but kindness and empathy won out. A handwritten note takes thought and time—and has real meaning because of it. I'm still basking in the warmth these cards and letters brought.

A great many people I met while crossing Europe also acted with kindness and empathy. So much of it still astonishes me. To invite a dirty, trail-worn stranger from another country into a home is a glorious act of *humanity* that I will never take for granted or forget. My gratitude also goes to everyone who gave a simple smile and shared a kindly word. These acts may have been small, but they had a profound and lasting effect. And, odd as it may still seem, I *really am* grateful for the people who withheld help and turned me away, for how it revealed the true power of kindness. I hope that others reading this will benefit from the enduring lessons these people unknowingly taught.

My two books have taken *far* longer to complete than The Walk itself. As with the physical journey, the writing journey couldn't have been completed on my own. Where Base Camp were essential for The Walk, so my wife, Joan, has been essential for the books. I don't know how many wives would put up with their husbands working for thousands of hours on a project that would never, in all likelihood, bring material benefit, but Joan did. Through her patience, encouragement and understanding Joan has shown the true depth of her love. She is one of a kind. I am fortunate beyond words.

My gratitude goes to the individuals who helped turn me into a writer through their support, particularly Geoff Birtles, former editor at *High Mountain Sports* magazine, who took a chance on an unknown writer thirty years ago; Cameron McNeish and John Manning, former editor and deputy editor of *The Great Outdoors* magazine, who gave me numerous opportunities to refine my craft; Emily Rodway and Carey Davies, former and current editors at *The Great Outdoors*, for their ongoing support and encouragement.

My two books would have been *far* poorer without the following beta readers: Mike Dano, Kate Gilliver, Ingrid Marshall, John Manning, Doug Skiba and Scott Spillman. These special friends gave hard, honest feedback, but I value them as much for their trust in how I'd take their criticisms as I do for the positive criticisms they gave. Ingrid Marshall deserves extra acknowledgement for going above and beyond with her feedback. She essentially became *On Sacred Ground*'s preliminary editor, and her guidance added real depth to several key passages. Her advice on one delicate section improved me as a person, for prompting me to try so much harder to see the world through other people's eyes. Someone in the publishing world should give Ingrid a job.

My trusted editor, Alex Roddie, did another extraordinary job with *On Sacred Ground*, surpassing his work on *The Earth Beneath My Feet*. From the start, Alex understood what I was trying to say, and made it his mission to help me say it. Aside from removing the many grammatical errors that littered the book, he also identified passages that needed improving, as well as several critical sections that hadn't yet been written but were definitely needed. A backpacker himself, Alex is also an extremely talented writer—his own work will stand the test of time. His deeply honest book, *The Farthest Shore*, is just the start. I am fortunate and grateful to have had his professional guidance, his advice, and his ongoing support.

Despite Alex's brilliant editing, further errors of my own still crept into the manuscript. I am indebted to my proofing editor, Moira Hunter, for hunting them down with great focus. Thank you, Moira, for being responsive, professional, and astonishingly observant. Any errors that remain are entirely my own!

Producing a book really does take a village. My gratitude goes to the many other 'villagers' who have helped: Bryan Palmintier, for his extraordinarily patient loan of a slide scanner; Victoria Wolf, for creating my website and ebooks, and for being so quick to respond each time extra tech support is needed; Dan Bailey, Tim Frenneaux, Eoin Hamilton, Dave Mycroft and Ash Routen, for giving my books extra exposure and increasing my audience; authors John D. Burns, Keith Foskett, Cameron McNeish, Ian Mitchell, Jim Perrin and Chris Townsend, for their professional endorsements. To have award-winning authors stake their own reputations on my book is profoundly humbling. Chris Townsend inspired me over thirty years ago when I first read his books—his support will be treasured for the rest of my life. My special thanks go to Jim Perrin for writing the foreword, and for his impactful words of encouragement. Jim's writings possess a depth I can only aspire to. I am awed that he feels that my own words are worthy of praise.

Finally, my ever-lasting gratitude goes to every single one of you who has chosen to read my books. There are many ways you could have spent your time —and yet here you are! *Straordinario!* I don't take this for granted; I never will. When I began writing, I had no expectation that my words would have meaning or value to anyone else, but many of you have written to say that they do. The emails I've received, and the online reviews that have been written, have moved me in ways I find impossible to express. Once again, no one *had* to write a word— so the choice to write has my enduring appreciation. I treasure these letters and reviews as much as I treasure any other part of The Walk—as much as 'Paradise Glade', the night with the Fleischers, and Nordkapp Day itself. Because of you, The Walk keeps giving. Because of all these new connections, my world keeps expanding. Because of you, I am reminded daily that I am *not* better off alone!

You have my heartfelt appreciation.

—Andrew Terrill, Golden, Colorado, May 2022.

A PLEA FOR THE HOMELESS

MY WALK across Europe raised awareness and funds for The Passage and the Cardinal Hume Centre. Both charities are still hard at work today, taking care of the immediate needs of individuals and families who no longer have homes, and providing a passage for them back into society.

Both charities still need support.

During my walk, a large number of people chose to help me, while a few chose not to. *What is it*, I wondered at the time, *that makes some people willing to help, and some unwilling? Why does one person open their home to a complete stranger without hesitation, and another person turn them away?*

By and large, most people *did* help. I received many acts of kindness and experienced a great deal of empathy. Over the miles, I learnt that even small acts add up. I'll never forget any of them, but one specific act is relevant here. It was made by a Norwegian campsite owner. She walked over to me in camp, holding a newspaper article about my walk that she'd just seen. 'Here, please,' she said, 'have the campsite fee back and also… here's a little extra to pass on to the homeless.'

If only, I'd wished at the time, *everyone who heard about The Walk back home was moved to help the homeless in a similar way.*

Many of the physical hardships I went through gave me an insight into what it might be like to live beyond society's edge. I even experienced a dark glimpse of the mental disintegration that can occur when one is looked at with disgust and is treated like dirt. Just imagine! Being treated as unworthy! Being turned away because of it! I am still shocked by the speed with which I began doubting my own self-worth. It made the fundraising side of The Walk feel even more important, and although I haven't dwelt on it excessively during either book I hope *you* will dwell on it now. Please pause for a moment. Picture yourself without a home. Picture everything you rely on—security, food, shelter, friends—picture it gone. Imagine people walking by, ignoring you as though you're not important. You'll soon believe you're not.

I hope you are in a position to help. It will take less than a minute of your time to follow one of the links on the next page, to donate a few pounds or dollars, to do one small act. But it *will* make a difference.

Actions make the world—another thought I had during The Walk. I lay in camp near the North Sea, considering all the kindness and empathy I'd experienced, and all the times when both had been lacking, when people couldn't be bothered to help, even in situations where they could have. Finally, I drifted off to sleep with the happy idea that I—small insignificant me—could make the entire world a better place, one small act at a time.

That's all it takes. One small act.

Below are details of The Passage and the Cardinal Hume Centre. No donation is too small.

***

THE PASSAGE

The Passage has been working with street homeless people in Central London for over forty years, providing resources which encourage, inspire and challenge them to transform their lives. We start by making contact with people on the street through outreach work. Our resource centre provides a warm welcome each day offering basic services of showers, clean clothes, and food and drink, followed by advice and help with a whole range of issues including mental health, substance misuse, physical healthcare, finding housing, employment and claiming welfare rights. We provide supportive hostels and follow-on support once people move into self-contained accommodation to avoid loneliness and isolation and the risk of repeat homelessness. We help over 3,000 individuals each year.

passage.org.uk/homelesswalk/

***

THE CARDINAL HUME CENTRE

Everyone should have a full life, but poverty at a young age can steal that potential. Too often poverty and homelessness in early life are repeated and compounded into later life. The Cardinal Hume Centre has been supporting people out of poverty and homelessness since 1986. Our approach is to build a relationship with each individual, to recognise everyone is different and often face complex and interrelated challenges. We proudly stick to the ethos of our founder, Cardinal Basil Hume. We provide a place of welcome, sanctuary and support to everyone who comes to the Centre. In any year we support more than 1,500 people with critical practical advice and support, our foodbank, access to our family area, and our hostel for young people.

cardinalhumecentre.org.uk/the-earth-beneath-my-feet

ABOUT THE PUBLISHER

ENCHANTED ROCK PRESS, LLC, is an independent book publishing imprint founded to celebrate the remarkable, fragile and enchanted planet we call home. Supported by publishing professionals, our mission is to share experiences that transport readers into the wild. We want to inspire people to step outdoors into our planet's enchanted places, and we want to do it in a way that encourages a thoughtful, joyful, and above all respectful approach.

As a small publisher, we face an uphill task (appropriately, given our mountain-themed subject matter) to reach a broader audience. If you have enjoyed this book, please tell other readers about it, and *please* consider leaving a review on Amazon, Goodreads.com, or elsewhere. Your review will make all the difference in the world. Thank you.

AUTHOR'S BIOGRAPHY

ANDREW TERRILL grew up in Pinner, suburban London, far removed from mountains and wild places. He didn't step onto a mountain until he was fifteen, but after that there was no going back. In the three and a half decades since, travelling on foot into wild nature has been a central part of his life. After completing several ultra-long walks, he settled in Colorado, where he now lives with his wife and two children. Open country lies just steps from his front door, and rarely a day passes without him visiting it, or a week without him sleeping in it. A regular contributor to *The Great Outdoors* magazine over the past two decades, *On Sacred Ground* is his second book. He has plans for further long walks.

Learn more at **andrewterrill.com**.